VISUALIZING PROJECT MANAGEMENT

MODELS AND FRAMEWORKS FOR MASTERING COMPLEX SYSTEMS

THIRD EDITION

KEVIN FORSBERG, PHD, CSEP
HAL MOOZ, PMP, CSEP
HOWARD COTTERMAN

WILEY

JOHN WILEY & SONS, INC.

Library of Congress Cataloging-in-Publication Data:

Forsberg, Kevin.
  Visualizing project management : models and frameworks for mastering
complex systems / Kevin Forsberg, Hal Mooz, Howard Cotterman.—3rd ed.
      p.   cm.
  Includes bibliographical references and index.
  ISBN-13 0-978-0-471-64848-2
  ISBN-10 0-471-64848-5 (cloth)
 1. Project management. I. Forsberg, Kevin. II. Cotterman, Howard. III.
Title.
  HD69.P.75F67   2005
  658.4′04—dc22

                                                            2005007673

Printed in the United States of America
10 9 8 7 6 5 4 3 2

*To those who master complexity and
provide us with simple, elegant solutions.*

FOREWORD TO THE THIRD EDITION

Today's industrial products, and many public sponsored projects, show a strong increase in functionality and complexity. Think of automobiles, mobile phones, personal computers, airplanes, or a space mission. To ensure success and cope with inherent risks of modern products, project management and systems engineering have become indispensable skills for forward-looking enterprises. They have been thrust into the center of attention of top executives. Both fields, project management and systems engineering, ensure success by focusing on technical performance, cost, and schedule—and beyond that on parameters such as return on investment, market acceptance, or sustainability.

Anyone who has lived with the space program, or any other high-tech industrial product development, can immediately appreciate this acclaimed book. It addresses and "visualizes" the multidimensional interactions of project management and systems engineering in several important ways. The book shows the interdependencies between the two disciplines and the relationships that each discipline has with the many other engineering, manufacturing, business administration, logistics, enterprise, or market-oriented skills needed to achieve successful products.

Since the early 1970s, many of the world's space projects have been planned and implemented through broad international cooperation. Having lived through some of these as engineer, project manager, and managing director, I well understand the need for simple and broadly accepted principles and practices for the practitioners of project management and systems engineering.

My years in industry gave me significant insight into the different engineering and project management cultures and practices prevailing in Europe and the United States. It enabled me to understand and easily interact with the different organizations that were involved in the most complex transatlantic cooperation of the 1970s. Remember, failures result not only from poor hardware engineering, software engineering, or systems or project management; they can also originate from differing cultural interpretations of engineering, communications, or management practices.

On more recent, highly complex international projects, such as the world's largest radar missions (SIR-C and SRTM) flown on the space shuttle, and the International Space Station (ISS), we learned again the lesson that project management and systems engineering, when focused on the essentials, are key ingredients to assured success.

At the Technical University of Delft in The Netherlands a few years ago, we initiated a new international postgraduate Master program of space systems engineering for senior engineers with a focus on modern "end-to-end" systems engineering. We emphasized the importance of multidisciplinary engineering, communication, and management interaction on the basis of a common use of terms and definitions. We also gave strong consideration to the fact that systems engineering and project management need to closely interact to achieve results.

The importance of this excellent book, able to encompass these two key disciplines, cannot be overemphasized. I was hence delighted to have been invited to write the Foreword for this third edition.

—Heinz Stoewer

Heinz Stoewer is the president of the International Council on Systems Engineering (INCOSE). Professor Stoewer started his career in aerospace. He spent a number of years in German and U.S. industry (MBB/EADS and McDonnell-Douglas/Boeing). In the 1970s, he was appointed the program manager for the Spacelab, the first human spaceflight enterprise at the European Space Agency. He eventually became a managing director of the German Space Agency. As professor for space systems engineering at the Technical University of Delft in The Netherlands, he initiated a highly successful space systems engineering Master program. Throughout his career, he has been aware of the need to interact effectively with compatriots in other fields and in other countries in areas covering the management of projects, systems, and software engineering.

FOREWORD TO THE SECOND EDITION

There are a thousand reasons for failure but not a single excuse.
Mike Reid

It is every manager's unending nightmare: In today's world of in-creasing complexity, there is less and less tolerance for error. We see this daily in the realms of health care, product safety and reliability, transportation, energy, communications, space exploration, military operations, and—as the above quote from the great Penn State foot-ball player Mike Reid demonstrates—sports. Whether the venue is the stock market, a company's customer base, consumers, govern-ment regulators, auditors, the battlefield, the ball field, or the media, "No one cares"—as the venerated quotation puts it—"about the storms you survived along the way, but whether you brought the ship safely into the harbor."

Over the course of my own career in aerospace, I have seen an unfortunate number of failures of very advanced, complex—and ex-pensive—pieces of equipment, often due to the most mundane of causes. One satellite went off course into space on a useless trajec-tory because there was a hyphen missing in one of the millions of lines of software code. A seemingly minor flaw in the electrical de-sign of the Apollo spacecraft was not detected until Apollo 13 was 200,000 miles from Earth, when a spark in a cryogenic oxygen tank led to an explosion and the near-loss of the crew. A major satellite proved to be badly nearsighted because of a tiny error in grinding the primary mirror in its optical train. And, as became apparent in the inquiry into the *Challenger* disaster, the per-formance of an exceedingly capable space vehicle—a miracle of modern technology—was undermined by the effects of cold temper-ature on a seal during a sudden winter storm. Murphy's Law, it would seem, has moved in lockstep with the advances of the modern age.

THEORETICALLY, SUCCESS IS MANAGEABLE

In the grand old days of American management, when it was presumed that all problems and mistakes could be controlled by more rigorous managerial oversight, the canonical solution to organizational error was to add more oversight and bureaucracy. Surely, it was thought, with more managers having narrower spans of control, the organization could prevent any problem from ever happening again. Of course, this theory was never confirmed in the real world—or as Kansas City Royals hitting instructor Charlie Lau once noted regarding a similar challenge, "There are two theories on hitting the knuckleball. Unfortunately, neither one works."

The problem with such a strategy of giving more managers fewer responsibilities was that no one was really in charge of the biggest responsibility: Will the overall enterprise succeed? I recall the comment a few years ago of the chief executive of one of the world's largest companies, who was stepping down after nearly a decade of increasingly poor performance in the marketplace by his company. He was asked by a journalist why the company had fared so poorly under his tutelage, to which he replied, "I don't know. It's a mysterious thing."

My observation is that there is no mystery here at all. After decades of trying to centrally "manage" every last variable and contingency encountered in the course of business, Fortune 500 companies found themselves with 12 to 15 layers of management—but essentially ill prepared to compete in an increasingly competitive global marketplace. Or as I once pointed out in one of my Laws, "If a sufficient number of management layers are superimposed on top of each other, it can be assured that disaster is not left to chance."

A NEW LOOK AT PROJECT MANAGEMENT

Today's leaders in both the private and public sectors are rediscovering the simple truth that every good manager has known in his or her heart since the first day on the job: Accountability is the one managerial task that cannot be delegated. There must be one person whose responsibility it is to make a project work—even as we acknowledge the importance of teamwork and "worker empowerment" in the modern workplace. In other words, we are rediscovering the critical role of the project manager.

The importance of the project manager has long been noted in our nation's military procurement establishment, which has traditionally considered the job to be among the most important and most difficult assignments in peacetime. Performed properly, the project management role, whether in the military, civilian government, or in business, can make enormous contributions and can even affect the course of history.

Challenges of this technology-focused project management role are particularly noteworthy for the insights they provide into the broader definition of project management. Perhaps the greatest of these is inherent in technology itself. In the effort to obtain the maximum possible advantage over a military adversary or a commercial competitor, products are often designed at the very edge of the state of the art. But as one high-level defense official noted in a moment of frustration over the repeated inability of advanced electronic systems to meet specified goals, "Airborne radars are not responsive to enthusiasm." In short, managerial adrenaline is not a substitute for managerial judgment when it comes to transitioning technology from the laboratory to the field.

Despite considerable tribulations—or, perhaps because of them—the job of the technology-focused project manager is among the most rewarding career choices. It presents challenging work with important consequences. It involves the latest in technology. It offers the opportunity to work with a quality group of associates. And over the years, its practitioners have generated a large number of truly enormous successes.

THE LURE OF PROJECT MANAGEMENT

This brings me to the broader observation that the project manager's job, in my opinion, is one of the very best jobs anywhere. Whether one is working at the Department of Defense, NASA, or a private company, the project manager's job offers opportunities and rewards unavailable anywhere else. Being a project manager means integrating a variety of disciplines—science, engineering, development, finance, and human resources—accomplishing an important goal, making a difference, and seeing the result of one's work. In short, project management is "being where the action is" in the development and application of exciting new technologies and processes.

The principles of successful project management—picking the best people, instilling attention to detail, involving the customer, and, most importantly, building adequate reserves—are no secret, but what is often missing in the literature on the subject is a comprehensive, easy-to-understand model. This is one of the many compelling aspects to Visualizing Project Management. The authors have taken a new, simplified approach to visualizing project management as a combination of sequential, situational management actions incorporating a four-part model—common vocabulary, teamwork, project cycle, and project management elements. The beauty of their approach is that they portray management complexity as process and discipline simplicity.

Kevin Forsberg, Harold Mooz, and Howard Cotterman are eminently qualified to compose such a comprehensive model for successful project management. They bring a collective experience unmatched in the commercial sphere. One author has spent his entire career in the high-tech commercial world; the two others have more than 20 years each at a company (Lockheed Corporation, which is part of the new Lockheed Martin Corporation) that established a reputation strongly supporting the role of the project manager. Collectively, the authors have spent many years successfully applying their "visualizing project management" approach to companies in both the commercial and the government markets. Their technical skill and work-environment experience are abundantly apparent in the real-world methodology they bring to the study and understanding of the importance of project management to the success of any organization.

SUMMARY

As corporate executives and their counterparts in the public sector expect project managers to assume many of the responsibilities of functional management—indeed, as we look to project managers to become "miracle workers" pulling together great teams of specialists to create products of enormous complexity—we need to make sure that the principles and applications of the project management process are thoroughly understood at all levels of the organizational hierarchy. This book will help executives, government officials, project managers, and project team members *visualize* and then successfully *apply* the process. I recommend this book to all those who aspire to project management, those who must supervise it in their organizations, or even those who are simply fascinated with how leading-edge technologies make it out of the laboratory and into the market.

—Norman R. Augustine

Norman Augustine retired in 1997 as Chair and CEO of Lockheed Martin Corporation. Upon retiring, he joined the faculty of the Department of Mechanical and Aerospace Engineering at Princeton University. Earlier in his career he had served as Under Secretary of the Army and prior to that as Assistant Director of Defense Research and Engineering. Mr. Augustine has been chairman of the National Academy of Engineering and served nine years as chairman of the American Red Cross. He has also been president of the American Institute of Aeronautics and Astronautics and served as chairman of the "Scoop" Jackson Foundation for Military Medicine. He is a trustee of the Massachusetts Institute of Technology and Johns Hopkins and was previously a trustee of Princeton. He serves on the President's Council of Advisors on Science and Technology and is a former chairman of the Defense Science Board. His current corporate boards are Black and Decker, Lockheed Martin, Procter and Gamble, and Phillips Petroleum. He has been awarded the National Medal of Technology and has received the Department of Defense's highest civilian award, the Distinguished Service Medal, five times. Mr. Augustine holds an MSE in Aeronautical Engineering from Princeton University.

ABOUT THE AUTHORS

Kevin Forsberg, PhD, CSEP, is co-founder of The Center for Systems Management, serving international clients in project management and systems engineering. Dr. Forsberg draws on 27 years of experience in applied research system engineering, and project management followed by 22 years of successful consulting to both government and industry. While at the Lockheed Palo Alto, California, Research Facility, Dr. Forsberg served as deputy director of the Materials and Structures Research Laboratory. He earned the NASA Public Service Medal for his contributions to the Space Shuttle program. He was also awarded the CIA Seal Medallion in recognition of his pioneering efforts in the field of project management. He received the 2001 INCOSE Pioneer Award. Dr. Forsberg is an INCOSE Certified Systems Engineering Professional. He received his BS in Civil Engineering at Massachusetts Institute of Technology and his PhD in Engineering Mechanics at Stanford University.

Hal Mooz, PMP and CSEP, is co-founder of The Center for Systems Management, one of two successful training and consulting companies he founded to specialize in project management and systems engineering. Mr. Mooz has competitively won and successfully managed highly reliable, sophisticated satellite programs from concept through operations. His 22 years of experience in program management and system engineering has been followed by 24 years of installing project management into federal agencies, government contractors, and commercial companies. He is co-founder of the Certificate in Project Management at the University of California at Santa Cruz and has recently developed courses for system engineering certificate programs in conjunction with Old Dominion and Stanford Universities. He was awarded the CIA Seal Medallion in recognition of his pioneering efforts in the field of project management and received the 2001 INCOSE Pioneer

Award. Mr. Mooz is a PMI certified Project Management Professional (PMP) and an INCOSE Certified Systems Engineering Professional (CSEP). Mr. Mooz received his ME degree from Stevens Institute of Technology.

Howard Cotterman has served The Center for Systems Management in capacities ranging from project manager to president, and has held executive positions at leading technology and aerospace companies, most recently as vice president of Rockwell International. Mr. Cotterman has successfully managed a broad range of system, software, and semiconductor projects, including Intel's family of microcomputers and peripherals. His 36 years of project management experience began with the development of IBM's first microprocessor in the mid-1960s and includes research, development, and manufacturing projects as NCR's Director of Advanced Development and at Leeds & Northrup where he was Principal Scientist. Mr. Cotterman was co-founder of Terminal Communications, Inc. and founder of Cognitive Corporation, specializing in knowledge management and online training. Mr. Cotterman received his BS and MS degrees in Electrical Engineering from Purdue University where he was a Sloan Fellow.

ACKNOWLEDGMENTS

The process models, best practices, and lessons learned embodied in *Visualizing Project Management* have been significantly enriched and refined in this *Third Edition* by collaboration among the many new contributors and by the reinforcement from successful project management and systems engineering practitioners.

We particularly wish to acknowledge the following contributors: Ray Kile for articulating the cause and effect relationships among the visual models, process improvement, and the achievement of peak performance; Frank Passavant for sharpening the core systems engineering messages, and particularly for his thoughtful and in-depth critique of requirements management and the Dual Vee; and John Chiorini for clarifying the synergies among our primary messages and those of the PMI® *PMBOK® Guide* and *INCOSE Systems Engineering Handbook*. We appreciate the substantial subject matter expertise contributed by Ray Kile relating to the SEI-CMMI® and cost estimating; by Jim Chism in clarifying the role of UML and SysML; and by Jim Whalen's DoD 5000 insights. We thank Marsha Finley for helping to identify the 100 most commonly misunderstood terms; Greg Cotterman for his contributions to Part I and to manuscript production; and Chris Fristad for his perspectives on the PMI® *PMBOK® Guide* and OPM3®. We are grateful to Neal Golub for agreeing to add his software project planning and estimation templates to our downloadable template database.

CONTENTS

INTRODUCTION

USING VISUAL MODELS TO MASTER COMPLEX SYSTEMS

The traditional telephone is heading for extinction—one more casualty of the Internet and evolution. Consider how quickly the cell phone grew from its modest beginnings as a mobile version of Alexander Graham Bell's telephone to being a complex entertainment, knowledge management, and communications system. But technology advance represents the most manageable facet of the complexity growth. Consider the business and social implications. Your boss will be able to contact you no matter where you are. Vacations will exist in name only.

While some organizations cite complexity as an excuse for late, flawed, and overrun projects, others welcome the challenge and strive to simplify and manage complexity as a competitive advantage. This book is dedicated to mastering complexity.

"The ability to simplify means to eliminate the unnecessary so that the necessary may speak."

Hans Hoffman[1]

IT'S ALARMINGLY COMMONPLACE FOR PROJECT TEAMS TO FAIL

Almost daily we are made aware of projects that have failed or haven't met customer expectations. Past examples include Iridium, Globalstar, and many others where the technical solution worked as specified but the business case was never realized. The English Channel tunnel has never achieved predicted revenues and the Boston "Big Dig" has overrun its $2.6 billion budget many times over

($14.6 billion and counting). At the other extreme, billions of dollars in failed projects have been attributed to minor technical problems, such as a missing line of code or crossed wires. Concurrent with these troubled projects are those that meet or exceed expectations. The Olympics are perhaps the best examples. Except for isolated instances such as Montreal, they routinely accomplish difficult objectives on time and usually with substantially—sometimes surprisingly—higher profits (Los Angeles Olympics profit was $100,000,000—ten times that expected). Product introductions such as the Apple iPod and the Toyota Lexus are among the excellent examples of projects that were very well executed.

> Since projects and project teams are temporary, their performance may be incorrectly attributed to the luck of the draw.

Widely varying project results would lead one to conclude—quite correctly—that project success is too often dependent on the specific team. But any team can succeed when it is committed to improving its processes and applying the fundamentals of project management and systems engineering comprehensively, consistently, and systematically.

RESPONDING TO THE ULTIMATE "WHY?"

Ironically, most of the billions of dollars lost in high-tech project failures have been traced to low-tech causes. Following each failure there is usually an extensive analysis that seeks to identify the root cause. Here's a representative list of reported root causes:

- No one communicated a change in design.
- A piece part was not qualified.
- A line of software code was missing.
- Two wires were interchanged.
- Unmatched connectors were mated.
- A review or decision gate was skipped.

We have only to ask "Why?" to see that these are symptoms of the real root cause. They are human errors—the results of behavior. Why wasn't the change communicated? Was it fear of interrogation? Why wasn't the part qualified? Was it a cost savings? And why weren't the interchanged wires detected? Was it incompetence or expediency? These are the ultimate "Whys?" that should be answered for every failed project. Chapter 4 addresses this question in a cultural context.

WHY DO COMPLEX SYSTEMS HAVE A DISMAL PROJECT PERFORMANCE RECORD?

Failure often results from flawed perception of what is involved in successfully managing complex system development from inception through completion. Even experienced managers often disagree on important aspects, like the blind men who encounter the elephant and reach different conclusions concerning the nature of the beast. In the parable, the man feeling the tail concludes the elephant is like a rope, while the man holding the trunk decides the elephant is like a snake. Project reality is such a complex organism that personal experience alone can result in biased and flawed views.

Being temporary, projects often bring together people unknown to each other. The newly formed group usually includes specialists motivated by the work itself and by their individual contributions. Teams of highly skilled technicians can make costly errors—even

THE FAR SIDE   By GARY LARSON

Visualization without confirmation through a common language can produce a flawed vision of reality. The results can be equally misleading whether we see the world through the optimist's rose-colored glasses or through a "buggy" lens as this Far Side cartoon depicts. (THE FAR SIDE © 1994 FARWORKS, INC./Dist. by UNIVERSAL PRESS SYNDICATE. Reprinted with permission. All rights reserved.)

fatal ones—simply because the members fail to understand or internalize a systematic approach for applying best practices to project management. A major factor critical to project success is the availability of an effective and intuitive management process—one the group will quickly buy into and build their team upon.

VISUALIZATION: A POWERFUL TECHNIQUE FOR ACHIEVING HIGH PERFORMANCE

No matter how much intuition you have, you can't rely on personal experience alone as you navigate through the increasingly complex and dynamic environment of projects. On the other hand, management excellence cannot simply be taught any more than excellence in Olympic gymnastics or being a great artist. Fortunately, complex systems do not require complex management, quite the contrary. The most effective project managers are able to decompose the apparent complexity of their project environment in order to view it more simply.

Psychologists agree that most people have insight and creative abilities far beyond those used routinely. This has been attributed to childhood education that favors left-brain (logical) modes of thinking, while downplaying the right brain's creativity. Albert Einstein is just one of many people believed to have overcome traditional Western society left-brain learning patterns. He was able to "see" three-dimensional pictures in his mind before he wrote equations. He emphasized the importance of visualization to his own working methods. Everything he did on the theory of relativity was already in the literature, but other physicists just couldn't visualize how to put it all together. Experts now believe that visualization, and the subsequent intuition improvements from right-brain thinking, can be developed with time and training.

Visualization can be a powerful technique for achieving high performance and success in business as it is in fields such as sports. Top athletes often perform successfully in their minds before competing. They experience their winning achievement visually—see it—even feel it. NASA researcher Dr. Charles Garfield reports that most peak performers are visualizers. Business people who need to persuade others, such as salespeople or entrepreneurs, prepare for the responses they expect by visualizing scenarios of their situation. Visualization—a right brain activity—is a vital characteristic of leadership, another right brain activity. We employ this technique to gain insight into the logical and systematic project management and systems engineering environments and processes—left brain activities.

Improved visualization and intuition can be developed with time and training.

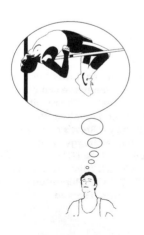

THE SIMPLIFYING POWER OF MODELS

Visual models enable us to see the big picture. They provide a powerful language for comprehending each key element in the project environment and for visualizing how each element relates to the whole and to the others:

- Models help us to explain and to understand how things work by simplifying complexity. Models enable us to visualize and characterize what to expect. What young science student hasn't been enlightened by a physical model of the reciprocating engine or of a molecule?
- Models can broaden our perspective as does a desktop globe or a model of the solar system.
- Models provide a common conceptual frame of reference just as a common vocabulary does for communications.
- Models can express rules and ideas more simply, models like pictures are worth more than a thousand words.
- Models clarify relationships, identify key elements, and eliminate confusion factors. In Thomas Kuhn's words, ". . . all models have similar functions. Among other things they supply the group with preferred and permissible analogies or metaphors."

> Model: A representation of the real thing used to depict a process, investigate risk, or to evaluate an attribute.

> "The power of a science seems quite generally to increase with the number of symbolic generalizations its practitioners have at their disposal."
>
> Thomas Kuhn

The appropriate models help avoid costly errors that can lead to failure. One of the major sources of project failure is flawed requirements and scope management. Models of the project environment, therefore, need to address the development and management of project requirements. Continuing to work on the project solution with an insufficient understanding of stakeholder requirements and a deficient requirements development process often leads to expensive time delays and redesigns. This doesn't have to be the case. A strong requirements development and management process model can provide that ounce of prevention.

> From road maps to wind tunnels, models help us avoid costly errors and dead ends— that is, if we're correctly modeling the right things.

THE INTEGRATED PROCESS MODEL

The most popular models in the development project environment focus either on project administration, technical development, or process improvement, often to the exclusion of the other areas.

All too often projects proceed with innovation and sophisticated development without paying heed to the evolving business case. Furthermore, the managers of supporting subsystems or items usually

Developers often focus on what is possible technically regardless of the constraints of cost, a limiting schedule, or what the customer requires.

have little knowledge of the driving business case and of the derivative cases at their level. This lack of awareness of the underlying business issues stems from inadequate collaboration between the business and technical disciplines and can lead to a wrong project solution that is ultimately rejected by the users, customer, or marketplace.

How then to best accommodate the evolving business case and to have it drive the technical and financial decisions throughout the project life cycle? The answer begins with internalizing the integrated process model presented here, tailoring the processes, and then putting the practices to work. The set of models presented in these pages builds on the natural synergies of project management and systems engineering, enabling project teams to:

- Develop new products and services that meet customer needs—the right solution the first time.
- Shorten time-to-market for new developments—effective business strategies and development tactics.
- Improve efficiency and productivity—organizational and personal capability maturity.
- Establish competitive positions in national or world markets—best in class processes leading to best in class performance.

To implement an effective process, any model must be intuitive because it is impossible to install if it can't be quickly understood and affirmed.

Installing an integrated project management and systems engineering culture, based on the models in this book, coupled with training and certifying key team members has significantly improved project success rates. Moving beyond success to a strong project culture and a predictable performance improvement program can represent a distinct competitive advantage.

Navigating the Book—Exploring the Models

This book is organized with three goals in mind:

The visual models presented here can broaden your perspective on all aspects of your project, enabling you to lead from your right brain and manage with your left.

1. Visualizing what's involved in mastering complex systems at the concept level. Part One introduces the integrated process model that enables you to visualize the major relationships.
2. Internalizing the processes and understanding how to leverage them. The chapters in Parts Two and Three correspond to the visual process model's building blocks and introduce supporting tactics, methods, and techniques.
3. Mastering complexity with a deeper understanding of systems engineering principles and their application. Part Four presents advanced topics that prepare you to confidently accept responsibility for the challenges of complex projects.

PART ONE

USING MODELS AND FRAMEWORKS TO MASTER COMPLEX SYSTEMS

As in previous editions, the wheel and axle model is the centerpiece—the basis for visualizing the overall project management process and for structuring the book's content. The theme of the book, and our metaphor for a great project team, is a symphony orchestra, each musician capable of solo performances, but committed

Note that the first violinist is systems engineering, the team's technical lead that, in project teams, frequently sets the pace and orchestrates the technical players in timing and intensity.

to teamwork. This edition emphasizes the pivotal role of systems engineering, the first violinist in the orchestra metaphor.

Visualizing Project Management, third edition, has four parts:

Part One draws on systems thinking to consider the project environment, highlighting the critical role of solution and stakeholder requirements.

Part Two applies our visual model to reveal the relationships and interdependencies among the major project success factors.

Part Three provides the tactics required to navigate skillfully in order to achieve the project goals.

Part Four describes how processes can best be deployed to achieve predictable performance improvements.

COPYRIGHTS AND SERVICE MARKS

PMI® and *PMBOK® Guide* are service and trademarks of the Project Management Institute, Inc. that are registered in the United States and other nations.

MARGIN NOTES

——— *PMBOK® Guide* ———
This form of margin note is used for PMI *PMBOK® Guide* references.

——— *INCOSE* ———
This form of margin note is used for *INCOSE Handbook* references.

This third edition uses two forms of margin notes. As in previous editions, margin notes are used to emphasize a point or to annotate a diagram, such as the systems engineering role in the first paragraph. The second form, shown here in the margin, is used to reference specific sections of the PMI *PMBOK® Guide* and the *INCOSE Systems Engineering Handbook, Version 3 (2006).*

SECTIONS

We occasionally refer to specific chapters by number and to a section nearby. *Sections* are delimited by headings in all caps and centered, such as this one.

1

WHY ARE PROJECT REQUIREMENTS A CRITICAL ISSUE?

In the mid- to late-1980s, cellular phones had very limited operational range and were generally used only in large cities. A strong business case for a satellite-based mobile phone was made and the Iridium Program was born. By the time the 12-year development and deployment was complete, GSM cellular technology had matured and spread through all markets. Only a fraction of the potential Iridium customers remained. The consortium, unable to pay the $5 billion debt, filed bankruptcy. A realistic business case, appropriately updated, would have revealed that the program could not survive—and it would have revealed the problem years before any satellites were launched.

"It was a painful lesson to learn, but it was an engineer's dream. . . . I had a great time, but, in the end, it taught me a great lesson in business planning. You need to minimize the investment as well as reduce the risks. We all need to think in terms of business, not straight engineering anymore."

Roger Taur[1]
Dr. Taur was a member
of the original Iridium
development team.

This chapter speaks to the challenges of maintaining consistency of the business case, the project scope, and customer needs. Subsequent chapters address the many creative ways to maintain this consistency, including opportunity management. In the case of the Iridium Corporation, opportunity seekers bought the assets for about 2 percent of the original investment. By late 2004, the new team had enlisted 100,000 customers and could be headed for success in a more limited market and greatly reduced investment (the original Iridium Corporation needed 1.6 million subscribers to survive).

Projects and their solutions are the lifeblood of most businesses. Projects are either the main business, as in construction, or they are expected to provide new products, as in most commercial product

For some businesses, such as aerospace and communications, project management is the lifeblood of the enterprise and systems engineering is the heart of project management.

companies. Whether for survival or to sustain market leadership, projects are the key to succeeding in world competition. Project success is delivering a result that does what it is supposed to; when it is supposed to; for the predicted development, operating, and replication costs; and with the reliability and quality expected.

THE MARKETPLACE DYNAMICS DEMAND MORE RESPONSIVENESS AND AGILITY

Tougher competition demands shorter time to market and squeezes the break-even point.

Marketplace shifts often force abrupt changes of direction. Longer projects face particularly elusive targets. Budget and contingency planning rarely account adequately for market shifts and schedule slips. A prolonged project can face inflated labor and material costs and eroded prices when it eventually shoulders its way into the marketplace. Competitive danger signs include:

- Shorter market windows with higher risks.
- More contenders carving available markets.
- Pricing pressure reducing profit margins.
- Plethora of emerging technologies.

Outside influence is persistent—an increasing distraction.

Conditions such as inflation/recession cycles, lack of borrowing power, and stockholder pressures have always existed, but not so tightly coupled with technology shocks and worldwide competition. Diversionary pressures include:

- High rate of technology change.
- More attention to legal, ethical, and fair conduct.
- Greater international involvement.
- Internet-based worker mobility.

The only certainty is uncertainty, especially with regard to project requirements. The Agile Alliance, an organization formed to address the conflicting demands on software developers, has issued a set of principles and practices to deal with changing requirements. This excerpt of their principles acknowledges the inevitability of changing requirements:

- Requirements are not negotiated up front, but rather evolve as a result of constant collaboration between the customer and development team.
- Welcome changing requirements, even late in development.
- Agile processes harness change for the customer's competitive advantage.

These tactics do apply to some environments, especially in smaller projects, but they could lead to failure in others. Development tactics are addressed in Chapters 7 and 19.

PROJECT SUCCESS DEPENDS ON DELIVERING THE RIGHT SOLUTION, DONE RIGHT—THE FIRST TIME

We refer to the purpose and final result of any project as the *solution*. Delighting the customer with the right solution could be delivering a product or service as expected, or even resolving a problem. "Done right—the first time" means it was developed as intended without burning out the team.

Projects usually exist to address a business opportunity; therefore, to achieve project success, all decisions must be consistent with the business case (also known as the mission case for some government projects). It is often difficult to achieve cooperation and balance among the business and technical aspects. Business cases and technical issues are often subject to conflicting priorities and external forces, such as those in the previous section.

> Business and technical conflicts are usually resolved through trade studies, negotiation, or similar processes.

MANAGE REQUIREMENTS TO MANAGE THE PROJECT

The Project Management Institute (PMI), the leading certification body for project management, defines project management as: *The application of knowledge, skills, tools, and techniques to project activities to meet project requirements.* Seasoned project teams view managing requirements and the project scope as the most critical elements of managing the project. The project and its requirements start with expressed needs and end only when those needs are satisfied as evidenced by successful user validation. Chapter 9 covers the end-to-end chain of technical and business development.

> Nonessential or overspecified requirements frequently result in missing schedule and cost targets.

Once technical and business requirements are established as consistent, the balance (referred to as *congruency*) needs to be maintained. The budget and schedule must enable achievement of the technical requirements. Conversely, the technical requirements must be achievable within the budget and schedule. Projects without congruency at the outset are usually doomed and unrecoverable unless the inconsistencies are resolved very early (Figure 1.1). In some industries, projects of this type are known as a "suicide run." Throughout a project's duration, there is continual pressure to change the

Figure 1.1   The "suicide run." Reprinted by permission of United Feature Syndicate, Inc.

established agreements. Schedules are compressed, available resources decreased, and technical features added. The project team must be able to recognize and respond to serious inconsistencies. When implementing schedule, budget, and technical changes, congruency must be reestablished or the project will fail.

REQUIREMENTS MANAGEMENT: THE INTERSECTION OF PROJECT MANAGEMENT AND SYSTEMS ENGINEERING

Why are project requirements a critical issue? The answer to this question lies partially in the pervasiveness of the requirements, the diverging interests of project stakeholders, and confusion over roles. Just as we have done up to this point, stakeholders talk about managing requirements without a common understanding of just what—and who—it involves (Figure 1.2).

The two key stakeholders on the project team are the project manager and the systems engineer. The previous section began with the PMI's definition of project management, which emphasized the role of requirements. While we support and applaud that emphasis, our definitions that follow reflect the *interdependency* of project management and systems engineering in regard to managing requirements.

Project management: The process of planning, applying, and controlling the use of funds, personnel, and physical resources to achieve a specific result.

Systems engineering: The process of managing requirements to include user and stakeholder requirements, concept selection, architecture development, requirements flowdown and trace-

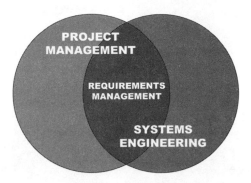

Figure 1.2   Requirements management: The intersection defined.

ability, opportunity and risk management, system integration, verification, validation, and lessons learned.

Requirements management: Management of the project business, budget, and technical baselines. The objective is to keep the three baselines congruent. The process includes baseline change management and authorization. Also included are requirements flowdown, traceability, and accountability.

The business case and the systems engineering management process provide the framework for requirements management—the place where project management and systems engineering intersect.

In many environments, project managers are held accountable for the cost and schedule performance of their projects even though the technical solution is being developed outside of their range of authority. Because the solution development usually consumes the largest portion of the budget and determines the schedule, this condition is likely to be unmanageable. Fortunately, this situation is changing as project management takes center stage and the project manager's role becomes better understood.

In environments where project managers are responsible for the development and deployment of the solution, the project manager should be skilled in the orchestration of solution development (systems engineering) or closely share that responsibility with someone who is.

The next chapter examines the intersection between project management and systems engineering in the context of the overall project solution environment.

In a recent meeting of one of the largest PMI chapters, only 22 percent reported having resource control.

2

VISUALIZING THE PROJECT ENVIRONMENT

Solutions to devastating events, such as forest fires, illustrate the power of systems thinking (Figure 2.1). For many decades, the conventional wisdom for controlling forest fires was to prevent them. This led to unacceptable fuel accumulation and even greater devastation over the long term when the accumulation did ignite in an uncontrollable rage. By considering the *bigger picture,* preemptive controlled burns emerged as the best solution. Similar bigger picture approaches have been used successfully for solving pest control and flooding threats.

Systems thinkers see the root causes and courses of action that control events.

When we fail to grasp the systemic source of problems, we are left to treat symptoms rather than eliminate underlying causes. Without systemic thinking, the best we can ever do is adapt or react. Systems thinking, powered by visual models, stimulates creative—rather than adaptive—behavior.

On most complex system development projects, the systems engineer is the champion and curator of the big picture, including the customer's perspective of the problem and the solution. To benefit from systems thinking, the project team needs to extend that viewpoint upward to the *bigger* picture of the project's overall environment.

Systems thinking encompasses critical thinking, solutions thinking, future and forward thinking, longer-term thinking, and

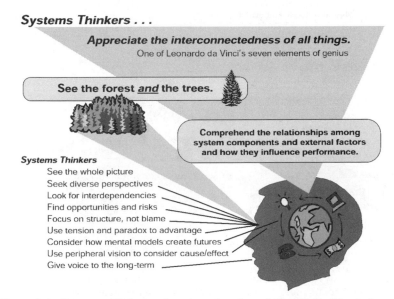

Systems Thinkers . . .

Appreciate the interconnectedness of all things.
One of Leonardo da Vinci's seven elements of genius

See the forest _and_ the trees.

**Comprehend the relationships among
system components and external factors
and how they influence performance.**

Systems Thinkers
See the whole picture
Seek diverse perspectives
Look for interdependencies
Find opportunities and risks
Focus on structure, not blame
Use tension and paradox to advantage
Consider how mental models create futures
Use peripheral vision to consider cause/effect
Give voice to the long-term

**Figure 2.1   Systems thinkers take a broader view of the world. Adapted
from _Systems Thinking Playbook,_ Linda Booth Sweeney and Dennis
Meadows, 1995.**

high-level thinking. It is not analytic thinking, which is tactical and parts oriented. To illustrate the stretch in our training events, we ask the participants to picture the class they are in as a system and to identify its major elements. The first responses typically focus on the actors, the materials, and the dynamics of the event itself. By asking the participants to consider everything they bring into the classroom, including environmental factors, the brainstorming session leads to a result similar to the bigger picture illustrated in Figure 2.2.

By providing frameworks and perspectives for systems thinking, models enable us to visualize the big picture, which is so vital to project management and systems engineering. In this chapter, we employ systems thinking to model and visualize the system solution environment to provide context as we zoom in on the area within which most of the system development decisions will be made, referred to as the *trade-off area* or, more simply, the *trade space*.

The final result of any project is a product, service, or even a problem resolution, all of which we refer to as the *system solution*. In the vernacular of systems thinking, a system and the project solution are used interchangeably.

Figure 2.2 Systems thinking focuses on relationships, multiple outcomes, holism and boundaries, the environment, the larger system, and feedback.

This next section characterizes the overall environment and space within which the solution is created in terms of:

- The available trade space.
- Models, frameworks, lessons learned, and best practices.
- Project stakeholders.

Subsequently, the remainder of this chapter zooms back out to the big picture to address the opportunities, risks, and ultimate payoff for those whose future depends on moving beyond project success to higher levels of performance:

- The professional atmosphere.
- Opportunities and risks.
- The payoff.

ZOOMING IN ON THE SOLUTION TRADE SPACE

Trade-off studies are used to select the best solution by evaluating the alternative concepts and architectures against a set of criteria. The trade-offs are performed within the project's trade space— the area bounded by project and solution constraints, as shown in Figure 2.3.

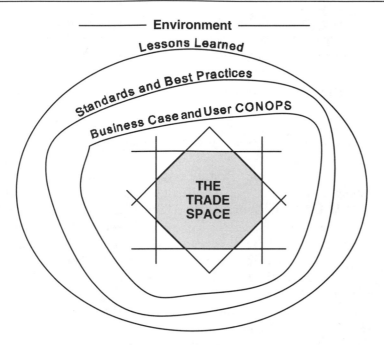

Figure 2.3   The trade-off area at the core of the environment.

Models, frameworks, and best practices influence the tactical approach and processes to be applied within the solution space. While these three terms are often used interchangeably, they are most valuable when their differences are understood and properly applied. In the context of project management and systems engineering, the following definitions and descriptions apply:

Models: A model is a representation of the real thing used to depict a process, investigate an opportunity or a risk, or evaluate an attribute. Properly constructed models are valuable tools because they focus attention on critical issues while stripping away less important details that tend to obscure what is needed to understand and to manage. Because they idealize a complex situation, a variety of different models can be constructed to represent the same situation. A useful model will be simple, but it must retain the essence of the situation to be managed—the driving force for the process model defined in the next chapter.

Frameworks: Within the solution space, a framework is a set of assumptions, concepts, values, and practices that constitutes a way of viewing reality. The Software Engineering Institute's (SEI) Capability Maturity Model Integrated (SEI-CMMI®) is

"Everything should be made as simple as possible—but no simpler."

Albert Einstein

the centerpiece of the SEI framework for assessing, rating, and subsequently improving an organization's performance. We discuss this framework further in Chapter 21.

Best Practices: Best practices are about doing what has been consistently demonstrated to work well—processes, procedures, and techniques that enable project success. Best practices need to be documented for the purposes of sharing, repetition, and refinement. Best practices are usually based on lessons learned by experienced project managers, as was done in developing the Project Management Institute's *A Guide to the Project Management Body of Knowledge (PMBOK® Guide).*[1] The *PMBOK® Guide* is updated periodically through feedback from practitioner experiences. The behavior-based process models in *Visualizing Project Management* integrate systems engineering and project management best practices, the latter being consistent with the *PMBOK® Guide.* Figure 2.4 continues the trade space delineation.

Figure 2.5 illustrates the solution space shrinking to the trade space (Figure 2.3), leading to the value-driven concept. The letters on the diagrams correspond to the following:

A. Stakeholder constraints imposed.
B. Legacy system conformance requirements.
C. Technology limitations.
D. The trade space where requirements are satisfied by performing trade-offs among alternative solution concepts.
E. The ideal concept fills out the trade space.
F. Low-value features are eliminated.

From a technical perspective, the ideal concept is one that fills out the trade space, pressing on all boundaries. However, a well-conceived business case provides a basis for determining the value of optional system features or capabilities. When low-value features are eliminated, the value-driven concept is realized as shown in step F of Figure 2.5. The widely practiced techniques of Value Engineering and Cost as an Independent Variable (CAIV) promote this approach.

IDENTIFYING THE PROJECT STAKEHOLDERS

The next step in characterizing the solution space is identification of the key stakeholders or groups. The project stakeholders fall into several categories:

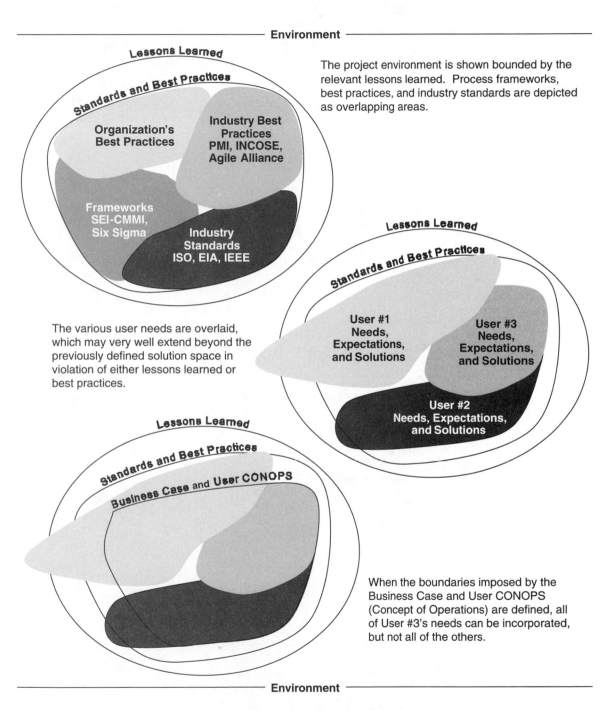

The project environment is shown bounded by the relevant lessons learned. Process frameworks, best practices, and industry standards are depicted as overlapping areas.

The various user needs are overlaid, which may very well extend beyond the previously defined solution space in violation of either lessons learned or best practices.

When the boundaries imposed by the Business Case and User CONOPS (Concept of Operations) are defined, all of User #3's needs can be incorporated, but not all of the others.

Figure 2.4   The project environment boundaries.

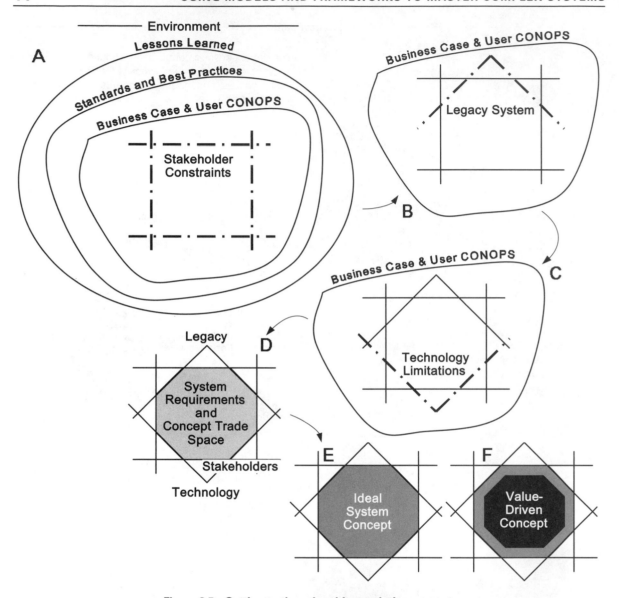

Figure 2.5   Getting to the value-driven solution concept.

- Customers and users.
- Project participants.
- Marketplace.
- Professional societies, regulatory bodies, and standards organizations.

The customers and users could be the same, but they are frequently different. For example, the project's customer could be the sponsoring organization's internal marketing department, which is serving as an intermediary for the final user or consumer of the project product or service.

Project participants include the core stakeholders: the project team, sponsoring enterprise, internal customers (such as the marketing/sales department), and functional organizations.

The marketplace has two key stakeholders: sales channels and competitors.

Professional societies, regulatory bodies, and standards organizations exert significant influence on project practitioners, the project vocabulary, and the solution space. Several of the key organizations are listed here and the most influential are profiled in Appendix B and in Part Three of our book *Communicating Project Management.*[2]

ASAPM—American Society for the Advancement of Project Management

DoD—U.S. Department of Defense

EIA—Electronics Industries Alliance

IEEE—Institute of Electrical and Electronics Engineers

IIE—Institute of Industrial Engineers

INCOSE—International Council on Systems Engineering

IPMA—International Project Management Association

ISO—International Organization for Standardization

PMI—Project Management Institute

SEI—Software Engineering Institute

SESA—Systems Engineering Society of Australia

THE PROFESSIONAL ATMOSPHERE

A large number of professional organizations and societies share their lessons learned, develop their own best practices, and offer various forms of support and mentoring to their members. They range in size from the Agile Alliance to the 28 separate professional societies that make up the half-million-member Institute of Electrical and Electronics Engineers.

The Agile Alliance is of particular interest because its methods (such as Extreme Programming) and feature-driven tenets are frequently misunderstood to conflict with a structured framework such as the SEI-CMMI. We view Agile methods as means for optimizing requirements flexibility and discovery while concentrating on constant improvement of the team's development practices.

From this perspective, agility may actually help an organization in achieving its capability and process maturity goals.

The SEI mission is to advance the practice of software engineering and to make predictable the acquiring, developing, and sustaining of software-intensive systems, from design through operation. The integrated systems engineering/hardware/software CMMI Product Suite was introduced in August 2000 to replace the Software Capability Maturity Model (SW-CMM) in use since 1987.

The SEI is one of the three professional organizations that, through continued growth in scope, influence, and collaboration, are expected to shape the future of the professional surroundings for projects. The Project Management Institute (PMI) and the International Council on Systems Engineering (INCOSE) represent the project management and systems engineering professional communities, respectively.

INCOSE expanded to international scope in 1995 and launched its Certified Systems Engineering Professional (CSEP) certification program in August 2004. The *INCOSE Systems Engineering Handbook,* the organization's certification guide, is referenced in margin notes throughout Parts Two and Three of this book using the INCOSE designation.

Holding a PMI PMP certification is the de facto basis for judging an individual's knowledge about project management, especially in the United States.

Professional certification of project managers and systems engineers is a strong short-term driver for career growth and personal development. Enlightened practitioners see certification as a means to establish and maintain their life skills rather than as an end in itself. For organizations, certification sponsorship represents a powerful motivator for establishing a culture of professionalism and personnel development.

OPPORTUNITIES AND RISKS

As the professional atmosphere improves, so does the local climate. Project practitioners can look forward to increasing opportunities to broaden their influence, enrich their knowledge, sharpen their skills, and advance their careers in the emerging era of professional collaboration. But we're not quite there.

Bad Habits Were Learned and Barriers Were Built

It starts with the universities and other institutions of higher learning that separate their Schools of Business from their Schools of

Engineering. New graduate engineers are ushered into the engineering environment and situated among other engineers—likewise the new recipients of a master's degree in business administration (MBAs) move into the nontechnical side of the business. Similarly, engineering and business staffs are often located in different buildings—possibly in different campuses or cities. Business and technical collaboration, if present at all, is not emphasized or facilitated. The barriers between disciplines grow. In many companies, organization structures keep technical and business management apart until the second level of management. It is often impractical to bridge the gap without abandoning one's career path.

Historically, associated professional organizations have further exacerbated this situation by not having a common vocabulary and not engendering collaboration.

Finally, technical and business professionals frequently establish their own independent customer contacts, each believing the other doesn't really know how to communicate with their custormer. Instinct replaces understanding, and when the product fails to satisfy, it is often attributed to the customer's "lack of appreciation."

Getting rid of past bad habits begins by recognizing them.

Breaking the Barriers—A Future of Collaboration and Integration

The concept of ensuring business-driven technical decisions throughout the project by integrating project management and systems engineering, while not new, is receiving renewed interest and investment in academic, government, and commercial venues. Several major universities, including MIT, Stevens Institute, and Stanford, are offering coordinated project management and systems engineering programs or are aggressively preparing to do so.

The growing professionalism, certification, and recognition of the systems engineering practice by INCOSE are deliberate steps to clarify the systems engineering role and recognize its significance.

The SEI provides a comprehensive framework for assessing an organization's system development process maturity and for establishing an integrated processes culture from the project to the enterprise level. Furthermore, the SEI-CMMI promotes blending of the engineering management disciplines and processes.

One of the primary purposes of this book is to encourage broader collaboration among individuals and between the disciplines.

While this transformation is breaking down historical barriers at the institutional level, the real change agents are the readers of this book who have a vested interest not only in acquiring the skills for mastering complex systems, but also in realizing the payoff.

THE PAYOFF: PERFORMANCE IMPROVEMENT

Near-maximum productivity improvements have already been wrought from conventional skills training and capital improvements such as computers and knowledge management. The integration of project management, systems engineering, and process improvement is being widely recognized as the wave of the future—the best means to improve project performance and ensure career advancements. Forward thinking organizations are laying a new keel based on this premise, which is the focus of Chapter 21.

3

MODELING THE FIVE ESSENTIALS

"Treasure hunters had no control. . . . They were subject to too many whims . . . that is why most of them failed."[1] Treasure-hunt projects are notorious for ad hoc management. By contrast, the story of the search for the SS *Central America* and the recovery of its treasure, as told in *Ship of Gold* by Gary Kinder, is one of the most dramatic illustrations of the power of blending business opportunity leadership with systematic engineering approaches.[2] During the early stages of the feasibility study, one of the key stakeholders made this observation: "Einstein didn't create anything new," said Glower. "Everything he did on the theory of relativity was already in the literature, but other physicists just didn't quite see how to put it all together."

This chapter is about visualizing "how to put it all together"—a management process much bigger than the sum of its parts—once the relationships among those parts are understood.

MODELING THE INTEGRATION OF PROJECT MANAGEMENT AND SYSTEMS ENGINEERING

The process model that frames this book was developed to provide a visual depiction of the integrated project management and systems engineering processes. We characterized the behavior of

"Principles that are established should be viewed as flexible, capable of adaptation to every need. It is the manager's job to know how to make use of them, which is a difficult art requiring intelligence, experience, decisiveness, and, most important, a sense of proportion."

Henri Fayol[3]

project managers, systems engineers, and teams that exhibited consistent successes as differentiated from behaviors that led to troubled and failed projects. Our resulting integrated process model is compliant with the many practices defined in the Project Management Institute's (PMI) *PMBOK® Guide* as well as those of the International Council on Systems Engineering (INCOSE).[4] The model is intended to:

- Communicate how a project should be managed.
- Encourage stakeholder involvement.
- Orchestrate the technical development process.
- Keep the health of the project transparent and available.
- Encourage pursuit of high-value opportunities while managing their risks.
- Trigger swift action to address problems.

VALIDATION CRITERIA FOR THE INTEGRATED PROJECT MANAGEMENT MODEL

Experts have identified the general criteria for effective models, to which we have added criteria specifically for project management and systems engineering:

- *Explicitly and operationally defined* structures and relationships.
- *Obviously valid and intuitive* to all project stakeholders. If a model has to be studied each time it's applied, it has minimal—perhaps even negative—value. It is difficult to install a process if the model isn't quickly understood and confirmed.
- *General applicability* throughout the project environment in a way that accounts for the complexity and dynamics of the project processes and the driving role of project requirements.
- *Differentiates sequence-driven* from situation-driven management. Viewing a project solely as a sequence of phases and events cannot properly represent management dynamics, processes, roles, and responsibilities.
- *Validated empirically* on real projects by real teams. This model is a result of the experiences—both successes and failures—of thousands of practitioners and hundreds of projects.
- *Easily remembered and effectively applied.*

FIVE ESSENTIALS FOR EVERY PROJECT

The dictionary defines a team as a group of people working or playing together to achieve a common goal. But anyone watching a swarm of 6-year-olds playing at soccer, with each child self-focused rather than on the team, knows that this definition is incomplete.

Imagine the challenges faced by a newly formed jazz group, composed of highly trained specialists, each capable of an excellent solo performance. Then consider one of the freest expressions of creativity in music—improvisational jazz. One of the apparent mysteries is that, while it seems free and unstructured, at the same time it doesn't result in uncontrolled noise. Music is produced, just as surely as music is produced by a symphony orchestra that is responding to a musical score.

However, each jazz session is unique—just like a project. It is improvisational and thus being created at the time. That music is reliably produced by the combined efforts of a group of jazz musicians suggests that there is an underlying process that facilitates the musicians in a group setting. In fact, jazz has rules. For example, each piece has a time signature. The musicians exercise creativity within their adopted boundaries and respect each other's contribution, just as project participants should.

When musicians of any kind come together for a short-term engagement they depend on five essentials:

1. Resources and environment (organizational commitment);
2. A common music communications language;
3. Teamwork;
4. A score or plan (cycle); and
5. Guidelines, rules, and techniques.

The process model for a successful project team is based on these same five essentials:

Organizational commitment: The foundation for the project that includes: (1) a culture responsive to the project manager; (2) the project team's charter to do the job; (3) the financial and other necessary resources; and (4) the tools and training for effective and efficient execution.

Communication: The language and the techniques used by a particular person or group to achieve understanding. In project management, this is the essential that enables team members to interact effectively and function as a team.

Teamwork: Efficiently working together to achieve a common goal, with acknowledged interdependency and trust, acceptance of a common code of conduct, and with a shared reward.

Project cycle: The project's overall strategic and tactical management approach that is performed in periods and phases punctuated by decision events. The broadest project cycle usually starts with the identification of user needs and ends with disposal of project products. The project cycle is comprised of three aspects: business, budget, and technical.

Management elements: The ten categories of interactive management responsibilities, techniques, and tools that are situationally applied throughout all phases of the project cycle by all stakeholders.

Visualizing the Relationships among the Five Essentials

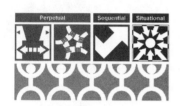

To aid in understanding and communication, the visual model differentiates between practices that are ever present (perpetual), those that are sequential, and those that are situational. When viewing the structure of each essential and the relationships among them, organizational commitment, communication, and teamwork are perpetual properties of the enterprise that transcend the boundaries of any single project.

The phases of the project cycle are sequential and should be tailored to each project. Project success usually depends on meeting the business objectives by performing a set of technical tasks within an authorized budget (cost and schedule). The three project cycle aspects (business, budget, technical) must be kept in balance.

The several hundred successful techniques and tools for both project management and systems engineering fit naturally into ten homogeneous groups.

The ten management element groups are situationally applied to the management of the project through the project cycle. There are several hundred *techniques* (practices such as using a spreadsheet or Gannt chart to depict a schedule) and *tools* (the means to perform a technique, such as Microsft Excel or Microsoft Project software) that successful project management and systems engineering practitioners use to address project situations. By grouping related techniques, we can identify homogeneous management elements. For instance, the work breakdown structure (WBS), WBS dictionary, project network diagrams, critical path analysis, scheduling, estimating, and others naturally fit into the planning element. Similarly, the techniques of measuring cost, schedule, and technical performance fit within the Project Status group. Iteration until all techniques and tools fit naturally into homogeneous specialties results in a ten-element structure.

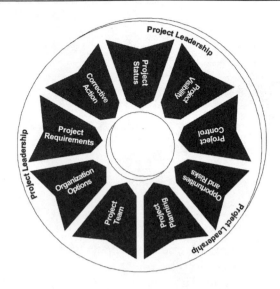

Figure 3.1 Management elements.

Techniques and tools are located within the element where their benefit is most significant. For instance, phase transition reviews (known as decision gates) provide the team with visibility as to what is happening, but the most significant benefit of decision gates is to provide project baseline approval and control. Therefore, decision gates are included in the Project Control group.

The first nine management elements are depicted as the spokes of a wheel:

1. Project Requirements,
2. Organizational Options,
3. Project Team,
4. Project Planning,
5. Opportunities and Risks,
6. Project Control,
7. Project Visibility,
8. Project Status, and
9. Corrective Action,

and are held intact by the rim, Project Leadership (Figure 3.1).

The project cycle is best visualized as an axle with the three congruent aspects—business, budget, and technical—depicted as its core (Figure 3.2). To illustrate the relationship between the situationally applied management elements and the sequential project cycle, a third dimension is required (Figure 3.3).

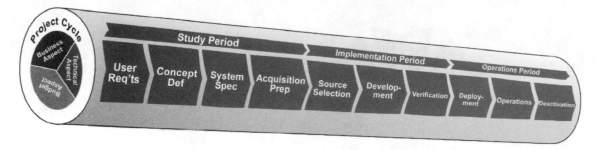

Figure 3.2   The project cycle portrayed as an axle.

The wheel progressing along the axle represents the project's logical sequence of events. Turning the dial—rotating the wheel—represents the dynamic selection and application of the technique(s) and tool(s) appropriate to the project situation at any point and to any aspect of the cycle. This sequential project cycle axle and the situational management wheel are supported by the ever-present piers of communication and teamwork on a foundation of organizational commitment. Without a solid foundation, the model collapses just as real projects do when management support and the infrastructure is inadequate.

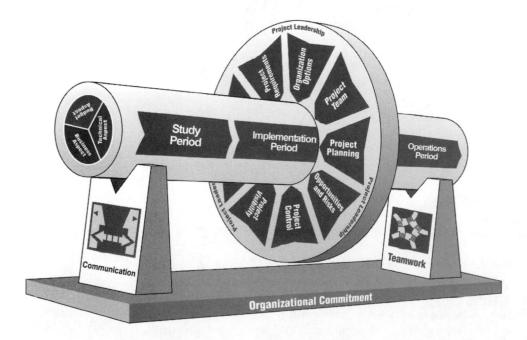

Figure 3.3   The wheel and axle model.

ELABORATION OF THE WHEEL
AND AXLE MODEL

This model has been validated by extensive project team experience and through its application as a template for evaluating troubled projects. Assessing how project teams address each aspect of the model can surface deficiencies and oversights in team conduct and management processes. Clients report that they have significantly improved project performance by basing their culture on this model. Even the most experienced project managers express a clearer understanding of their roles and increased confidence in their project execution.

 Organizational Commitment—The Springboard for Successful Projects

Project success is rooted in the foundation support systems that enable effective teams. That support can be demonstrated every time executive management charters a new project by authorizing the leadership role(s) and resources. The foundation is solidified by an organizational culture that recognizes project management and systems engineering as a team sport with the project manager calling the plays. The foundation is further reinforced by infrastructure that includes tools and training to support the project team in the achievement of its specific objectives.

Forward-looking organizations are equipping their teams with both PM and SE computer-based tools that facilitate planning and tracking of progress, technical analysis of concepts, and assistance in conducting trade studies such as decision support systems. INCOSE is currently leading the development of a common graphical template for expression of both requirements and concepts that will be adopted and supported by multiple tool vendors.

Enterprise culture, team behavior, and interpersonal relationsips are key factors of the organizational commitment. The answer to the ultimate "Why?" raised in the Introduction and addressed in the next chapter is to be found in the execution of this essential.

A useful executive management project support technique is monthly and/or quarterly reviews that address progress and shortcomings with the objective of helping to resolve issues that can benefit from higher level assistance such as added or different resources, high-level customer communication, pressure on suppliers, and the like. These reviews should not be a forum for blaming and criticizing team members or they will lose their effectiveness as a positive contribution to the project team support system.

Communication Based on a Common Vocabulary—An Ever-Present Challenge

The imagery of a jazz group or a symphony orchestra illustrates the interdependency among the five essentials. Removal of just one essential leads to vulnerability and instability. For example, imagine the confusion triggered by simple misunderstandings if you were to try to recover lost luggage in a foreign country without knowing the language.

The orchestra metaphor also reminds us that most of the orchestra's communication is based on a graphical vocabulary (notes) and the physical motions and facial gestures of the conductor that musicians understand. During a performance, no words are used, yet communication is timely and effective. To be an effective team member, an orchestra member must be conversant in both the graphical and physical languages. Similarly, team members must be conversant in the project's languages and communication techniques. Graphical languages, such as the Unified Modeling Language™ (discussed in Chapter 9), and tools such as Microsoft Visio and PowerPoint, aid communication and are commonly used in project related communication. While these tools may not always create substance, they do help display the results of team creativity and design evolution.

We are constantly reminded of the consequences of communication breakdown in our consulting and training sessions. Several terms we use to teach the practice of project management are confused with similar or identical terms used, with different meaning, in the context of a domain specific business or technical field.

A prominent project management word, *status*, has nothing to do with prestige. The project management context is usually unambiguous, but what troubles some people is the common practice of using *statusing* as a verb.

Vocabulary problems lead to conflict and serious misunderstandings. Therefore, a common vocabulary is necessary before you can effectively communicate about the project and develop the necessary teamwork. Furthermore, the common vocabulary of projects should include both project management and systems engineering terms. *Communicating Project Management*, a companion to this book, addresses communication techniques of many types and provides an integrated vocabulary with definitions for project manage-

---

The trend toward emerging technology specialties, each with its own language, coupled with the global and temporary aspects of projects, necessitates the definition of a common vocabulary for each project—even small ones.

All project practitioners should understand earned value and the implications of incremental and evolutionary development.

ment, systems engineering, and software engineering, including the Software Engineering Institute's CMMI® glossary.[5] The Glossary to this book defines terms that are frequently misunderstood and contribute to confusion.

Project Teamwork among All Stakeholders

Project stakeholders consist of people and organizations that can affect or be affected by the project.

Teamwork is often defined as working together to achieve a common goal. However, this definition falls short of the scope of the teamwork required in the project environment. The work portion of teamwork—that is, the creative effort needed to harness the creativity of all stakeholders—is usually not well understood. Because of this, real teamwork is only partially achieved. For teamwork to flourish, each of the following fundamentals must be developed and nurtured:

- Common goals;
- Acknowledged interdependency, trust, and mutual respect;
- A common code of conduct;
- Shared rewards; and
- Team spirit and energy.

Most project teams, including stakeholders, fail to adequately address these teamwork factors. Of these five factors, the most often overlooked is the common code of conduct. All too often, managers assume that a code of conduct is implied and understood even though it hasn't been explicitly defined and agreed to by all participants. This can lead to tension and separation among the team members, destroying teamwork. Many authors, including Jackman[6] and Kinlaw,[7] have addressed the issues involved in achieving successful teamwork.

Without a commitment to and implementation of teamwork, daily project activity would resemble rush hour in the subway. It's difficult to imagine a talented group of musicians making good music without a common score and a conductor. Even in self-directed teams, the leadership role is filled circumstantially by strict adherence to proven processes supported by all team members. And while it is possible for a leaderless group to become a team complete with teamwork, it is a time-consuming process at best and likely to fail in today's rapid-paced virtual project environments. With company survival often riding on project successes, we doubt

Conflict and confusion may drive team members into incorrect practices—even to performing incorrect work.

The visual evidence of teamwork . . .

The coffeepot is never left empty for teammates!

that most CEOs would gamble on the odds of creating effective leaderless project teams—any more than ticket buyers would gamble on the performance of a conductor-less orchestra.

With adequate organizational commitment and an established vocabulary, the project team will be equipped to tailor the project cycle to match the challenges of their project.

 The Sequential Project Cycle—The Template for Achieving Predictable Performance

All projects have a cycle. It may not always be documented and it may not be fully understood, but there is a sequence of phases through which the project passes in pursuit of the project's opportunity (Figure 3.4).

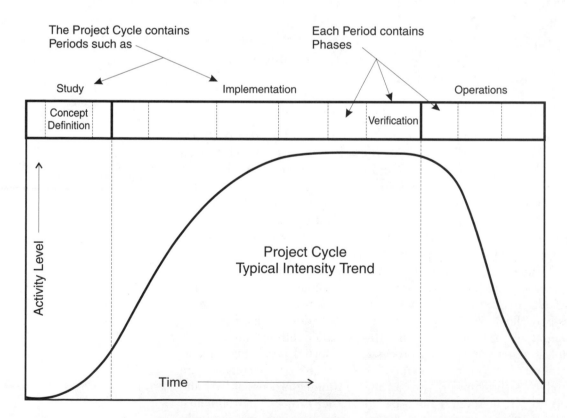

Figure 3.4   The sequential project cycle.

Professional project management organizations usually have a standard or template project cycle that embodies their proven approach and lessons learned. That reference cycle serves as a foundation for achieving predictable performance from project to project and is tailored to the special characteristics of the project at hand. The resultant project cycle then becomes the parent or driver of the project's logic network (represented by, e.g., PERT and GANTT charts) that will be developed during planning.

The project cycle for development projects should represent system solution maturation. It usually contains Periods (such as Study, Implementation, and Operations), and Phases within the Periods (such as Requirements Development and Concept Definition). Phases include activities such as Trade-Off Candidate Concepts, products such as System Concept Document, and decision gates or phase transition reviews such as System Concept Review (Figure 3.5).

The PROJECT CYCLE		
	Budget	These events involve planning for, and securing, project funding to fuel the project through the cycle.
	Periods	
	Phases	
	Activities	Specific actions taken to meet the goals of the project, e.g., Define user requirements, Trade-off candidate concepts, Develop user validation approach.
	Products	The output of activities—to be approved at the Decision Gate, e.g., System Concept Document Specifications, drawings, and manuals, Internal hardware and software feasibility models, Deliverable hardware, software, and documentation.
	Decision Gates	Predetermined decision check points to be satisfied before advancing to the next set of activities, e.g., System Concept Review.

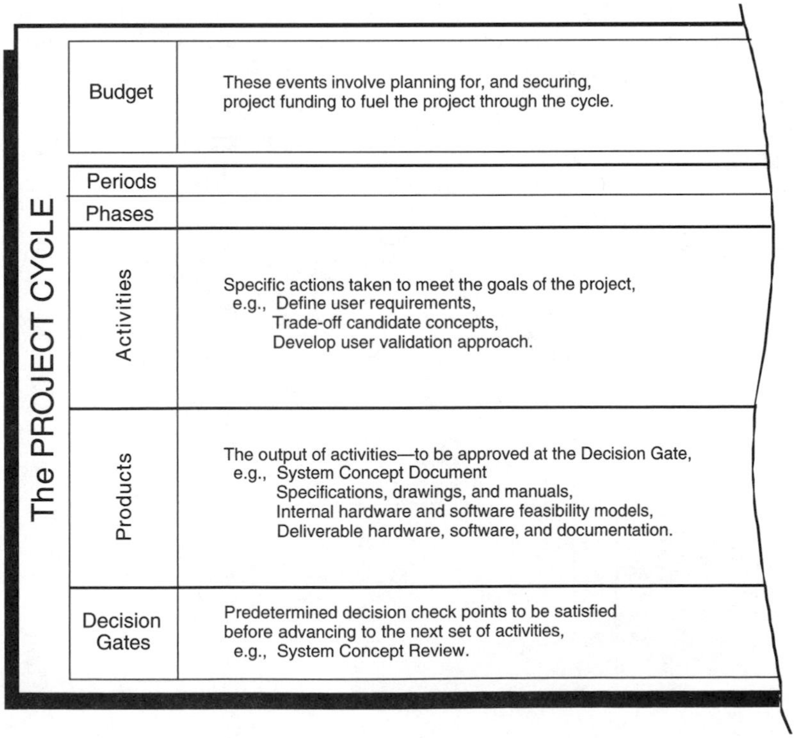

Figure 3.5 Recommended format for the project cycle.

Known by a variety of names that help to characterize it, the project cycle has been called: budget cycle, acquisition cycle, implementation cycle, and others. These are typically condensed functional views of portions of the overall project cycle.

A complete project cycle is usually designed to achieve the project strategy and includes the tactical development and integration methods determined for the project.

There are three aspects of any project cycle that are best envisioned as layers: business, budget, and technical. Each layer uses the common periods and phases but contains its own set of activities and products. The interwoven events of the three aspects constitute the total project cycle that is sometimes referred to as the project opportunity cycle. The project cycle should span from user wants to project deactivation or any reduced span appropriate to the project's scope (Figure 3.6).

The business aspect of the cycle contains the overall business tactics for accomplishing the business or mission case that is the root justification for pursuing the project opportunity. The business aspect includes such activities as teaming, alliances, licensing, market analysis, market testing, and other events relevant to the business case success. Important business decision gates include

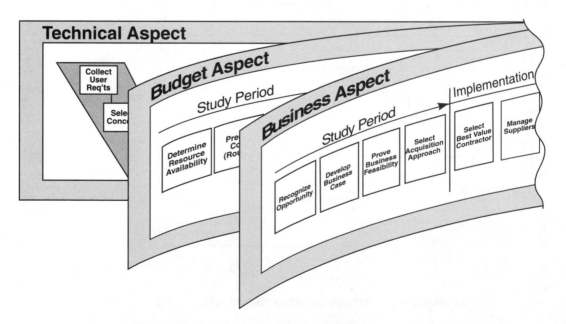

Figure 3.6   The three aspects of all projects.

approval of the overall program plan and contracting and subcontracting milestones.

The budget aspect contains the management approach (tactics) for securing and managing the funding of the project. It includes development of the detailed project "should cost" and "should take" estimates and the events associated with applying for and getting approval for the project funds. It also contains the financial management approach, such as phased work release timed with funding availability and cash flow management.

The technical aspect identifies the activities and events required to develop the optimum technical solution in the most efficient manner, a systems engineering responsibility. Tactics such as unified, incremental, linear, or evolutionary development and single or multiple deliveries should be reflected within the technical aspect of the cycle. While the business aspect is the driver of the project for development projects, the technical aspect will contain the arrangement and sequence of periods and phases to best produce the system solution. The technical cycle will usually frame the project network and will most likely represent the critical path.

THE PROJECT MANAGEMENT ELEMENTS—TEN CATEGORIES OF SITUATIONAL TECHNIQUES AND TOOLS

Technical, schedule, and cost performance are not naturally compatible and synergistic. They are opposing forces in dynamic tension that require compromise based on knowledge of the project's priorities and health. The management elements, summarized here, provide the necessary techniques and tools that can be situationally applied to manage the project through the project cycle.

Many texts and organizations attempt to apply the Fayol model to projects (depicted in the first column of Table 3.1). While the Fayol model and its more recent derivatives (second column) have a timeless validity to ongoing general management, they have critical deficiencies related to project management and the relatively short duration of projects. They fail to address the unique role of requirements as the project initiator and driver. Even more significantly, they do not provide enough detail to manage highly complex project processes, particularly those of high-risk, emerging-technology projects. To provide greater comprehension of what is required, we have expanded these models. The resulting ten elements, applicable to all phases of the cycle, identify those indispensable responsibilities of

> Technical, schedule, and cost performance are opposing forces in dynamic tension that require compromise.

> The wheel-and-axle process model adds details that too often are misunderstood, minimized, or ignored in practice. Lack of attention to these details is precisely the kind of omission that dooms projects.

Situational management depends on the proper application of each technique . . . skillfully.

Projects sometimes fail by flawed application of excellent techniques.

project management and systems engineering that are too often misunderstood, trivialized, or ignored in practice. This is not an academic reorganization. Lack of attention to these techniques leads to omissions that often doom projects.

The added and changed elements are shown in bold. For project control, the distinction between being proactive and reactive, noted in the last column, is particularly significant. Project Control embodies those techniques that help ensure that events happen as planned, and that unplanned events do not happen (proactive), whereas the three variance control elements define the means for detecting and correcting unplanned results (reactive).

Table 3.1   Relating the ten elements to traditional models

Fayol (1916)	Recent Derivatives	Our Ten-Element Model	Rationale for Expansion	Major Focus
		Requirements	Failure to manage requirements, which initiate and drive projects, is the major cause for failure.	Formulate *Proactive*
Organizing	Organizing	Organizing		
	Staffing	**Project Team**	Teams are newly formed for each project and include subcontractors and outsourcing.	
Planning	Planning	Planning		
		Opportunity and Risk Management	Usually ignored in the project environment and a significant cause of project failures.	
		Project Control	Often improperly implemented as monitoring. Many failures are due to a lack of proper controls.	
Controlling	Controlling	**Visibility**	Visibility systems must be designed and implemented to keep all stakeholders informed.	Variance control
Coordinating		**Status**	Hard measurement of progress and variance, as opposed to the more typical activity reporting.	*Reactive*
Commanding	Directing	**Corrective Action**	Innovative actions required to get back on plan.	
		Leadership	Creation of team energy to succeed to the plan.	Motivate

Because they are situational, the techniques must be applied responsively, relative to the active project phase and the team or individual circumstances at the time. An example is the Organization Options element that is applied frequently (almost continually) as the project moves from phase to phase and changes its organization form to best satisfy the objectives of the active phase. In addition, the organization option for a supplier or an internal manufacturing department is likely to be considerably different from that of the project office. Similarly, the element of Project Visibility will call for those techniques that are best suited to the active project-cycle phase and the geographic distribution of stakeholders.

> The project risk, size, and management style determine the extent of application, but not whether a particular element will be present or not—all are essential for project success.

The ten project management elements (Table 3.1) are the team's tool chest containing the best available techniques and tools in each category. This implicitly depends on the team being skilled in the application of all of the techniques and tools—which is often not the case. Projects do fail by flawed application of excellent techniques.

It is becoming increasingly popular for organizations to select a tool suite for project management and systems engineering functions. Microsoft Project is by far the most popular project planning tool set. Risk management tracking is another popular tool capability. While the tools don't discover the risks, they do help track the mitigation progress. Many systems engineering tools are available and range from requirements management all the way to executable simulations. Some are feature rich and require training to realize their full capability.

The ten elements are summarized in Chapter 8 and discussed in detail in Chapters 9 through 18.

PART TWO

THE ESSENTIALS OF PROJECT MANAGEMENT

P art Two devotes one chapter to each of the five essentials of the process model introduced in Chapter 3.

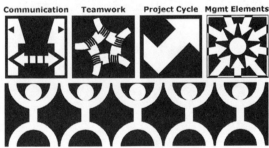

Previous editions of *Visualizing Project Management* describe four essentials of project management: vocabulary, teamwork, the project cycle, and the ten management elements.

 While the project environment and enterprise infrastructure have always been considered key to the four essentials, our lessons learned in building and sustaining project cultures have illuminated the critical importance of organizational commitment as the foundation and enabler for the other four essentials.

Nonverbal languages play an increasing role in project management and systems engineering, particularly in the graphical expression of requirements. We must, therefore, be more precise with our own process model vocabulary. While a concise vocabulary is a vital project success factor, it is now more properly characterized as part of project communication.

The next five chapters, and the ten that follow in Part Three, include margin notes (as defined in the opener to Part One) to correlate the functional attributes of the five essentials with industry practices set forth in the PMI *PMBOK® Guide* and the *INCOSE Systems Engineering Handbook*.

4

ORGANIZATIONAL COMMITMENT

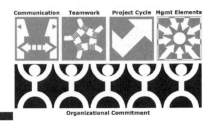
Commitments are sometimes triggered by a life-threatening event. In the case of one high-tech company, it was the corporation's life at risk. A sharp drop in proposal win rates was further complicated by a declining economy. Customers rated the company high on creativity and quality, but unacceptably low on managing development projects. The 25 largest contracts (Top 25) were all behind schedule—by as much as 50 percent—and all were over budget. Prospects for recovery were grim. A 20 percent layoff, the first in the company's 20-year history, was further evidence of the problems.

Despite the short-term crisis (or because of it), the company president acknowledged the need for a long-term solution at the culture level. His team selected our company to establish the necessary processes facilitated by a training program. Everything we provided was based on the foundation concepts of this book.

Top management was trained first. Over the next two years, all professional staff—from accounting to marketing to engineering—were required to take two weeks of training in project management, systems engineering, and project business management. One year into the program, despite no significant improvement in business results, the president insisted on staying the course of rebuilding the company's culture. He reinforced this commitment with a performance improvement incentive program tied to measurable results. By the end of the second year, all projects showed significant improvement and the Top 25 were all performing within budget and on schedule to the amazement and delight of the executive team and their customers. The next 15 years saw four presidents and many Top 25 project changes, but with only one exception the on-time, in-budget, high-quality results continued with significant client award fees and profit.

—— PMBOK® Guide ——
The *PMBOK® Guide* does not directly address organizational commitment.

However, *PMBOK® Guide* Sec 1.5.3 *Understanding the Project Environment,* 2.3 *Organizational Influences,* and 9.2 *Acquire the Project Team* contain relevant information.

—— INCOSE ——
INCOSE also does not directly address organizational commitment. Sec 7.2 *Enterprise Environment Management,* 7.3 *Investment Management,* and 7.5 *Resource Management* are consistent with this chapter.

"Commitment unlocks the doors of imagination, allows vision, and gives us the 'right stuff' to turn our dreams into reality."

James Womack[1]

Education programs are usually among the first casualties of a company's recovery, but that's the time they're most needed and have the highest impact.

In the cited company, ESL, the commitment unlocked the doors of imagination, allowed the vision, and provided the organization with the right stuff. They cultivated a learning organization long before the phrase was coined.

This ESL story illustrates many of the key messages that follow, particularly the importance of setting the overall objectives, establishing priorities, staying the course and:

- Building a project culture, starting at the top,
- Obtaining buy-in through shared discovery, and
- Keeping the faith in the vision by staying focused on the long view.

Many organizations are benefiting from their own decision to invest in a project culture, one in which project management and systems engineering are integrated as a core competency and as a competitive force. What's unusual about this case is the company's commitment of energy and resources in a deteriorating situation where the typical response is to cut all discretionary spending. ESL survived and prospered because organizational commitment started at the top, providing the fabric of the culture.

ESTABLISHING A PROJECT CULTURE WITH ALL THE RIGHT STUFF

Much more has been said than done about meaningful and lasting culture changes. Establishing a culture is not about creating a social club with a certain theme. All organizations exist to accomplish something; they have a core mission—a purpose. The delivered system is the end; the project culture is the means.

By project culture, we mean an enterprise-wide belief system that empowers the project manager to get the job done while openly addressing the critical balance needed between the enduring functional organizations and the relatively short-term project teams. What is needed is a project culture that views and rewards the project stakeholders inclusively; that is, by including all stakeholders, not just the assigned team members.

Dr. Judd Allen likens the stages of cultural change to those of farming:[2]

- Analyze and plan:
  Prepare the soil.
- Introduce systems and processes:
  Plant the seeds of change.

- Integrate, train, and mentor:
  Water and fertilize—the seeds take root.
- Evaluate and extend:
  Harvest and gather new seeds to plant.

The Role of Executive Management

When a company forms a new division, the top executive makes an announcement alerting everyone in the company. Personnel assignments are announced and roles and responsibilities are defined. In particular, relationships between existing and new organizations are clarified. In an effective project culture, each new project should be viewed as a temporary new division, with the project manager in the role of the general manager.

Executive management must determine the project manager's level of authority and then hold him or her accountable consistent with that defined authority. To hold the project manager accountable for cost and schedule with no power over the technical content is irresponsible and unfair.

Just as every project needs a champion, the project culture needs its champions—the organization's chief executive and appropriate top management. This is a proactive role as represented by the qualities in the middle column of the following list, yet many executives provide only lip service (the last column). As an example of lip service, it serves little purpose to charter a project team and project manager if the cultural support isn't already in place:

Culture Ingredient	Proactive Management	Lip Service to Project Team
Project manager authority	Fully empowered	Responsibility only
Communications	Open to broad scrutiny	Arbitrary
Project training	Available to all levels	None
Management support	Continuously involved	Impossible edicts
Management process	Kept up-to-date	Counterproductive
Funding and budgets	Planned and realistic	No budget authority
Project controls	Comprehensive	Arbitrary

Why are some executive management teams reluctant to make necessary cultural commitments? As managers rise in the

Table 4.1   A project culture depends on proactive management

	Proactive ☺	Reactive 😐	Slow React 🙁	Lip Service 🙁 🙁	No Interest 🙁 🙁 🙁
Project manager authority	Fully empowered	Selective delegation	Reluctant to delegate	Responsibility without authority	Unspecified
Communications	Open to broad scrutiny	Formal	Defensive	Avoided	Closed to any scrutiny
Project training	All levels	Project team	Managers only	None	None
Management support	Continuously involved	Reference manual	Reluctant	Impossible edicts	Sink or swim
Management process	Up-to-date	Standard	As customer demands	Counter-productive involvement	None
Funding and budgets	Planned	Controlled	By variances	No budget authority	Excess spending with cash cow
Project controls	Comprehensive and effective	Basic	Force fit	Arbitrary	Uncontrolled

organization, they often suffer a gradual loss of perspective regarding the change process itself. Too many executives are reluctant to leave their comfort zones and depart from tradition. They typically don't embrace or emphasize disciplined project management or systems engineering on any level. Their behavior can range from resistive to showing no interest at all as contrasted with the ideal proactive management attitude (Table 4.1).

Career Paths

Many companies treat project management and systems engineering as roles or assignments rather than as professional career paths. Others provide career paths with compensation linked to demonstrated proficiency levels. These companies also encourage certification, usually with financial support. In companies where project management is a defined career step to general management, the project manager position may be positioned more senior than a functional manager. This approach ensures that functional managers view the project manager as a customer. Cultures that are not project-oriented, where functional management is perceived as a step up from project management, generally exhibit less effective project execution.

The Learning Organization—Getting to the Ultimate "Why?"

Referring to the farming metaphor described previously, cultural change starts with preparing the soil and turning over a few rocks by analyzing the organization's behavior. This begins by determining why projects fail as addressed in the Introduction.

> A learning organization is one that identifies ways in which it could strengthen itself and successfully incorporates those ideas into its culture and operations.

This analysis requires an open culture where participants learn to "admire" and solve problems, not to hide or excuse them.

A Culture of Learning

To install and sustain a project culture, project teams and stakeholders need ongoing training beginning with training in the culture itself. A project culture views project management and systems engineering as essential core competencies—life skills to be sustained and improved. Companies serious about their project performance provide both project management and systems engineering training and encourage certification in both disciplines—the PMP and CSEP discussed in Chapter 2. Organization performance improvement is also encouraged through capability assessments and ratings such as SEI-CMMI and ISO certification levels of achievement.

Enlightened organizations treat professional certifications as a means to encourage professionalism and self-improvement, but not as an end in themselves. Support considerations should include budgeting time for certification training and ways to recognize and reward the accomplishment.

Lessons Learned

Many projects fail by repeating the *lessons learned*—the technical or business mistakes of others. For example, the SeaSat Satellite failed in orbit when an arc across the solar-array-slip rings caused a catastrophic power supply failure. About a year earlier, a prior project at the same company had solved this problem, which had been discovered in a thermal vacuum chamber test before their launch. This finding was not communicated to the SeaSat team. Lessons learned developed by project teams after project completion can be invaluable to other project managers, present and future. But there is usually no convenient mechanism for the lessons to get into the hands

> Don't fix the blame . . .
> fix the problem.

(and minds) of those who would benefit most. There may even be a cultural bias against exposing prior failures. Furthermore, project teams are dispersed to other projects just at the time they should be documenting their learning experiences. Perhaps Thoreau had this predicament in mind when he queried, "How can we remember our ignorance, which our growth requires, when we are using our knowledge all of the time?" One of the most neglected project management concepts is lessons learned from prior failures and successes. Later, we treat lessons learned as one of any project's requirements artifacts. In some U.S. government Request for Proposals (RFPs), the solicitation requires bidders to explain how they plan to respond to relevant lessons learned. The bidders must research and consider relevant lessons as part of the requirements.

If You Can't Change the People, *Change the People*

Few people embrace culture change. Some resist change openly (or worse, subversively). While it is important not to give up on someone prematurely, one person with a bad attitude can destroy teamwork and drag down the team as well as affect the organization's project culture. When removing an uncooperative team member, the manager needs to let the others know why, in direct, factual terms.

THE PROJECT ENVIRONMENT

Projects defy tradition. Traditional management methods simply don't apply.

Projects are quite different from traditional operations. A common form of development project is exemplified by a construction industry project or by DoD- and NASA-contracted developments that typically create projects among many geographically and nationally dispersed companies. When the project team has completed its objectives, it is disbanded and its members seek new assignments through their skill-center home organization. Still other projects are formed with one organization at the core that then uses other companies, divisions, and subcontractors as skilled resources. In all cases, project team members typically serve two managers: one for the project duration focused on tasks, and the other, the functional manager, focused on career and technical performance (providing the guarantee for the project assignment).

The evolution of a typical project, such as a new product or service development, usually follows three periods or stages (Figure 4.1).

Traditional management approaches deal well with the first and third of these three periods. For development projects, they typically

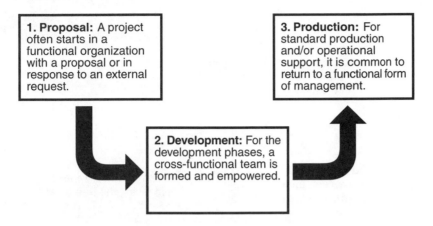

Figure 4.1   The evolution of a typical project.

do not work well during period two—the heart of project management. Traditional working conditions have meant stability, continuity, and security to the personnel. Conventional wisdom and traditional management textbooks have long emphasized the need for the manager to create a productive work environment and a consistent climate including:

- Stable work environment.
- Minimum of conflict among employees.
- Ambitious employees driven to be their personal best by perks and personal competition.
- Simple, clear reporting structure and organization.
- Responsibility matched with authority.
- Maximum creative freedom.

There's very little of this list that relates to the project environment. Conventional wisdom seldom holds true for projects. In many cases, it's dead wrong.

As depicted by Figure 4.2, projects are as important to institutions as leaves are to a tree. Traditional management models focus on the enduring organizations—the roots—such as functional departments. By contrast, project management is more narrowly focused on the specific objectives of the project at hand. Like task forces and other temporary groups, project teams are drawn from various long-term permanent organizations. But, unlike other temporary groups, projects are managed to a defined plan including a budget, schedule, and specific output—usually a product or service. Projects are requirements driven. The customer or user defines the

> Conventional wisdom seldom holds true for projects. In many cases, it's dead wrong.

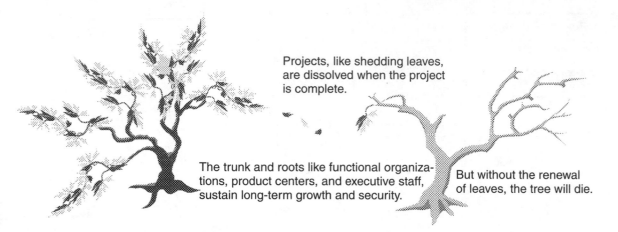

Projects, like shedding leaves, are dissolved when the project is complete.

The trunk and roots like functional organizations, product centers, and executive staff, sustain long-term growth and security.

But without the renewal of leaves, the tree will die.

Figure 4.2   Projects are like the leaves on a tree.

requirements to be met by the project team. This may be done through an intermediary such as the marketing organization.

Unlike the activities that occur wholly within traditional, functional organizations, project work depends on lateral flow across domain specialties. Therefore, projects lend themselves to some form of matrix organization (see Figure 4.3). Horizontal dotted-line interfaces need to be encouraged and strengthened rather than used reluctantly as exceptions to the linear chain of command.

The vast majority of projects exist in the matrix environment where there is a small project office (typically under 5 percent of the total project team), and project managers rely on borrowed or con-

---

Projects should not be forced into traditional structures used for repetitive or long-term work.

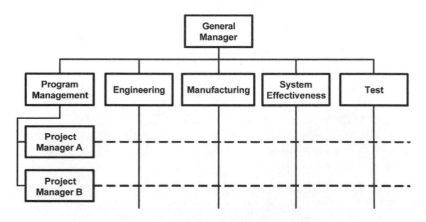

Figure 4.3   Typical matrix organization.

tracted personnel to do the required work. Individuals on the project often answer to the project manager as well as their functional manager. This is a very powerful and positive structure, but the project managers, functional managers, and all of the project team members must understand their respective roles or it can fail. Management understanding of—and support for—the project environment is required at all levels, from executive to first-line managers, from engineering to manufacturing, from contracts to procurement.

To effectively install project management and systems engineering, a foundation is necessary. An executive should issue the project charter to authorize the project, appoint key personnel, and establish the working relationships including the code of conduct and spirit of the relationships.

If the functional managers control what their people do, project managers become powerless and are reduced to being project coordinators and monitors, simply reporting on what is happening and why projects are not meeting their objectives. Alternatively, if the project manager has full control, the functional departments become "body shops," supplying people on demand and removing them when budgets are cut. Such managers are often judged by how little overhead funds are used to sustain their people, in which case it is difficult to build a core corporate technical competence. These undesirable extremes can be balanced when executive management works with all organizations to define their roles and responsibilities in the project environment and culture.

> Project management and systems engineering are difficult to describe succinctly.

PROJECT RESOURCES

Project management and systems engineering require substantial support systems. There is extensive planning, coordinating, communicating, measuring, analysis, controlling, statusing, reporting, and a host of other activities requiring thoroughness and attention to detail. Timeliness is of the essence since corrective action must be swift if projects are to meet their cost and schedule constraints.

The increasing complexity of projects is exacerbating this challenge as the number of entities and interfaces soar exponentially. No longer are hand-entered tables and matrices effective and efficient.

Supporting systems for planning, work release, cost collection, status reporting, earned value, technical performance, personnel management, material and parts procurement, subcontractor management, and so forth should all be designed to support the project with a minimum of overhead and bureaucracy. Well-managed companies have

> *INCOSE*
> The *INCOSE Handbook* Sec 7.5 *Resource Management* cites the necessity of coordinating project staffing with the resource needs of the entire enterprise.

planning centers, planning software, cost collection daily, cost reporting in real time (either daily or weekly), requirements-management software, system-simulation software, decision-analysis software, lessons-learned databases, and other support systems.

Forward-looking organizations are equipping their teams with both PM and SE computer-based tools that facilitate planning and tracking of progress, technical analysis of concepts, and aid in informed trade studies such as decision support systems. INCOSE is currently leading the development of a common graphical template for expressing both requirements and concepts, which is to be made available by multiple tool vendors.

A major support environment issue is authority of the project manager, which must be determined by executive management. There is a very wide dynamic range for this position that extends from no power to supreme dictatorial power. In government-related projects performed to defined contract terms and conditions, it is not uncommon for the project manager to have complete authority over the project. In these cases, the project is run as a line of business with cost-center performance. In this environment, the project manager decides and implements with autonomy and is held accountable for the results. The project manager "buys" internal services by issuing work tasks with associated budgets. If internal support systems fall short, the authority extends to cancelling the internal services and acquiring the support from whatever organization can provide it, even from a competitive source. Buyers like their supplier project managers to enjoy this level of authority. In this environment, the concept of "make a promise, keep a promise" has a chance of working because of the threat of work cancellation.

The other exteme is caused when functional organizations are funded on an annual basis by general management rather than by the project managers. Project managers must then solicit functional support by requesting it (begging for it) followed by managing the resource with no authority or financial power. In extreme cases, it comes down to the project manager having to complain to senior management to get the support needed to complete the project as planned. Because the functional managers own the resources, they are the ones that determine the project priorities and the effort expended on them. In this environment, the concept of "make a promise, keep a promise" almost always fails.

The organization's culture should recognize and respond to the project manager as the overall authority of the project and to the chief systems engineer as the senior technical authority of the project and the keeper of the customer's perspective. Functional man-

----- *PMBOK® Guide* -----
The *PMBOK® Guide* Sec 2.3.3 *Organizational Structure* illustrates the degree of authority of the project manager as a function of the type of organization created by general management.

agers should view the project manager as their customer with customer satisfaction as their ultimate driver. Functional managers should be willing to guarantee the performance of their specialists and be willing to step in and rectify substandard performance.

ORGANIZATION COMMITMENT EXERCISE

Based on your current or recent work experience, list the tangible evidence of organizational commitment. Include executive support, career paths, processes, tools, and training.

Make a second list of those organizational actions that would significantly improve the project team's ability to succeed.

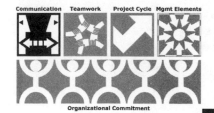
Communication Teamwork Project Cycle Mgmt Elements

Organizational Commitment

5

PROJECT COMMUNICATION

"The greatest problem in communication is the illusion that it has been accomplished."

George Bernard Shaw

─── *PMBOK*® *Guide* ───

This chapter is consistent with *PMBOK*® *Guide* Ch 10 *Project Communications Management.*

• 10.1 *Communication Planning.*

• 10.2 *Information Distribution.*

─── INCOSE ───

This chapter is consistent with *INCOSE Handbook* Sec 5.2 *Planning* and Sec 5.7 *Control Process.*

─── *PMBOK*® *Guide* ───

Communication process areas are portions of three of the five *PMBOK*® *Guide* Chapter 3 Process Groups:

• 3.2.2 *Planning.*

• 3.2.3 *Executing.*

• 3.2.4 *Monitoring and Controlling.*

"The Board believes that deficiencies in communication, including those spelled out by the Shuttle Independent Assessment Team (1999), were a foundation for the [*Columbia*] accident [on February 1, 2003]."

From the Final Report of the *Columbia* Accident Investigation Board, August 2003.[1]

Communication problems are the root cause of many project failures. Miscommunication routinely leads to conflict that can destroy teamwork. Techniques for communicating in the project environment and a common vocabulary are prerequisites for developing teamwork and for us to be able to discuss the remaining Essentials, Teamwork, the Project Cycle, and the Ten Management Elements.

It is beyond the scope of this book to enumerate the thousands of communication techniques that can benefit projects of all sizes and complexity and to define the countless terms from which a project-specific vocabulary can be assembled. We draw on excerpts and examples from our companion book, *Communicating Project Management,* and refer to several other sources that we have found especially valuable.[2]

Communicating is difficult enough in familiar work, social, and family settings. The project environment can be particularly challenging. Due to their temporary nature, projects often bring together people who were previously unknown to each other, which is reason enough for miscommunication, especially in the early project

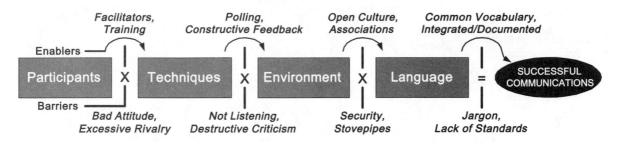

Figure 5.1   The Project Management Communication model.

phases. Because projects also integrate people with very different backgrounds, they represent a microcosm of a general organization or company. Negative labels, such as *geek* and *bean counter,* exemplify some of the attitudinal barriers that interfere with project communications, not to mention the vocabulary ambiguities among the various disciplines. As illustrated in Figure 5.1, communication results can only be as good as the least of the multiplication factors in this product:

Participants × Techniques × Environment × Language = Communications

Several general models have proven helpful in visualizing and understanding the communication process. Many models dating from the late 1940s are referred to as *transmission models* because they approach communications as an information transfer problem based on some variation of four fundamental elements:

Sender (or Source) > Message > Channel (or Medium) > Receiver

The transmission models have also influenced early studies of human communication, but many theorists now consider them to be misleading. These models and their derivatives focus more on the study of message making as a process rather than on what a message means or how it creates meaning.

The issues of meaning and interpretation are reflected in the model depicted in Figure 5.2, introduced in 1960, which emphasizes the interpretive processes. Berlo defined five verbal communication skills: speaking and writing (encoding skills), listening and reading (decoding skills), and thought or reasoning (both encoding and decoding).

For those interested in a deeper understanding of the theories underlying these and other models, we offer these references.

> To press a suit means one thing to a tailor and something very different to a lawyer.

> ——— *PMBOK® Guide* ———
> *PMBOK® Guide* Figure 10-3 identifies components of communication as:
> - Encode.
> - Message.
> - Medium.
> - Noise.
> - Decode.

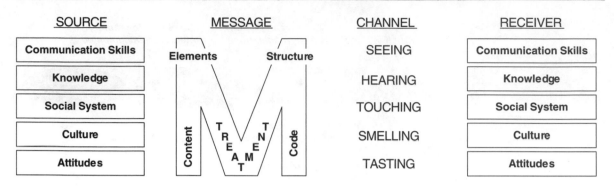

Figure 5.2   David Berlo SMCR model.

Theories of Human Communication by Stephen Littlejohn is considered the seminal text in the field.[3] Richard Lanigan in *Phenomenology of Communication* focuses on semantics—what a message means and how it creates that meaning.[4]

The remainder of this chapter speaks to the communications issues of project teams by considering each of the four communication model factors: participants, techniques, environment, and language (Figure 5.1).

PARTICIPANTS AND THEIR INFLUENCE ON PROJECT COMMUNICATIONS

We often think of project participants as being limited to the team members. But from total influence and broader communications viewpoints, the participants encompass a wide array of stakeholders, including:

- Functional and middle management;
- Executive management;
- Closely related stakeholders, such as policy makers, contractors, customers, and potential users; and
- Global stakeholders, such as professional associations and standards organizations.

Stakeholders all bring their own vocabulary, behaviors, communication styles, attitudes, biases, and hidden agendas to the project environment.

Personal Behaviors and Communication Styles

To communicate effectively, we all need to be aware of differing behaviors and styles and their potential impact. Leaders often need to adapt their own style rather than "shape up" the other person.

There are numerous texts and self-study guides for analyzing your style tendencies and preferences. In Chapter 18, we summarize two models proven to be particularly effective. However, the details of any specific self-typing or group analysis scheme are less important than the process itself—exploring your own preferences and stretching your range of styles. To benefit from that process, you have to be self-aware and open to discovery.

Models help discern cognitive preferences and do not represent behavioral absolutes. They provide insight into how we gather information, process it, and communicate. Regardless of your preferred style, your actual style at any time should be affected by factors such as the maturity level of team members and the gravity or priority of the situation. Variety and shifts in style are not only necessary—they're healthy. Communicating in projects requires flexibility and adaptability in dealing with the task at hand, the personalities involved, events, and the situation. As the Columbia Accident Investigation Board noted, "In highly uncertain circumstances, . . . management failed to defer to its engineers and failed to recognize that different data standards—qualitative, subjective, and intuitive— and different processes—democratic rather than protocol and chain of command—were appropriate."[5]

Attitudes and Biases Can Build Bridges of Understanding or Destroy Projects

We refer to negative personal biases regarding important project management techniques as the *hidden enemies*. For example, our surveys of approximately 20,000 managers regarding their attitude about red teams revealed that only 20 percent of project participants have a positive attitude about this important document evaluation and communication technique.

The Berlo SMCR Model (Figure 5.2) identifies attitude as one of five facets that affect personal communications. (Some models combine Berlo's social system facet with culture.) An inappropriate attitude or bias regarding project subject matter or a specific technique, once understood, can usually be dealt with rationally and amicably. But undisclosed attitudes toward oneself or toward another in the communications loop are a much more significant barrier. If you

Red team—objective peer or expert review of documentation and presentation material to identify deficiencies and recommend corrective action.

(See the Glossary for a more complete definition.)

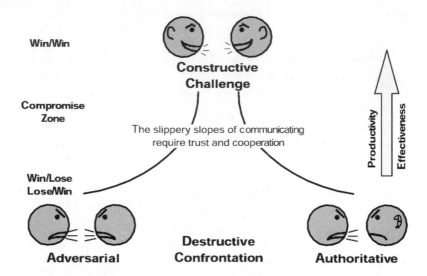

Figure 5.3   Attitude: The slippery slopes of communicating.

have a low opinion of the person with whom you're dialoging, you will certainly formulate your message differently from the way you formulate it for your respective collaborators. It is regrettable that the type of productive dialog illustrated at the top of the mountain in Figure 5.3 is so unstable and susceptible to sudden erosion and decline.

Constructive challenge (Figure 5.3) is a problem-resolving technique that depends on good communication skills and a positive attitude. Known as *constructive confrontation* in some circles, it can easily turn destructive without the right intentions, skills, or the commitment to immediately solve problems. To keep the process constructive and effective the following ground rules apply:

- On recognizing a problem, go directly to the most likely problem solver—independent of organization structure.
- Confront the problem, not the person, and use facts.
- Exclude personalities from the discussion.
- Work jointly toward resolution, holding each other accountable for the shared responsibilities.

Used skillfully, this approach eliminates whining and solves problems quickly. Some leading companies have built this practice into their culture. But when used in name only, as a weapon in rivalry or for other wrong purposes, it can destroy teamwork and the project. Excessive rivalry can be just as destructive at the individual level as it is at the global level. As long-time participants in professional associations and industry standards organizations, we have observed a trend of increasing cooperation among the key project disciplines. We ad-

—— PMBOK® Guide ——
The *PMBOK® Guide* Chapter 10 *Project Communications Management* recommends that meeting owners should plan for conflict resolution to ensure meetings are productive.

dress this collaborative spirit in several sections. Unfortunately, this industry-level collaboration frequently fails to permeate the very organizations and projects that form their constituency. Sometimes this is a result of competitive pressures. More often, it is ignorance or misdirected ambition.

In the face of management and global barriers, how can project managers ensure effective communications on their own project? Just like every other responsibility within a project, it starts at home—by taking responsibility for communicating skills, attitudes, and training at the individual and team levels. You, as project manager, need to assess the skills within your team and take the appropriate measures, which often start with good guides such as those identified in the next section.

The project participants have the greatest potential to promote understanding by proactively strengthening the other three communication factors: technique, environment, and language. When you or other key stakeholders anticipate a communication breakdown or encounter a barrier, the best strategy may be to turn to a nonstakeholder for objective feedback or assistance. For example, the initial project planning session is often held before the newly formed project team has coalesced; therefore, they may benefit greatly from an outside facilitator, one who is skilled in the subject matter as well as the art of communicating among disparate factions. This approach can:

- Accelerate the convergence to a workable plan,
- Provide valuable on-the-job communication training,
- Lead to the building and realization of teamwork, and
- Serve as a model for future conduct.

TECHNIQUES FOR COMMUNICATING IN PROJECTS

Exchange and *feedback* are key words in describing communication techniques. Whether engaged in a simple conversation or conducting a multifaceted design review, the most powerful techniques are those that result in some kind of exchange or feedback.

The next paragraph provides guides for communication techniques that are particularly helpful. While many of the suggestions offered in these sources may seem like common sense, they help focus on critical points that may be taken for granted, such as preparing for a one-on-one conversation, testing a potentially touchy conversation, or actively listening to what other people say. In addition, they offer some helpful conversational strategies and tips for determining when a meeting is going off course.

In her book, *Communicate with Confidence!,* Dianna Booher provides a compilation of 1,042 tips, all with explanations.[7] The compilation is directed toward better governance with words, both written and oral. The book by Harkins and Bennis describes proven communication techniques for improving growth and productivity.[8] Kegan and Lahey offer practical solutions to several communication barriers.[9] The article by Brown and Isaacs elevates the casual conversation to business process status.[10]

We previously discussed the situational nature of communications, particularly in projects. In addition to being aware of your own and others' communication styles, you need to consider your purposes, such as:

- Social (entertainment, enjoyment, or passing time).
- Relationship (build rapport, teamwork, trust, and commitment).
- Information exchange (present, learn, and share).
- Collaborate (work toward common goals or outputs).
- Resolve problems (address issues, remove barriers, vent hostility).
- Influence (persuade, negotiate, or direct).

You may find it useful to identify your purposes and describe your situation in order to anticipate the way in which you and the others involved may respond. Start by identifying your motivation source (personal need served).

Over the course of a project, shifts in purpose and situations occur almost routinely. For example, you may start a project with generous support from the functional engineering department, only to witness that support later wane as another project competes for the same resources. Apply the following when collaboration suddenly turns to negotiation:

- Identify or reinforce the common vision or expected outcome.
- Identify the interests of each party in the outcome.
- Have each party prioritize his or her interests.
- Generate alternative solutions.
- Choose the solution that satisfies the most interests of both parties.

We next discuss communication techniques that are often overlooked or underused to the point of project failure.

View Dialog as a Core Process

Fundamental communication techniques are brought into play whenever one project member engages another in conversation. The potential impact of the ubiquitous one-on-one conversation is too often ignored or taken for granted. The caricatures in Figure 5.3 illustrate a few of the situations we have all been in—on one side or the other.

Hundreds of valuable and creative conversational techniques are explored in the sources listed earlier. Brown and Isaacs cite research demonstrating that informal conversations can often be much more powerful and satisfying than formal communication processes. They offer this thesis: "Consider that these informal networks of learning conversations are as much a core business process as marketing, distribution, or product development. In fact, thoughtful conversations around questions that matter might be the core process in any company—the source of organizational intelligence that enables the other business processes to create positive results."[11] We hasten to add that, while informal conversation techniques can be effective, their utility and power is greatly diminished when they are practiced as a substitute for inadequate project visibility and statusing processes.

By definition, deep dialog goes beyond an informal conversation. It extends to the exchange of constructive feelings and attitudes in order to reach a common understanding. The practice of this communication technique is a good sign that teamwork is flourishing. Openness and sharing can elevate passive dialog to active collaboration and create an environment for resolving conflict, but it requires the investment of time. One useful technique is to selectively schedule meetings with no fixed agenda to facilitate open-ended discussions.

To promote dialog as a core process, consider these ground rules:

- Test assumptions and inferences.
- Share all relevant information.
- Focus on interests, not positions.
- Be specific and use examples.
- Agree on what important words mean.
- Explain the reason behind one's statements, questions, and actions.
- Disagree openly.
- Make statements, then invite questions and comments.
- Do not take degrading "cheap shots" or otherwise distract the group.
- All members are expected to participate in all phases of the process.
- Exchange relevant information with nongroup members.
- Make decisions by consensus.
- Do self-critiques.

Be Proactive—Use Glance Management

The most important job for the project manager or technical leader is to be in touch with the team members. You cannot manage your project by sitting in your office all day waiting for people to come to you. Management-by-walking-(or wandering)-around (MBWA) is a vital skill. Yet project communications often suffer because team leaders spend too much time managing by PowerPoint and e-mail. By occasionally circulating among team members in their work setting, team leaders can resolve—or at least learn about—issues that may never make it to a formal review, address morale or even technical problems before they become issues, or simply enter into a brief conversation that helps maintain an open culture. In Chapter 14, glance management and MBWA are discussed in more detail.

Improving communications through brevity when less is more. Very often, the real impact of communication doesn't occur until the information is recalled. As a rule of thumb, retention halves for each of five communication steps, which leaves us with eight minutes in the bank for a two-hour investment:

We *hear* half of what is said	2 hours
We *listen* to half of what we hear	1 hour
We *understand* half of what we listen to	30 minutes
We *believe* half of what we understand	15 minutes
We *remember* half of what we believe	8 minutes

Beyond two hours in a single session, another factor takes over—fatigue.

Hiding problems by saying nothing is not a positive application of this technique.

Observing and Listening—Encouraging Communications by Remaining Silent

Perhaps the most difficult communication technique of all is effective listening. We all know this from our own experiences and from the proliferation of great thinkers who have lamented the lost art of listening. Do you sometimes find yourself practicing one of the following nonlistening behaviors?

- Dreaming—thinking of other things.
- Acting—focusing on delivery methods rather than content.
- Rehearsing—formulating responses or rebuttals.
- Placating—agreeing, just to be nice.
- Derailing—switching.
- Debating—discrediting or discounting the message.
- Filtering—hearing selectively or with bias.
- Knowing-it-all—succumbing to the urge to talk.

"The more you say, the less people remember."

Anatole France

"It's a toss-up as to which are finally the most exasperating—the dull people who never talk, or the bright people who never listen."

Sydney Harris

One listening technique we favor begins by turning off the natural tendency to immediately react to what you're hearing. It requires turning up the gain on your receiver—and turning off your transmitter to fully experience the power of remaining silent. Sometimes your silence can speak volumes. This is especially difficult if you are an expert in your field or a high-level manager and believe that you know it all. But that's one of the most critical listening situations for understanding and removing barriers, learning fresh ideas, building rapport, and demonstrating positive leadership at the project level. Imagine the positive outcome if NASA management had *really* listened to the *Challenger* and *Columbia* interactions discussed earlier.

Polling Techniques—Overcoming the Danger of Remaining Silent

What do you do when people withhold their interpretations for the wrong reasons?

In her Tip 40, Dianna Booher asserts that you need to hear silence as it is intended (and we add, not as you want to interpret it).

She points out that people who believe that silence is consent are in for a big disappointment. She identifies 16 meanings for silence, including reflection, confusion, anger, revulsion, rebuke, shock, and powerlessness.[12] We add one that often dooms projects: fear.

Polling is a communication technique that has been traditional in aerospace programs for years. It consists of addressing individually each representative in a launch operation and recording his or her decision as to proceeding with the launch. Every individual has the right and obligation to stop a launch if his or her area is not launch worthy.

The power of using this technique, and the danger of inappropriately omitting it, is illustrated by ABC Television's faithful reenactment of the *Challenger* launch decision telephone conference with Thiokol. It shows a team of responsible Thiokol engineers being overpowered by their management, who are determined to please NASA officials with a favorable launch decision even though the engineers believed that the low launch temperature was far too risky for the solid rocket booster O-rings. NASA attempted to ensure that Thiokol's decision was based on team consensus by asking over the conference call telephone, "Is there anyone in the room with a different opinion?"[13] The engineers fearfully remained silent, their facial expressions and body language telling the true story of their discomfort with the reckless decision. NASA management was unable to see

> "He knew the precise psychological moment to say nothing."
>
> Oscar Wilde

> "The best way to persuade others is with our ears."
>
> Dean Rusk

> "There are no facts, only interpretations."
>
> Friedrich Nietzsche

the telling body language so that critical communication did not occur. Had NASA recorded a poll requiring those present to state their name and launch decision, the launch probably would have been postponed.

Make Meetings Meaningful—and Don't Neglect to Follow Up

This subject is addressed in Chapter 15, where meetings are referred to as the project manager's dilemma. High-value meetings are critical to project success while ineffective meetings can be worse than wasteful—they can destroy morale.

Constructive Feedback—Ensuring That the Exchange Is Understood by All

You haven't fully communicated until your intended meaning is confirmed through your audience's response or by some other form of feedback. For instance, the buyer and seller in the cartoon in the margin have very different views of what a "house" should be.

The importance of this communication technique is not only critical when eliciting requirements, but at every step in the project cycle. Feedback provides the basis for project decisions:

> *Fast* feedback enables *fast* decisions.
> Fast *honest* feedback enables fast *sound* decisions.

Projects are driven by the project cycle with its reviews and decision gates. Since these events bring together the key stakeholders, they offer one of the most powerful and efficient opportunities for project communications. But unless that all-important feedback loop is reinforcing and constructive, the experience will be worse than no communications at all. Some situations can benefit greatly from a two-way feedback agreement to establish trust and create a comfortable environment for candor. Here's one approach to consider:

> In order for us to be effective, I give you permission to be totally honest with me. (As long as you focus solely on work content and don't attack me as a person.)
>
> I will do my best to comprehend your message and to remain calm and objective as we resolve the issues together.
>
> In turn I intend to be honest and forthright with you.

Feedback works best as part of an organizational culture that encourages it to be given and received without reservation. Keep these guidelines in mind:

Effective	*Ineffective*
Frank and objective	Emotional and personal
Specific and complete	General and vague
Actionable	Not actionable
Facts	Opinions
Timely	Ill-timed

Before providing feedback, consider the categories depicted in Figure 5.4. Your approach should take into account the potential for conflict (e.g., the degree of criticism or counseling), the sensitivity of the receiver, and your own skills.

In the management of projects, access to facts is necessary but not sufficient. There must be confirmation that key decision makers are cognizant of the relevant facts and are bringing them to bear on decisions important to the project. This is best accomplished at decision gates where proof of concept performance and proof of design producibility provide the basis for moving ahead. In the conduct of decision gates, constructive challenge and constructive feedback are key to achieving confidence. Receivers must be open to this input and concentrate on hearing the suggestions and solution as best intentions. No matter how caustic the delivery may be, don't react as if you are attacked personally or you may end up shooting the messenger and inhibiting future valuable information.

Decision gates are not the only forums for constructive feedback. Others include: personnel performance reviews, project status reviews, fee evaluation reviews, proposal evaluations, proposal debriefings, peer reviews, red team reviews, and tiger team reviews. There is no limit to the additional informal opportunities and methods for providing essential, ongoing feedback, including conversation around the water cooler.

> "The secret of running a successful business is to make sure that all key decision makers have access to the same set of facts."
>
> Jack Welch[14]

Feedback Categories

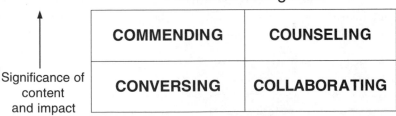

Figure 5.4   Providing feedback.

We have found peer reviews to be very effective when the review methods of all parties are aligned. There are three distinctive types of peer reviews for content and quality:

Type 1—Please Comment
- Author requests comments.
- Commenter provides comments without expecting feedback.
- Author decides what will be incorporated and what will be ignored.

Type 2—Collaborate to Consensus (C2C)
- Author requests C2C.
- Reviewer(s) provides comments and expects discussion or debate resulting in consensus.
- Both are willing to vigorously defend the agreement.

Type 3—Red Team Reviews are used when comparing to a reference such as a request for proposal or an industry standard.
- Reviewers score against preestablished criteria.
- Reviewers assess strengths and weaknesses.
- Reviewers recommend improvements.
- Authors discuss details with the reviewers to ensure understanding of the scoring, strengths, weaknesses, and recommendations, but not to debate their validity.
- Authors respond to the reviewers' suggestions as the authors deem appropriate.

THE ENVIRONMENT

This section considers the organization's project environment, which has about as much variation as does the world's political landscapes—from free and open to dictatorial and suppressive.

Effective leaders need to be able to listen, and not doing so can have dire consequences. In the final report on the Columbia Accident Investigation,[16] the Board noted the similarities between the two shuttle disasters and commented:

> Risk, uncertainty, and history came together when unprecedented circumstances arose prior to both accidents. For *Challenger,* the launch time weather prediction was for cold temperatures that were out of the engineering experience base. For *Columbia,* a large foam hit—also outside the experience base—was discovered after launch. . . . In both situations, all new information was weighed and interpreted against past experience. . . . Worried engineers in 1986

"A major obstacle to the development of a common language is our relative insularity. In the same way that physical isolation breeds language dialects, our intellectual isolation has bred project management dialects."

William Duncan[15]

and again in 2003 found it impossible to reverse the Flight Readiness Review risk assessments that foam and O-rings did not pose safety-of-flight concerns. . . .

In the *Challenger* prelaunch teleconference, where engineers were recommending that NASA delay the launch, the Marshall Solid Rocket Booster Project Manager repeatedly challenged and discredited Thiokol's risk assessment. Similarly, *Columbia's* Mission Management Team Chair made statements reiterating her understanding that foam was a maintenance problem and a turnaround issue, not a safety-of-flight issue.

> In both cases, engineers presented concerns as well as possible solutions—a request for images of *Columbia* and a temperature constraint on *Challenger's* launch. Management did not listen to what their engineers were telling them and instead overruled their informed technical recommendations.
> *The organizational structure and hierarchy stifled effective communication of technical problems.*

A Balanced Environment Encourages Feedback

An organization's culture and process should not become one where feedback providers must spend excessive time massaging the message so as not to irritate the receiver. Speed and clarity must prevail in the interest of achieving swift but informed decisions.

Feedback receivers must develop immunity to being offended in the interest of swift, clear communication. A Teflon coat or thick skin helps. The receiver also needs to give the provider some slack.

Stovepipes and Silos

One form of organizational isolation is known as *stovepipes* or *silos*. This jargon refers to virtual barriers proudly built by functional teams of a single discipline or power group. If not carefully managed, we might end up with "we creators" and "those bean counters" or, as another example, "our night shift" and "that dazed shift" or any other equally derogatory division. These virtual barriers, which are so proudly built, not only partition and inhibit communication but also foster negative communication that alienates and punishes. One of the authors would visit customers without informing his marketing personnel because he felt they were not technically qualified. This practice is seriously wrong and can be disastrous for any project depending on free and open communication to ensure the best decisions.

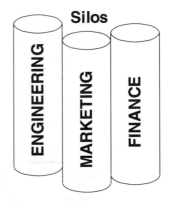

LANGUAGE AND VOCABULARY—THE MANY MEANS USED TO EXPRESS THOUGHTS

By language we mean everything from a common vocabulary to appropriate attire and body language, and we also include the effective use of silence. Some simple advice regarding body language: Believe the body language you're seeing if it conflicts with the words you're hearing. Likewise, intonation speaks louder than words.

Verbal communication problems are sufficiently widespread that they are spawning a niche business. Some consultants are finding that by the time project requirements are translated into implementation tasks communicated either orally or in written form, the resulting task may have little to do with satisfying the project's requirements and objectives. These consultants report eliminating at least 40 percent of potential project work deemed irrelevant to the intended outcome, significantly reducing the project's cost. The cause of this inefficiency is illustrated by the parlor game where a story is passed around the table. When the last person recites the story to the group, there is usually little similarity to the original. This same message erosion can occur in the project environment as contract terms are converted into system requirements, which are converted into concepts and architectures with design-to specifications. Designers then respond to the specifications without ever having seen the parent documents. This environment is one where misinterpretation can occur and grow unchecked. One of the roles of systems engineering is to audit project work in the light of the customer's objectives to ensure that all work is properly contributing to the planned result.

Graphical languages, such as UML and SysML (discussed briefly at the end of this section and in more detail in Chapter 9), are playing an increasing role in project communication, particularly for complex systems where words may not be enough (or may be too much).

To communicate clearly, you first have to *think* clearly.

To Communicate Effectively, You Have to Think Clearly and Use a Common Vocabulary

The successful practice of project management and systems engineering involves areas of conflict that can only be resolved with a clearly defined vocabulary.

John Beckley articulates the essence of clarity: "It isn't hard to write something which, if a person takes the time to study it, is absolutely clear. But writing that has to be studied is not good communication. The meaning of good writing is so immediately clear and obvious, it doesn't have to be studied."[17] Beckley tells the following story about a man who wrote to a government bureau asking if hydrochloric acid could be used to clean the tubes in his steam boiler:

> This was the bureau's reply: "Uncertainties of reactive processes make the use of hydrochloric acid undesirable where alkalinity is involved."
>
> In appreciation, the man wired back: "Thanks for the advice. I'll start using it next week."
>
> Washington wired back urgently, but still in the bureaucratic jargon: "Regrettable decision involves uncertainties. Hydrochloric acid will produce sublimate invalidating reactions."
>
> This extra courtesy prompted this acknowledgment: "Thanks again. Glad to know it's okay."
>
> Finally, another urgent, but unmistakable, message: "DON'T USE HYDROCHLORIC ACID! IT WILL EAT THE HELL OUT OF YOUR TUBES!"

Our society criticizes attorneys and politicians for their confusing, often incomprehensible, prose. It seems intended to obscure rather than to clarify events. But in a similar fashion, managers and technical people often use confusing jargon.

Unfortunately, Orwellian "doublespeak" has proliferated to all segments of politics and business, often in the form of jargon that finds us blaming everything on "paradigms" or a lack of "infrastructure." On the other hand, capitalizing on new technologies and practices can be facilitated by emerging, appropriately defined jargon.

Acronyms can simplify communication if they are uniformly understood by the team. Remember to leave the jargon behind and spell out the acronyms when making presentations or writing for audiences outside the project environment. If acronyms are used, define them as they are introduced and provide a glossary.

The truly impressive communicator doesn't set out to impress anybody—just tries to get ideas across in the simplest, clearest fashion. Such a person is likely viewed as an outstanding communicator and project contributor.

We All Speak the Same Language, Don't We?

Many words, which are viewed as synonyms in common usage, have unique and distinct meanings in a technical sense. Stress and strain, commonly used interchangeably to refer to personal anxiety, refer to quite different technical phenomena, as do the project management terms verification and validation. Few people confuse bread with its

> "Snow jobs"—intended or not—can backfire. Your words may mean something quite different to your listener.

> Jargon needs to be used as a means, rather than becoming an end, for communicating.

> All too frequently, when an engineer sounds as if she's speaking a foreign language—one composed mostly of acronyms—it's because she wants to.

chief ingredient, flour, but the ingredient cement is often used incorrectly to refer to concrete. Not many people care, but the distinction is critical if you are a civil engineer or a building contractor.

The assumption that we have a common language when we don't can have far worse consequences than trying to communicate nonverbally. After all, as jargon proliferates, the language of choice will often revert to the more trustworthy standby: body language.

A leading corporation asked us to participate in a team building session convened to identify the opportunities, associated risks, and appropriate actions for a new team. It was the first time the complete team had been brought together, so the project manager opened the meeting with a 40-minute overview of the project. We jotted down approximately 20 terms we didn't understand and later asked the team members which of the terms they understood. Over half of the group didn't understand any of the 20 terms. Without a clarifying reference, the team didn't get the important message the project manager was trying to convey. But each member remained silent, being too embarrassed to ask and assuming the others knew. The most dangerous assumption was on the part of the project manager, who assumed everyone understood.

A major corporation signed a contract with a foreign government to rebuild that country's entire communication structure without understanding the meaning or implications of many of the contract provisions. The resulting five-year, multibillion dollar project was completed on time but at zero profit—not a career-enhancing outcome.

To prevent misunderstandings, one U.S. government agency includes electronic and printed versions of their terminology manual with their request for proposal (RFP) so that all received proposals are based on identical definitions. Similar techniques are proliferating to other project environments.

Each project needs its own terminology baseline. To make this point in our training sessions, we ask the class to define several commonly used terms. We frequently select the following five from a substantial list of misunderstood terms: prototype, baseline, qualification, verification, and validation.

The class participants always argue among themselves as to the correct meanings. The debate continues inconclusively until the organization's project management terminology manual is used to clarify the meanings.

There is a need for a common vocabulary at the project level because most enterprises don't have a common vocabulary and words are used differently across projects, companies, and industries. Furthermore, broad-based terminology manuals are often imprecise.

The term *qualified* was not understood and not responded to during the prelaunch readiness review of the space shuttle *Challenger*, leading to the O-ring failure and causing the tragic deaths of seven astronauts. One of the decision makers in the Flight Readiness Review asked, "It's my understanding that the Solid Rocket Boosters are qualified by contract for operation between 40 and 90°F. . . . Are the solids qualified to 40 degrees or aren't they?"[18] The question was never answered, and since the predicted temperature at launch was 29°F there should have been no question about postponing the launch.

The process of creating a terminology manual of any kind is not trivial. Consider the plight of James Murray when he agreed in 1878 to take the assignment as editor to create the Oxford English dictionary.[19] The job had been scoped several years earlier as a two-year project involving 60,000 definitions. It was completed 50 years later with over six million definitions (estimating project size and duration has never been easy). However, the process we use today to build a terminology manual is not unlike that used by Murray, where multiple sources must be consulted to create a meaningful document.

When building a project-management terminology manual, one would think that, in the present era, existing sources in the disciplines supporting projects would provide a strong starting point. However, in reviewing one 387-page dictionary of mechanical design, we could not find common project terms such as prototype, engineering model, mock-up, specification, or qualification.[20] Yet, it is the mechanical designer who must implement those concepts on any project involving hardware. Fortunately, the software profession has been more aware of the need for accurate definitions; four of these five terms were found in the appendix to a software tutorial.[21]

When we turned to a well-respected reference from the project-management field, we were astounded by the absence of the term *requirements*, which not only represents the intersection of project management and systems engineering but drives them both. We devote Chapter 9 to this topic. The PMI *PMBOK® Guide* uses *scope* to refer to requirements.[22] Though these words are not identical in meaning, this clearly illustrates the need for terms to be carefully defined on your project. It also emphasizes the need for completeness. *Requirement* is a term widely used in high-technology industries, and *scope* is widely used in the construction field.

A terminology database, tailored to the project at hand, can go a long way toward fixing the problem. It needs to consider the terminology appropriate to the industry, company, and the specific project. The cardinal rule in constructing a project vocabulary is to make sure every item added is justified. It must contribute more to

——— **INCOSE** ———

The *INCOSE Handbook* defines *baseline* as, "a specification or product that has been formally reviewed and agreed upon, that thereafter serves as the basis for further development, and that can be changed only through formal change control procedures."

——— **PMBOK® Guide** ———

The *PMBOK® Guide* Glossary defines *baseline* as "the approved time phased plan . . . plus or minus approved project scope, cost, schedule, and technical changes."

——— **PMBOK® Guide** ———

Both the *PMBOK® Guide* and the *INCOSE Handbook* include glossaries of terms.

A secondary benefit of a project-terminology database is the increase in everyone's sensitivity to the need for precise communications.

Why use "utilize" when you could utilize "use"?

understanding than it detracts as potential excess verbiage. Try first to use ordinary language to represent a needed concept, using short words where possible. Only if the resulting expression is unduly burdensome should a new term or acronym be coined or borrowed from a related field or industry. In the latter case, the use of the existing nomenclature should clarify, rather than mislead, through its similarities.

When Words Are Not Enough (or Too Much)

Flowcharts and behavior diagrams have long been used for expressing ideas and designs. In recent years, these forms of graphical communication are replacing the written word as a means to express project requirements and as a primary artifact throughout system development. The emerging role of the Unified Modeling Language™ (UML) and SysML in systems engineering is discussed in detail in Chapter 9 and in Appendix C.

The need for more precision to express requirements and concepts for complex systems is one reason for the growth in popularity of graphical languages and diagramming. The other main driver, analogous to the growth of the ubiquitous spreadsheet made into a household utensil by Lotus123, is the availability of productivity tools that support language standards such as UML and that integrate with other productivity tools.

Some Critical Decision Gates Have Critically Confused Titles

While the definition of decision gates involves more than terminology, some titles themselves have been a historical source of confusion. We will use this section to clarify particularly egregious nomenclature. Decision gates are discussed in more depth in the next chapter.

Professional societies have defined decision gates that are common to both government and commercial projects. Since these definitions are being broadly adopted by commercial industry in international environments, it is important to alert new users to misleading nomenclature. Some decision gate titles are incorrectly based on their position relative to design approval (e.g., being preliminary to or critical to design approval). There is no universal set of terms all agree to. The Preliminary Design Review is also called an Initial Design Review by some and a High Level Design Review by others. The intent of these three reviews is similar, but not identical. The terminology we have selected is in wide use and clearly represents the concepts we wish to convey.

The Preliminary Design Review (PDR) is actually the final "design-to" of the concept, specification, and verification plan review. PDRs are really Performance Guarantee Gates because test and analytical evidence should prove that all performance numbers are achievable, that no significant performance risk remains, and the end product will satisfy the customer. But in many PDRs you can count on only three things: coffee, donuts, and pictorials of the project approach. Specifications (major evidence to be evaluated) are often conspicuous by their absence, as are verification plans, having not yet been developed. Because it's preliminary, the audience is easily contented, although it should not be. This confusing terminology may well cause the team to not deliver their decision gate products. Countless hours are wasted in PDRs that don't satisfy the criteria for the review.

> There is nothing preliminary about the Preliminary Design Review. It would be better called the Performance Guarantee Gate.

All decision gates are the final points for important project decisions. Even though one of the better-known decision gates is called a Critical Design Review (which is the "build-to" design review), all decision gates are critical events in the project cycle. Critical Design Reviews (CDRs) are really Production Guarantee Gates because test and demonstrations should prove that building and coding to the proposed documentation is achievable with acceptable risk and that the end product will satisfy the customer. That is, the design approach and processes are well understood and are repeatable.

> There is nothing uniquely critical about the Critical Design Review. It would be better called the Production Guarantee Gate.

The most critical of all design reviews is the System Concept Review where the system concept is approved, thereby committing to the associated life cycle costs and risks of the concept selected.

> The most critical decision gate is the System Concept Review.

Formal Is as Formal Does (Not as Formal Says)

We often find that *formality* is erroneously associated with the amount and appearance of documentation, rather than properly relating to project conduct that's in accordance with established forms, conventions, and requirements.

Formality has to do with team adherence to baselined principles and practices regardless of the elegance of their documentation. Well-documented projects are sometimes undisciplined, ignoring their own documentation and operating in an informal mode. Conversely, we have witnessed projects with almost no documentation that operated in accord with the requirements and conventions adopted by the project—a very formal and binding discipline.

Formality relates to whether the agreements (oral or otherwise) are "binding." A "make a promise, keep a promise" culture is formal.

Accountability—Walking the Talk

Accountability is an important part of every project's vocabulary.

Project managers should hold their teams accountable to the project vocabulary. It is reasonable to have team members certify that they have read the baseline project terminology and that they are committed to using it.

PROJECT COMMUNICATION EXERCISES

Jot down your definitions for prototype, baseline, qualification, verification, and validation. Compare what you have to the definitions in the Glossary.

For your project, identify the means used for communicating and prioritize them as to their importance. Based on the information provided in this chapter, identify potential improvements.

Rank the four communication model factors (*participant behaviors, techniques, environment,* and *language*) as to their relative contribution to your project communication problems. Identify several examples of situations or behaviors that illustrate your highest-ranking problem areas and compare your results with others in your organization.

6

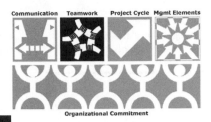

TEAMWORK

There was a period during which the U.S. government taught adversarial project management. The theory was that contractors being told they were not measuring up would cause a positive reaction—work harder to improve—thereby benefiting the government. Teamwork waned, as did morale. One government agency, the CIA, did not subscribe to this philosophy and decided to find a better way to enhance teamwork and enhance both creativity and productivity. In 1988, Len Malinowski was assigned to develop a precedent-setting project management training program. It was to baseline the combined best practices in both project management and systems engineering for the entire agency. Len took this learning experience one step further, campaigning to team the government project manager with the related contractor project manager. Security and ethics barriers were thrown at Len, but he prevailed and the two-week, off-site learning experience was based on the teamwork concept. Thirty-five hundred personnel in team pairs learned of each other's objectives, methods, and biases. At the same time, they learned a common vocabulary and a common approach to managing technical development projects. As a result, project performance dramatically improved throughout the agency. The program logo (at the end of this paragraph), prominent throughout the training materials, stressed the importance of teamwork. The relationships were characterized as partners hooked at the hip while in an arm's-length business relationship. The most successful learning experiences occurred when an entire project team of government, contractor, and subcontractor personnel was trained as an intact team at project start-up.

User   Project Office   Contractor   Subcontractor

"Coming together is a beginning. Keeping together is progress. Working together is success."

Henry Ford

—— *PMBOK® GUIDE* ——
This chapter is consistent with *PMBOK® Guide* Sec 9.3.2 *Develop Project Team: Tools and Techniques.*

—— *INCOSE* ——
The *INCOSE Handbook* emphasizes the value of teamwork in the introductory sections and in Section 5, *SE Project Management Processes.*

Of all the challenges facing project teams, the greatest involves the people themselves.

T eam effectiveness relies on many things, including chemistry, attitudes, and motivational sources. Achieving real teamwork depends on three steps:

1. Forming a group capable of becoming a team,
2. Creating and sustaining a teamwork environment, and
3. Inspiring teamwork success through leadership.

In this chapter, we focus on the second of these: creating and sustaining a teamwork environment. Team formation emphasizes the techniques for selecting the right people and defining their roles—an ongoing process throughout the project cycle. The motivational techniques needed to sustain the project team are an integral part of leadership.

WHY DO SO MANY TEAMS FAIL?

Few terms are as evocative of today's desired work setting as *team* and *teamwork*.

Teamwork, so essential to effective project performance, receives considerable attention today. We want our project staffs to become empowered teams—perhaps even self-directed teams. We organize our work groups into integrated project or product teams. We use Red Teams for peer review and Tiger Teams to solve problems. To manage quality achievement, we team with our customers. We have Continuous Improvement Teams. We agonize over the impact of telecommuting on teamwork. And then with all this emphasis on teaming and teamwork, we still collect groups of people, tell them they're empowered, leave them alone, and hope that a functioning team somehow emerges from that forced proximity of a small conference room or an Internet facilitated collaboration.

If that wished-for team fails to emerge from the self-discovery process, then we resort to an event called a "team build" at an off-site location. The staff discusses goals and generates mission statements. The event is full of good social activities—perhaps the traditional "build a tower out of drinking straws"—and even some outward-bound type of outdoor experience like a "trust fall." Then, full of sociable camaraderie, we go back to work and watch the team that started to jell so nicely in the woods or at the conference site fall quickly and quietly apart, back into the collection of individuals that we started with (Figure 6.1).

Once a group is formed, the people tend to believe they are a team even when they're not.

When teamwork fails, it's seldom due to lack of good intentions.

Failure usually results from a lack of a common approach to accomplish the work as a team. Inadequate leadership fails to create the environment in which teams can flourish. Furthermore, potential team members are seldom trained in how to share their efforts to

The special recognition usually given to the "team" portion of teamwork makes members aware of the need for cooperation.

Yet many teams fail.

Most team efforts fail because of insufficient attention to the   involved.

Figure 6.1   The "work" in teamwork.

accomplish team goals. The team may also assume they know more about teamwork than they actually do. So we need to be able to differentiate between superficial teamwork and the real thing.

THE FUNDAMENTALS OF AN EFFECTIVE TEAMWORK ENVIRONMENT

Effective teams share several common characteristics. They can articulate the common goal that they are committed to achieve. They acknowledge their interdependency with their teammates, coupled with mutual respect. They have accepted boundaries on their actions—a common code of conduct for the performance of the task. They have accepted the reward of success they will all share. Add team spirit and a sense of enjoyment when working together, and the result can be a highly effective and efficient team that produces quality results.

One of our metaphors for a team is an orchestra with a common score and a conductor. A successful performance depends on the direction of the score (project plan) and a single point of accountability for setting the tempo. However, having a conductor just wave the baton (or a project manager authorize tasks, which is the functional equivalent in today's project environment) is insufficient to build and sustain a team.

The image of an orchestra performance reflects today's real project environment and the nature of operating project teams.

Our dilemma today is that we can't take the time or risk for self-directed group discovery. And merely having a project manager and a kick-off event is insufficient to sustain real teamwork. So, where do the shared goals, the sense of interdependency, the common code of conduct, and the shared rewards come from? That's the work of creating teamwork.

Fundamental 1: Common Goals

Significant involvement leads to a sense of responsibility for—and therefore, commitment to—project goals.

In contrast to a conventional, ongoing functional department, project teams are usually comprised of a heterogeneous group of people from various functional responsibilities. For this reason, as well as the nature of project people and the teamwork culture, each team member wants involvement and proactive participation in management activities. These include planning, measuring, evaluating, anticipating, and alerting others to attractive opportunities and looming risks.

Building teamwork begins with clearly defining the individual and joint objectives and outlining the various roles and responsibilities required to accomplish the objectives. Gaining consensus for the top-level goal is often easy. You must probe to the second or third tier to reveal and resolve overlaps and gaps. Having that team activity available, ask each member of the group, "Now that you understand the content of the tasks, do you really want to be a member of this team?" A "yes" identifies a potential team member.

Fundamental 2: Acknowledged Interdependency and Mutual Respect

We concur with Stephen Covey's assertion: "The cause of almost all relationship difficulties is rooted in conflicting or ambiguous expectations around roles and goals."[1] In the team environment, mutual respect, relationships, roles, and interdependencies are inextricable and develop in concert.

At the project's beginning, a revealing team effort is defining roles. After team orientation and goal setting, the task of preparing personal task descriptions provides a maturity calibration point and offers a revealing way of getting feedback regarding team role perceptions. The following are steps for the team to acknowledge interdependency and to establish expectations:

- Define the specific functions, tasks, and individual responsibilities.
- Develop an organizational structure and define team interdependencies.
- Define the scope of authority of each member.

Some roles are assumed, undeclared, and/or undefined, including personal activities such as tutor, interpreter, cheerleader, or troubleshooter. While there are usually formal, written responsibilities for project managers and leaders, team members' roles are too frequently unwritten. In her book, *Star Teams, Key Players*, Jackman emphasizes the responsibility of each team member for ensuring outstanding performance of the team by becoming a key contributor.[2] As each member is added to the team, it is a wise, proactive practice for that new member to define his or her roles and to have those roles acknowledged by the rest of the team and the project manager. Then the roles are adjusted as appropriate, to create both team synergy and minimize discord.

Later, in the planning process, the cards-on-the-wall technique (discussed in Chapter 12) provides a highly effective team building opportunity. As the schedule network evolves, personnel interdependencies are easily recognized.

You can have well-defined responsibilities, but if the interdependencies are not acknowledged, there is no basis for teamwork—only a well-structured individual effort. For interdependencies to be recognized, there must be an acceptance of, and respect for, the roles that must be filled by each team member.

Like teamwork itself, mutual respect is easier said than done. You need to be aware of, acknowledge, and accommodate both strengths and weaknesses—both yours and others'.

Role biases can be major roadblocks to respect, and that can lead to potholes, as one of the authors learned long ago when mixing asphalt for a road-resurfacing project. The contractor personnel took great pleasure in fooling the state inspector. A faulty scale allowed too much sand in the mix, causing the inspector to approve every bad batch. The workers thought it was a great joke until they depended on those roads. Many years later, the potholes are still a grim reminder of the deficient mix, and especially of the lack of appreciation for the inspector's vital role.

Role biases can be particularly true of the project management and systems engineering disciplines. Systems engineers often see themselves as the key technical contributors carrying the rest of the project on their "technical backs." They sometimes believe that no one else is capable of communicating with them or of appreciating their "contributions." Likewise, project managers believe systems engineers have little regard for cost and schedule. This book is intended to help overcome these communication and teamwork barriers by providing the information necessary for the entire team to participate in determining the system solution approach.

Roles and mutual dependencies need to be acknowledged by all project members.

Mutual respect means accepting the need for the role performed by each team member and respecting his or her competency, especially if it is outside your field of expertise.

In a production environment, manufacturing often sees quality assurance (QA) as an enemy to be circumvented rather than a vital member of the team necessary to project success. Conversely, QA has been known to stop production lines just to exercise its authority.

The space shuttle tile program, which developed and produced the external heat shield for the orbiter vehicle, demonstrates how teamwork, based on mutual respect, can mean the difference between success and failure. In the transition from research to production, problems occurred that no one knew how to solve. Manufacturing and QA personnel worked together very effectively, helping each other resolve the many technical challenges. Responsibilities for traditional QA tasks were even shifted between organizations when people on the production line found a better way. A true cooperative and lasting team spirit, based on mutual respect, was developed between manufacturing and QA.

Though respect is earned, it begins by putting your critical attitude aside and giving others the benefit of the doubt without being condescending or patronizing. By keeping an open mind, you can acquire respect for your lack of specific skills, for another's competency, and for traditionally adversarial roles.

Fundamental 3: A Common Code of Conduct

The right time to address legal and ethical issues is when they are only potential problems—before they become a career-limiting lesson learned. When it comes to conduct, just as in planning, an ounce of prevention is worth a pound of cure.

Legal and ethical issues have been receiving widespread attention in the news media as more and more companies restate their earnings. The most obvious conduct issues are usually well-documented prohibitions by company or government policies. But they may not be well known to all team members. And the gray (or ambiguous) areas, especially those involving contractor and customer interfaces, may not be understood or interpreted consistently. The project manager is responsible for reviewing these issues, together with the relevant company policies, to ensure that all team members are sensitized to areas of risk. Figure 6.2 lists legal conduct issues for review with the team.

Ask yourself, "Would I be embarrassed if my behavior appeared on the front page of the newspaper?"

Ethical conduct issues are more difficult to enumerate. Ultimately, you have to depend on personal values to navigate through the possible conflicts that can occur between company practices, laws and regulations, and management direction. When dichotomies persist, these guidelines may help:

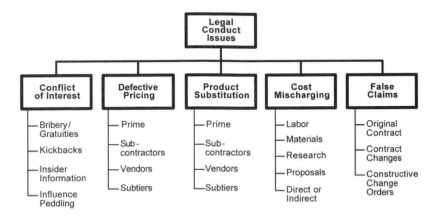

Figure 6.2   Legal conduct issues.

PMBOK® Guide
PMBOK® Guide Sec 9.3.2.4
Develop Project Team: Ground Rules relates to the team's code of conduct.

- Seek higher management guidance to confirm difficult choices for conflicts among the various codes of conduct.
- If asked to operate in a potentially improper manner, make sure that the request is written and verify it with the cognizant authority. Do nothing that violates your personal ethics.
- Report any improper conduct, anonymously if necessary.

To be effective, a common code of conduct needs to:

- Resolve potential sources of conflict,
- Clear the air on gray areas, and
- Cover areas not addressed by other standards such as:
  —Working on new scope in response to an oral request and
  —Threshold value of a change proposal.

Ask each potential member of the team, "Will you commit to abide by these rules of conduct?"

A "no" will surface issues to be resolved.

Categories to consider include:

Customer relations.
Personal use and care of company property.
Attendance and work hours.
Safety.
Sexual harassment.
Smoking, alcohol, and drug abuse.
Gambling.
Falsification of records.

Acceptance of gifts.
Standards of quality.

Fundamental 4: Shared Rewards

Money spent on pizza for all
may be more effective than a
bonus given to the most outstanding contributor.

Shared recognition for contributing team members of a successful
project is often far more important than cash bonuses. People are
motivated to do a good job and to cooperate with one another when
they are confident that their individual and team performance will
be publicly recognized and appreciated by their peers and their
management.

—— *PMBOK® Guide* ——
PMBOK® Guide Sec 9.3.2.6
*Develop Project Team: Recog-
nition and Rewards* provides
additional reward information.

Effective cash rewards begin with fair and equitable compensation for team members. You can also devise awards that can
be earned by the entire team. The concept of shared rewards
suggests dividing a bonus pool equally by the number of participants. With this approach, the lowest paid receives the highest
percentage compared to base compensation causing a ground swell
of enthusiasm.

A Hyundai executive was forced to resign because he rewarded
370 quality management division employees for the dramatic improvement in Hyundai quality, which surpassed even Toyota. His
error was that he failed to reward all 35,000 Hyundai employees.
Hyundai ultimately agreed to include all employees, as the union
contract required, and paid $29 million to the 35,000 employees (ap-
proximately $830 per person).

Fundamental 5: Team Spirit and Energy

Instilling teamwork cooperation often begins with unin-
stalling the "me-first"
competition culture deeply
scripted in most people by
their education and business
experience.

This quality depends on personal attitudes as well as company culture and begins with:

- An agreement to pool resources.
- Interdependence rather than independence.
- Desire to do whatever is necessary to succeed.
- Placing team needs above one's own needs.
- Never asking the team to do what you are not willing to do.
- Setting the example for others to follow.

Allow the team to come to
consensus even though you
know the answer and could
tell it to them. They will feel
more energized about the
solution if it is theirs.

Independent thinking alone is not suited to the interdependent
project reality. Putting the team ahead of oneself, however, does
not mean the elimination of strong pacesetters. Driving personalities need to exercise their assertiveness and energy without domi-

nating their teammates. This sometimes involves subtle leadership techniques.

TECHNIQUES FOR BUILDING AND SUSTAINING TEAMWORK: THE *WORK* OF TEAM*WORK*

Creating and sustaining effective teamwork requires ongoing work on the part of all team members. Many team building efforts fail either because essential techniques are unknown or applied inappropriately by participants unaware of the situational nature of project management and leadership.

While team building is a total team responsibility, we will focus first on what the project manager can do to foster and nurture a fledgling team. First, we need to refine our image of the team as an orchestra led by the project manager. In the project reality, the project manager is both the composer and the conductor. To quote Peter Drucker, "This task requires the manager to bring out and make effective whatever strength there is in his or her resources—and above all in the human resources—and neutralize whatever there is as weakness. This is the only way in which a genuine whole can ever be created."[3]

Like any other development process, there is a gestation period involved. The project manager must avoid over directing and smothering the team. Alternatively, too much freedom can cause a new team to founder. The project manager must:

- Clearly define unambiguous responsibilities,
- Define and communicate a project process and style,
- Delegate wherever possible,
- Empower the team to be accountable,
- Balance support with direction as required,
- Train the team, by example, to operate as a team,
- Deal with underperformers who drag the team down,
- Establish team-effort rewards, and
- Design the tasks and work packages in a way to encourage teamwork.

The leadership techniques discussed next pertain especially to building teamwork.

The Team Kick-Off Meeting—A Teamwork Opportunity.

The kick-off meeting should be a working session. When properly led by the project manager, it can provide each team member with a

---

Teams don't always need managers to do things right, but leaders always need teams doing the right things.

The project manager is the most responsible for sustaining a whole that is larger than the sum of its parts.

—— *PMBOK® Guide* ——
PMBOK® Guide Sec 9.3.2.3 *Develop Project Team: Team Building Activities* cites the value of project-related team-building events.

The kick-off meeting may be the best opportunity the project manager has to communicate the project vision to the team in relationship to their work.

sense of organization, stability, and personal as well as team accomplishment. Proper leadership includes a detailed agenda. In *Dynamic Project Management,* the authors offer a detailed agenda for the team kick-off meeting.[4] Emphasizing this opportunity to commit the team members to a common goal, they list ten meeting goals, which we have paraphrased:

> As in football, a successful kickoff has the team lined up and heading for the common goal (post).

1. Introduce project team members.
2. Define the overall project (objectives, goals, strategy, and tactics).
3. Describe key deliverables, key milestones, constraints, opportunities and risks.
4. Review the team mission and develop supporting goals interactively.
5. Determine reporting relationships and interaction with other teams.
6. Define lines of communication and interfaces.
7. Review preliminary project plans.
8. Pinpoint high-risk or problem areas.
9. Delineate responsibilities.
10. Generate and obtain commitment.

A video recording of the kick-off meeting is an important resource to bring new team members up to speed as they join the project.

Team Planning and Problem Solving

> Planning is a continuing activity, not a one-time event.

In a team context, planning and problem solving are excellent team building techniques, offering opportunities for training, environment setting, and reinforcement. For planning and network development, we use a technique called cards-on-the-wall, described in Chapter 12, to actively involve the project team in the planning process. It facilitates team development of the tactical approach and buy in on the planned actions. Once created, the plan will need to be revisited by the team at each phase transition point to ensure that it remains valid and that current plans respond to previous lessons learned.

Defining and Communicating a Decision Process and Style

Even though leadership style and the decision process will vary with the project situation, most managers have a preferred or default style that needs to be communicated to the team. This is detailed in the section on leadership in Chapter 18. In many project environments, a consensus decision process fosters teamwork and is more effective than the extremes of unilateral or unanimous decision making, depicted in Figure 6.3.

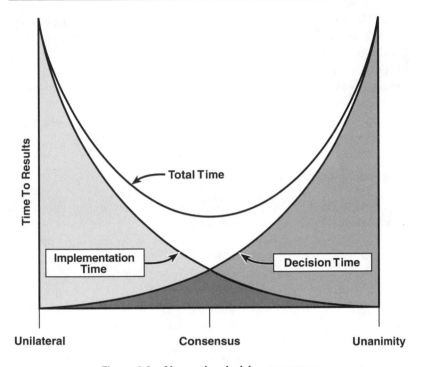

Figure 6.3   **Alternative decision processes.**

A consensus decision process consists of a thorough discussion until all team members have had a fair hearing and all members are committed to accept and support the group decision. Reaching a consensus may require compromises, but it does *not* involve:

- Voting or averaging,
- Bargaining or trading-off, or
- Steam rolling or flipping a coin.

Consensus decision making is most effective when:

- You don't know who has the expertise,
- Your facts are insufficient to decide and you need the judgment of a group of involved personnel, and
- You need the commitment of the group for the implementation.

Setting the decision environment is not a one-time activity. Let's say you've decided to operate throughout the project on a consensus basis. You find that it works well for team planning of the project, but not as you get into the actual work. Individual contributors with differing work habits and desire for flexible work

Management styles need to be appropriate to the situation. The key to success is in communicating your style appropriately as well.

schedules make consensus building at each decision point cumbersome. Finally, as you hit a real crisis in the program, you can't wait for the team. You make a decision unilaterally and that irritates everyone on the project. The urgency of the situation called for a change in style—an important right for the leader. But teamwork suffers when you change your style without letting the team know when or why a change is necessary. An effective leader reveals the reasons when making a change in management style.

The Project Information Center

A project information center—or project-specific web site—should portray timely, accurate, and relevant information.

Sharing information with the team is a way of reinforcing the vision and setting a good communications example. A room, wall, or web site where staff can review current information on the project in near real time offers an efficient means to share information. Current information also enhances the team's ability to reach a shared reward. But what information do you share and how often do you share it? Typical project dynamics suggest that selecting relevant information throughout the project is essential because as the project changes so does the type of information needed, as well as its timeliness. Out-of-date status charts and schedules vividly reveal a lack of attention to the details of project management and the lack of importance you place on team communication.

Dealing with Underperformers Who Drag the Team Down

When removing a team member, the manager needs to let the others know why—in direct, factual terms.

All too often project managers are reluctant to lose a warm body because of scarce replacements. This can be shortsighted. The underperformer may represent more of a drag than his or her contribution represents. It also sends the wrong message to the remainder of the team. They need to know exactly what kind of performance it takes to earn job security.

Team Events and Celebrations

Be careful not to leave someone out!

These are opportunities for creative team building. Events that simulate the project environment through outdoor activities, for example, are extremely useful at start-up time. There is also a continuing need for team rebuilding throughout the project as new challenges are faced and especially as new project members join. The techniques useful in the later stages of the project should focus more closely on actual project issues where lessons learned can be incorporated into the event.

Look for positive events and report them publicly at staff meetings and project reviews. Enlist the customer when appropriate. Go off-site—even if only for pizza and beer (no money is no excuse).

Training

Either as formal courses and seminars or as an integral part of any team activity, learning events can contribute significantly to teamwork. Project management and systems engineering courses, such as those we conduct for our clients, are only the starting point for training an ongoing management responsibility. Project managers should make opportunities for team members to share their learning experiences.

—— PMBOK® Guide ——
PMBOK® guide Sec 9.3.2.2
Develop Project Team: Training covers the role of training in team development.

Reward Achievement

Remember that rewards come in many forms and, wherever possible, should recognize group contributions, as do the shared rewards discussed earlier.

Rewarding achievement is the one technique that most consider easy to apply. There is a talent, however, in rewarding performance effectively. For example, if you like to start meetings by recognizing good performance, you're obliged to make sure you're aware of the supporting details. Many a compliment backfires by irritating someone else who contributed to the work while the recipient was just the most visible (or worse, the highest ranking). Paying for accomplishments is another traditional reward that has to be done judiciously.

Good performance needs to be rewarded—what gets rewarded gets done.

Reinforcement

Techniques that emphasize working as a team include: focusing on the common goal once established and accepted by the team; maintaining respect for the functions, roles, and positions within the team; acceptance of interdependencies; continued acceptance of the evolving common code of conduct; and adjusting the shared rewards as the project matures. The leader must emphasize the essentials of teamwork throughout the project. Posters and slogans around a team room (reminding people of important aspects) can be helpful.

Team members should take any opportunities to reinforce the team principles presented in training sessions.

WHEN IS YOUR GROUP REALLY A TEAM?

Teamwork is something everyone claims to believe in. People tend to believe they're a team, even when they are not. It would be useful to

You need to confirm that your leadership is working on an ongoing basis as measured by observable behavior.

have a means to assess if your team really is one. Kinlaw has drawn on his decades of experience in working with both industry and government teams to create a "superior team development inventory (STDI)."[5] His inventory questionnaire is presented in the appendix of his book. The surest way to get off on a false start is to convene the troops for a kick-off session that is little more than a pep talk. It may cause good feelings but it will not last. Likewise, it is equally ineffective to use teamwork techniques only as reactions to problems.

Positive Teamwork Indicators	*Negative Teamwork Indicators*
A positive, cooperative climate prevails.	A climate of suspicion and distrust exists.
Information flows freely between team members.	Information is hoarded or withheld.
No work is considered beyond an individual's job description. If it needs to be done then someone is doing it.	Finger pointing and defensiveness prevail.
Interpersonal interactions are spontaneous and positive.	Counterproductive subgroups and cliques begin to form.
The collective energy of the team is high.	Fear of failure causes individuals to avoid or postpone making important decisions.
Real teamwork focuses the energy of a diverse group of individuals, having different personality traits and skills, to optimally accomplish a common goal.	The absence of teamwork doesn't lead just to low productivity, it creates a counterproductive environment that saps the energy of the group and demotivates the individuals.

TEAMWORK EXERCISE

From your personal experience, work related and otherwise, identify those teams that exhibited good and poor teamwork. For each team identified, evaluate to what extent they implemented the four fundamentals to effective teamwork.

Factor	Score	Reason	Recommended Improvement
Common goal			
Acknowledged interdependency and trust			
Code of conduct			
Shared reward			
Team spirit			

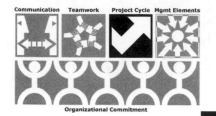

ESSENTIAL 4

7

THE PROJECT CYCLE

—— PMBOK® Guide ——
This chapter is consistent with
PMBOK® Guide, Sec 2.1, *The
Project Life Cycle*

—— INCOSE ——
This chapter is consistent with
INCOSE Handbook Sec 3
Generic Life Cycle Stages.

The impact of not establishing a gated project cycle can be substantial, as in the case of a national Health Maintenance Organization (HMO) in the construction of new medical facilities. In the absence of a defined project cycle, the HMO's management did not get involved in detailed design decisions. Further, there were no binding decision gates that involved the appropriate using stakeholders to get formal approvals of the configuration before proceeding. For example, the doctors (the operational users) were not required to approve the dimensionally correct floorplan (an early concept artifact) that vividly displays how the hospital is laid out to support the required medical functions. As a result, after the hospitals were constructed, the doctors directed considerable redesign and rework before accepting occupancy—a costly and time-consuming impact. A gated project cycle, requiring doctor approvals, was adopted to correct this process deficiency.

An appropriate project cycle
contributes significantly to
doing the right project right
the first time.

The project cycle is the sequential Essential of project management and systems engineering. It's about progressing from stake to stake—the decision gates and other timeline events. Figure 7.1 illustrates the project cycle format. This chapter presents the significant features of a basic project cycle with a single thread from beginning to completion. Many projects are more complex, so Part Four provides additional detail on the principles, techniques, and terms introduced here, such as the characteristics of unified, incremental, linear, evolutionary, and agile development, baseline management, and the Waterfall, Spiral, and Vee models.

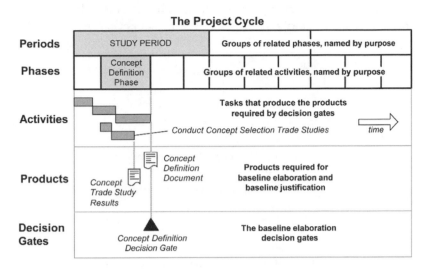

Figure 7.1   The project cycle format.

DEFINING THE RIGHT ROAD TO SUCCESS

In our training and project management experience, we encounter the following unfortunate situations; those teams that:

- Accept and follow a standard project cycle because it's dictated by their customers or management.
- Don't define a project cycle, not having previously heard of the concept.

The former tolerate the concept because compliance is directed, and the latter resist it because it appears rigid and bureaucratic. Both are victims of a failure to appreciate the power of the project cycle as a reliable road map for an enterprise and as a flexible and effective navigation tool to execute individual projects correctly the first time.

In the absence of a defined-management approach, and without the defined milestones (decision gates) to ensure progress and baseline approval, project teams are left to create an ad hoc sequence of events believing they are navigating correctly.

Staying competitive often requires a short time to market. An institutionalized project cycle based on time-proven lessons learned can be tailored up or down, but only if you first know the preferred route.

This chapter presents a baseline template that can be applied to a wide range of development projects in all environments, whether

We define the *project cycle* as an orderly sequence of integrated activities, performed in phases, leading to success.

Even though all projects travel through a sequence of phases, the road may not be clearly understood.

"We all want progress, but if you're on the wrong road, progress means doing an about-turn and walking back to the right road; in that case, the man who turns back soonest is the most progressive."

C. S. Lewis

government, commercial, or nonprofit. This framework facilitates the sequential proactive management of projects that is:

- Orderly,
- Methodical, and
- Disciplined.

Since not all events and features in our template are universal in application, you should create your own version. To tailor a project-specific cycle, each entry must be evaluated, resulting in a conscious decision to include it or not. This avoids errors of omission while taking advantage of proven baseline.

An effective way to build a tailored project cycle is to take these four steps:

1. Decide on the appropriate periods or stages (Study, Implementation, or Operations) for your project. The periods are related to the evolving system solution, which paces the project. The development of the system is what is maturing and is a measure of progress.
2. Identify the decision gates and the associated phases within the periods that are required to ensure the best value system development steps. There are always decision gates at the end of each phase; additional decision gates are often beneficial within a phase.
3. Define the products or artifacts (documents, models, test articles, etc.) that must be in evidence and ready for baselining at each decision gate to ensure that the project has delivered to the objectives of the phase or subphase and is ready to move forward (exit and entry criteria).
4. Define the tasks required to create the products or artifacts. These tasks will provide the input for building the project network and schedule (discussed in Chapter 12).

Our baseline project-cycle template contained in this book is divided into three periods or stages: the Study Period, the Implementation Period, and the Operations Period. These periods correspond to the major objectives of the system solution as it matures from an identified user need through concept determination, implementation, and ultimately to production and user operation. Figure 7.2 depicts representative government and commercial periods and phases along with our project cycle template. The NASA cycle comes from two references, one for the systems engineering cycle and the other for program or project management.[1] The U.S. Department of Defense cycle comes from a recent publication.[2] The ISO/IEC cycle comes from ISO-15288.[3]

Eliminating a feature from a proven template must be justified.

— *PMBOK® Guide* —
The *PMBOK® Guide* Sec 2.1.1 *Characteristics of the Project Life Cycle,* provides relevant discussion.

Many disciplined companies follow some version of a project cycle that is divided into periods and further subdivided into phases.

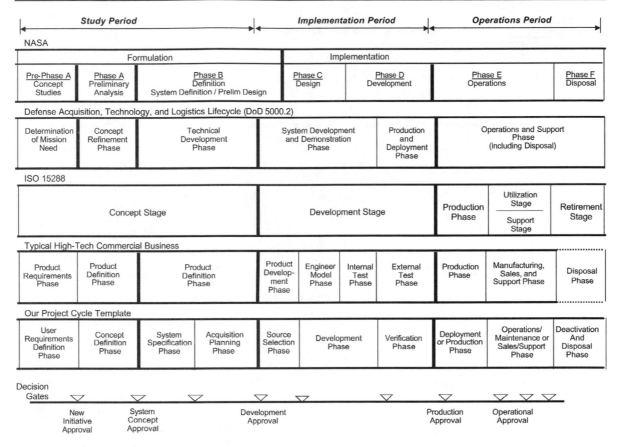

Figure 7.2 Project cycle templates.

In their book, *Microsoft Secrets,* Cusumano and Selby describe the Microsoft project cycle for new product development.[4] The Microsoft cycle, which typically lasts from 12 to 24 months, has three phases (Planning, Development, and Stabilization). Each of the phases has detailed activities, products, and decision gates. The final decision gate, at the end of the stabilization phase, has a title that should delight Microsoft product users: "zero bug release." Although their terms differ somewhat from those used in Figure 7.2, their description of the cycle maps exactly to our baseline model.

All cycles begin with a user needing something. Typically, customers determine the need and the user requirements and then contract with one or more providers (ultimately, the project team) to develop the product or service. Customer types include government agencies, commercial enterprises, or a company's internal marketing department.

Even though projects can be initiated very differently, they are subject to similar project management and systems engineering processes once the requirements are established.

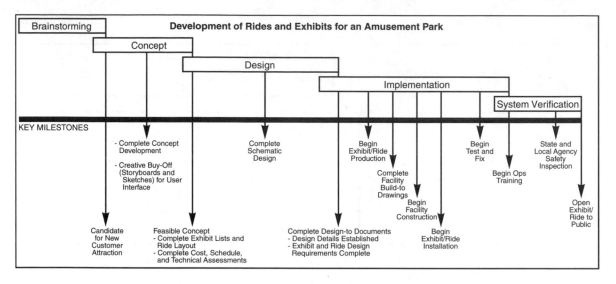

Figure 7.3   Project cycle chart for amusement park exhibits and rides.

—— *PMBOK® Guide* ——
The *PMBOK® Guide* Sec 2.1.2
Characteristics of Project Phases identifies "initial," "intermediate," and "final" as phases of a project.

—————— *INCOSE* ——————
The INCOSE *Life Cycle Stages* identifies stages as:

• Pre-concept exploratory research.
• Concept.
• Development.
• Production.
• Utilization.
• Support.
• Retirement.

Highly creative commercial organizations benefit from having a defined requirements-driven process. The development of new amusement park attractions usually begins with "blue sky" explorations and concludes with a new exhibit or ride (Figure 7.3). Many theme park organizations, including Walt Disney Imagineering, follow a cycle like this.[5] Note that this cycle closely matches the processes illustrated in Figure 7.2.

In government acquisitions and larger commercial projects, team members and managers may change with the project-cycle period. For example, in the case of a Department of Defense (DoD) project, once a mission need is identified, a project champion is selected and a core team is formed to develop the user requirements and to produce the tender or bidder documents. That core team may change during the implementation period, although some team members may stay to provide continuity throughout the three periods. Bidders will generally form a proposal preparation team, the core of which may also continue through all or part of the implementation phases.

Large, decentralized corporations often follow the government practice of having separate customer (e.g., product marketing) and provider (e.g., product development) teams. In this case, the marketing team will prepare the user requirements for the product development team.

Large commercial suppliers of systems built up from their "standard" components offer another example. The sales team signs a contract with defined requirements. The implementation team manages the project after contract signing and procures, installs, and verifies the system. Their project cycle should reflect the activities and products for the required modifications, verification, and readiness to hand off to the operations team.

Smaller commercial projects are more likely to consist of a single project manager selected as soon as the scope and nature of the project is established and who will serve throughout delivery. Even in this case, the size and composition of the project team will likely change as appropriate to the periods and phases.

> The project periods often represent natural boundaries to team responsibilities and composition.

THE STUDY PERIOD YIELDS A HIGH RETURN ON INVESTMENT

The Study Period typically determines the scope, feasibility, and funding of a project (Figure 7.4), therefore, making or breaking candidate projects. Yet, important cost estimation studies are often circumvented in the rush to implementation. High-level government panels, such as the Hearth commission and Packard commission, concluded that hasty Study Periods, resulting in flawed or incomplete requirements, are the major cause of project failure. Their findings continue to be reverified; the General Accounting Office (GAO) reported in 1999 that high-tech government projects continue to fail for low-tech, often mundane, reasons. Typically these low-tech reasons are flaws built in as a result of incomplete studies as well as improper implementation of an otherwise sound project management process.

> A major cause of project failure is insufficient focus on product opportunities and inadequate attention to resolving development risks during the study period.

Flawed Study Period project estimation seems to be the root cause of the predicted several billion dollar overrun for the twenty-first century construction of the Oakland-San Francisco Bay Bridge. The cost problem is so severe that a change in design concept is being considered even though construction is well underway. In addition, the public is calling for an investigation of the study period managers, CalTrans.

The Big Dig in Boston, with an overrun several times the original estimate, is another example of flawed project scope and cost determination in the Study Period and scope creep during implementation.

The project team generally must engage in considerable analysis and negotiation in order to develop the requirements. The project

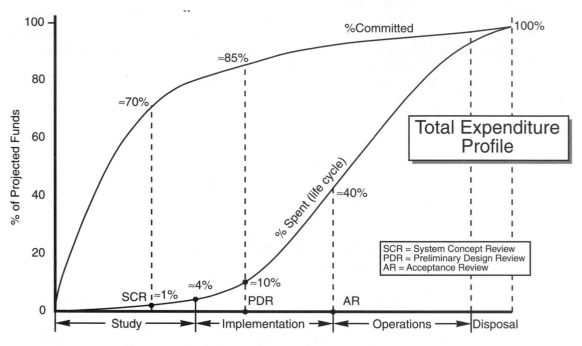

Figure 7.4   Typical expenditure profile: Committed versus spent.

manager and systems engineer must work as a team to ensure that the technical requirements match the business case objectives.

A comprehensive analysis can often prevent the time lost and the funds wasted on requirements-driven rework as illustrated in Figure 7.5. This figure is uncommon since most organizations do not collect the necessary data to create this relationship. The chart author, Werner Gruhl, worked in the comptroller's office at NASA Headquarters and had access to actual project costs by category for both the study and development periods. He also knew the development costs as estimated at the end of their study period, and he knew what the project requirements were at the start of the development effort. He was able to adjust for financial distortions caused by events beyond the control of the project team. For instance, the most expensive part of the Hubble Space Telescope Program was not the mirror or the spacecraft itself, but rather the three years of environmentally controlled storage of the completed satellite following the *Challenger* accident. Mr. Gruhl was able to compare the actual costs incurred for the work that was planned at the start of the development period to the estimated costs for that same effort. This resulted in the "Final Overrun as a Percent of the Commitment

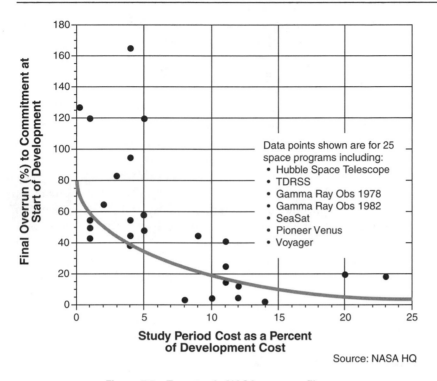

Figure 7.5   Twenty-six NASA program files.

(Estimate) at the Start of Development." The horizontal axis is the ratio of the cost of the study period to the cost of the development period. He did this analysis for 26 space projects. The conclusion is that greater investment in the study period will yield a more accurate estimate of the ultimate cost of development, enabling the project manager to manage the implementation period effectively.

As an example, if you estimate the development cost for your project to be $10 million, and if you have spent less than $1 million on the study period, there is a high probability that you will have an overrun in excess of 20 percent. After unacceptable project performance in the early 1990s, NASA implemented an executive requirement that any project that is predicting greater than 15 percent development cost growth must appear at a Cancellation Review to "show cause" why the project should not be cancelled. Study period interest increased as a result.

Our baseline cycle template provides four phases within the study period: User Requirements Definition, Concept Definition, System Specification, and Acquisition Preparation. Systems engineering has primary responsibility for the technical decisions during these phases, but the project manager must ensure consistency with the business case and with customer needs.

User Requirements Definition Phase

The major objective of the User Requirements Definition Phase is to determine exactly which of the user's many requirements will be included in, and satisfied by, the responsive project. In some cases, user requirements may be more comprehensive than can be reasonably incorporated into a single project and those of lower priority are rejected. Also included in this phase is the development of stakeholder requirements that impose constraints on the solution trade space. This phase is essential in both government and commercial projects because it is key to correctly bounding the project and avoiding over specification and grandiose expectations. It is also essential to establishing the feasibility of meeting the user's requirements, because what may seem reasonable at the first communication may be too challenging—or even impossible—to meet at a subsystem or component level.

Concept Definition Phase

The objectives of the Concept Definition Phase are to evaluate system concept alternatives, to select the best value concept and its architecture, to develop the associated life-cycle budgetary should-cost estimate, the target should-take schedule, and finally, to identify opportunities to pursue and risks to mitigate. During this phase, estimates of required funding are updated as the credibility of the basis of the estimates is improved.

There is a pitfall, however. During this phase, aggressive selling of a project concept is often necessary to secure the funding to move ahead to the implementation period, and in so doing unachievable expectations (both for cost and schedule) are often established. The Boston Big Dig, the Denver Airport, and the Oakland-San Francisco Bay Bridge projects take their place with colossal projects of prior centuries, such as the Panama Canal. All of these projects were (or will be) successfully completed, but with huge cost and schedule growth—and with career-limiting impact to the succession of project managers who each advanced the project incrementally forward. The proactive defense against false expectations is a comprehensive study period to size the project correctly.

A positive example is provided by the project team that managed the Øresund Bridge-Tunnel project (between Copenhagen, Denmark, and Malmö, Sweden, at the time the world's longest bridge) from concept development through construction. Starting on a predicted decade-long effort in 1991, they spent three years in the study period, and then finished the bridge early (July 2000) and within budget.[6] In addition, they are currently meeting their traffic growth prediction, which is more than the English Channel Tunnel has achieved. It can be done.

System Specification Definition Phase

The objective of the System Specification Definition Phase is to quantify the system and interface requirements for the selected concept and to perform technology opportunity investigations and risk reduction actions in areas where technical feasibility is uncertain. Experimentation and modeling should ensure that all specified performance is achievable and affordable. There can be substantial cost and schedule penalty if this is not done properly. One program consisting of incremental delivery of satellites over a 15-year period encountered significant problems in initial manufacturing. The first system was years late and could only be delivered with a waiver of specification requirements. But as evidence of a nonachievable specification, the last satellite in the series, due to launch in 2008, will also require the same waiver because it still will not be able to meet the initial specifications.

Acquisition Preparation Phase

The final phase of the study period, the Acquisition Preparation Phase, is used to prepare for the implementation period. It includes development of the schedule and budget for acquiring or developing the proposed system and ensures the availability of the funding at the level of the most-probable cost for the project. This phase also defines the method of acquisition, identification of participants in the acquisition process, and identification of candidate suppliers, which may include internal organizations. The final event is to obtain approvals needed to proceed with the project. For internal development projects, the final event in the study period is to present the technically substantiated business opportunity to executive management and secure their commitment.

THE IMPLEMENTATION PERIOD IS FOR ACQUISITION OR DEVELOPMENT

The Implementation Period consists of three phases: Source Selection, System Development, and Verification. In government projects, the implementation period may be referred to as the Acquisition Period. In this case, it sets the contractual foundation for procuring the project and initiates the process of building the buyer-seller team that will work together through at least development.

Source Selection Phase

The objective of the Source Selection Phase is to choose, through fair and open competition and through the comprehensive evaluation of contractor proposals, the "best value" bidder. For acquisition projects, the buyer releases the Request for Proposal, receives and evaluates bidders' proposals, and negotiates a contract with the selected bidder. For internal developments, the implementation period may have one or more Source Selection Phases for individual increments of the system. These phases often occur after the "design to" specifications are available.

System Development Phase

In both external and internal developments, the objective of the System Development Phase is to design and build the first article or develop the service concept if the solution consists of services only.

Verification Phase

In the Verification Phase, the project team integrates and verifies (by inspection, test, demonstration, or analysis) the system or service in accordance with defining specifications. These activities prove that the solution has been built right. It is high risk to deploy the system without verification. However, this sometimes happens when executive management eagerly deploys a new system for reasons outside the project's scope or beyond the control of the project manager. Skipping verification is almost always far more costly in time, money, and reputation than following the proper sequence.

President Carter agreed to build a new embassy in Moscow, even though his security team said they could not verify the structure would be secure. After five years, the six-story building was nearing completion when the project had to be stopped because listening devices were found to be cast into the concrete of the Russian-built columns and beams. The building stood idle for almost a decade. A modified version, built by U.S.-security-cleared workers, was completed in 2001, 22 years after the project was initiated.

More recently, the Bush administration mandated deployment of the $15 billion missile defense system without a single successful system test. As widely reported in major U.S. news media, even though no flight tests had been conducted previously, 7 untested missiles were already in underground silos by the end of 2004 with 12 more scheduled for 2005 deployment. "Pentagon officials defend what they call a 'spiral development' approach to the program, saying it's designed to put a missile defense system into operation rapidly by simultaneously deploying, evaluating and upgrading components. 'This is not a traditional development program, where operations begin only once testing is complete,' Taylor said [Chris Taylor is a spokesman for the Missile Defense Agency]."[7] In this case, spiral development means uncontrolled management practices that bear very little resemblance to the Spiral Model discussed later in this chapter.

> There is technical logic for the recommended sequence of stages and phases. Perceived political necessity cannot overcome engineering reality. Deploying a system before a successful system test is high risk.

THE OPERATIONS PERIOD IS FOR FULFILLING USER NEEDS

The Operations Period proves that user needs are fulfilled through realizing the project solution. It consists of three phases—the first is called either Deployment or Production, depending on the main purpose, such as a system acquisition versus a commercial product to be manufactured and marketed. The second phase is Operations and Maintenance or Sales and Support, again named to reflect the purpose or emphasis. The third and last phase of the Operations Period is Deactivation for both government and commercial projects.

Deployment and Operations/Maintenance Phases

In government acquisition projects, the objectives of the Deployment Phase are to transfer the system from the contractor's facility to the operational location and to establish full operational capability. Operations and Maintenance consists of operating and maintaining the system in conformance with user requirements and identifying system improvements for future implementation.

Production and Sales/Support Phases

In commercial projects, the objective of the Production Phase is to transfer to manufacturing operations, often accompanied by a hand off to a new project team dedicated to the production function. Finally, the system is delivered to users in the marketplace and the Sales and Support Phase begins. During this time, the project team handles design changes justified by manufacturing or by market demands.

Deactivation Phase

The Deactivation Phase disposes of all elements of the project. To facilitate this requirement, many products are being built with the requirement that they be totally recyclable. Early planning for a deactivation phase is vital in certain projects. The NASA Skylab randomly fell to earth in an uninhabited part of Australia. Pieces of a Russian satellite fell uncontrolled onto Canada. Love Canal and other super-fund sites are also examples of inadequate deactivation planning. (Super-fund refers to U.S. government money set aside for high-priority environmental clean up.) Deactivation and disposal considerations should be a part of the concept selection criteria.

Recycling considerations, now mandated by some European countries, have long been normal design and manufacturing practice at BMW. Environmentally oriented thinking and practices geared toward closed-loop recycling are today as much a part of the company's culture as "Sheer Driving Pleasure." Integrating the Recycling and Dismantling Center into the automobile development process has resulted in car designs that consider the full product life cycle—all the way to recycling. Starting in 2006, manufacturers in the European Union retain lifetime responsibility for the environmentally sensitive materials in their products.

THE IMPORTANCE OF DECISION GATES

Decision gates are used to review and approve the baseline elaboration.

A *decision gate* (also referred to as a control gate or quality gate) is a baseline approval event in the project cycle, sufficiently important to be defined and included in the schedule by executive management, the project manager, or the customer. Decision gates represent major decision points in the project cycle. They ensure that new activities are not pursued until the previously scheduled activities, on which the new ones depend, are satisfactorily completed and baselined. The primary objectives of decision gates are to:

Decision gates focus the creativity where it is most needed.

- Ensure that the elaboration of the business and technical baselines are acceptable and will lead to satisfactory verification and validation.
- Ensure that the next phase team is prepared, and that the risk of proceeding is acceptable.
- Continue to foster buyer and seller teamwork.

While many decision gate titles sound like design reviews and are often conducted as such, they are business reviews addressing these questions:

Decision gates, although heavy in technical content, are business reviews. They need to occur throughout the project phases to control all three project cycle aspects: business, budget, and technical.

- Does it still satisfy the business case?
- Is it affordable?
- Can it be delivered when needed?

Too often decision gates like Preliminary Design Review (PDR) and Critical Design Review (CDR) are conducted as technical reviews rather than combined technical and business reviews. Market demand, affordability, and realistic schedules are important decision criteria leading to concept selections and should be updated and evaluated at every decision gate. Inadequate checks along the way can set up subsequent failures—usually a major factor in cost overruns and delays. At each decision gate, the decision options are:

—— *PMBOK® Guide* ——
The *PMBOK® Guide* Sec 2.1.2 defines phase-end gates and notes that they are also called "phase exits," "phase gates," or "kill points."

The critical role of gates in approving the elaboration of the baseline is not addressed.

Acceptable: Proceed with project;

Acceptable with reservations: Proceed and respond to action items;

Unacceptable: Do not proceed; repeat the review when ready; or

Unsalvageable: Terminate the project.

Upon successful completion of a decision gate, the elaborated baseline, usually in the form of artifacts (documents, models, or other products of a project cycle phase), is put under configuration management, requiring buyer and seller agreement to incorporate changes. All future creativity must be based on the updated baseline.

Decision gate definitions should identify the:

Each decision gate's definition should be included in the project's terminology database.

- Purpose of the decision gate,
- Host and chairperson,
- Attendees,
- Location,
- Agenda and how the decision gate is to be conducted,

——— *INCOSE* ———
INCOSE Handbook Sec 3.2
covers decision gates as
related to the development
maturity of the project or service.

Decision gate approval must
involve the necessary disciplines and stakeholders and
must be based on hard evidence of compliance.

- Evidence to be evaluated,
- Actions, and
- Closure method.

A broadly employed decision gate, the System Requirements Review (SRR), should be held to confirm that a provider adequately understands the customer's requirements. It usually occurs near the beginning of the project cycle and involves the primary customer and the primary provider. Subsequently, it occurs when any new provider is added to the project, the primary provider then becoming the customer of the added provider.

The consequences of conducting a superficial review, omitting a critical discipline, or skipping a decision gate altogether are usually long-term and costly. The executives at a leading conglomerate literally choked on their new product (a microwavable meal) when they set out to investigate its market woes. When challenged to evaluate their own product, the executive group identified 28 product deficiencies that should have been caught during the project cycle, well before product introduction to the marketplace. A few of the more significant flaws included: when positioning the open carton to read the heating instructions, the contents spilled; the instructions, printed in black on a dark blue background, weren't legible; the specified microwave heating time was insufficient to heat the food, but when the time was increased adequately food material migrated into the plastic container material.

Car design flaws and recalls provide many examples of the hazards of skipping decision gates or omitting critical skills, such as human factors, in the baseline decision process. Such problems can also result from inadequate concurrent engineering, a subject addressed in Chapter 9.

Even when appropriate decision gates are mandated, such as in building construction, there is little chance of success if the participants do not scrutinize the artifacts. A neighbor of one of the authors had a custom-designed home built with an attached garage. He requested that one garage bay be designed extra wide and extra high to accommodate his recreation vehicle. After the building was finished according to the drawings and passed all inspections, his vehicle did not fit. He found the architect's error on the drawings, which he had personally approved and signed 10 months earlier—a mistake costly to him.

After completing a new post office building in a major U.S. city at a cost of $140 million, the city engineers found that post office trucks would not fit into the enclosed loading dock. Similarly, normal food service trucks are too large to service Denver Airport's concourse restaurants.

THREE ASPECTS OF THE PROJECT CYCLE: BUSINESS, BUDGET, AND TECHNICAL

The three aspects of the project cycle can be viewed as layers (Figure 3.6 and Table 7.1). Each layer—business, budget, and technical—contains its own logic set. The interwoven events for the three aspects constitute the total cycle, which can also be considered as the project opportunity cycle. The project cycle can span from user wants to project disposal or a reduced scope in accordance with the project objectives.

The *business aspect* (Table 7.1) drives the project and is based on the business case that justifies the pursuit of the opportunity. The business aspect contains the necessary business events related to customer management, justifying the project, business alliances, the overall business management events, and associated contractor and subcontractor management. Also included are the tasks necessary to solicit, select, and manage vendors. In the government project environment, the business case is usually called the mission case. The business aspect starts with seeking value-driven project opportunities to help achieve the strategic objectives of the enterprise. Trade-offs are made to select those projects suitable for the organization's portfolio as justified by the business case. The business case analyzes the project's fit within the organization's business objectives, the investment required, the expected market and market share, the

Table 7.1 The three aspects of the project cycle

	Study *Figuring out what to do*				Implementation *Doing it*			Operations *Using it*		
Period Phase	User Require-ments	Concept Definition	System Spec	Acquisition Prep	Source Selection	Develop-ment	Verification	Deploy-ment	Ops and Maint	Deactiva-tion
	Is it worth doing? How to acquire?				*Are we getting value?*			*Are we glad we did it?*		
Business aspect	Recognize opportunity	Develop business case	Prove business feasibility	Select acquisition approach	Select best value supplier	Manage suppliers. In-process ROI projections		Manage doers	Improve; add value	Evaluate ROI
	Can we afford to do it and is money available?				*Are financials on plan?*			*Was it financially worth it?*		
Budget aspect	Determine resource availability and source	Predict should-cost and phasing	Refine should-cost and phasing	Ensure phased resource availability	Determine most probable cost	Manage budgets, funding, and value		Manage value	Manage value	Provide closure
	What is the problem and the solution?				*How to do it and prove it?*			*Is the customer smiling?*		
Technical aspect	Collect user requirements, user CONOPS, and select system requirements	Select concept; develop system CONOPS	Prove technical feasibility. Develop spec	Identify capable suppliers	Select capable supplier	Manage design-to, build-to. Buy, build, code. Ensure integration and verification		Ensure validation	Provide technical support	Provide technical support

profit expected, and the associated risks. It's essential that the business case is accurate in predicting both the need and the demand for the product or service and what customers will be willing to pay. Perhaps most important of all, the business case must be kept up to date as the business environment evolves.

To get approval to start a new project, the project champion must create an attractive business proposition and then aggressively sell it to the stakeholders. In their eagerness to get approval to proceed with their project, some project champions exaggerate the return and minimize the costs of development, so the seeds of failure are sown early—and it is often a business constraint that forces creation of an unworkable technical solution, which is then driven to the point of collapse. That is what happened to NASA's "faster, better, cheaper" approach in the 1990s. Early successes seemed to validate this business approach, but budget cuts were made for each successive project until ultimately the "cheaper" attribute drove the design teams to create fragile technical solutions taking shortcuts to proven processes resulting in too many failures (NASA has abandoned "faster, better, cheaper" in favor of a more balanced and traditional approach).

History offers many examples of setting out on a flawed base, driven by an aggressive business case. The French selected Ferdinand de Lesseps to head their Panama Canal effort because of his Suez Canal experience. His experts recommended:[8]

> The business case must be updated to reflect changes in the business environment that could significantly impact the justification for the project being in the portfolio or continuing at all.

- A sea-level canal (no locks), just like the Suez canal,
- Reducing the time to complete the canal from 12 years to 8 years,
- Reducing the projected cost from $240 million to $169 million,
- Reducing the contingency in the cost estimates from 25 percent to 10 percent, even though the cost estimate did NOT include paying interest on the capital, the large cost for purchasing the Panamanian railroad, administrative costs during construction, and sums due the holder of the canal option in the selected area,
- While reducing the estimated cost, the reviewers increased the anticipated volume of excavation by 50 percent.

De Lesseps made one trip to Panama, spent a week touring the proposed route, and then returned to speak to potential investors. In his speech he further cut the predicted costs from the optimistic $169 million to $132 million (compared to the $240 million engineering estimate). He also discounted the deadly climate as, "an invention of adversaries" (ultimately over 20,000 died from malaria and yellow fever). The ultimate failed French effort cost about $287 million, the largest expenditure on any single peaceful undertaking of any kind.[9]

The roots of the failure were that estimates were based on what the team (De Lesseps) thought they could sell, not what it would actually take to do the job. This process is still alive and well. From mega projects (i.e., space station, Boston Big Dig) to small ones, intentional underestimates to "get the job going" are common. In every such case the initial project manager starts off with a severe handicap and is on a suicide run.

These disasters could have possibly been avoided by having each project-cycle decision gate reaffirm the business or mission case and carefully adjust to the ever-present dynamics of the market. This is particularly relevant and meaningful because most project team members do not know and cannot articulate their project's business case nor the business case at their level of responsibility.

Sometimes financial challenges are created by external project stakeholders and are outside project control. The agreement between the governments of Sweden and Denmark established the rules governing the Øresund bridge-tunnel construction and operation. "The agreement stipulates that the Øresund Bridge and its operations must be financed by toll fees (the road section) and fees from the rail operators. However, it was subsequently decided that the operators are now liable for Value-Added Tax (VAT) on revenue from the road traffic. As competing ferry routes do not pay VAT, the bridge operators cannot compensate for VAT payments by increasing charges on private vehicles. This has led to lower-than-expected income."[10]

The original budgets and schedules for the bridge and tunnel were met, but the change in revenue rules forced a longer bond repayment schedule.

The business aspect of the project cycle also reflects the approach to acquisition and fielding, including competitive source selections, if required. During the acquisition period, the focus is on supplier management and on the trading of features and benefits in the marketplace as designers and producers seek to enhance the project's concept. Then as production and fielding begin, the activity shifts to customer service and increasing value by continuous improvement in both service and product performance. Incremental or version upgrades are the generally accepted way of implementing this approach. In software, this is done with timely enhancements and automatic downloads that keep users at the state of the art.

The *budget aspect* of the project cycle depicts the activities and events necessary to secure funding and to fuel the project throughout its project cycle. The executive's challenge is to prioritize the projects (by business case) and then to allocate available funds among the proposed and active projects. The project manager's challenge is to secure the necessary funds for the project at hand and to properly manage them.

Government and commercial organizations usually have to operate within a total budget, typically established on an annual cycle. New project initiatives have to compete with ongoing projects for a share of the total budget. This reality may present difficult timing constraints, especially with increasingly narrow market windows.

The budget aspect for government projects is complex, involving both the executive and legislative branches. In the past, projects were often approved without knowledge of or preparation for the operating costs that often loomed as the most significant. Now life-cycle costs are included when estimating project cost.

The budget activities and business management activities are combined with the technical aspect (Table 7.1) to yield the complete project cycle. The technical events of development projects are usually the most significant force driving project length and development cost, and they're often the most difficult to manage. For these reasons, we will treat the technical aspect in more detail than the other two aspects. However, this does not mean that the business and budget aspects should be discounted. If the project is to succeed on both financial and technical criteria (the only true definition of success), all three aspects of the project must be skillfully balanced using ultimate project value as the driver.

> The technical aspect usually drives the project's length and cost.

SYSTEMS ENGINEERING IS VITALLY IMPORTANT TO THE TECHNICAL ASPECT

> Systems engineering is doing the right thing right, the first time.

> ——— *INCOSE* ———
> The relevant section of the *INCOSE Handbook* is Sec 1.2 *The Purpose and Scope of Systems Engineering.*

The *technical aspect* starts with user needs, which are developed into system functional and performance requirements by adjusting, adding, and eliminating requirements to yield a set that has the promise of being satisfied while providing sufficient value to be supported. Concept trades are then performed to determine the best value concept to satisfy the system requirements. The System Concept Baseline is decomposed into the entities of the system and the concepts and specifications for each entity. The resulting decomposition represents the system architecture. This process and the resultant artifacts define the concepts for all the entities down to the lowest-configuration item (LCI) from the systems engineer's viewpoint. The technical artifacts should also define the approach for system integration and for the verification and validation at each level of integration, including that the final result satisfies the ultimate customer and users. That is the essence of the systems engineering process.

Systems engineering's role is sometimes confused with that of design engineering. Systems engineering does not create the design; rather, it creates the requirements, concepts, and architecture that are documented in baseline specifications and other artifacts. Starting with the User Requirements Document, systems engineering is responsible for conducting the analysis and trade studies that lead to the concepts and their specifications.

One of the most important responsibilities of systems engineering is the overall system architecture. As Rechtin and Maier noted, "Clearly, if a system is to succeed, it must satisfy a useful purpose at an affordable cost for an acceptable period of time. . . . But of the three criteria, satisfying a useful purpose is predominant. Without it being satisfied, all others are irrelevant. Architecting therefore begins with, and is responsible for maintaining, the integrity of the system's purpose."[11] Stevens et al. said, "Architectural design defines clearly what is to be built. This is potentially the most creative part of the system process, and the point at which the cost of the system is largely fixed."[12]

Examples of systems engineering failures illustrate the distinction. In the initial B-1 bomber, the advanced electronic and counterattack systems interfered with each other—the plane's own electronic countermeasures for jamming enemy systems jammed its own B-1 targeting electronics—yet the design engineers met the individual specifications for each system. On the Blackhawk helicopter, the "fly-by-wire" system failed when exposed to radio broadcast at short range—a test flight crashed when flying over a radio station. On the commercial front (waterfront, that is), a shipping container from a British exporter was fully loaded with hair dryers for sale in the United States. The dryers were built only for 50-cycle, 220-volt power. The exporter did not know that the U.S. commercial home products operate on 60-cycle, 110-volt power.

The systems engineering manager should direct the overall process toward achieving the optimum technical solution, including:

- Systems engineering planning,
- Requirements development and management,

> Systems engineering defines what is to be done technically; functional engineering decides how to do it.

- Requirements analysis and audit,
- Concept and architecture development,
- Performance management,
- Baseline management,
- Design audits,
- Interface control,
- Opportunity and risk management, and
- Verification and validation management.

The systems engineering process progressively flows down from system and entity concepts and requirements to the lowest level of decomposition (e.g., hardware and software units), usually the lowest configuration item or lowest replaceable unit (LRU). Each level of decomposition represents one or more entities or configuration items (CIs) that make up the system at that level. A CI typically requires its own:

- Specification (functions, performance, interfaces, design constraints, quality attributes),
- Design reviews,
- Qualification testing and certification,
- Acceptance reviews, and
- Operator and maintenance manuals.

A CI should be selected to facilitate management accountability and replacement capability. For example, a car and a car battery are both CIs to the consumer, because they can be readily acquired and replaced. However the battery's individual cells are not a CI, because they cannot readily be purchased and replaced by the consumer.

MODELING THE TECHNICAL ASPECT

There is no universally accepted approach to managing the technical aspect of projects.

This section summarizes several historical and current models used to represent the technical aspect. While these models enhance the visualization process and provide insight into specific characteristics of the product development cycle, they all have important omissions. Part of the problem is that there is no widely understood or universally accepted model for managing the technical aspect of projects. While a variety of models are available, some err in the sequencing of project events while others focus on entity development and ignore the management of architecture complexity.

We often hear strong preferences voiced for one model to the exclusion of all others. This is dangerous. It is important to take advantage of the wide array of management models by understanding their strengths and limitations and then applying them appropriately. For example, some models are useful primarily for visualization and comprehension while others are better suited for day-to-day management. Our critique has two purposes:

1. To use the strengths and contributions of each model to enhance understanding and the visualization process.
2. To become aware and learn from the important omissions in popular portrayals of the project management and systems engineering processes.

> Most approaches fail to differentiate among ongoing processes and sequential and situational events.

The circular model in Figure 7.6 was previously used by a leading government agency to manage complex technical projects. This model's visible flaws, noted in the diagram, are highly instructive. In this and other linear, sequential models, continuously present situational activities, such as risk analysis and management and configuration management, are incorrectly depicted as sequential events rather than continuously applied processes.

Some early models, such as DoD STD 2167A, depict hardware-related events as independent from software-related events (Figure 7.7). The message that these two vital development paths can and should be managed separately until final system integration resulted in hardware-software incompatibility for many projects. This model

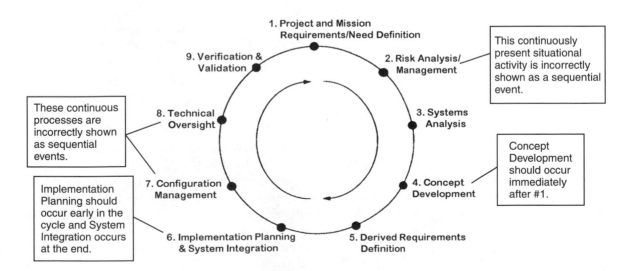

Figure 7.6 This circular model has several flaws.

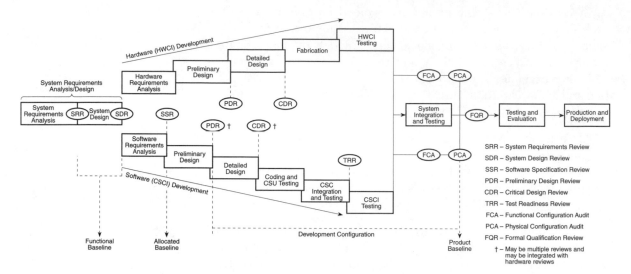

Figure 7.7   **Hardware- and software-related events are erroneously separated.**

was in use for several decades, but was abandoned in the mid-1990s when the Department of Defense directed its staff and contractors to apply commercial standards for software development.

The 2167A model (Figure 7.7) and the Waterfall Model (Figure 7.8) require that work downstream should not begin until upstream uncertainties are resolved and major reviews (decision gates) have been satisfied. The Waterfall, developed by Dr. Winston W. Royce, is so named because software development is depicted as flowing from the top to the bottom in discrete, sequential, linear phases.[13] The model represents the software development cycle as a series of steps progressing diagonally from upper left to lower right. In complex, high-risk projects, this is inappropriate. Rona Stillman, a computer scientist at the U.S. General Accounting Office, maintains that, "The waterfall model is risk-averse. It encourages unrealistic cost and schedule estimates and the appearance of problem-free development." There is often a need to initiate software design and coding, as well as hardware modeling, earlier in the development cycle to ensure that the requirements are properly understood and to prove technical feasibility. For these reasons, many organizations do not embrace these and similar technical development models.

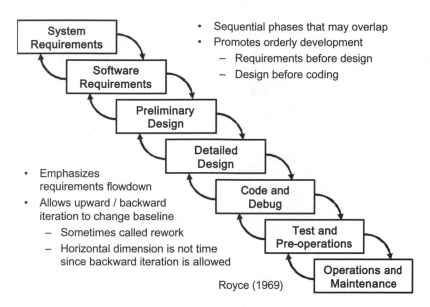

- Sequential phases that may overlap
- Promotes orderly development
  - Requirements before design
  - Design before coding

The Waterfall Model replaced hacking with a repeatable, phased software-development process.

- Emphasizes requirements flowdown
- Allows upward / backward iteration to change baseline
  - Sometimes called rework
  - Horizontal dimension is not time since backward iteration is allowed

Royce (1969)

Figure 7.8   The Waterfall Model.

The Spiral Model (Figure 7.9) is an excellent risk-driven model that attempts to address the shortcomings of the Waterfall. This model was developed by Dr. Barry W. Boehm to resolve the Waterfall deficiencies.[14] Dr. Boehm addresses the need for early requirements understanding and feasibility modeling including operational scenario modeling. Many software organizations use the Spiral as their development method and model. Microsoft, for instance, uses a process that is, ". . . similar to the risk-driven, incremental 'spiral' life cycle model."[15] The Spiral is another view of the technical aspect of the project cycle that emphasizes early risk analysis and software "prototyping." While it does achieve the objective of early risk mitigation, the spiral representation can be confusing. The circular time representation is inconsistent with traditional left-to-right time representations and risk management is portrayed as a sequence of serial analyses (in the upper left quadrant) preceding and delaying low-risk product development rather than offering the option of performing risk management as an ongoing, parallel part of the development process. In addition, all risk management is shown to cease once the concept represented by the operational prototype is available, giving the impression that the required detail design, coding,

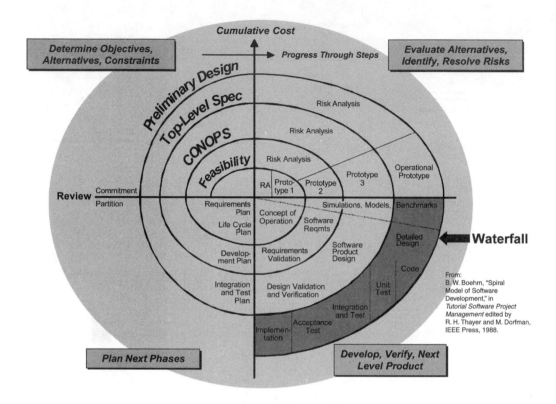

Figure 7.9   The Spiral Model.

and testing will be risk free as in the Royce Waterfall representation. This is rarely the case. To draw on the Spiral's strengths for risk management, we return to it in Chapter 13.

VEE MODELS: TOOLS FOR VISUALIZING AND MANAGING TECHNICAL DEVELOPMENT

Why the Vee Is a V

The V form most accurately represents system evolution from the perspective of system decomposition and integration activities.

The Vee models are valuable tools for visualizing and managing the systems engineering process.

Project cycles progress from left to right in a series of phases usually depicted horizontally consistent with the conventional time axis. However, some models have altered the depiction to emphasize selected attributes. In the Waterfall, the series of phases descend from the upper left down to the lower right. Emphasis here is on the flowdown of requirements as the system detail is elaborated. The Spiral Model's phases are shown wrapped around a center point in the form of a spiral; emphasis is on repetitive modeling (each revo-

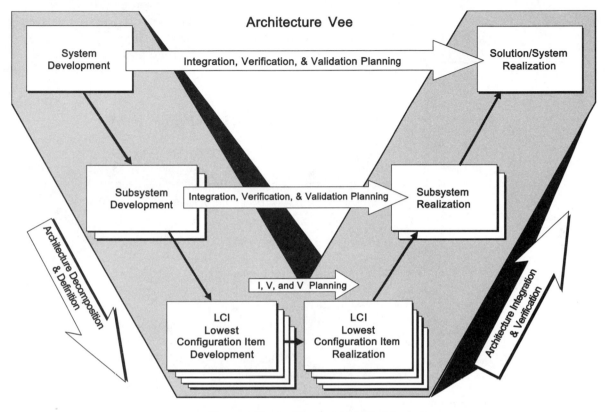

Figure 7.10   Architecture Vee Model.

lution) to address known risk. The final wrap of the spiral, however, contains Royce's Waterfall.

As depicted by the Waterfall, system decomposition extends from the needs of a user or customer down through concept development and subsystems to low-level entities. In reality, the entities are then built and integrated with others up through system realization. The resulting Vee form (Figure 7.10) most accurately represents system evolution from the perspective of decomposition and integration activities.

There can by any number of levels in the decomposition. As a reference, the *INCOSE Handbook* defines seven decomposition levels (system down to part). For simplicity, the basic Architecture Vee is illustrated with three levels, refering to the lowest level as the LCI from the architectural perspective of the systems engineer.

At each decomposition level, there is a direct correlation between activities on the left and right sides of the Vee. This is deliberate. For

——————— *INCOSE* ———————

The *INCOSE Handbook* defines these seven decomposition levels:

1. System.
2. Segment.
3. Element.
4. Subsystem.
5. Assembly.
6. Subassembly.
7. Part.

example, the method of verification to be used on the right must be determined on the left—at the time requirements are first defined—for each set of requirements developed at each level. This minimizes the chances that requirements are specified in a way that cannot be measured or verified.

System Decomposition and Definition

Decomposition: The hierarchical, functional, and physical partitioning of any system into hardware assemblies, software components, and operator activities that can be scheduled, budgeted, and assigned to a responsible manager.

Definition: The *design to, build to,* and *code to* artifacts that define the functional and physical content of every entity.

The increasing thickness of the Vee (orthogonal to the paper) is symbolic of the number of entities at each decomposition level, which relates to system complexity. Referring to Figure 7.11, the concept of the evolving baselines, progressively increasing in architecture depth and under change control, is represented by the Vee core. The left leg of the Vee represents system decomposition and definition and the right leg represents integration and verification.

Our Vee model supports the real-world need for exploratory technical investigation early in the cycle to pursue opportunities and reduce risk. For example, we encourage early hardware and software requirements-understanding models and technical feasibility models. This helps clarify user requirements and ensures that customer requirements are achievable. Early participation of domain experts is essential to the credibility of this process. Upward iteration with the user is often needed to get buy-in to the opportunities and to manage the risks in the continuous process of user requirements clarification. The details of these "off-core" studies are explored in greater depth in Chapter 13.

Time and project maturity flow from left to right on the Vee; therefore, once a decision gate is passed, backward iteration is not possible. However, vertical iteration is encouraged all the way up to the user and user requirements and down to the lowest-level hardware component or software unit (along the "time now" vertical line). This is the typical activity at every "time now" point progressing along the core of the Vee. Changes in user requirements

Business case and budget allocations flow down with the technical requirements and constraints. When properly allocated, each entity receives a business case and a budget. Hence, all three aspects of the project cycle take a Vee form to faithfully represent the solution development path.

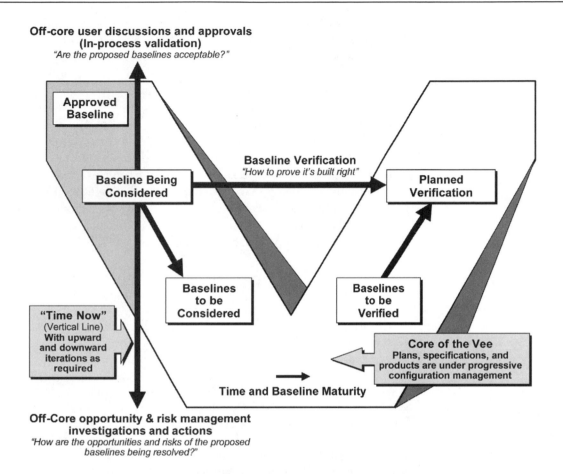

Figure 7.11   Vee Model: Decomposition and definition.

introduced after the PDR will impact baselined concepts and their design-to specifications and may best be held for later versions or releases. If substantive changes to user requirements must be made subsequent to the PDR, then the project should be reset to the position, within the Vee, of the requirement impact. The repeat of much of the development sequence may be faster because of previous experience and lessons learned, but all affected phases and decision gates must be repeated in view of the major change in requirements.

As the project progresses, requirements flowdown analyses and opportunity and risk investigations continue. This is shown in Figure 7.11 by the vertical off-core activities that descend to the decomposition level necessary to evaluate available opportunities or to satisfy concerns. For instance, if there is a question about new material or piece part technology, the downward off-core activity will descend to the material or part level where modeling can prove that incorporation will be beneficial.

While technical feasibility decisions are based on these off-core activities, only the decisions at the core of the Vee are put under configuration management (change control). Off-core analyses, studies, and modeling are performed to substantiate the core decisions. The studies ensure that opportunities have been assessed and are being managed and that risks have been mitigated or determined to be acceptable. The laboratory or model shop off-core analysis may not require rigorous controls and will usually be repeated at the appropriate decomposition level to justify baselining the result.

The Vee development approach is consistent with—and supports—the current best practices in iterative evolutionary software development. If iterations are expected to be part of development, the architecture must be robust and flexible enough to adapt to the evolving requirements. As Craig Larman states:

> The Unified Process (and most new methods) encourage a combination of risk-driven and client-driven iterative planning. This means that the goals of the early iterations are chosen to pursue the opportunity of a solution by: (1) identifying and driving down the highest risks, and (2) building visible features that the client cares most about. Risk-driven iterative development includes more specifically the practice of architecture-centric iterative development, meaning that early iterations focus on building, testing, and stabilizing the core architecture. Why? Because not having a solid architecture is a common high risk.[16]

The project development process is dynamic. Throughout the project cycle there is iteration at all levels, studying user needs, investigating alternate concepts, performing analyses, building models, and conducting evaluations. The Vee model establishes order out of what might emerge as a chaotic process. The baselines on the core are the anchor for the "time now" iterations, but these baselines can be revised through the change management process. The upward iterations address the evolution of user requirements, while downward iterations evolve improved solutions. This iterative, evolutionary process can continue for as long as the project team desires, constrained only by the user's schedule, the customer's budget, and the project's ultimate objectives.

Beware, however, of system-level changes made late in the development process. Such changes carry a high risk that the consequences will not be completely identified and implemented. The cause of the *Apollo 13* disaster was traced to a late change.[17] It took a sequence of five events to trigger the disaster, but the root cause was an increase in the spacecraft bus voltage incorporated after the PDR. All hardware was modified to accommodate the voltage increase except for one part that was eventually overstressed by the higher voltage and sparked the explosion that almost caused the fatal failure of the mission.

During the development of the Space Shuttle, a series of drop tests were performed to verify the landing characteristics of the orbiter. A full-scale engineering model (named the Enterprise), with pilots on board, was carried on the back of a Boeing 747 to a high altitude and released to glide back to the Dryden Flight Test Facility and verify landing behavior. Because this vehicle would not go to orbit, and hence did not have the high-temperature reentry, sheets of styrofoam were machined and bonded to the external surfaces to simulate the tile contours. The styrofoam was painted green to simulate the color of the insulation tile coating being used at that time. During the year it took to prepare the orbiter engineering model, work continued on the tile project to develop a better coating. A new black coating passed a series of verification and qualification tests, and, because it was superior in most respects to the green coating, the black coating was adopted as the updated baseline. A few days before the flight test of the full-scale orbiter model was to begin, an executive on the shuttle project decided that even though the color of the vehicle had nothing to do with the landing tests, it would be better for publicity if the orbiter was painted black on the bottom.[18] The RF signals to transmit the test data should be unaffected by the vehicle color. So the vehicle was repainted. This change, being considered so trivial, did not go through the change control process. During checkout just before the test was to start, it was found that no signals could be transmitted or received. The black paint that covered the antennae contained lampblack, which was opaque to RF. Thus, RF opaque lampblack covered the antennae. Considerable rework was required before the tests could start. No change is a small change.

As a design matures, concept and design iterations must decrease and ultimately stop. When design solutions are under configuration management, engineers and designers can often see further potential improvement. Just remember the post-PDR decision gate motto: "Better is the enemy of good enough." Late changes trigger continually changing requirements to other areas, usually with broad and expensive impact to the system.

Agile software developers have adopted the motto, "Embrace change," and have designed their development processes to accommodate frequent changes. However, there should be limits. If the team is developing network software for a cellular wireless system, and after PDR the customer decides that the system should be based on satellite communication, the impact to project cost and schedule will be substantial. There is another post-PDR rule: "Meeting customer requirements and walking on water are equally easy—when both are frozen."

System Integration and Verification

System Integration and Verification ascend the right side of the Vee.

> *Integration:* The successive combining and testing of system hardware assemblies, software components, and operator tasks to progressively prove the performance and compatibility of all entities of the system.
>
> *Verification:* Proof of compliance with specifications.
>
> *Validation:* Proof of user satisfaction.

Validation is about building the right thing.

Verification is about building it right.

The method of verification to be used at each level on the right Vee leg must be determined as the specifications are developed at the corresponding decomposition level on the left Vee leg.

The critical aspects of the integration and verification process are indicated in Figure 7.12. Note the overt distinction on the right leg of the Vee between verification and validation. Verification is the process of proving that each entity meets its specifications. Validation is the process of demonstrating (as opposed to proving) that the users are satisfied, regardless of the specified performance.

A complex verification process may overdrive cost and schedule and be the determining factor when considering alternative decomposition and integration concepts.

As the integration and verification processes ascend the right Vee leg, anomalies encountered should involve systems engineering in anomaly identification, assessment, and resolution. Issues that cannot be resolved but can be tolerated may require a waiver or deviation from the customer in conjunction with a modified as-verified

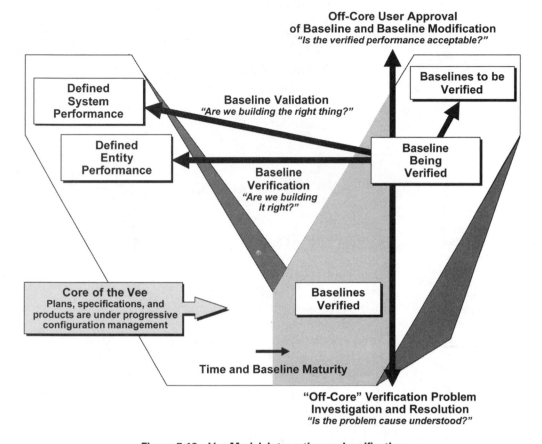

Figure 7.12 Vee Model: Integration and verification.

baseline. In some environments, a deviation (to a specification) is granted before the fact (the requirement does not need to be met), while a waiver is granted after the fact (the entity is built and fails verification). In many organizations, the terms are used interchangeably, just as concrete and cement are used (incorrectly) as synonyms in common usage.

Applying the Vee to Business and Budget Aspects

If the technical aspect naturally tracks the Vee form, what about the business and budget aspects? Do they also form a Vee or some other shape?

In the management of many projects, the business and budget aspects do not track the Vee shape of the technical aspect. But they should. For comprehensive project management, all tasks for all system entities should have individual business cases and commensurate budgets. For this to occur, the business case and budget allocations must flow down with the technical requirements and constraints. When properly allocated, the lowest configuration item manager will receive a business case and a budget. Hence, all three aspects of the project cycle take a Vee form to correctly represent the system development path.

TECHNICAL DEVELOPMENT TACTICS

Evolutionary development provides for investigation and experimentation to develop a capability. Delivery is usually in entity versions each delivering improved performance. Individual increments can be developed using the evolutionary approach.

The strategic goals of a project will drive the development tactics. A single instance of the basic Vee Model represents the most straightforward tactical approach: a unified, linear development with a single delivery. If a project goal is to upgrade the system over time with newly developed improvements, then a system architecture with increments configured for easy upgrading and fielding is the best tactical method. This alternative to a unified method deliberately decomposes the concept into modular entities to be developed *incrementally,* that is, separately for later integration as is done in the auto industry. If a goal is to migrate technology into the system over time, then an *evolutionary* development method may be appropriate. The concepts of incremental and evolutionary development are only summarized here. Chapter 19 addresses technical development tactics in more depth.

INCOSE

INCOSE Handbook Sec 3.4 identifies life cycle development approaches such as:

• Single Thread Development.
• Incremental Development.
• Evolutionary Development.

If some user requirements are too vague to permit final specification at the design-to decision gate (PDR) or if the development process itself uncovers unforeseen needs and system applications, a tactic is to proceed with a combination of straightforward (linear) development and evolutionary releases, typical of commercial software development. We illustrate this combination in a product structure with four increments: A, B, C, and D. Figure 7.13 depicts a combination of development tactics selected to meet specific strategic objectives: The evolving product breakdown structure is shown in the margin.

Development and delivery decisions are usually driven by the business case in response to the demands of the market or the customer. While the project manager should be well versed in the business case, the systems engineer usually has the best appreciation for the flexibility of the project to accommodate and benefit from the various tactical development and delivery methods dis-

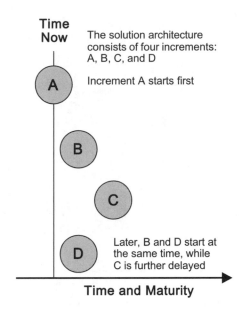

Figure 7.13a   Solution initiation.

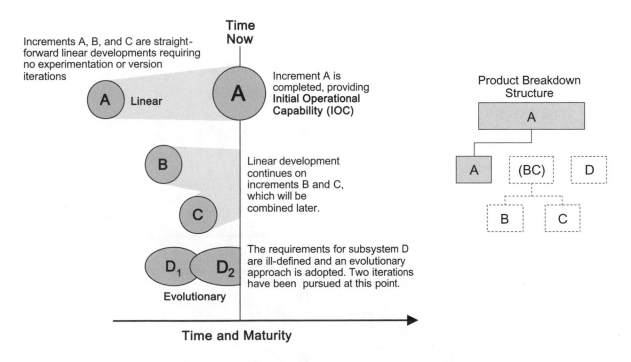

Figure 7.13b   Increment A completed, providing initial operating capacity.

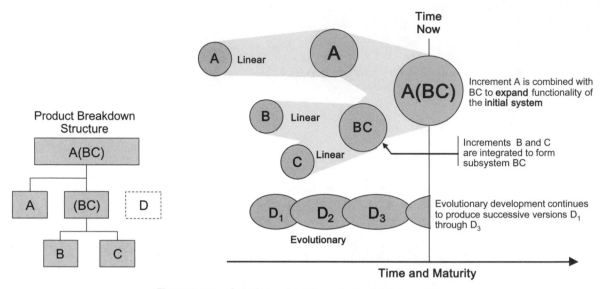

Figure 7.13c   Solution subsystems A, B, and C complete.

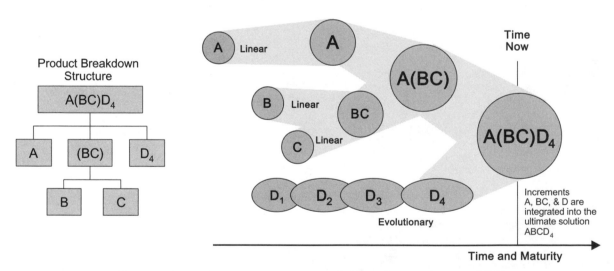

Figure 7.13d   All increments are integrated to form the enhanced system.

cussed here. To arrive at the best decision for the sake of the market and the project, the project manager and the systems engineer should collaborate until consensus is reached. Then, the decision should be baselined and broadcast to the project team so that the tactics can be built into the tailored project cycle and all subsequent planning.

TECHNOLOGY INSERTION

Projects are sometimes initiated with known technology shortfalls or anticipate an emerging technology. Technology development can be done in parallel with the project evolution, shown in Figure 7.14,

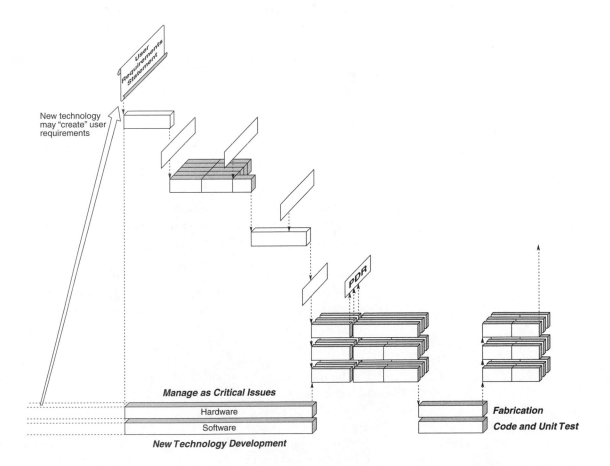

Figure 7.14   Technology insertion.

and inserted as late as the design-to decision gate when the performance of the new technology must be specified and guaranteed. In the example, the required technology development is represented by a horizontal bar shown off-core at the level where it will impact the project if expected performance is not available. Technology development should be managed and statused by the project manager and systems engineer as an opportunity critical to the success of the project.

BASELINE MANAGEMENT

Baselines contain all the business, technical, cost, schedule, and deliverable requirements that are sufficiently mature to be accepted and placed under change control, usually at decision gates or phase transition reviews. The project team then relies on these baselines as the approved state of the project for further elaboration. Projects should be managed to a coordinated business or mission baseline (contract, schedules), budget baseline (should cost, most probable cost), and technical baseline (requirements, concepts, specifications, verification plans, etc.).

Baseline management is accomplished by configuration management including a formal change control regimen that, for each type of artifact, establishes:

- The event that places that artifact under change control,
- The method for considering change, and
- The required change approval, usually involving both a buyer and a seller.

The overall objective of baseline and change management is to establish a reliable knowledge reference for the project business and design maturity. This is necessary for accurate communications among supporting business, technical, training, sparing, replication, and repair personnel. The change control process, addressed in Chapter 14, is usually initiated by the first official artifact of the project, which in many cases is the contract (for internal projects the contract may be a memorandum from management). This first artifact is usually business based and provides the overall objectives and business (or mission) case for the project. It is especially important that this artifact be managed so that any changes to the business or mission case are properly accounted for and responded to. Too often, projects drift from their initial, undocumented objectives, no longer reflecting what was originally or even currently intended.

It is common over the life of a project for the sponsor to change, bringing new personalities and requirements to the project. These new requirements should receive disciplined change management so that they are properly interpreted and accommodated with commensurate changes in budget and schedule constraints.

The technical baseline is often initiated by the User Requirements Document—usually the first technical artifact to be placed under formal configuration management. As the project cycle progresses, systems engineering together with the contributing engineering disciplines produce a series of technical baselines consistent with the maturation of the solution and the phases of the project. Examples of technical baselines are:

User Requirements	As-Replicated (Production Release)
System Requirements	As-Built
Concept Definition	As-Tested
System Specification	As-Deployed
"Design-to"	As-Operated
"Build-to" (Pilot Production)	

Changes to the business, budget, or technical baselines require joint action (review and approval) by the customer and the provider. In the case of commercial projects, the customer is often represented by the marketing manager or general manager. In this case, the business baseline is established by the initial agreement between executive management and marketing as to the project scope, funding, and schedule.

For contractual work authorized by an external customer, the provider's business baseline is usually a contract. Business baseline changes require contract action, and for large federal government contracts funding changes may even require congressional action.

Systems engineering should work closely with the business manager (both customer and provider) so that the technical requirements are congruent with business and budget baseline provisions. When there is a reduction of funds, systems engineering and the project manager have to ensure there is a commensurate reduction in technical scope and work content.

Baseline management is discussed in more depth in Chapter 14.

TAILORING THE PROJECT CYCLE

A project for hosting the Olympics is unlikely to perform well if it is following the technical project cycle tailored for developing a toothbrush as illustrated in Figure 7.15.

Each project, or at least each project type, needs a project cycle tailored to the strategic objectives and the tactical approach to achieving those objectives. Major project types, which usually have a template project cycle and are common to both the government and commercial environments, include:

- *System development*—creation of a new product to meet a need. (*Example:* mobile telephone system)
- *System integration*—combining of existing entities into a functioning system. (*Example:* automated manufacturing facility using commercially available equipment)
- *Production*—process improvement of product replication to existing documentation. (*Example:* reduce cost of building computers)

—— *PMBOK® Guide* ——
Both the *PMBOK® Guide* and the *INCOSE Handbook* cite the need to tailor generic cycles to the specifics of the project. *INCOSE Handbook* Sec 8 describes tailoring of the cycle.

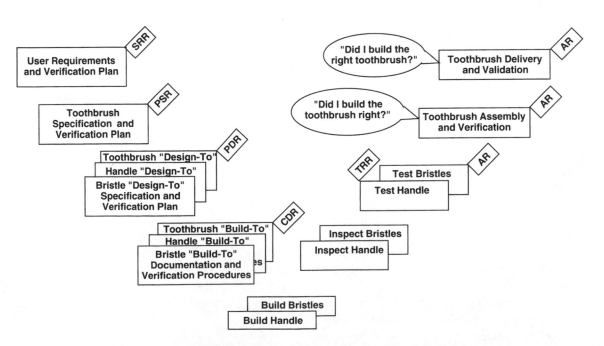

Figure 7.15   A technical project cycle tailored for developing a toothbrush.

Table 7.2 Project Types Characterized by Driving Force and Risks

Project Type	If Driven By	Then the Risk Is
System development #1	Performance	Cost, schedule
System development #2	Cost	Performance, schedule
System integration	Compatibility	Entity availability
Production	Cost	Performance, quality
Research and development	Technology	Strays from corporate needs
Facility	Schedule	Quality, cost, trades personnel

- *Research and development*—discovering a new approach to solving a problem. (*Example:* use biological models to increase computer capabilities)
- *Facilities*—produce a new facility to meet a prescribed need. (*Example:* Airport, hospital, wafer production facility)

Each project type is characterized by its driving opportunity and risk factors. Table 7.2 is ordered by degree of risk and management complexity, with system development projects at the high end. There are exceptions: A company depending on specialized technology research for the bulk of its income could attribute the highest risk to research projects. Some pharmaceutical companies fit this category. Likewise, a company that develops very simple and predictable products, such as campaign buttons, but depends on very low-cost production, will view manufacturing projects as high-risk.

The project cycle template developed by your organization needs to be adapted to each project based on the:

- Project type, content, scope, and complexity.
- Management environment—customers, contractors, and top management.
- Mandated constraints.
- The management style.
- Balance between project opportunities and risks.

The customer and provider project managers should jointly define their project cycle, the content and conduct of the decision gates, and the nature and content of the required decision gate artifacts.

Tailoring may add or delete project cycle features as shown:

> Most well-known examples of failures and lessons learned come from big projects. That's because failures of small projects get little publicity.

> Deviations from the relevant template cycle need to be substantiated with solid rationale.

Feature Modified:	Example Modification
Phases	Deactivation Phase added
	Source Selection Phase deleted
Decision gates	Consent-to-Pour-Concrete Review added
	Qualification Acceptance Review deleted
Products and activities	Field Test Model added
	On-Site Training deleted

> The tailoring process is one of the most important aspects of project planning.

Tailoring requires foresight and informed judgment on the part of everyone involved, orchestrated by the project manager. We recommend these tailoring steps:

> Select the phases.

- Phase selection is based on project type (development, research, product integration, production, facilities, service); content (e.g., the hardware/software balance); tactical development and delivery method (unified, incremental, linear, evolutionary, single, multiple, as defined in Chapter 19); scope; and complexity.

> Select the baseline management decision gates.

- Decision gate selection is based on the baseline sequence and artifacts to be developed and managed. Decision gates should always occur at phase transitions and are often beneficial within some phases. Some decision gates can be included to help keep the project sold to supporting organizations. Too few decision gates allow the project to operate without control. Too many may overburden the project with superfluous administration.

> Select the lower level decision gates.

- Interim gates should be chosen to enhance opportunities and to minimize risk. Plan interim decision gates to ensure readiness for the baseline management decision gates.

> Identify decision gate products.

- Identify the products (artifacts) required at the decision gates: documents, deliverables, models, and agreements.

> Identify all activities.

- Identify the activities necessary to produce the products required at each decision gate.

> Review pertinent lessons learned.

- Validate the project cycle against past experience. Consider and apply lessons learned from related projects and previous contract experience, secured directly from project officials and in contract files.

> Get executive concurrence.

- To obtain approval for your project cycle, develop justification for all deviations from the organization's template. Although tailoring is encouraged, changes need to be justified.

Specific internal and external standards may be an explicit feature of your project cycle template. Those standards, as well as all requirements and standards, should be appropriate to the reliability and risk level of the project. Those embodied in contracts need to be critically reviewed as part of the tailoring process. Situations that prompt tailoring of standards include:

- Inappropriate application of standards.
- Blanket imposition of standards.
- Underimposition of standards.
- Implementation of a "no-tailoring" policy subsequent to contract award.
- Cost versus benefits of standards implementation is ignored.
- The inappropriate imposition of high reliability or severe environmental standards.
- Standards applied arbitrarily, "just to be safe."
- Extensive and uncontrolled cross-referencing of standards.
- Imposition of obsolete standards.
- Application of government standards where commercial practices are acceptable.

These tailoring techniques are applicable to standards and other artifacts, especially contract terms and conditions:

- Specify exact applicable paragraphs.
- Specify exempted provisions.
- Specify tailored values for referenced standards.
- Expand referenced standards as necessary.
- Specify exact documentation deliverables.
- Extract selected standards and include in contract documentation.
- Allow contractor choices when risk is acceptable.
- Prioritize requirements.

SHORTENING THE PROJECT CYCLE TIME

The increasing challenges of time to market and technical obsolescence are familiar pressures for shorter schedules. Not only are shorter schedules less expensive, but they free up skilled personnel who are usually needed on other projects.

The project cycle is the driver of subordinate project networks and, consequently, the project schedule and its critical path (Figure 7.16).

Approaches to shorten the schedule should begin at the broadest level—the project cycle. Techniques such as shortening the critical path or running multiple shifts will be addressed in Chapters 12 and 17.

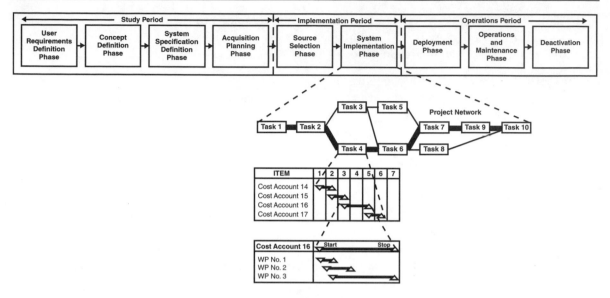

Figure 7.16   The project cycle template drives the network.

The best way to ensure the shortest schedule and quality results
is by applying a strategically and tactically correct project cycle
managed by qualified and motivated personnel. Consider reducing
the technical risks and other impediments by selectively using previously developed or previously qualified products.

The Geostationary Operational Environment Satellite (weather
satellite) project team decided to shorten the project cycle by gambling on a short cut.[19] To reduce the predicted four-year development, the study period was deleted. The satellite was delivered nine
years later, an embarrassing five years late. Technical feasibility development under the direction of creative scientists was performed
concurrently with ongoing system development. This approach eventually drove costs and schedules to multiples of the original predictions. Conversely, properly planned technology insertion projects
have succeeded in many instances at NASA and elsewhere.

When exceptional performance is required, the project team
should be staffed with experts and co-located to facilitate efficient
communications and reduce distractions. This approach is called
skunk works after Kelly Johnson's Lockheed organization that produced quantum leaps in technology in very short time spans.[20] Johnson's team applied project cycle discipline, baseline management,
change control, and decision gates. The team applied all practices
using a "sweet spot" approach that was simple, yet formal, with low
amounts of documentation.

The pursuit of "better, faster, cheaper" has caused some teams to discard the discipline of the gated project cycle or to skip selected phases and decision gates without due regard for the consequences. This approach has proven to be unacceptably risky and multiple failures have confirmed that proven practices were often eliminated in the desire to meet a "faster, better, cheaper" mandate.

The key to success is to tailor a gated cycle, based on a proven template, so that it is lean, efficient, and effective. Decision gates should add the value of baseline review and approval without causing schedule delay or stalling ongoing progress. In a skunk works environment, decision gates are usually working sessions, but retain the discipline required for ensuring binding and informed execution. Decision gates should not require lengthy and cumbersome processes and should not include people who are peripheral to the baselining decision. For example, to skip a Consent-to-Pour-Concrete Review is irresponsible and can result in a misplaced or poorly constructed foundation. The review should take just a few minutes requiring only an inspection of the layout, forms, steel, concrete mix, and the personnel credentials.

The following are inspiring examples of successful transitions to faster cycle times:

Product	Implementation Period in Months	
	Original	*Improved*
HP computer printer	54	22
Ford automobile	48	16
Ingersoll-Rand air grinder	40	15
Warner clutch brake	36	10

PROJECT CYCLE EXERCISE

You and your partner are preparing to build a custom home on a site yet to be selected. You want to ensure a smooth process and that you remain friends with each other and with all the other stakeholders when it is completed.

To minimize risk, you are to create your preferred project cycle complete with periods, phases, and decision gates by formulating the three parallel congruent aspects (business, budget, and technical).

For the business aspect, consider: site location; resale; community trends; school districts; selection of architect, engineer, and contractor; whether you will act as general contractor or not; community approval; architecture committee approval; planning permits; building permits; and certificate of occupancy. This is not a complete list. Add to it as necessary to ensure consideration of all stakeholders. Make sure your phases and decision gates structure an orderly progression and provide the necessary agreements.

For the budget aspect, consider: target budgets, should-cost estimates, available assets, loan qualification, loan commitments, progress payments, funds disbursements, management reserve, contractor holdbacks, performance bonuses, and penalties. This is not a complete list. Make sure your phases and decision gates structure an orderly progression and provide the necessary agreements.

For the technical aspect consider: zoning, community or subdivision themes, concept development, design-to specifications, build-to artifacts, code compliance, quality control, material control, and inspections. This is not a complete list. Make sure your phases and decision gates structure an orderly progression and provide the necessary agreements.

Your final product should be a three-row project cycle, one row for each of the three aspects. The columns should represent periods and their phases. For example, the first period might be the study period with the first phase defined as Owner Requirements Definition. This is the phase in which you and your partner establish requirements, along with the overall budget and schedule, for the project, independent of the selected site or building design.

8

THE TEN MANAGEMENT ELEMENTS

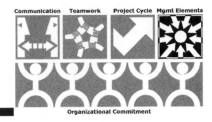

Effective management can indeed move mountains. One of the management breakthroughs in the Panama Canal project was the realization that the major challenge was logistics— how to relocate what amounted to a mountain of dirt, instead of the prior view of digging a big ditch.

In a very different logistics challenge, that of supporting the Gulf War with a military force equal to the population of Alaska, General William G. Pagonis offers several management lessons. In his book, *In Moving Mountains,*[1] Pagonis outlines his management style, which includes:

- Constant informational flow on index cards to all levels of the organization,
- Daily bulletins and stand-up meetings (limited to 30 minutes and anyone interested, regardless of rank, can attend), and
- Articulation of each leader's management style, "so that subordinates need zero time and energy guessing how the manager manages."

General Pagonis also had some sage advice regarding project planning, control, and execution. "If you have good people, and if you have the capability to expand and delegate, and you have a centralized plan, imagination and ingenuity will always win. I believe in centralized control and decentralized execution."

——— *PMBOK® Guide* ———
The *PMBOK® Guide* identifies nine knowledge areas.

——— *INCOSE* ———
The *INCOSE Handbook* cites 16 technical and 10 project management processes. These are analogous to the ten project elements described here but do not correlate exactly as these elements are behavioral rather than functional.

This chapter and the ten that follow are about those good people; the planning, control, and execution together with organizing the project and installing the management processes. The integrated process model (wheel and axle), introduced in Chapter 3, helps to visualize project management and to appreciate the functional relationships. The wheel depicts the first nine situational management elements as the spokes of a wheel, held together by its rim, Project Leadership.

"Effectiveness lies in balance," is Stephen Covey's way of expressing the need for a sense of proportion. Too much focus, he quips, ". . . is like a person who runs three or four hours a day, bragging about the extra ten years of life it creates, unaware he's spending it running."[2]

THE ELEMENTS

The *elements* are the project's tool chest, with project management and systems engineering techniques and tools sorted and grouped into like categories requiring ten drawers. The ten categories of management responsibilities, functions, techniques, and tools are all essential to orchestrating the team and developing the project's system solution. They apply to:

- All types of projects.
- All phases of the project cycle.
- All organizations participating in the project.

An important facet of the wheel metaphor is the actual interdependence of the spokes of a wheel. The wheel is structurally much greater than the collection of its parts. But, one weak spoke reduces its overall effectiveness. The elements are described briefly in the following section and are then detailed in the ten corresponding chapters that follow.

Project management and systems engineering techniques and tools share the same drawers because they are most commonly used together.

Project Requirements

Project Requirements is all about managing the three baselines: business, budget, and technical. It covers both the development and management of requirements. Included are business, budget, and technical requirements and spans from project conception to deactivation. Business requirements include, for example, the business or mission case; contracts involved; stakeholder constraints; industry standards, policies, and trends; and funding sources. The budget

——— *PMBOK® Guide* ———
This element is consistent with *PMBOK® Guide* Ch 5 *Project Scope Management.*

——— INCOSE ———
This element is consistent with *INCOSE Handbook* Sec 5.6 *Technical Processes and Decision-Making Process.*

aspect covers the securing of funding and the spending plan. The technical aspect covers system maturation across requirements identification, substantiation, concept selection, architecture selection, decomposition, definition, integration, verification, and validation. The requirements element is situational rather than sequential since new requirements, which can be introduced at almost any point in the project, need to be managed concurrently with the requirements already driving the development. While the project's business case drives this element, systems engineering accounts for most of the execution.

Organization Options

Organization Options considers the strengths and deficiencies of various project structures (wiring diagrams), how each resolves accountabilities and responsibilities, and how each promotes teamwork and communications. Complex projects do not have to result in complex structures, and there is no single "best" organization. There are many options including matrix, integrated product teams, and integrated project teams—even skunk works, where exceptional systems engineering has been demonstrated.[3] (The skunk works is a name adopted by the highly creative Lockheed aircraft development organization.) The Organization Options element is personnel-independent and offers a basis for selecting and changing the structure appropriately as the project progresses through project cycle phases from inception to deactivation.

—— *PMBOK® Guide* ——
This element is consistent with *PMBOK® Guide* Sec 2.3.3 *Organizational Structure,* Ch 4 *Project Integration Management,* and Ch 9 *Project Human Resources Management.*

—— *INCOSE* ——
This element is consistent with *INCOSE Handbook* Sec 5.3 *Organizing Process.*

The Project Team

The Project Team element addresses staffing the organization. Selection criteria should consider character attributes, qualifications, and the specific skills demanded by the challenges of each project phase. Competency models that include necessary attributes and qualifications should form the basis of selection for key positions such as the project manager, the business manager, the systems engineer, the planner, and the subcontractor manager. The preferred management approach requires that the team participants be matched to the requirements of the project cycle phase.

—— *PMBOK® Guide* ——
This element is consistent with *PMBOK® Guide* Ch 9 *Project Human Resources Management.*

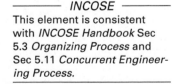
—— *INCOSE* ——
This element is consistent with *INCOSE Handbook* Sec 5.3 *Organizing Process* and Sec 5.11 *Concurrent Engineering Process.*

Project Planning

Project Planning spans the team's conversion of the project's requirements into team task authorizations, including delivery schedules and resource requirements. But it doesn't end there. Too often

—— *PMBOK® Guide* ——
This element is consistent with *PMBOK® Guide* Ch 6 *Project Time Management* and Ch 7 *Project Cost Management*.

———— *INCOSE* ————
This element is consistent with *INCOSE Handbook* Sec 5.2 *Planning*.

—— *PMBOK® Guide* ——
This element is consistent with *PMBOK® Guide* Ch 11 *Project Risk Management*.

———— *INCOSE* ————
This element is consistent with *INCOSE Handbook* Sec 5.8 *Risk Management Processes*.

planning is done once and is then forgotten as the project strays from its intended path. Plans must be kept current, reflecting new information and actual progress. The planning process should include both manual and computer tools that support the development of the best tactical approach for accomplishing the project's objectives. We encourage the use of the cards-on-the-wall technique described in Chapter 12 to develop the project's task network and schedule.

Opportunities and Risks

Opportunities and Risks is about pursuing opportunities and managing their risks. It encompasses the identification, evaluation, and management of both opportunities and their associated risks. It spans the techniques for determining and quantifying the value of potential actions to enhance the opportunities and those necessary to mitigate the risks. Opportunities and risks may be identified at any point in the project cycle, so the techniques and tools of this element must be applied perceptively as the project progresses through the cycle. Although an integral part of planning, it is common for both of these factors to be treated superficially by the project team and many projects have failed as a result. The conventional mode of focusing the team just on risks tends to foster negativism. An alternative is to have the team seeking and seizing opportunities to excel and then to examine and manage the risks of those opportunities. This approach encourages innovation and fosters positive teamwork. The uniqueness and importance of opportunities and risks and how they should be managed justifies treatment as a separate element.

Project Control

—— *PMBOK® Guide* ——
This element is consistent with *PMBOK® Guide* discussions on control in Sec 5.5 *Project Scope*, Sec 4.5 *Monitor and Control Project Work,* and Ch 8 *Project Quality Management*.

———— *INCOSE* ————
This element is consistent with *INCOSE Handbook* Sec 5.7 *Control Process* and Sec 5.9 *Configuration Management*.

Project Control is often misunderstood because many projects have a project controls organization that reports activity and status rather than actually controlling anything. Controlling the project is necessary to ensure that planned events happen as planned and that unplanned events don't happen. Control methods should apply to all three baselines (business, budget, and technical). In our approach, proactive control is recognized as process control where every aspect that needs to be controlled must have a control standard, a control authority, a control mechanism, and a variance detection system. Using schedule control as an example, the standard is the baselined master schedule, the authority is the business manager, the mechanism is the change board, and the variance detection is schedule status. Categories of controlled processes may include baselines, configuration, security, safety, requirements, manufacturing processes, software development environment, schedule, cost, and so on. Reactive control consists of corrective action initiated in response to unacceptable variances. Many projects fail when control systems are not established or are circumvented.

Project Visibility

Project Visibility encompasses all of the techniques used by the project team, including external stakeholders, to gather data and disseminate information to ensure that the health of the project is transparent to the project team. It includes techniques like management by walking around (MBWA) and project information centers as well as electronic techniques such as voice mail, e-mail, and video conferencing. The visibility system and associated techniques must be designed to serve the active project phase, the organizational structure, and geographic complexity.

—— *PMBOK® Guide* ——
The *PMBOK® Guide* and the *INCOSE Handbook* do not specifically address visibility as a management technique category, although both cite the need to monitor ongoing work.

Project Status

Project Status is frequently confused with project activity rather than performance metrics. Project Status is comprehensive measurements of performance against the plan to detect unacceptable variances and determine the need for corrective action. Status should encompass schedule, cost, technical, and business progress. The evaluation and measurement should also include the rate of change of variances if not corrected. Technical Performance Measurement and Earned Value Management are included in this technique and tool set.

—— *PMBOK® Guide* ——
This element is consistent with *PMBOK® Guide* Ch 5 *Project Scope Management*, Ch 6 *Project Time Management*, and Ch 7 *Project Cost Management*.

—— *INCOSE* ——
The *INCOSE Handbook* Sec 6.3 addresses *Technical Performance Measurement*.

Corrective Action

Corrective Action is the culmination of variance management and emphasizes that reactive management is necessary and proper for effective project management. Corrective Actions are taken to return the project to plan and usually take place as a result of project statusing. The techniques may include overtime, added work shifts, an alternate technical approach, new leadership, and so on. Projects that ignore variances and fail to implement corrective action are usually out of control.

—— *PMBOK® Guide* ——
This element is consistent with *PMBOK® Guide* treatment of corrective actions in each knowledge area.

—— *INCOSE* ——
The *INCOSE Handbook* addresses deviations from specifications.

Project Leadership

Project Leadership is the mortar that holds the other elements of project management and systems engineering intact and ensures that

—— *PMBOK® Guide* ——
Both the *PMBOK® Guide* and
the *INCOSE Handbook*
address the importance of
leadership but neither
embraces leadership as a
separate knowledge area or
management category.

all are being properly implemented and applied. Leadership depends on the ability to inspire—to ensure that project members are motivated on both the individual and team levels to deliver as promised within the desired project management culture. Leadership emphasizes doing the right things, while doing things right is a primary management responsibility. Leadership depends on the skillful application of techniques such as handling different personalities and maturity levels, and team composition and rewards. History has confirmed that, without strong leadership, the team is likely to stray from sound fundamentals and implement high-risk, failure-prone short cuts. If the team members are fully trained in the worth of the elements and are believers in the process, then the need for strong leadership is reduced.

PROJECT MANAGEMENT ELEMENTS EXERCISE

Make a list of every project management technique that you can think of. Then group them according to the ten project management element categories. When a technique serves more than one element, locate it in the element with the most significant impact. For instance, a decision gate often provides visibility, status, and control of baseline evolution; however, the primary purpose is baseline control.

Example:

Requirements	*Organization Options*
Specification	Functional organization
Lessons learned	Integrated product team
Process standard	Matrix organization

PART THREE

THE TEN MANAGEMENT ELEMENTS IN DETAIL

The axle and wheel in the following figure depict the relationship between the sequential and situational essentials of our model. The project cycle, represented by the axle, is the time-phased backbone of the project and identifies the tactical approach, project deliverables, and the sequence of major events. The movable wheel is the project's tool chest, representing the ten categories of processes, techniques, and tools that the enterprise encourages and supports for skillful application. In organizations that employ the CMMI, ISO, or Six Sigma frameworks, these processes and techniques are usually controlled and well documented to ensure proper application. Likewise, the knowledge areas identified in the PMI *PMBOK® Guide* and the best practices in *INCOSE Systems Engineering Handbook* can be organized and mapped into these ten categories to complete the interrelated set of management methods for consistent deployment.

The ten management elements facilitate the tactical approach to realizing the strategic goals of the project.

Each chapter in Part Three is devoted to one of the ten management elements—the spokes of the wheel.

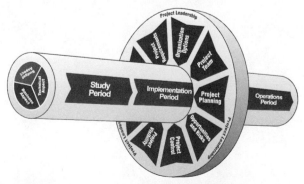

Skillful application of a feature-rich tool chest is becoming increasingly relevant to mastering complexity.

The techniques and tools in each category are applicable to project management and systems engineering as well as to hardware and software development. In today's evolving tool environment, including more extensive use of symbolic languages, widespread tool knowledge is rare. Care must be exercised to guard against flawed communication through improper tool or language application. A shift in the tactical approach, or the introduction of unfamiliar, sophisticated tools, may require specialized training.

9
PROJECT REQUIREMENTS

A major challenge in expressing project ideas in writing is the selection of words that accurately represent the things themselves. Unfortunately, poorly chosen or missing words often create major problems. This excerpt from the 1907 specification for the Wright brothers' first production contract may be the ancestor of one of our most abused requirement clichés, the ubiquitous "user-friendly."[1]

the Government and trial flights will be at Fort Myer, Virginia.
8. It should be so designed as to ascent in any country which may be encountered in field service. The starting device must be simple and transportable. It should also land in a field without requiring a specially prepared spot and without damaging its structure.
9. It should be provided with some device to permit of a safe descent in case of an accident to the propelling machinery.
10. It should be sufficiently simple in its construction and operation to permit an intelligent man to become proficient in its use within a reasonable length of time.

> 10. **It should be sufficiently simple in its construction and operation to permit an intelligent man to become proficient in its use within a reasonable length of time.**

14. Bidders must state the time which will be required for delivery after receipt of order.

JAMES ALLEN
Brigadier General, Chief Signal Officer of the Army

SIGNAL OFFICE
Washington, D. C., *December 23, 1907.*

Wright Brothers' production contract, circa 1907.

. . . Requirements only half a word:
user requirements, customer requirements, stakeholder requirements, contract requirements, internal requirements, baselined requirements, unbaselined requirements, concept independent, concept dependent, allocated requirements, derived requirements functional requirements, performance requirements, design requirements, verification requirements, requirements musts, requirements wants, requirements weights.

—— *PMBOK® Guide* ——
This chapter is consistent with *PMBOK® Guide* Ch 5 *Project Scope Management* and Ch 10 *Project Communication Management.*

—— *INCOSE* ——
This chapter is also consistent with the entire content of the *INCOSE Handbook.*

It is always a challenge to ensure that the requirements and their implications are understood. When the U.S. Signal Corps in 1907 released the invitation to bid on a heavier-than-air flying machine, their overall objective was clear, even though the specification had many unclear details. At that time, it was not certain that anyone could satisfy the requirements. Technical experts argued, "there is not a known flying machine in the world which could fulfill these requirements."[2] Only the Wright brothers knew the project was achievable and that the U.S. Army had written the specification based on the Wright brothers' claim that they had already built machines that proved feasibility of the concepts. The army expected only 1 bid, but received 41. There were 40 bidders who had little chance of succeeding because they did not have a clear understanding of what the vague requirements really implied, and what would be needed to meet them. Two contracts were awarded, but only the Wright brothers delivered.

SIGNS OF OUR IDEAS

"We should have a great many fewer disputes in the world if words were taken for what they are, the signs of our ideas only, and not for the things themselves."

John Locke[3]

Nonessential or overspecified requirements frequently result in missing schedule and cost targets.

Project requirements start with what the user really needs (not what the provider perceives that the user needs) and end when those needs are satisfied as evidenced by successful user validation. In the end-to-end chain of technical and business development, there is an ongoing danger of misunderstanding and ambiguity. This often leads to nonessential, overspecified, unclear, or missing requirements, as illustrated by Figure 9.1—a cartoon familiar to every marketing student. Beyond just humor, this illustrates the current drive toward graphical representations of system and mission requirements, solution concepts, and solution behavior.

Overcoming Paradigm Paralysis

Recognizing a user need and having a great idea for solving it are not enough. Consider the typewriter. Viewing it as a widely used office appliance for more than a century, one could conclude it had been an instant success. On the contrary, acceptance was so slow that its promoters nearly abandoned it as a failure. It took more than a decade for users to realize that they needed the typewriter.[4]

In more recent history, the word processor had a similar slow beginning. Users (mostly typists) did not appreciate the significance of the new technology. When surveyed in 1970 about what could improve their productivity, many typists requested a way to correct the spelling of the last word typed before the text was transferred to the paper. Typewriters were then produced that displayed one line of text on a built-in one-line screen, with software to check spelling. It took several years for users to understand that, if the software

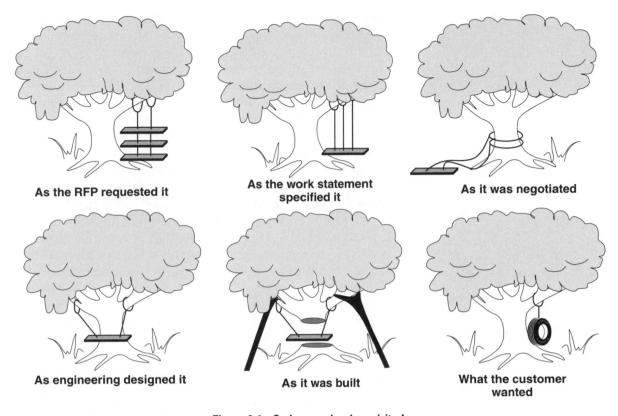

| As the RFP requested it | As the work statement specified it | As it was negotiated |
| As engineering designed it | As it was built | What the customer wanted |

Figure 9.1   Swings, a classic revisited.

could handle one line, a larger screen would allow composition and spell checking paragraphs and even whole pages.

For several years, management strongly resisted the concept that a word processor was a tool that engineers and managers should use. The executives who viewed word processors as typewriter replacements could not make the paradigm shift needed to envision a time when it would become commonplace for engineers and executives to create their own text documents.

Reliance on the wrong users can be misleading. Clayton Christensen presents a strong argument in his book, *The Innovator's Dilemma*,[5] that relying on current users may prevent you from taking advantage of an emerging technology poised to sweep away your current product. Competitors and new entrants with a more accurate vision may capture your business. Christensen uses the computer hard disk and its evolution to illustrate his point. Early mainframe computer manufacturers used 14-inch hard drives. When smaller, lower-capacity 8-inch drives were demonstrated, disk manufacturers asked

> Project requirements end only when the user has been satisfied.

the mainframe manufacturers for their user requirements. Computer manufacturers were not interested in the smaller drives because the smaller size advantages could not offset the associated higher cost per megabyte and the associated reduction in storage capacity and speed. Established disk manufacturers stopped their small drive development. However, emergent disk drive companies found minicomputer manufacturers who were willing to pay a premium for reduced physical size. Within a few years, the 8-inch drive matured and surpassed the larger drives in capacity and speed while maintaining a lower price. The emergent companies had captured the new market. Christensen said, "Ultimately, every 14-inch drive maker was driven from the industry." What is compelling about his thesis is that this cycle was repeated at every change in disk size evolving from 14 inch to 8 inch to 5.25 inch to 3.5 inch to 1.8 inch. The emergent firms that developed a new market became the established firms that were in turn driven out of business by the next technological advance. Christensen said, "The problem established firms seem unable to confront successfully is that of downward vision and mobility. . . ." He noted that disk manufacturers, held captive by their customers, delayed in making the strategic commitment to lead the market transition.

When Users and Developers Converge

It is important to decide on the approach to developing requirements, as it will directly affect the team's ability to perform successfully.

Most projects start with relatively well-defined user or customer requirements that can be further refined and developed by a structured process. These processes are based on frameworks, methods, techniques, and tools all rooted in lessons learned and best practices. Projects managed to these principles can usually be accurately planned and predicted.

However, many projects start with ill-defined user and customer requirements, leading to their discovery by the development process itself. Today, Rapid Application Development, Agile Development (including Extreme Programming), Hardware Model Shop Development, and others are flexible approaches to simultaneous discovery of both requirements and their solutions. Schedules and costs for these projects are difficult to predict.

Many techniques have been developed to help project champions more effectively discover and elicit user needs, and more effectively market solutions to meet those needs. One such technique, Quality Function Deployment (QFD), has proven to be very useful and enduring.[6] QFD defines and prioritizes product quality (requirements satisfaction) from the users' perspective, and conveys to

---

INCOSE

INCOSE Handbook Sec 4.6 cites user involvement in the Implementation Process as a best practice and lack of user involvement as a traditional problem area. The *INCOSE Handbook* also emphasizes user involvement in:

- Sec 4.7 *Integration Process.*
- Sec 4.8 *Verification Process.*
- Sec. 4.9 *Validation process.*

On most projects, new requirements are introduced throughout the project cycle.

the designers what to emphasize. It then maps the system features to the prioritized requirements vividly illustrating both unsatisfied requirements and satisfaction overkill. This and other techniques are illustrated in the following section on the decomposition analysis and resolution process.

There is a notable trend that impacts the timely development of user requirements. In his book, *Business @ the Speed of Thought,* Bill Gates emphasizes the orders of magnitude reduction in time required to gather data on customer interests and customer reactions to fielded products.[7] He discusses how corporations such as Coca-Cola and Jiffy Lube have made very effective use of such data mining to better profile user interests and needs to improve their responsiveness and competitive position.

Rapid access to data via the Internet does not alter the basic development processes. As noted in Chapter 7, Microsoft follows a project cycle consistent with our template.[8] Gates's vision of the next decades reemphasizes the need to continually hone project management and systems engineering processes.

Getting the right set of users' requirements is a major challenge facing the systems engineer, the project manager, and marketing organizations. For new products or for substantially new applications of existing ones, some combination of incremental and evolutionary development is often the most effective approach to adjust to changing market demands.

The Chain of Requirements Baselines

The project's customer usually controls the definition of user requirements. The provider further refines these requirements within the baseline definition. User requirements are typically the first to be baselined and placed under configuration management. An example is when a couple decides to build a house, they each make a list of their individual requirements. The combined list is the User Requirements Document (URD). Paired with this set of requirements is the context of implementation or user Concept of Operations (CONOPS), which describes the project's solution space, behavior, and environment.[9] In general, CONOPS is similar to, but broader than, current system or software "use cases." This is changing with the development of SysML, the object-oriented systems engineering modeling and design language. The Object Management Group (www.omg.org) is designing templates for systems engineering scenarios and use cases to include all the content necessary for a complete CONOPS. The intent is to eliminate the need for a separate CONOPS document.

The CONOPS for a house characterizes the community, climate, and infrastructure associated with the selected building site and describes how any house solution is expected to be used by the residents.

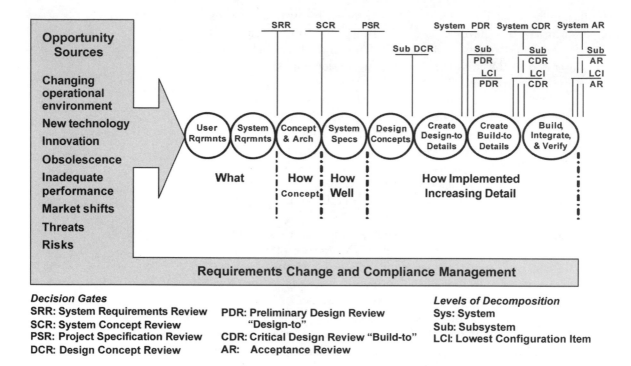

Figure 9.2   Requirements management: The chain of requirements baselines.

System development proceeds from system requirements to the creation of the "design-to" and "build-to" artifacts (documents, drawings, architectural models, engineering models, etc.) for every entity of the architecture. Each entity can adopt linear, unified, incremental, or evolutionary development, but for simplicity of explanation we use linear development here. The process is applied repeatedly until the requirements have been elaborated to piece part and process details (Figure 9.2).

REQUIREMENTS MANAGEMENT: A CRITICAL ACTIVITY THROUGHOUT THE PROJECT CYCLE

We must concern ourselves with both requirements development and requirements management. The requirements artifacts, which are products of the project-cycle phases, detail the maturing system solution.

The requirements management element is situational since new requirements can be introduced into the project at almost any time

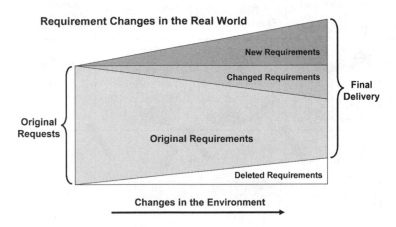

Figure 9.3   Requirements change environment.

and decomposition level, to be managed concurrently with the maturing baselines. In fact, the current trend is to embrace requirements changes to keep abreast of both the moving business case and emerging technologies. Figure 9.3 illustrates the real world of changing requirements. Failure to respond to the changing environment can cause project failure—a situation often experienced in today's project environment.

REQUIREMENTS MANAGEMENT COMPLEXITY

Requirements management encompasses the transfer of business and technical details among the domain specific participants. In the information transfer, voids and conflicts will emerge if the communication is imprecise or misunderstood. Much like in the parlor game of passing a story from one person to another among the attendees, there is a danger that the end result is not what the originator intended. Requirements management and requirements management artifacts must be configured to ensure undistorted communication. Figure 9.4 illustrates the challenge to be addressed.

FROM REQUIREMENTS TO SYSTEM SOLUTIONS

The sequential facet of requirements development is represented by the core of the Vee Model (Figure 9.5), as described in Chapter 7. A simple three-level hierarchy is shown here, with the system at the

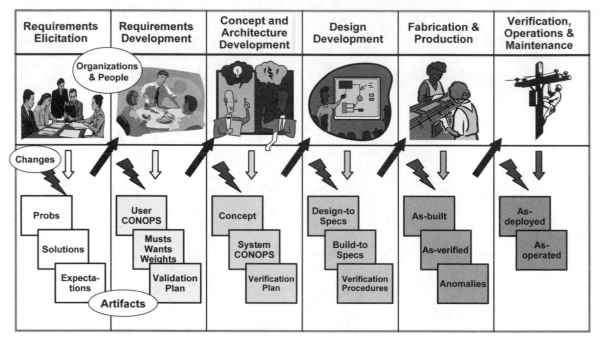

Figure 9.4   Requirements management complexity.

top level. At the lowest level, there can be many configuration items (CIs), and so the Vee is shown thicker at its base. On the left leg of the Vee, requirements are identified and concepts are created. On the right leg, the completed configuration items are verified and integrated into subsystems, which in turn are verified and integrated to make the system.

System development is described by the process called Decomposition Analysis and Resolution (DAR; Figure 9.6). The DAR process guides the systems engineering activities that flow down and define the requirements for each entity and how they should be satisfied or resolved. Systems engineering typically manages the DAR process.

The Verification Analysis and Resolution (VAR) process (Figure 9.7) defines the tasks spanning from assembling of parts and processes and the coding of software through integration, verification, and validation. As integration and verification activities are conducted, verification anomalies that occur must be resolved to a satisfactory conclusion or the project will stall. The VAR process illustrates the activities required to resolve anomalies to the satis-

―――― *PMBOK® Guide* ――――
The *PMBOK® Guide* Sec 5.4 *Scope Verification* presents verification as stakeholder formal acceptance of deliverables.

―――――― *INCOSE* ――――――
The *INCOSE Handbook* and this book define the stakeholder formal acceptance activity as *Validation*. Verification is proof of specification compliance.

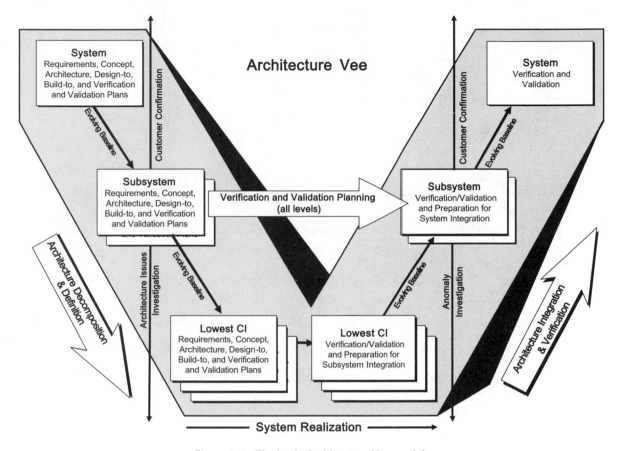

Figure 9.5   The basic Architecture Vee model.

faction of the customer. Systems engineering typically oversees the VAR process.

For a given decomposition level of the Architecture Vee, say a subsystem, the DAR represents the development of the solution and the elaboration detail required for that subsystem. For Commercial-Off-The-Shelf entities (COTS), the build-to detail is not required because it already exists. The DAR process is repeated for every architecture entity from the system, down to the lowest-configuration items, such as computer software units. Likewise, the VAR process is applied to each entity on the right leg of the Architecture Vee. Figure 9.8 illustrates the DAR and VAR processes applied in a plane orthogonal to the Architecture Vee. DAR and VAR processes are applied separately to each entity when there are multiple entities at a

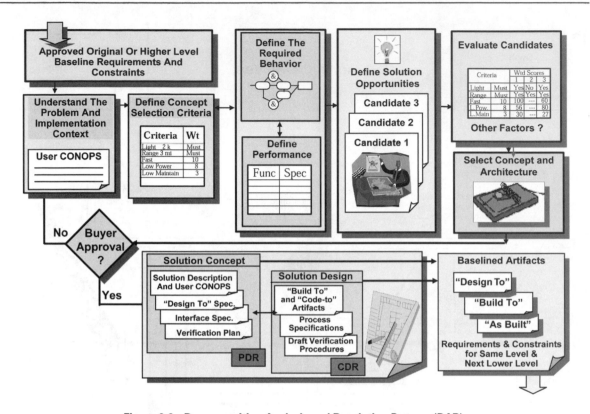

Figure 9.6   Decomposition Analysis and Resolution Process (DAR).

given level in the architecture hierarchy (e.g., in Figure 9.8 two sub-systems are shown).

To understand the complete sequence—one that represents best practices—requires the more detailed view of the intersecting Vees provided in Chapter 19.

——— *INCOSE* ———
INCOSE Handbook Sec 4.4
Architectural Design Process
treats both concept and architecture determination within
the Architectural Design
Process.

THE DECOMPOSITION ANALYSIS AND RESOLUTION PROCESS ENSURES THE DESIGN SATISFIES USERS AND STAKEHOLDERS

The DAR is the essence of systems engineering in which trade studies ensure the best value concept and architecture at every decomposition level. This section addresses each of the activities in the DAR process illustrated in Figure 9.6.

To illustrate the DAR process, this section uses one author's experience in remodeling his home. Further, the example demonstrates

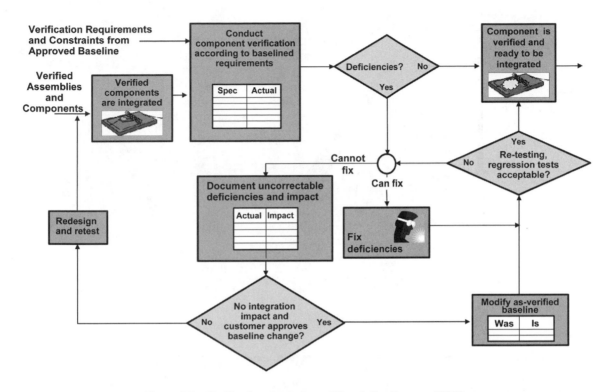

Figure 9.7   Verification Analysis and Resolution Process (VAR).

the benefits of using this process—even for simple or familiar projects. In this case, the process is applied to selecting a home-heating system. For this heating system, the "higher-level requirements and constraints" include personal comfort zones, aesthetics, and the existing house structure. The margin notes relate this example to the DAR steps that follow.

The Sources and Techniques for Determining Requirements

For each entity, the DAR process is initiated and driven by higher-level requirements and constraints. These come from already approved baselines such as the service utilities provided to a structure and the influences of users and stakeholders at the system level and at succeeding levels of decomposition down to the level under analysis.

To ensure all requirements have been elicited from users and stakeholders, a check-and-balance system should be implemented, usually consisting of multiple techniques. Some examples follow:

The sources for remodeling requirements include building codes, and most important, the users' comfort. The Context of Implementation is the historical climate of the area, the expected energy loss of the structure, the constraints of the existing structure, and the available utilities.

What did you like and dislike about heating systems with which you have had experience?

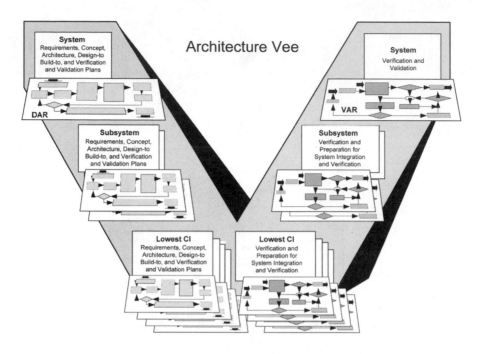

Figure 9.8   The DAR and VAR processes applied to the Architecture Vee.

────── *PMBOK® Guide* ──────
The *PMBOK® Guide* Sec 2.2
Project Stakeholders covers the
significance of stakeholders to
project success and Sec 10.4
Manage Stakeholders covers
stakeholder management.

The *PMBOK® Guide* does not
address stakeholder management as critical to Requirements Management.

Technique	• Comments and suggestions.
Documentation review	• Review best available data and records before interviewing stakeholders.
Interviews	• Face-to-face stakeholder discussions.
	• Best conducted using a checklist.
	• Document and prioritize requirements and constraints as they are identified.
Focus groups	• Ask open-ended questions.
	• Used to identify issues and establish realistic expectations.
Surveys	• Questionnaire to sample users.
	• Quantitative type questions.
	• May require statistical analysis.
	• Must be comprehensive and unambiguous.
Comment cards	• Provides feedback on an existing product or service.
Observation and confirmation	• Verify that users really do what they say they do.

Prioritization is perhaps the most significant technique for proactively managing project requirements and avoiding overspecified and biased solutions. The extent to which management discipline can be exercised by putting first things first obviously depends on knowing and understanding priorities. If they are not explicitly stated in contracts, and they usually are not, they must be understood by the time the user requirements and system requirements artifacts are baselined and placed under change control. Requirements prioritization is essential to the implementation of design-to-cost, cost as an independent variable (CAIV), and in pursuing value-driven solutions.

Prioritization is usually done in two forms: weighted criteria for trade-off analysis and independent priority levels (at least three levels: must, want, and nice to have).

> In our heating system example, fast temperature response, low noise level, minimum dust, and "set it and forget it" operation ranked much higher than cost.

Understand the Context of Implementation

The context of the implementation describes the environment within which the project solution must operate. To understand the context, you need to define the system boundaries and include all interface and operational factors such as reliability, maintainability, availability, human factors, and security. In addition, brainstorming sessions can help to verify your understanding. Ask probing questions and *listen*. It's often helpful to verify the understanding with a customer approved behavioral model.

The contractor in Figure 9.9 had a clear understanding of the requirements, but was a little short on understanding the context.

> For example:
> San Francisco Bay area—mild weather; no freezing, but rapid changes of up to 25°F with fog patterns; maximum outside temp of about 90°F (32°C) and minimum of about 32°F (0°C).

Define the Problem to Be Solved and Establish Weighted Evaluation Criteria

At each level of decomposition, the problem is defined by the higher-level baseline (e.g., user requirements, entity requirements, concept, and specification at each level). Each requirement should include weighted evaluation criteria, together with applicable scoring methods to represent how well any candidate solution satisfies the criteria. Concept selection criteria can become unwieldy if dozens of criteria are used in evaluating candidate concepts. A more practical approach is to select the most challenging, high-priority factors to drive the selection. To illustrate the point, consider the selection criteria for a new family car. Critical safety and performance factors may be difficult to achieve and should be included. However, a black color and an automatic transmission, while absolute "musts," are easy to achieve and should not complicate the evaluation.

> The problem to be solved is maintaining a comfortable home temperature under all conditions. The evaluation criteria include a fast reaction time, economical fuel, clean (low dust), low noise, fully automatic operation, and low initial cost.

THE FAR SIDE   By GARY LARSON

Suddenly, a heated exchange took place
between the king and the moat contractor.

**Figure 9.9   The Far Side © 1996 Farworks, Inc., distributed by Universal Press
Syndicate. Reprinted with permission. All rights reserved.**

You also need to decide the risk philosophy because risk tolerance drives risk management. Answers to the following typical questions will help establish the risk philosophy for your project:

- What are the consequences of system failure?
  Loss of life, mission failure, enterprise embarrassment, cost,
  schedule, technical, or safety.
- What is the technology maturity? Can "off-the-shelf" enti-
  ties be used?
  Consequence of delivering a new, but obsolete, system versus a
  state-of-the-art system with no logistics.
- What are the opportunities of and for the system? How will
  they be managed?
- What are the future growth expectations?

- What are the risks to, in, and from the system? How will they be managed?

Risk philosophy (tolerance) is often expressed in terms such as "single thread design," or "no single point failure modes in mission critical functions" or in a reliability rating such as 0.03 percent failure probability.

The risk philosophy will drive these risk adjustment decisions:

Risk Decision	Decision Range
Design for growth	Planned or none
New technology	High use to no use
Expendable margins	High margins to no margin
Reliability	High to low
Part derating	Substantial to none
Redundancy	Full to none
Inspection	100 percent to none
Qualification	Required high margins to none
Verification	100 percent unit verification to none
Certification	Full pedigree proof to no proof
Sparing	Full to none
Cost	Mandatory constraint to desirable target
Schedule	Mandatory constraint to desirable target
Other market applications	Planned to none

Behavior Diagram (Example)

Define the Required Behavior and Performance.

The objective is to describe the behavior of the essential system functions. This can be done in narrative form, but the trend is toward graphical techniques such as the functional flow diagrams shown here, which are usually more effective. When characterizing behavior, use action verbs such as *detect, trigger, initiate, deliver,* and *cancel.* For example, the accompanying margin note is the narrative description of the behavior for the house heating system.

The two methods for flowing requirements to lower-level entities are derivation (analysis) and allocation (past experience and judgment). In the derivation method, the requirements for each succeeding architecture level are established on the basis of quantitative analysis. Allocated requirements are based on past experiences and rules of

The required behavior is that the heating system detect the difference between the temperature setting and the current ambient temperature. The system then introduces heat until that difference is close to zero.

The performance requirements are:

1. Detection of temperature differences of two degrees.

2. Maximum of five-minute heater response to bring the temperature back to the set point.

thumb, and, therefore, their validity and applicability must be confirmed as the design evolves. Incorporating COTS or existing objects into the solution also contributes to defining allocated requirements.

Develop the Candidate Logical or Physical Solutions

For this example, the heating candidates are electrical and hydronic baseboard, electrical radiant ceiling, hydronic-in-slab, and forced-air heating.

Identify potential solutions that satisfy the functional and performance requirements, using past experience, analytical approaches, brainstorming candidate concepts, or other means. Assess the candidates and develop system discriminators for each viable one. Discriminators may be technical, cost, schedule, or risk. Avoid rejecting "obvious misfits" prematurely until they have had fair consideration.

The hydronic-in-slab solution provides the opportunity for quiet, dust-free heating. The risk: Glycol pipes in slab floors are difficult to repair.

- Develop the top-level architectures to understand each candidate's relative complexity.
- Flowdown functional and performance requirements. (Lower-level requirements will usually be concept and architecture specific.)
- Identify critical issues (may require investigating down to hardware part or software unit level).
- Use available performance history or hardware and software feasibility models to determine and confirm achievable performance values.

Select the Best Solution

By using the weighted concept selection criteria previously defined, make an informed selection of the best solution (Figure 9.10). Score each candidate solution against the criteria. This ultimately leads to a comparison of weighted scores and the basis for rational design choices that meet the highest priority requirements.

In our example, none of the standard conventional solutions meet all of the criteria. Radiant solutions are too slow; forced air is too noisy and dirty.

The techniques for weighting criteria include: weighting against a fixed standard, weighting relative to the most important criterion or best alternative, and pair-wise comparison (e.g., Analytical Hierarchy Process[10]). The decision criteria may need to include subjective criteria obtained from many individuals. These weighted criteria can be decided by consensus, voting (permitting multiple votes per individual), or the geometric mean of individual scores. If at all possible, the customer or user should confirm that the decision criteria and weights are appropriate for concept selection. This helps avoid decisions that are based on incorrect assumptions.

A Heating Debate

The heating system selection process had to be repeated with new candidate solutions. Radiant systems were analyzed to try to improve response times and no practical solutions were found. Forced air was analyzed for ways to reduce noise and dust. One creative contractor suggested suspending a forced-hot-air system in the thermal- and sound-insulated attic on shock- and vibration-isolated rods hung from the rafters to minimize noise and to ground residual vibration to the outside walls and foundation. By achieving further isolation with flexible fabric ducting and clean air with an electronic air filter, all criteria could be met with a modified forced air system. This was the system selected for implementation.

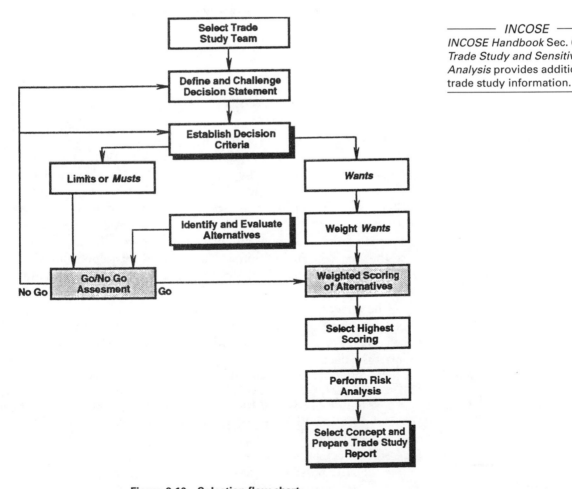

_____ INCOSE _____
INCOSE Handbook Sec. 6.4
*Trade Study and Sensitivity
Analysis* provides additional
trade study information.

Figure 9.10   Selection flow chart.

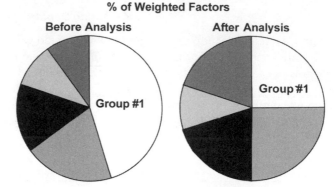

% of Weighted Factors

Group #1 was determined to be over driving the selection criteria.

Figure 9.11   Sensitivity analysis (example).

It is a good practice to perform a sensitivity analysis of the weighted criteria to ensure that the criteria weightings are not distorted. For instance, if more than half of the decision criteria weightings are concerned with vehicle appearance factors such as color, shape, and upholstery, then a vehicle selection decision may be inappropriately driven by aesthetics rather than performance, safety, and reliability features. Figure 9.11 illustrates the weighting criteria before and after sensitivity analysis revealed a skewed distribution.

One of the most powerful ways to compare alternatives is to use the decision analysis process developed by Kepner and Tregoe.[11] The weighted comparison matrix shown in Figure 9.12 illustrates the process.

The selection process is not complete until "other factors" have been considered. The highest scoring candidate may not be the best choice if other factors, not in the evaluation criteria, significantly impact the decision. The final step in the decision process is to evaluate the other factors in the following five steps:

1. Assess other factors of the most promising alternatives:
   • Consider both business and technical issues.
   • Determine the consequences.
   • Estimate probability and impact.
   • Identify possible actions to take advantage of opportunities or mitigate risks.

Selecting Candidates for Further Consideration

Decision Statement:	Select the best vehicle to meet the needs of the Patrick family. (Mom, dad, and three kids, ages 5 to 16)												
Evaluation Criteria:		**Alternative 1** Mid-Size Domestic Car			**Alternative 2** Japanese Sports Car			**Alternative 3** Domestic Mini-Van			**Alternative 4** Italian Sports Car		
Musts (Go/No-Go):													
• Under $25,000		✕			✕			✕			–		
• Transport 5 people		✕			–			✕			–		
Wants:	Weight	Comments	Raw (R)	R*W	Comments	Raw (R)	R*W	Comments	Raw (R)	R*W	Comments	Raw (R)	R*W
• 25 mpg (10.6 kpl)*	8	26.2 mpg avg. (11.2 kpl)	10	80				25.1 mpg avg. (10.7 kpl)	7	56			
• Carry garden supplies	10	Trunk only	2	20				Good capacity	10	100			
• Crash safety	9	Rated high on tests	10	90				Meets min. reqmts	7	63			
• Use on dates (16 yo.)	4	Considered "Cool" by peers	10	40				"Parents" type car	5	20			
Max Score (10xW):	310												
Total Score:				230						239			

* 1 mpg (miles per gallon) = 0.426 kpl (kilometers per liter)

Note: Scores that are within 10% are essentially equal

Figure 9.12   The Study Process, based on Kepner-Tregoe Decision Analysis Methodology.

2. Evaluate failure modes and effects of the promising candidates:
   • Determine impact on the system.
   • Determine approach to mitigate effects (e.g., requirements for increased reliability, fault tolerance, or fail safe operation).
   • Incorporate in the solution.
3. Adopt other factor actions identified in step one.
4. Rescore candidates with actions incorporated.
5. Reconsider the effect of residual factors.

Quality Function Deployment—House of Quality

A second method for comparing the relative value of concepts is the application of QFD (also known as the House of Quality since the graphic representation is in the shape of a house with a pointed

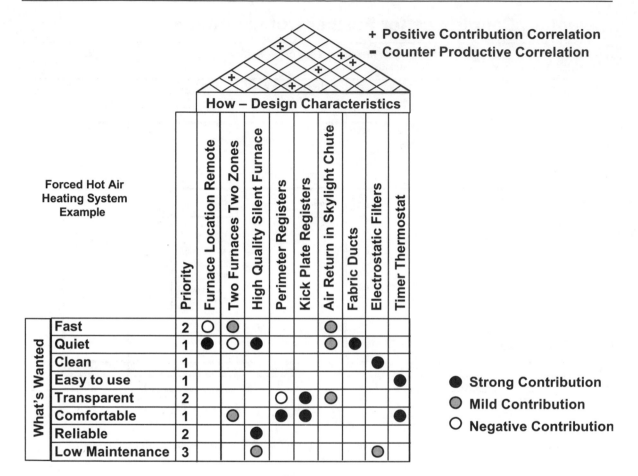

Figure 9.13 Quality Function Deployment example.

roof). The purpose of QFD is to map prioritized requirements against solution (concept) features to determine unsatisfied requirements and requirements overkill. Figure 9.13 is a completed example for the heating system used in this chapter. Note the first and second columns contain rows of prioritized requirements and their weights. The remaining columns are the concept features with column and row intersections revealing degrees of coincidence. The roof structure reveals intersections of correlation and conflict.

Architecture Selection

Once the concept is chosen, the "best" of alternate architectures must also be selected. There are usually multiple ways in which a system or solution architecture can be decomposed. Ease of integration, ease of upgrading, simplicity of management accountability, or ease of development, among others, usually drives the selection. The product breakdown structure represents the architecture and is driven by the integration approach. Figure 9.14 illustrates four integration approaches to a single concept and architecture.

The following are two dramatic examples of how innovative architecture selection at the second level of the product breakdown structure resulted in huge leaps in schedule performance.

The first involved the ship building industry, which typically built ships by laying the keel on the launching ways (the ramp used for launching the completed ship) and then expanding the structure, followed by each trade, in its turn, installing the plumbing, electrical, propulsion, and so on. This architecture made it impossible to work multiple trades in parallel as many had to wait their turn to participate. Additionally, only one ship could be constructed at a time on the launching ways, thereby seriously constraining the total throughput. The launching ways literally were the critical path.

Bath Iron Works in Maine had incentive contracts with bonuses for early delivery. They envisioned the ship as a series of fully integrated modular slices allowing simultaneous participation of all

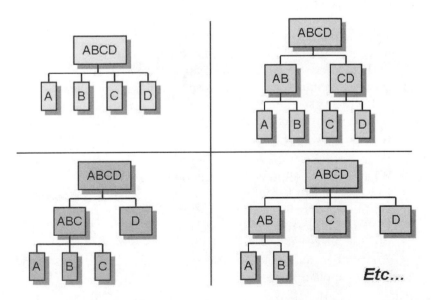

Figure 9.14 The Product Breakdown Structure provides a road map for integration.

trades on multiple modular slices of the ship. Additionally, time on the critical-path launching ways was greatly reduced, thus providing increased throughput. Ship delivery was so rapid that the U.S. Navy had difficulty finding parking places for the ships.

The home building industry achieved similar breakthrough results in terms of construction time. The city of San Diego, California, held a home construction contest to determine just how fast a three-bedroom house could be constructed, starting with bare ground and using no prefabricated modules. Like the shipyard, the building industry also was hampered by the serial trades sequence. Two contractors excelled by changing the second level of their product breakdown structure (PBS) from the usual trades-defined PBS elements such as framing and plumbing. They defined instead fully integrated PBS modules, such as north wall and roof assembly. This allowed a crew of 300 to work in parallel. Two houses were built on bare lots, which had to be fully landscaped and ready for occupancy in less than three hours each. Since the focus was on speed of construction, and not low-cost replication, this new approach did not "sweep the industry." However, it is an amazing example of creativity.

These two illustrations highlight the importance of selecting the proper architecture. Today, antivirus software companies structure their software architecture to facilitate easy updating and we routinely download new versions of one or more of the architecture increments to combat new viruses.

The specification for the selected concept and architecture prepares the team for elaboration of the details at each level of decomposition. The creation of the design-to and build-to artifacts completes the DAR process at each level. The approved baseline now includes the concept, architecture, design-to specifications, and the decision-support artifacts such as trade-off analyses. Each concept specification must answer the following:

- What is the problem to be solved, and in what context?
- What is the proposed concept?
- What must the solution do? (Functional Performance)
- How well must the solution do it? (Quantitative Performance)
- Within what context and interfaces?
- Is there a preferred architecture?
- What is the risk tolerance (risk philosophy)?
- How will customer satisfaction be determined (verification and validation planning)?

This results in the approved higher-level baseline for the next lower architecture decomposition level.

In our example, "forced hot air" becomes the requirement for lower level decisions such as furnace and filter selection, furnace room, ducting design, foundation design, wall design, and service locations.

The DAR process is repeated until all architecture entities, down to the lowest configuration item, have been baselined. The baselining of any one entity at a level requires collaborative development with interfacing entities to ensure mutual compatibility.

THE VERIFICATION ANALYSIS AND RESOLUTION PROCESS

The companion to the DAR process is the VAR, a process repeated through the integration and verification sequences as new groups of entities are combined to ultimately form the system (Figure 9.7).

The VAR process is an integral part of requirements management. It provides the framework for verifying each level of integration according to the verification criteria embodied in the entity specifications. Conventional wisdom is that tests are more perceptive than analysis because tests encompass the "real-world" issues that are very hard to model analytically. But beware—tests can introduce complications of their own and can mask the actual condition or behavior. In the spring of 1999, an expensive system was in its final system test. The system incorporated explosive bolts. The bolts were to fire only on operator command. Analysis predicted that voltage transients at system start-up could cause the explosives to fire prematurely, but laboratory tests repeatedly indicated no anomalies.

The first time the system was put into operational use, the explosive bolts fired on system start-up, just as the analysis predicted. The lab tests had, in fact, experienced a high voltage transient the first time the system was turned on, but it was never repeated on many subsequent trials that day, even after sitting idle for several hours. So the test director concluded there were no transients and the system was safe. In fact, it took a day of idle time for the transient to reoccur—but in the press of time, that test was never rerun. The test omission allowed a defective solution to be installed, resulting in a multimillion-dollar loss.

The improper setup of a test device allowed the flaw in the Hubble mirror to go undetected for six years, until the telescope was in orbit and the problem was there for all to see. The unfortunate fact is that the flaw was detected six years prior to launch. Those troubling data were ignored until it was too late. In college, we often ran lab experiments until we got the right answer, then we quit and ignored the prior failures. Such habits have carried over to the

The success of the VAR process is rooted in left Vee planning for right Vee execution.

──── *INCOSE* ────
INCOSE Handbook Sec 4.7 *Integration Process,* 4.8 *Verification Process,* and 4.9 *Validation Process* provide additional information.

workplace with serious consequences. In a project, all anomalies must be fully resolved or you risk finding bad news when its impact is devastating.

Verification may be done by analysis, inspection, demonstration, or test. With the previous cautions in mind, testing is the preferred approach in most situations, supplemented by the other techniques as necessary. Depending on the objectives, various types of tests are performed:

Engineering:	Prove feasibility and demonstrate performance to support the design process.
Informal:	Demonstrate readiness for formal testing (customer acceptance).
Formal:	Produce acceptance of verification data. Verifications are witnessed by the customer.
Qualification:	Demonstrate that the design will perform in its intended environment *with margin* (temperature, vibration, shock, humidity, transaction overload, unexpected power shutdown and recovery, etc.).
Acceptance:	Demonstrate that the deliverable item is built with sufficient quality that it replicates the qualification item performance and that it will perform as intended in the operational environment.
Environmental:	Simulate the operating environment by subjecting the test article to temperature, vibration, humidity, acoustic, shocks, salt spray, radiation, and so on. Can also be used to stress parts to find weaknesses.
Life:	Demonstrate system life and failure modes in the expected environment. Accelerated life tests may be used to shorten test duration if accelerated exposure does not distort the expected results.
Reliability:	Demonstrate system failure rates and failure modes.
First Article:	Demonstrate quality of first manufactured article.
Nth Article:	Demonstrate that the quality of any selected unit has not degraded from the first article. Sampling plans may be used when sufficient data have been gathered to provide a reliable statistical basis.

PROJECT REQUIREMENTS TRACEABILITY AND ACCOUNTABILITY

The identification and management of the proper "parentage" (parent-child relationships) from the highest-level system requirements to the lowest-level configuration item requirement and to verification requirements and methods is referred to as *Requirements Traceability*—a requirements management responsibility.

Requirements development, analysis, and management are sufficiently complex to require computer-based tools to facilitate the interactive mapping and change management. A comparison of many of the commercial requirements traceability tools available can be found on www.incose.org.

The purpose of requirements accountability is to ensure that all requirements have been responded to and have been verified by test, inspection, demonstration, and, where the foregoing are not possible, simulation and analysis. Systems engineering is responsible for auditing the verification results and certifying that the evidence demonstrates conclusively that the requirements have been achieved. A compliance matrix, called Requirements Traceability and Verification Matrix (RTVM), presents the verification results, and is often used as the certified evidence for customer acceptance.

MANAGING TO BE DETERMINED AND TO BE RESOLVED REQUIREMENTS

Unresolved requirements should be viewed as liens against the baseline and must be resolved as early as possible to reduce programmatic risk. Undefined requirements are referred to as *To Be Determined* (TBD). TBDs are a risk to the project since their impacts cannot be priced or scheduled. When the TBD is defined, it may have an impact that leads to contractual actions, such as an engineering change proposal, to adjust the contract baseline or a request for equitable adjustment.

Requirements whose definition is approximately but not exactly known are called *To Be Resolved* (TBR). Usually, rough estimates of a TBR's impact can be made and accommodated in the contract baseline. However, there is always a risk that the resolution of a TBR may be beyond the schedule or cost baseline, resulting in a contract action to adjust the baseline.

Formal work-off plans must be developed for both TBDs and TBRs, including "must have" delivery dates (Figure 9.15). Failure of

---

In traceability, a child may have many parents.

INCOSE

INCOSE Handbook Sec 4.2 *Stakeholder Requirements Definition Process* initiates the requirements management process.

It's naive to believe that TBDs and TBRs can be resolved with no impact to cost or schedule.

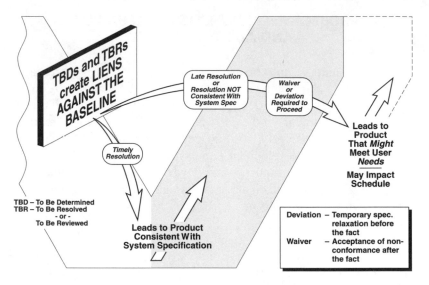

Figure 9.15   Resolve TBDs and TBRs early.

the customer to deliver on these negotiated delivery dates may be grounds for contract-based constructive change claims, including compensation.

THE POTENTIAL FOR LOW-RISK HARDWARE AND SOFTWARE SOLUTIONS

Previously Developed Products consist of COTS, Government-Off-The-Shelf (GOTS), and Nondevelopment-Item (NDI) hardware and software products. Because others have already accomplished the development, these products offer potential low-risk solutions to those who can benefit from their reuse. However, they are not risk free because interface, performance, and technical support problems may override whatever advantages they may appear to have. Thorough investigation is required to examine both the opportunities and risks of the intended reuse. The push for better, faster, and cheaper products in both the commercial and government environments has created added pressure to use COTS and NDI entities. In most cases, this is exactly the right thing to do. However, the pressures to shorten the schedule, as well as reduce costs, have caused use of existing entities without fully understanding their limitations. Avoiding these problems will be discussed in Part Four.

In today's office automation systems and business information systems, there are high percentages of COTS in use. In command and control systems, the percentages are markedly lower. This is understandable, recognizing the proliferation of high-quality and reliable business applications and the comparative nonexistence of commercial multipurpose interactive command systems.

Users of COTS products seek to realize reduced development time and costs and to achieve known and predictable performance. Users also expect to rely on long-term technical support. While these advantages are attractive, the user may actually experience substandard performance, difficulty in producing integration code, rights to data issues, and no technical support due to modification of the product or later version releases superseding the chosen product.

In evaluating COTS products, requirements should be prioritized to facilitate selection between candidate COTS products, none of which may satisfy all requirements. Therefore, a best available choice may have to suffice.

The following twelve lessons learned regarding the use of COTS or other previously developed products is an alert to potential problems:

1. COTS may be more or less capable than needed.
2. Required features may be dropped by the vendor in later upgrades.
3. Bugs in present versions may never be fixed.
4. Upward compatibility may not be assured.
5. Interface hardware and software is often required.
6. COTS may be difficult to integrate with other parts of the solution and once integrated its performance may not be easy to predict.
7. Source code may be required but difficult to get. The source code may have to be held in an escrow account.
8. Capability certifications are difficult to achieve.
9. Altering the COTS item voids its warranty.
10. Vendors abandon products at their convenience.
11. Training may not be available.
12. Life-cycle costs depend on supplier commitment to the product line.

REQUIREMENTS MANAGEMENT TOOLS

From an information systems viewpoint, the handling of requirements data is similar to inventory control. Both involve complex, interrelated tables; cross-references; and "where-used" indices. Manual tools such as card files and index tables are readily available.

General-purpose database applications, many of them inexpensive desktop products, can be further customized to address a specific project or even an organization's tailored project template.

Currently, there are a number of specialty requirements management tools available, some with extended capabilities such as system simulation, behavior analysis, and trade-off analysis. Most of these tools are found in the systems engineering domain and at systems engineering conferences rather than in the project management domain.

The International Council on Systems Engineering (INCOSE) maintains a web site (www.incose.org) with a compilation of about 1,500 systems engineering tools.

Several popular graphical tools, such as SmartDraw and Microsoft Visio, incorporate templates for behavior diagrams and process flowcharts using the Unified Modeling Language™ (UML).

A REQUIREMENTS MODELING LANGUAGE— THE EMERGING ROLE OF SYSML

Appendix A contains an overview of the emerging role of UML and SysML in systems engineering. Large, complex systems must be structured in a way that enables scalability, security, and robust execution under stressful conditions, and their architecture must be clearly enough defined so that they can be built and maintained. A well-designed architecture benefits any program, not just the largest ones. Large applications are mentioned first because structure is a way of dealing with complexity. The benefits of structure (and of modeling and design) compound as application size grows large. The Object Management Group's Unified Modeling Language (UML) helps specify, visualize, and document models of software systems, including their structure and design, in a way that meets all of these requirements.[12] Fortunately, these same benefits can be extended to systems engineering.

To develop any complex system requires a team of engineers working at the system level to analyze the needs of the stakeholders, define all the requirements, devise the best concept from several alternatives, and define the system architecture. The system team must also provide the designers with all of the models and visualizations that describe the architecture down to the lowest decomposed level. David Oliver in his book *Engineering Complex Systems with Models and Objects* states, "These descriptions must be provided in the representations, terminology, and notations used by the different design disciplines. They must be unambiguous, complete, and mutually consistent such that the entities will integrate to provide the desired emergent behavior of the system."[13] So how does the systems engineer benefit from UML, designed primarily for software personnel?

First, there are many systems being developed that use object-oriented software development. As such, the current structured approach to systems engineering poses a communication barrier between the systems engineer and the software developers due to differing visual representations. Basically, there is the lack of a common notation, semantics, and terminology as well as a definite tool incompatibility. This gap needs to be bridged to take full advantage of object-oriented design and full use of UML. To be effective, in addition to the structure language (UML), one needs a systems-engineering method consistent with that language and additional systems-engineering notation.

In November 2000, the INCOSE Object Oriented Systems Engineering Methodology (OOSEM) Working Group was established to help further evolve the methodology.

──────── *INCOSE* ────────
INCOSE Handbook Sec 6.2
Object Oriented Systems Engineering Method provides additional information.

The OOSEM working group goals are to:

- Evolve the object-oriented systems engineering methodology.
- Establish requirements and proposed solutions for extending UML to support-systems engineering modeling.
- Develop education materials to train systems engineers in the OOSEM systems-engineering method.

OOSEM includes the following development activities:

- Analyze needs.
- Define system requirements.
- Define logical architecture.
- Synthesize candidate allocated architectures.
- Optimize and evaluate alternatives.
- Validate and verify the system.

These activities are consistent with the systems engineering Vee model and process that is applied at each level of the system hierarchy. Fundamental tenets of systems engineering, such as disciplined management processes (i.e., risk, configuration management, planning, measurement), and the use of multidisciplinary teams, must be applied to support each of these activities to be effective.

SysML is to be a customized version of UML 2 to support the specification, analysis, design, verification, and validation of complex systems that may include hardware, software, data, personnel, procedures, and facilities. The customization effort began on September 13, 2001, with a meeting of an OMG chartered group called the Systems Engineering Domain Special Interest Group (SEDESIG). "The goals of that group were to:

- Provide a standard SE modeling language to specify, design, and verify complex systems.
- Facilitate integration of systems, software, and other engineering disciplines.
- Promote rigor in the transfer of information between disciplines and tools."[14]

It is expected that SysML will be formally adopted by OMG in 2005.

REQUIREMENTS ELEMENT EXERCISE

The objective of this exercise is to provide experience in developing and stating requirements using a method of musts, wants, and priorities.

You have decided to purchase a new vehicle. You have not yet decided on the model or brand and want to make certain that you select the best solution for your needs. Make a list of your "musts" (will not buy without them), "wants" (not mandatory, but desirable), and weight the "wants" according to their importance.

The "musts" need to be strictly quantitative, such as, "must cost less than $35,000" or, "must have four or more doors." Qualitative statements such as "must be low maintenance" do not qualify as a "must." It is acceptable to have an evaluation factor in both categories. For instance, "must stop from 70 mph in 170 feet (110 kph in 52 meters)" can be a "must" and "short braking distance" can be a "want" to give credit to those that pass the "must" and are better than others at braking.

Once you have identified the "musts" and "wants," prioritize the "wants" by selecting the most important "want" and assign it a weight of 10. Determine the relative importance of the other "wants" and weight them accordingly. If two or more "wants" are of equal importance, they will have equal weights. The final list with weights provides the evaluation criteria against which alternatives can be scored. Now, conduct a sensitivity analysis to ensure that the weights are properly apportioned to your selection objectives so that the many entertainment and convenience features are not unbalancing the selection.

Rate the vehicle that best satisfies a "want" with a score of ten for that "want." Score the other alternatives relative to that "want." Equal scores are acceptable. Multiply the criteria weight by the alternative score results to arrive at a weighted score for each "want" factor. Sum the scores to determine the overall ranking.

10

ORGANIZATION OPTIONS

MANAGEMENT ELEMENT 2

Lockheed's wide-body L1011 was heralded by both pilots and passengers as an excellent aircraft. However, Lockheed's creditors and stockholders were not complementary, since the L1011 was a financial albatross, taking the corporation to the brink of bankruptcy. How is it that this technical winner, superior in many ways to its DC-10 competitor, was such a financial loser? A significant contributor was the conflict built into the organization. Functional departments reporting to the general manager were expected to respond to a staff project manager. The general manager allocated resources directly to the functional departments, such as marketing, engineering, manufacturing, quality, and product test. The project manager was then expected to manage these stovepipes without resource control or other authority. L1011 team members reported that the engineering manager actually barred the project manager from attending change control meetings. This ineffective structure resulted in futile turnstile changing of the project manager and, at the same time, ongoing change of the aircraft baseline without commensurate sales-price adjustments. The general manager should have assumed the role of the project manager or chartered the project manager with the financial resources and the authority to buy necessary services from the best source. In the latter case, the project manager would have been the functional organizations' customer.

"Confusion is a word we have invented for an order which is not understood."

Henry Miller[1]

─── *PMBOK® Guide* ───
This chapter is consistent with the *PMBOK® Guide* Sec 2.3 *Organizational Influences* and Ch 9 *Project Human Resources Management.*

─── *INCOSE* ───
Related areas are the *INCOSE Handbook* Sec 5.3 *Organizing Process* and Sec 5.11 *Concurrent Engineering.*

A s Peter Drucker puts it, "At best an organizational structure will not cause trouble."[2] As the previous situation illustrates, the wrong organizational structure will not only cause trouble, it can destroy the project.

In the case of the L1011, the only person with the authority to maintain consistency between the business goals and the technical solution was actually the general manager, not the project manager. While this organization is not ideal, it could work if the project were properly chartered and stakeholder roles and responsibilities were defined and properly executed (e.g., if the general manager actively resolved emerging conflicts).

A great deal has been written about organizational theory—a favorite topic of industrial psychologists. The variations on form and order are limitless, as are the behavioral implications. Experience reveals that the point of confusion usually occurs when the order, though rationally structured by management, is not adequately explained to those who must operate by it—team members and others who participate in the project. This confusion is largely eliminated when individual, as well as organizational, roles and relationships are determined by a defined process. Preferably, the structure itself implies much of this order; for example, the logical path to problem solving, conflict resolution, and information. But even so, these need to be explicitly defined in the organization charter and reinforced by the project manager.

This chapter addresses organization options independent from the physical or geographical location. The growing trend toward telecommuting and "virtual" teams may have little effect on the organization structure but it may significantly impact communications and teamwork, so those trends are addressed in Chapters 5 and 6.

Each project manager faces the task of changing the organization structure to suit the changing phases of the project cycle.

The project manager must also ensure that supplying organizations, including subcontractors, also have effective organization structures. One of the authors had a major subcontract where the project manager did not have resource control and was essentially impotent to manage. To fix the problem, a contract change was made to ensure that the subcontractor's project manager was given resource control by his management. Improved performance was a direct result of the directed change.

While effective management, leadership, and teamwork are more important success factors than structural details, the optimal organization can contribute significantly to project performance and efficiency. In most organizations, the project manager does not

Organization: A reporting structure in which individuals function as a unit to conduct business or perform a function.

have freedom to reshape the external reporting relationships of the project unless the project is the major part of the corporation or the project is a major customer of a subcontractor. For instance, you usually do not have the freedom to choose a functional structure in a matrix-oriented corporation. If you are in a well-established, traditional hierarchical organization, then trying to convert to a matrix or trying to introduce cross-functional project teams can be a major and distracting challenge.[3] However, understanding the organization strengths and weaknesses of various options will allow you to work more effectively within your constraints and to push for change when there is a high return in doing so. Chapter 11 covers the project team, the associated management element focused on building a working organization.

The organization's design should promote the team's dominant interfaces and preferred communication channels. Its purpose is to ensure that project requirements are met, hence, the importance of designing the organization after the requirements of the project are established and understood. As a practical matter, the core team (initially consisting of the project manager, systems engineering manager, and other lead positions) is probably involved during the study period.

Most projects are best served by some form of matrix organization combined with elements from pure functional organizations and others from pure project form, each addressing a specific subproject or support function. We address the primary reasons for selecting each form after reviewing their relative strengths and weaknesses.

> The organization design should respond to what it will take to satisfy the requirements.

FUNCTIONAL ORGANIZATIONS

The functional organization is the traditional business structure. It has prevailed throughout the manufacturing-driven, industrial era. With a few exceptions, the functional organization has proved its effectiveness for single-technology companies having one high-volume product line serving a common market with a common manufacturing process and/or a business segment with relatively slow or predictable technical changes. One notable exception is a company serving a broad common market, but also having one large customer with special requirements that requires the focused attention of a project manager. A semiconductor company, for example, supplying standard parts might benefit from a separate product or project organization to serve customers requiring "ruggedized" versions of the same products.

The following sections explain the strengths and weaknesses of common organizational structures. It is beneficial to understand how to deal with the weaknesses of your configuration.

Pure Support (Functional) Skill Centers

Strengths	*Weaknesses*
+ Skill development.	−Customer interface unclear.
+ Technology development.	−Project priority unclear.
+ Technology transfer.	−Confused status communications.
+ Low talent duplication.	−Project schedule/cost controls
+ High personnel loyalty.	are difficult.

As organizations grow to multiple projects/products with multiple markets/customers, the pure functional organization (Figure 10.1) often proves ineffective. For example, one of our clients was trying to manage approximately 50 project/product lines through a traditional functional organization. When a customer called the salesman to find out how their project was doing, the following scenario often occurred. The salesman would refer the customer to one of the functional departments, such as engineering or production. The functional managers would either pass the inquirer along to others or respond inappropriately, being aware only of the status of their portion of the work. For projects that were in the design or production phase, the customer might end up talking to an engineering manager or to production control, who would either give partial or misleading information or avoid blame by disclosing the internal problems of other departments. This resulted in the frustrated customer calling the president for better service. The president would raise that cus-

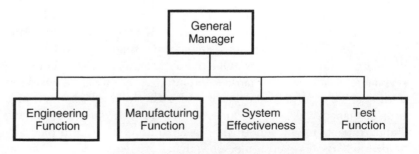

Figure 10.1   Pure support skill centers.

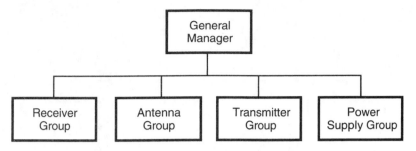

Figure 10.2 Pure support product centers.

tomer's priority to the top, causing all the other projects to suffer as the priorities in design or on the shop floor shifted. Priorities would change daily as the top position was given to the most recent squeaky wheel. This confusion in managing priorities and determining status usually leads to setting up product centers or divisions (Figure 10.2).

Pure Support (Functional) Product Centers

Strengths	*Weaknesses*
+ Product development.	−Customer interface unclear.
+ Technology development.	−Technology transfer difficult.
+ High personnel loyalty.	−Project priorities unclear.
	−Communications confused.
	−Schedule/cost controls are difficult.

THE PURE PROJECT ORGANIZATION

The pure project organization, shown in Figure 10.3, is composed of separate autonomous units, each being one project. They often evolve from functional or support organizations with the success of a high-priority task force as a model. Because the project manager has full line (hire and fire) authority over the team for the project's duration, this structure maximizes the project manager's control and the clarity of the customer interface. However, the project manager may become consumed by human-resource issues. Unfortunately, the dramatic success of a single, high-priority task force is not easily replicated when multiple projects are competing for key company resources and priority.

—— *PMBOK® Guide* ——
The *PMBOK® Guide* Sec 2.3.4
The Role of the PMO in Organizational Structures cites the
value of a Project Management Office (PMO) for all organizational structures but
particularly for projectized and
matrix organizations to oversee project management and
work prioritization.

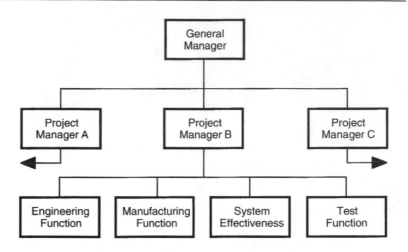

Figure 10.3   Pure support organization.

Pure Project Organization

Strengths	*Weaknesses*
+ Accountability clear.	−Talent duplication.
+ Customer interface clear.	−Technology awareness.
+ Controls strong.	−Technical sharing.
+ Communications strong.	−Career development.
+ Balances technical, cost, and schedule.	−Hire/fire.
	−Staffing irregular workloads.

Project organizations are relatively costly because of the inability to share part-time resources and they may also cause isolation of personnel from the company's strategy and technology focus. There is also a natural tendency for team members to be kept on the project well beyond the date that is justified. Team members are typically dedicated full time—another contributor to the inefficiency of this organization. This is one of the reasons that some functions such as personnel (human resources) and finance are often maintained as central support organizations, with talent assigned to projects as required.

THE CONVENTIONAL MATRIX ORGANIZATION

The strengths of a matrix
organization can usually be
increased by effective
leadership.

Most organizations are a blend of functional and project structures in the form of a matrix with solid (hire/fire management) vertical

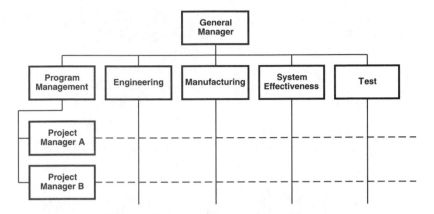

Figure 10.4   The conventional matrix.

lines and dotted (task assignment or borrow/return) horizontal lines. The most common form of matrix has the team members connected to project managers by dotted lines and connected to their functional managers by solid lines as shown in Figure 10.4. These structures combine the best aspects of the pure functional and pure project organization forms, as demonstrated by their relative strengths.

An effective matrix structure is perhaps the strongest of all project management organizational options. The key word is "effective." To succeed, all participants have to understand their roles and responsibilities. The project team member has two bosses, but this should not cause conflict to the project team member if it is clear that the project manager defines only what is to be done and the functional manager defines how to do it. All three authors worked for decades in highly efficient matrix environments in a variety of situations. As consultants, we have also witnessed poorly implemented matrix organizations. In fact, in the large-scale mergers that have occurred in the 1990s many organizations lost their formula and their current matrix structures are staffed with unhappy team members. A well-functioning matrix organization is like a bicycle— it is dynamically stable but statically unstable.

Those readers familiar with military resource deployment have seen a similar battlefield evolution brought about largely by technology. Traditional, vertically organized functional branches (army, air force, and navy) are rapidly being "matrixed" into battle units or task groups. This counterpart to the business task force consists of tightly coordinated resources under the direction of, perhaps, a tank commander, for the period of one engagement. The infantry, armor, aircraft, and even ships form a team, coupled more by computer

—— *PMBOK® Guide* ——
The *PMBOK® Guide* Sec 2.3.3 *Organization Structure* differentiates three matrix structures:

1. Weak.
2. Balanced.
3. Strong.

The differentiator is the location of budget control; functional managers (weak) and the project manager (strong).

The military matrix in the field is analogous to the conventional matrix on the business battlefield.

communications than by voice. These task groups, after having carried out their mission, return to their permanent units available for other deployments.

Conventional Matrix Organization

Strengths	Weaknesses
+ Single point accountability.	−Two boss syndrome.
+ Customer interface clear.	−High management skill level required.
+ Rapid reaction.	
+ Duplication reduced.	−Competition for resources.
+Technology development.	−Lack of employee recognition.
+ Career development.	−Management cooperation required.
+ Disbanded easily.	

Functional organizations that have evolved to product centers may transition to a matrix organization based on those product centers. While this structure does offer some of the advantages of the conventional matrix, it combines the disadvantages of both the matrix and the product-centered functional organization. It tends to inhibit both technology and career development and requires greater integration skills. The following discusses variations of the conventional matrix that have proven to be effective.

Conventional matrix organizations can operate in one of two ways. In the first, the project manager borrows people from the support managers and provides daily supervision and funding. In the second form, the project manager "subcontracts" the work to the support manager, providing a task statement and funding. For example, a key technology development may require the combined talents and synergy of a team of specialists working in close proximity. This need may best be met by the specialists meeting periodically without disrupting their ongoing work routine.

The compound and collocated matrix forms offer effective compromises between the project and conventional matrix structures.

THE COMPOUND OR COLLOCATED MATRIX ORGANIZATION

Some environments may benefit from variants of the conventional matrix form. To compensate for structural and/or personnel shortcomings, most large projects will introduce pure functional structure and/or pure project structure sections to form a compound matrix. For example, critical resources (either administrative or technical) may report directly (solid line) to the project manager or, alternatively, be collocated with the project office. The latter,

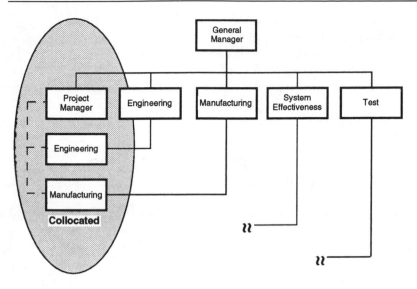

Figure 10.5   The collocated matrix.

known as the collocated matrix, is shown in Figure 10.5. It provides for maximum focus on project objectives with a corresponding disadvantage: isolating the project team members from the company's overall strategic operations.

The Collocated Matrix

Strengths	Weaknesses
+ Single point accountability.	−Technology awareness.
+ Clear customer interface.	−Management support.
+ Good control.	−Technical sharing.
+ Single location.	−Staffing irregular workloads.
+ High personnel loyalty.	−Personnel evaluation by
+ Career development.	functional manager.

In some project intensive environments, such as the aerospace industry, and in geographically dispersed multinational companies, the relationships are sometimes reversed. In the hybrid matrix, the team members are connected to the project manager for the duration of the project by solid lines approaching a pure project organization. In this case, the functional departments are small core staffs responsible for long-term strategic technology and concept development—perhaps even common component or subsystem development. For example, the corporate engineering manager typically

The hybrid matrix retains the focus and most advantages of the pure project organization while improving efficiency.

looks for means to avoid duplication, share technology, and provide for professional development. He or she may have line/budget authority for proprietary technology development projects—some or all of which may be performed by direct reports. Another variation shares a common (typically high-tech) manufacturing operation, but assigns the production engineering function, usually part of the manufacturing function, to the project.

DESIGNING AND MAINTAINING A RELEVANT STRUCTURE

All decision criteria should be prioritized.

A single government agency or company will often simultaneously use several organization options for project management. Furthermore, each project will typically evolve through several structures during its life and the project manager and customer can significantly influence the option selected. Deciding on the initial structure involves both subjective criteria, such as prior organizational experience, and objective criteria, such as the availability and location of resources. The guidelines that follow are for simple projects or subprojects:

- *Pure Functional* organization is the best match for a single project that is relatively independent in interface or technology. Pure functional is not preferred for management of multiple projects.
- *Pure Project* is a good choice for projects for which schedule, security, and/or product performance is paramount and cost is relatively unimportant.
- *Conventional Matrix* works well if the project manager has authority to manage the funds and has business relationships with supporting managers, including formal work commitments and participation in project planning. The matrix fails when the project manager is seen only as a coordinator with the support managers operating on a "best effort" basis.
- *Collocated Matrix* should be considered for high priority projects dependent on critical resources and/or technologies and when ongoing involvement with company strategy and long-term business goals are secondary.

INTEGRATED PROJECT TEAMS AND INTEGRATED PRODUCT TEAMS

There are many ways to develop an organizational structure. Some managers begin by assuming a starting form, perhaps a conventional matrix, and then they modify it to resolve staffing barriers. We prefer a process that matches the organization to the requirements (as segmented into major work packages by the work breakdown structure). In this process, the total project is viewed as a set of simple projects, defined by the nature of their deliverables and/or resource requirements (Figure 10.6). The terminology for this approach is Integrated Product Teams.

Matrix refinements, such as Integrated Project Teams and Integrated Product Teams, have solved product responsibility issues; however, these forms bring a new set of issues regarding system integration and responsibility for the perpetuation of the enterprise, such as technology development and technology sharing. The role of systems engineering, always important, becomes crucial when integrating a system developed by multiple product teams.

> Integrated Project Teams and Integrated Product Teams instill responsibility and accountability.

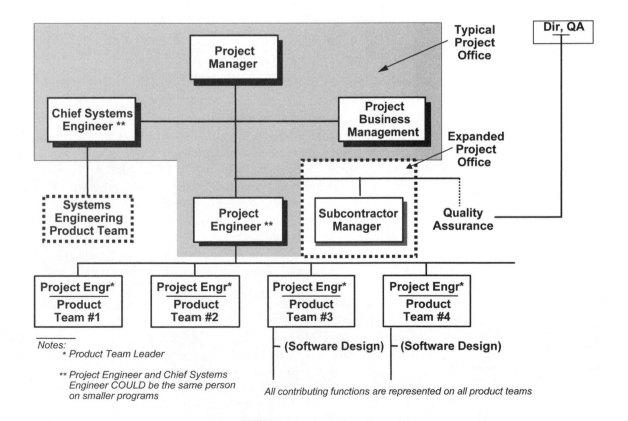

Notes:
* Product Team Leader

** Project Engineer and Chief Systems Engineer COULD be the same person on smaller programs

All contributing functions are represented on all product teams

Figure 10.6 Typical project team organization.

When defining the original structure, you need to plan responses to the inevitable project-cycle dynamics. Without anticipating changes, you may find yourself evaluating the following symptoms and thrashing through crisis-driven reorganizations. While no organization is expected to be perfect, some may be flawed to the extent that project success is at risk. Before reorganizing, be sure it is justified. The authors of *Dynamic Project Management* offer these symptoms of an inappropriate organization to watch for:

> Is there a [lack of] product pride and ownership among the team members?
>
> Is too much attention typically given to one particular technical function, to the neglect of other technical components?
>
> Does a great deal of finger-pointing exist across technical groups?
>
> Is slippage common, while customer responsiveness is negligible?
>
> Do project participants appear unsure of their responsibilities or of the mission or objective(s) of the project?
>
> Are projects experiencing considerable cost overruns as a result of duplication of effort or unclear delegation of responsibilities?
>
> Do project participants complain of a lack of job satisfaction, rewards, or recognition for project efforts?

The authors observe that, "Unfortunately, when symptoms of inadequate organizing appear, some companies typically respond by applying more time, money, or resources to the already weakened and inadequate project organization. If the problem truly is an inappropriately structured project organization, simply addressing the symptoms while ignoring the basic problem itself may leave the organization and its people frustrated and demoralized, as projects continue to slip and conflict continues to grow."[4]

On the other hand, each of the symptoms previously discussed, taken separately, could have little to do with the organization and a lot to do with leadership, or the lack thereof. One has to look closely at the combinations and patterns to conclude that reorganization is indeed needed.

The single biggest error in organization design is overcomplexity or redundancy leading to confused responsibility. We've defined several complex configurations and suggested others in an effort to define the problem and provide choices. However, some configurations such as the hybrid matrix are suitable for only the very largest projects or for an entire multidivisional corporation.

Complex projects need not lead to complex structures.

WIRING IN THE SYSTEMS ENGINEER

Regardless of the organization form, the systems engineer is the technical leader for the project and should be prominently positioned and directly connected to the project manager. In some cases, the systems engineer is staff to the project manager. For larger projects, the systems engineer as a direct report supervises a requirements development staff and a separate integration and verification staff. This configuration provides the checks and balances to ensure the right solution is being built right. It is undesirable for the systems engineer to report directly to the engineering department and then be loaned to the project manager. In that structure, the systems engineer will be biased to satisfying the engineering position rather than that of satisfying the client. Chapter 11 suggests a structure to enhance the teamwork within the project office level.

MATRIX MANAGEMENT OPERATIONS

While matrix structures often result in turf conflict and reduced morale, this can be prevented by using a fairly simple technique. The technique is for the project office and the functional managers to collaborate on an operating procedure to clarify the roles, responsibilities, and relationships in the potential conflict areas of the dual-manager environment. One well-developed matrix organization defined its operating procedures and relationships in 26 areas. Figure 10.7 is a template for this procedure. Note that the most important column is the Relationship column. This column should stress a collaborative team relationship for the good of the project and the project's customer.

ORGANIZATION OPTIONS EXERCISE

You've been appointed the project manager for a new nine-month project. The first three months are allocated to design, four months for product development, and two months to testing and delivery. Design will require four skilled experts. The development will require a large number of technicians working in four separate locations, one of which is overseas. Test, integration, and final delivery will be performed in your plant 30 miles from your office location. Your company typically uses matrix management and all technical resources

PROJECT FUNCTION	RESPONSIBILITY		RELATIONSHIP
	PROJECT MANAGER	**FUNCTIONAL MANAGER**	
Contract Negotiations	Responsible for developing negotiation strategy and is accountable for negotiation results. Carries primary responsibility for resolution of technical definition and programmatic issues.	Contracting Officer (Contract Administrator) chairs the negotiating team and is responsible for documenting the negotiation proceedings and obtaining final execution of the contract. Carries primary responsibility for resolution of contractual and cost issues.	Contract negotiation is a team effort, and close rapport must exist among all negotiating team members.
Assignment of key personnel	Responsible for identifying the time-phased needs for personnel and the skills required. Responsible for providing adequate advance notice of return.	Assigns key personnel to the project with the concurrence of the Project Manager. Responsible for the performance of the assigned personnel to deliver in accordance with the terms of the "contract" with the project manager	The Functional Manager adds, removes, rewards and disciplines personnel utilizing supporting information from the Project Manager. Key personnel will not be added to the project or removed without the concurrence of both.

Figure 10.7   Matrix management operating procedure template.

exist within the company; however, other projects frequently compete for the same resources. You can elect to borrow staff by name or contract for services by department, but you must decide which mode best suits your needs. You are aware that another project of significance is about to start and will probably need similar resources to yours.

List the advantages and shortcomings of matrix management in this context. Define actions you should take to minimize potential staffing difficulties.

11

THE PROJECT TEAM

MANAGEMENT ELEMENT 3

One of the authors had a contract with a premier tape recorder supplier for an existing flight-proven tape recorder. One day the company announced that several of its team had quit. As it turned out, they were the finest of the engineering team. Costs began to accelerate and schedules began to slip as the company futilely staffed the project with unskilled personnel.

Before long it became apparent that there was no hope of achieving delivery as contracted. The contract was terminated and a new contract was awarded to the new company the departing engineers had formed. It was a painful decision and not without risk as the new company was a start-up and the new recorder design had to be qualified before being certified for flight. Credibility is a major factor in building a team and, in this case, the contract had to follow the technical capability of the team. There was no other viable choice.

"The meeting of two personalities is like the contact of two chemical substances: if there is any reaction, both are transformed."

Carl Jung

—— *PMBOK® Guide* ——
This chapter is consistent with the *PMBOK® Guide* Ch 9 *Project Human Resources Management* and Sec 4.1 *Develop Project Charter.*

In Chapter 6, we focused on instilling teamwork, a perpetual property of projects and the third Essential to successful project management. We now look at team formation, a situational process ongoing throughout the project cycle, as each phase requires a different mix of talented individuals. As Lewis comments in his book, *Team-Based Project Management,* "Teams don't just happen—they must be *built.*"[1] Forming the team requires six steps:

1. Defining the project manager's roles, responsibilities, and authority.
2. Selecting the project manager.

Forming the team starts with selecting the right people and defining their roles.

Figure 11.1   The project team.

3. Chartering the project and confirming the project manager's authority.
4. Staffing the team.
5. Selecting the right subcontractors.
6. Managing the organization's interfaces and interrelationships.

The Project Team element goes beyond the traditional staffing function and includes management of the interfaces with supporting organizations, contractors, upper management, and the customer (which may be the internal marketing/sales department) (Figure 11.1).

—— *PMBOK® Guide* ——
The *PMBOK® Guide* Ch 9 *Project Human Resources Management* identifies four process groups:

• Human Resource Planning.
• Acquire Project Team.
• Develop Project Team.
• Manage Project Team.

ATTRIBUTES AND COMPETENCIES

When selecting individuals to populate an organization there are two primary factors that should be considered. The first is the attributes of the individual and whether those attributes fit the organization you have or plan to have. Attributes have to do with personal conduct and behavior such as being prompt, honest, forthright, communicative, alert, self-reliant, trustworthy, and a host of others. We would not want to make up our team of lazy, dishonest, or unproductive individuals. Reference checks and interviews tend to focus on evaluation of a person's attributes. In making reference checks, get the referred-to person to name yet another qualified reference so that you base your judgment on people not directly named by the candidate. You will be surprised and enlightened by what you learn from the second-generation references.

The second factor is the competencies of the individual and how skillful he or she is within the claimed competencies. An individual may be competent enough to be certified by an authorizing body and at the same time have no valuable skills except being able to pass evaluation tests. Many people will claim successful past project performance when they had little to do with it. In some cases, they happened to be on staff to the movers and shakers of the project and are eager to claim the credit for themselves.

Rigorous evaluation against predetermined criteria is valuable to ensure the proper mix of attributes and competencies for each project position. The competency model to follow is both a technique and a tool to help make an informed decision. Hiring decisions should not be made without one.

> —— *PMBOK® Guide* ——
> The *PMBOK® Guide* Sec 9.1.3.1 *Human Resource Planning* identifies resource planning output as:
> * Roles to be performed.
> * Authority needed.
> * Responsibilities to be carried out.
> * Competency needed.

DEFINING THE PROJECT MANAGER'S ROLES, RESPONSIBILITIES, AND AUTHORITY

The project manager's roles are broad—like those of general managers—and range from administration to technical to leadership.[2] However, there is a shorter-range focus than that of a line manager who is responsible for the long-term strength of the organization. By contrast, the project manager should be correctly focused on the relatively short-term results of the project. In many environments, the project manager is viewed as the general manager for the project and, although the project assignment may be for a relatively short duration, the project manager may also be charged with eternalizing the project through follow-on and derivative business.

> —— *PMBOK® Guide* ——
> The *PMBOK® Guide* Sec 2.3.3 *Organizational Structure* covers alternative matrix management structures and the authority of the project manager.

> A major challenge is to make both the customer and the organization successful by leading the project team.

Roles	*Complications*
Manage the project throughout the project cycle.	Meet an aggressive schedule.
Balance technical, schedule, and cost performance.	Managing changing requirements and implementing emerging technologies.

Roles	*Complications*
Solve problems expeditiously as they arise.	Perform within the budget by using unlimited funds and resources.
Inspire and motivate the entire team.	Optimize the mix of dedicated, shared, and contract personnel.

Project management challenges are often exacerbated by an imbalance among:

- *Responsibility*—the duty or obligation to complete a specific act or assignment.
- *Authority*—the power to exact obedience and make decisions to fulfill specific obligations.
- *Accountability*—being answerable for success or failure.

Broad responsibilities increase the need for information and force the project manager to cross organizational lines, which is similar to a general manager. But without the general manager's formal authority, the project manager (equipped with implied authority) must often depend on interpersonal skills and negotiating abilities to influence others.

While the range of the project manager's authority varies greatly, effective project management policy should require that:

- The project manager has financial control.
- The support managers view the project manager as their customer.
- A culture of "make a promise, keep a promise" exists.
- Delineation of responsibilities is understood and agreed to.

Before selecting the project manager, the responsibilities need to be determined. They should include responsibility for:

- Establishing the project vocabulary;
- Establishing the team and teamwork environment;
- Inspiring and motivating the team;
- Ensuring all project requirements are defined and that they flow down to the lowest level;
- Leading the planning and managing to the plan;
- Pursuing opportunities and managing risk;
- Ensuring controls are in place and effective;
- Controlling the evolving baseline through a change control system;
- Ensuring that visibility techniques are in place and are effective;
- Determining the frequency and content of project status reviews, and
- Executing timely action to correct variances from the plan.

The project manager must have total project responsibility and accountability, yet often has too little authority.

The project manager must have authority for resource control and must be able to start and stop work.

SELECTING THE PROJECT MANAGER

There are many sources for ideas for a new project. When an idea seems promising enough to pursue, a project champion is either appointed or someone seizes the opportunity to aggressively evaluate the opportunity (the user's needs and potential return from meeting them) and to estimate the resources required to pursue the opportunity. The champion also evaluates the risks inherent in satisfying the user and other stakeholders. Even on projects that ultimately involve billions of dollars, the project champion usually works alone, with occasional input from domain experts, to create the first estimate of the project plan. If it is decided that a study team is warranted, the project champion may be the appropriate one to lead the early effort or even the entire study period. At the end of the study period, the project requirements should be adequately understood and the project manager for the implementation period should be selected. It is unusual for the project champion to continue in this role.

Selecting the implementation-period project manager is a critical matchmaking task for executive management. In too many cases, the project manager is selected before the requirements and the organizational form of the project are determined. This should be reversed to match the project manager skills with known challenges of the job.

The project manager should be carefully selected because the right choice is critical to project success. The project manager must fulfill the requirements of the customer or user; must answer to senior management by generating a fair return on investment; and must provide a stimulating, positive work environment for the project team, while at the same time satisfying personal family obligations and goals.

Our experience reveals that strong leadership can compensate for insufficient authority. Peters and Waterman report a high correlation between project success and the leadership qualities and/or delegated authority of the project manager.[3] In many types of projects, leadership qualities are more important than authority. But this should never be taken for granted. It is essential that the project manager operates as a manager/leader rather than just as a coordinator/monitor and has effective business interrelationships with the managers supporting the project.

When selecting any team member, it is beneficial to have an objective basis for evaluating the most critical competency factors for the project. This example competency model (Table 11.1) illustrates only a portion of a comprehensive set of management skills.

---- *PMBOK® Guide* ----
The *PMBOK® Guide* Sec 1.5 *Areas of Expertise* identifies five areas of knowledge and skills necessary on the project team:

- The *PMBOK® Guide*.
- Application area (knowledge, standards, and regulations pertinent to the project domain).
- Understanding of the project environment.
- General management knowledge and skills.
- Interpersonal skills.

The project manager has roles in three different arenas: the customer's, executive management's, and the project team's.

Table 11.1 Competency Model Excerpt

Rating Factor	Weight	Basic	Score	Advanced	Score	Expert	Score
Project management training		Has had some project management training		Has had the company's or equivalent project management training		Has earned the company's, PMI, or equivalent certification in project management.[*]	
Project management experience		Has served as a deputy or assistant project manager		Has been a successful project manager		Has managed several successful projects	
Contracting and negotiating		Is knowledge-able of types and applications of relevant contract types		Has participated in developing contract negotiation strategies		Has consider-able experience in contract negotiation strategy and participating in negotiations	
Sub-contracting		Is knowledge-able in the difference between purchasing and subcontracting		Has participated in the selection and award of subcontracts		Has successfully managed subcontractors	
Decision analysis		Is aware of the importance and practice of Analytical Decision Process[†]		Has been trained in Analytical Decision Process[†]		Has been trained and routinely practices Analytical Decision Process[†]	

[*]PMI (Project Management Institute) certification as a Project Management Professional is based on a comprehensive examination.
[†]Analytical Decision Process was originated by Kepner Tregoe Associates (Princeton, New Jersey).

The base structure for most projects is some form of matrix, designed to take advantage of critical technical demands, to accommodate unique management strengths and weaknesses, and to balance short-term project priorities with the long-term priorities of the company and/or functional organizations. All matrix forms are characterized by complex interpersonal relationships requiring that the project manager be selected more on the basis of behavioral (e.g., negotiating and leadership) skills than on technical skills. However, the project manager should be "conversant" in the project domain and cognizant of the systems engineering process. Systems engineering experience is very beneficial preparation for the challenges of project management. The person selected must have the right combination of attributes and qualifications. ". . . the ideal project manager would probably have doctorates in engineering, business, and psychology, with experience at ten different companies in a variety of project positions, [yet] be about twenty-five years old."[4] In addition to the required skills, the project manager should exhibit the following capabilities:

- Leadership and team building;
- Entrepreneurial and business acumen;
- Balance between technical and business capabilities (generalist); and
- Planning, organizing, and administration abilities.

Since balance and synergy between business and technical capabilities is critical, some organizations require a program manager to have had experience as a chief systems engineer. Yet, other organizations are having success by installing project managers with a business management background strongly supported by a qualified systems engineer to manage the technical development.

CHARTERING THE PROJECT AND CONFIRMING THE PROJECT MANAGER'S AUTHORITY

The first step in gaining recognition for a new project and team is to formally charter the project manager and project office. High-level authorization of the project's charter mitigates the historical handicap mentioned earlier—project management responsibility without commensurate authority. Harold Kerzner offers this sage advice: "Generally speaking, a project manager should have more authority than his responsibility calls for, the exact amount of authority usually depending upon the amount of risk that the project manager must take. The greater the risk, the greater the amount of authority."[5] Here again, taking risk really means pursuing opportunity. The greater the opportunity, the greater the required authority.

The project manager's authority should be documented when the project is chartered. The project's charter, represented by the sample letter shown in Figure 11.2, performs several key functions:

Document the charter and get your management to sign it.

- Identifies the project and its importance to the organization.
- Appoints the project manager and other key personnel.

MEMORANDUM

Date:

To: All Functional Managers; President's Office; List

From: Vice President, Special Projects

Re: Establishment of the Advanced Systems
Development Project

I'm pleased to announce that, after tough competition, we have been selected by the customer as the prime contractor for the Advanced System Development. We have pursued this prestigious opportunity aggressively and we are now committed to providing this state-of-the-art system.

To carry out this critical project, I am establishing the ASD Project Office with Fred Jones as Project Manager, reporting directly to me. I have delegated to Mr. Jones the authority to manage all activities necessary to fulfill our contractual obligations by working directly with our key subcontractors. Mr. Jones will be held fully responsible and accountable for the technical, schedule, and financial success of this project.

Others with key responsibilities for the ASD project are: Joan Wait as System Engineering Manager, Jim Wu as Business Manager, and Mary Fay as Contract Administrator.

The Program Implementation Review will be held 30 days from today with the primary objective of executive approval of the total Project Plan. At that time, I expect to approve the necessary funding, under Mr. Jones's control, for the next period of the project.

Congratulations to all of you who contributed to this important win! I am asking for your full support for Mr. Jones and his team in this most important business opportunity.

Our customer is counting on us to perform and, in turn, I am counting on you to deliver as we have promised in our proposal.

/signed/
Vice President,
Special Projects

Figure 11.2 The project team charter.

- Establishes top-level responsibilities and authority.
- Positions the support organizations and their authority.
- Places subcontractors in a service relationship.
- Acknowledges the project team.
- Establishes the funding and spending control.
- Confirms that the cognizant executive started the project and chose the manager.

Figure 11.2 sets the tone for teamwork by accepting personal accountability for the proposal made by the team. This may seem like an obvious gesture, but even though accountability, unlike authority, can never be delegated, not all senior managers publicly acknowledge their accountability for the team's efforts. Publicizing such memoranda is effective.

The project manager's authority needs to be confirmed and reaffirmed daily. Authority is a way of thinking that starts by delegation at the top and is accepted and seized by the project manager. Continuing authority is based on the project manager earning the respect of the organization through being effective and credible. As Kerzner observes:

> Authority can be delegated from one's superiors. [Personal] power, on the other hand, is granted to an individual by his subordinates and is a measure of their respect for him. A manager's authority is a combination of his power and influence such that subordinates, peers, and associates willingly accept his judgment.

> In the traditional structure, the power spectrum is realized through the hierarchy, whereas in the project structure power comes from credibility, expertise, or being a sound decision maker.[6]

STAFFING THE TEAM

The stages of staffing correspond to the project phases and funding milestones, beginning with selection of the core team. We frequently refer to just the project manager when discussing management responsibilities, authority, and accountabilities, but there are three critical roles of the project office (Figure 11.3).

The *systems engineer/technical manager*—second only to the project manager in responsibility and accountability—is responsible for the technical integrity of the project while meeting the cost and performance objectives of project requirements. The systems engineer is a key participant in the planning process and provides technical management of the systems engineering process directed at achieving the optimum technical solution. To ensure

---

PMBOK® Guide
The *PMBOK® Guide* Sec 4.1 *Develop Project Charter* covers project charters, starting with the Project Statement of Work.

The organization's culture should view the project manager as the customer.

While the proper chartering is necessary for establishing the project manager's authority, it is far from sufficient.

For small projects, two or three roles of the triad may be performed by the project manager.

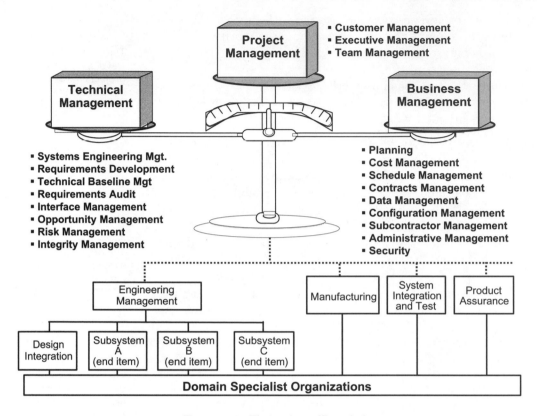

- Customer Management
- Executive Management
- Team Management

Project Management

Technical Management

Business Management

- Systems Engineering Mgt.
- Requirements Development
- Technical Baseline Mgt
- Requirements Audit
- Interface Management
- Opportunity Management
- Risk Management
- Integrity Management

- Planning
- Cost Management
- Schedule Management
- Contracts Management
- Data Management
- Configuration Management
- Subcontractor Management
- Administrative Management
- Security

Engineering Management

Manufacturing

System Integration and Test

Product Assurance

Design Integration

Subsystem A (end item)

Subsystem B (end item)

Subsystem C (end item)

Domain Specialist Organizations

Figure 11.3   The project office triad.

the appropriate balance between technical and business factors, it is highly desirable to have a systems engineering manager or chief systems engineer responsible for:

- Requirements management, analysis, and audit.
- Orchestrating technical players in timing and intensity.
- Baseline, opportunity, risk, performance, and verification management.
- Interface control.
- Design audits.
- Understanding and managing to the customer's perspective.

For small projects the project manager will typically perform the systems engineering function.

The *business manager* is responsible for all business aspects of the project including planning, scheduling, and contractual matters, as well as legal, moral, and ethics issues. The business manager also assists the project manager in implementing planning, control, visibility, statusing, and corrective action systems.

Before personnel staffing selections occur, the required functions and related skills should be determined. The nature of the project will dictate the core team functions, for which the project manager should prepare job descriptions. Most job descriptions should be based on the task descriptions developed within the Work Breakdown Structure (WBS). These job descriptions are not only important in the selection process, but they are the basis of negotiations within the matrix structure.

Those who thrive in the project environment will typically be adaptable and interdependent as well as independent and results driven. To paraphrase Stephen Covey, independent thinking alone is not suited to the interdependent project reality. "Independent people who do not have the maturity to think and act interdependently may be good individual producers, but they won't be good leaders or team players."[7]

While all team members are selected on the basis of both skills and personal attributes, it is particularly important that the core team have previous project experience, preferably at the task and project management levels.

As each member is added to the team, it is wise for new members to define their roles and to have these roles acknowledged by the rest of the team, beginning with the project manager. Doing this early affords the opportunity to make adjustments to create synergy and minimize discord. Until the detailed planning is done, roles and responsibilities may have to be defined in general terms with later refinement consistent with the planning results.

Outsourcing is an increasingly popular alternative to applying direct project staff. Subcontractors, vendors, and consultants can be a cost-effective way to fulfill functional capability. However, you should be just as diligent in selecting external sources as you are in selecting employees, including reference checks, facility tours, and key person contract clauses.

THE IMPORTANCE OF CONCURRENT ENGINEERING

The project team needs to consider, *from the outset,* all elements of the project cycle. Involving all stakeholders in the development process is known as *Concurrent Engineering* (Figure 11.4). For example, airline pilots should participate in the concept definition of a new plane to properly influence the operational aspects of the system.

Concurrent Engineering is the concept that all stakeholders need to be considered throughout the project cycle in order to produce the best product.

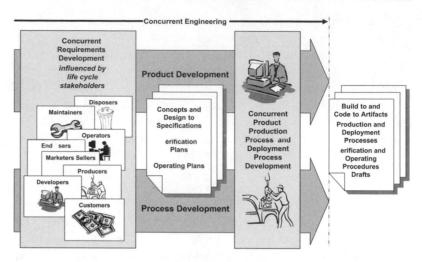

Figure 11.4   Concurrent engineering fosters stakeholder influence.

——— INCOSE ———
INCOSE Handbook Sec 5.11
covers *Concurrent Engineering*.

Systems engineering must
ensure the timely involvement
of all disciplines.

Likewise, the baggage handlers should influence that part of the design pertinent to their operations. Similarly, recent generations of computer architecture have benefited greatly from having software engineers involved in the hardware design. Concurrent engineering also promotes simultaneous product and process development to ensure that efficient producibility is designed in.

Systems engineering is responsible for involving the key personnel (to address human factors, safety, producibility, inspectibility, reliability, maintainability, logistics, etc.) in each phase. This does not require a dedicated team of specialists. However, it does require a proactive systems engineer who can ensure domain specialists are appropriately applied to pursue high value opportunities and their risks.

MANAGING THE MAJOR INTERFACES AND INTERRELATIONSHIPS

The authors of *Dynamic Project Management* have likened matrix interactions to those of a marketplace. "Negotiations concerning assignments, priorities, equipment, facilities, and people are constant. Matrix team members often complain of the continuous meetings, but it is through such meetings that the characteristic decentralized decision making occurs."[8]

The complex relationships and confusing lines of authority in the project/functional lattice demands thoughtful planning. As illustrated in Figure 11.5, the project manager identifies what is to be

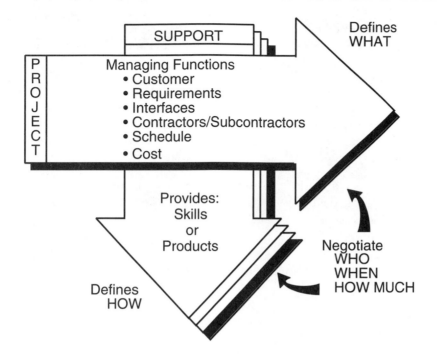

Figure 11.5   Matrix functions chart.

done, primarily by means of work authorizing agreements or MBOs derived from the requirements. The functional organizations are responsible for defining and negotiating with the project manager how the tasks are to be performed and then implementing them.

Both project- and support-management responsibilities are assigned by executive management. The project manager ensures that project objectives are achieved on schedule and at the lowest cost compatible with user/contractual requirements. The support managers ensure the performance of specific project requirements as defined and authorized by the project manager. In addition, as the advocate for technical excellence, each support manager is responsible for:

- Performing for executive management in support of all projects.
- Performing as agreed with each project manager.
- Maintaining personnel expertise consistent with emerging technology and industry best practices.
- Recommending creative ways to meet project objectives.
- Providing function's cost, schedule, and technical opportunity and risk assessment.

- Assigning skilled personnel to support projects.
- Actively participating in problem solving and conflict resolution.
- Correcting deficiencies in performance.

One of the most significant techniques for minimizing confusion and avoiding excessive interaction is to clarify roles and responsibilities where conflict in authority and function are likely to take place. The critical areas of potential conflict that should be resolved are:

- Project direction, objectives, priorities, planning, reviews, status, and controls.
- Assuring project effectiveness and customer commitments.
- Proposal preparation, contract negotiations, and contract management status.
- Technical, schedule, budget, and make versus buy decisions.
- Assignment of key personnel and establishment of employee objectives.
- Communications, correspondence, and data requirements.
- Point of contact for customer, upper management, and support interfaces.

A technique for managing any form of matrix organization is the Project Work Authorizing Agreement (PWAA) or an equivalent method for authorizing work. The PWAA is a contract between the project office and the supporting organizations. As illustrated in the next chapter on planning, it contains task definition, budget, schedule, performer's commitment, and project office authorization (Figure 11.6). Companies or organizations that have a formal, quantified, and measurable MBO program can make use of that system to supplement, or in the case of simple projects, substitute for the more definitive PWAA. These methods are addressed in Chapters 12 and 16.

> Teams rarely go wrong by themselves—more often they suffer from lack of direction and false assumptions.

These are common expectations of executive management, the customer, and the team members:

- *Timely, accurate information*—for teams to work well, information and ideas have to flow smoothly.
- *No surprises*—for cooperation to grow, communication must be complete and candid. There is no place on a project team for a problem withholder.
- *Credit given where credit deserved*—the rewards must match the risks and recognition given for both individual and team efforts.

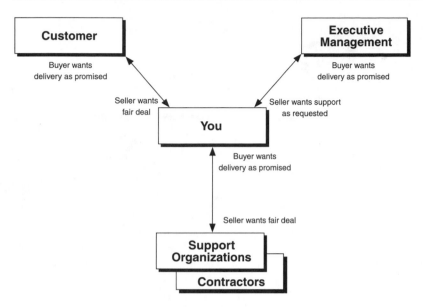

Figure 11.6   The buyer/seller viewpoints.

Matrix operations depend on their project manager being viewed as a buyer of services provided by the support managers.

PROJECT TEAM EXERCISE

The objective of this exercise is to provide experience in identifying the issues facing a project manager in staffing a project.

You are the project manager for a project your company is bidding and, if successful, it will position you and your company for significant growth. Unfortunately, the last similar project was poorly staffed and the delivered product required extensive rework before being acceptable to the customer. Your company's reputation has suffered and management is concerned about a repeat.

You have been asked to prepare a staffing plan. The project is predicted to last 18 months, and will require the equivalent of ten full-time people although actual head count will vary, beginning with just a few key designers, expanding to a larger staff of development people, testers, and so on, and then tailing off to key engineering staff during final testing and delivery. All staff will report to you for the duration of the project and will be collocated in your facility.

What information should you develop to guide your staffing plan?

MANAGEMENT ELEMENT 4

"It is a bad plan that admits of no modification."

Publilius Syrus

—— *PMBOK® Guide* ——
This chapter is consistent with the *PMBOK® Guide* Ch 5 *Project Scope Management,* Ch 6 *Project Time Management,* Ch 7 *Project Cost Management*

—————— *INCOSE* ——————
This chapter is consistent with *INCOSE Handbook* Sec 5.2 *Planning Process.*

Planning is performed in each project-cycle phase to prepare for the subsequent phases.

Project planning is an iterative process on several levels, as well as an ongoing one.

12

PROJECT PLANNING

Planning must reflect the tactics selected to achieve the project's strategic objectives including the integration sequence of the various system entities. The infamous Denver Airport construction project failed to do this and suffered huge overruns and schedule delays as a result. Even though baggage handling is a key part of any airport, the Denver Airport state-of-the-art baggage handling system was an afterthought not factored into the concept, the architecture, or the operating scenarios. As a result, the baggage system had to be designed and installed within the inadequate physical constraints of existing designs and operations already under construction. Furthermore, the constraints also prohibited an effective backup system. Unfortunately, the approved Denver Airport plan was never rebaselined to accommodate the add-on baggage handling capability as it should have been. As a result, the costs soared from $1.7 billion to more than $4.8 billion, a 200 percent overrun, and the operational readiness was delayed 16 months.

PLAN THE WORK AND WORK THE PLAN

We define planning as the process that determines beforehand the tasks necessary to complete the project. Planning continues and the plan evolves as the project progresses through the phases of the project cycle. A plan contains at least:

- *What* is to be done.
- *When* it should be done.
- *Who* is responsible for doing it.

A complete plan adds physical and financial resource profiles.

At the highest total project level, planning is performed in each project-cycle phase to prepare for the subsequent phases. The lowest level of iteration occurs within each activity—such as iterating through network development and task schedules to determine and shorten the critical path. While the emphasis, level of detail, and opportunity and risk factors change from one phase to the next, the process that follows is relevant to every project phase.

Project planning and statusing are directly related to each other and inextricably linked. You select the status methods before planning, since the planning needs to support and relate to the statusing method and its intended granularity. For example, to benefit fully from the power of earned value, tasks need to be defined in sufficient detail to minimize the need to judge percent complete. The preferred method is to establish interim milestones with related percentages. For instance, a report might earn 10 percent for the outline, 30 percent for the first draft, 10 percent for red team review, 30 percent to incorporate improvements, and 20 percent to produce the final version. We address earned value in Chapter 16.

Many experts see earned value as a planning technique as well as a method to status the project.

The project plan (Figure 12.1) is usually composed of a set of specialty plans. Some plans, such as the acquisition plan and the source selection plan, apply only to projects that need to evaluate and select competitive suppliers. The implementation plan for solution development is common to all development projects and will

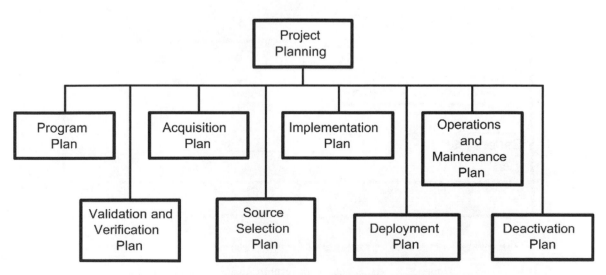

Figure 12.1   The total project plan consists of multiple plans.

be used throughout this chapter to illustrate the overall planning process.

IMPLEMENTATION PLANNING: CONVERTING THE PROJECT REQUIREMENTS INTO ORDERLY WORK

We define *implementation planning* as the process of converting all project requirements into a logically sequenced set of negotiated work authorizing agreements (Figure 12.2) and subcontracts.

Project Work Authorizing Agreements are internal contracts containing:

- Task description.
- Schedule for deliverables.
- Time-phased budgets.
- Agreement by the implementer.
- Agreement by the project manager.

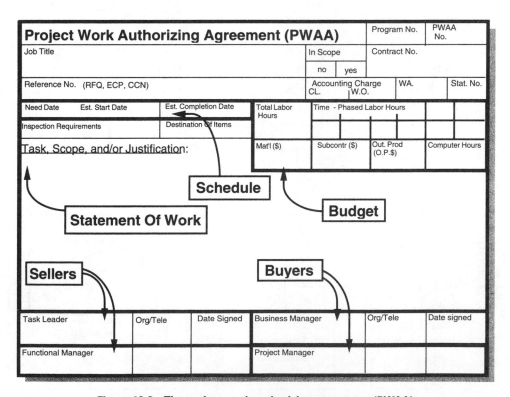

Figure 12.2   The project work authorizing agreement (PWAA).

Subcontracts are external contracts containing all of the previous items plus:

- Contract terms and conditions.
- Legal authority to perform.
- Conditions for default.

THE PLANNING PROCESS: SIMULATING THE PROJECT

Figure 12.3 shows an overview of the plan development objectives and process, highlighting the role of the project manager in integrating the customer's objectives with those of the enterprise's management. It emphasizes a major reason projects fail: insufficient team interaction. Productive interaction helps motivate and commit the team. But it has to be a meaningful interactive process. The most difficult project objectives offer the best team brainstorming opportunities. When the team members resolve strategies and tactics to achieve their objectives and develop the plan, their investment skyrockets—they become committed to implementing "their" plan.

A significant contributor to poor planning is lack of a systematic and structured process. As emphasized in Chapter 2, to test for a sensible plan it is important to be able to envision it—to be able to

> Implementation planning is driven by the project's objectives, the need to communicate, and the need to obtain agreements and commitments.

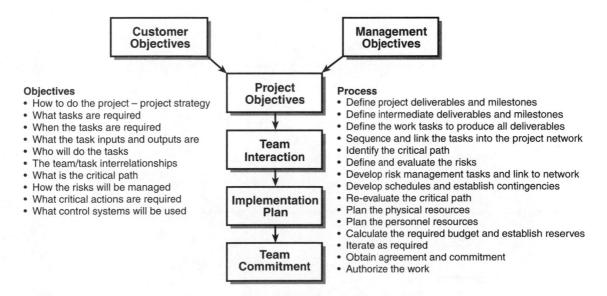

Objectives
- How to do the project – project strategy
- What tasks are required
- When the tasks are required
- What the task inputs and outputs are
- Who will do the tasks
- The team/task interrelationships
- What is the critical path
- How the risks will be managed
- What critical actions are required
- What control systems will be used

Customer Objectives

Management Objectives

Project Objectives

Team Interaction

Implementation Plan

Team Commitment

Process
- Define project deliverables and milestones
- Define intermediate deliverables and milestones
- Define the work tasks to produce all deliverables
- Sequence and link the tasks into the project network
- Identify the critical path
- Define and evaluate the risks
- Develop risk management tasks and link to network
- Develop schedules and establish contingencies
- Re-evaluate the critical path
- Plan the physical resources
- Plan the personnel resources
- Calculate the required budget and establish reserves
- Iterate as required
- Obtain agreement and commitment
- Authorize the work

Figure 12.3 Planning objectives, process, and drivers.

decompose it into deliverables and then to simulate the flow of the work in a visual walk-through. Our planning process steps converge on a cards-on-the-wall (COW) networking technique that provides this visualization. The main process elements are listed in Table 12.1.

This approach, shown as a flowchart in Figure 12.4, offers a systematic way to transform the project activities into a baseline plan suitable for both proactive and reactive management. In the remainder of the planning section, we will address each flowchart element in detail.

The goal of planning parrots the project goal: to ensure that all commitments to the customer are met. To get there, we start the

Table 12.1   The Planning Process: Major Elements and Techniques

Key Element	Process	Primary Technique
Products	Decomposing deliverables into their hierarchical (architecture) structure—from senior most down to the lowest level internal and external deliverables.	Project Product List and Fact Sheets
Development strategy and tactics	Determining the development strategy and tactics such as fast time to market and unified, incremental, linear, and/or evolutionary development with either single or multiple deliveries.	Application of the "Vee model"
Opportunity and risk tactics	Identifying opportunities and associated risks and the customer-compatible opportunity and risk actions with preventive, causative, and contingent action plans.	Lessons Learned
Tasks	Defining the tasks needed to develop each deliverable.	Work Breakdown Structure
Network	Logically arranging the interactive tasks to portray the best value development and delivery approach.	Cards-on-the-wall network, followed by a computerized network and critical path determination and analysis
Schedules	Scheduling each task according to the calendar and resource availability and then refining and shortening the critical path where possible and meaningful.	Scheduling software
Resources	Defining resources (personnel, equipment, finances) needed to accomplish each task on schedule.	Spread sheets and cost estimating models
Commitments	Committing the necessary resources and funds to carry out the plan.	Project Work Authorizing Agreements

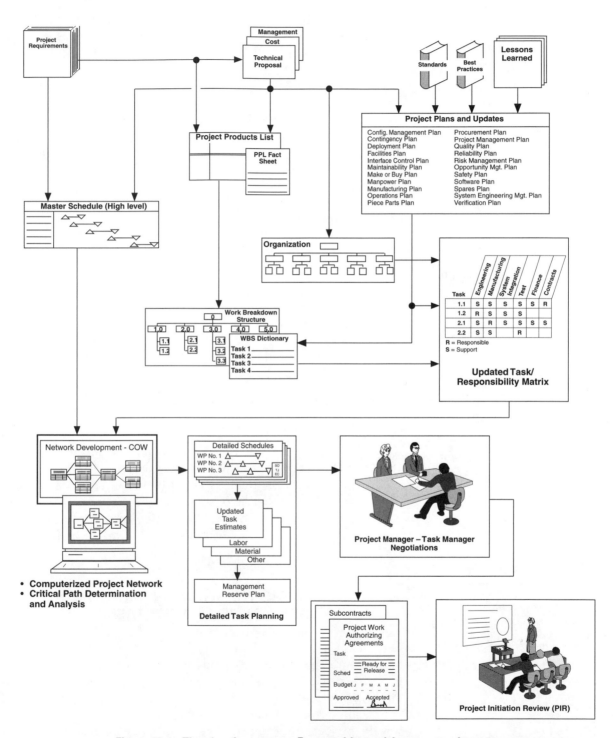

Figure 12.4 The planning process: From problem solving to commitment.

planning with the project requirements that include the Statement of Work (SOW), the milestone schedule (Master Schedule), cost targets, and definition of all deliverables. The Master Schedule identifies the overall start and stop dates and all major milestones.

DETERMINING THE PROJECT DELIVERABLES

The Project Products List and Fact Sheets are techniques that facilitate this step.

One of the first planning steps is to determine all of the project deliverables and to provide a narrative description of each. The Project Products List (PPL) is derived from the decomposition and definition of the system and is a list of all external deliverables and internal deliverables, in all forms produced, with the quantities required. Examples of the different forms of products that could be produced are:

- Drafts.
- Simulations.
- Models (user requirements understanding, technical feasibility, physical fit, field test, preproduction, etc.).
- Qualification units.
- Deliverables.
- Spares.

An example of a hardware PPL and a software PPL are shown in Figure 12.5. Other PPLs would include support equipment, documentation, and services.

A Project Product List Fact Sheet should accompany each PPL (Figure 12.6). Its purpose is to provide a description and expected use for each item. It is usually written by the most knowledgeable expert available, whether he or she is to work on the project or not. The fact sheets are used by project participants to plan and estimate labor and material for each deliverable to facilitate costing and pricing.

DEFINING THE WORK BREAKDOWN STRUCTURE AND THE TASKS

As the keystone of the plan, the WBS depicts the project decomposition and the associated tasks.

The WBS for development projects is best depicted as the system architecture consisting of system, subsystems, and components rather than by discipline or functional organization (such as engineering, manufacturing, test, etc.). The WBS is represented graphically or in an indented list (Figure 12.7) and illustrates the way the project will be integrated, assigned, and statused. The WBS

Project Products List

Title: Propulsion System Dual Tank Configuration (WBS 11.01.02)

Project Office Approval

Item no	Nomenclature and WBS Number	Drawing Number (or similar to)	Make or buy	Status Des	Status Hdwe	TF	PF	TS	SI	FT	Q	DV	F	S	Remarks
1	Propulsion Module (10.01.02 .19)		M	N	N							1	2		Assemble, Install & Test
2	Propellant Tank (10.01.02.07)	8160485 - X (2P64002)	B	M	N			2		1	2	4	1		Spherical Version Of 2P64002 (cylindrical)
3	Reaction Engine Module (10.01.02.06)	8160481 -X (2P64000 - 13)	B	M	N	14	16	1	2	2	32	2			RRC Intelsat V 0.5 LBF Thruster Mounted In Pairs On An REM
4	Latching Solenoid Valve (11.01.02.11)	2P60481 - 3 or equivalent	B	E	N			4	1		4	8	1		
5	Service Valve (11.01.02.11)	2P60483 - X	B	E	N			3			3	6	1		
6	PR XDucer (11.01.02.15)	8111210 - X	B	M	N	1		4	1	1	4	8	1		Modify To Increase Shielding For New
7	Filter (11.01.02.10)	8103465 - 15	B	E	N			4			4	8	1		Radiation Environment

Legend:
Status: N = New, M = Modified, E = Existing
"Category": TF – Technical Feasibility Model, PF – Physical Fit Model, TS – Thermal Simulation Model, SI – System Integration Model, FT – Field Test Model, Q – Qualification Unit, DV – Development Vehicle, F – Flight, S – Spares

Page 1 Of 2

Also software
Also support equipment
Also documentation
Also services

PROJECT PRODUCTS LIST — Software

WBS NO. 1.3.7.1
SUBSYSTEM Data Compression
WORK PKG NO. 1.3.7.1.0
Date June 12
Revision 1.2
Page 1

LEGEND
STATUS: N - New, M - Modified, E - Existing
PRODUCT LEVEL: CSCI – Computer Software Configuration Item, CSC – Computer Software Component

NOMENCLATURE	MNEMONIC	CI	CSC	User Rqmt's Model	Technical Feasibility Mdl	-01	-02	MAKE (M) OR BUY (B)	SOFTW. DESIGN	PROGR. CODING	EST. LINES OF CODE	SECURITY CLASSIF.	REMARKS
Data Base Core	RDMS	X		X	X	X		M	M	N	125K	Uncl	Convert to Ada
Report Writer	WRIT		X	X		X		M	N	N	87K	Uncl	
Graphics	GRAF		X			X		B	N	N	42K	Uncl	
Dictionary	DICT		X				X	M	N	N	65K	Uncl	

Figure 12.5 Project product list (PPL) examples.

Item:	Pressure transducer
Part No:	8111210 - 503
Source:	Electromech, Inc.
WBS No:	11.01.02.15
Description:	This transducer is identical electrically to existing part no. 8111210-501. The envelope is to be modified to increase heat survivability. The shield concept must be proven by tests of the development model. The shielding design must be qualified by selected qualification tests per the test plan.

Figure 12.6　PPL fact sheet example.

is critical to project planning because it is the basis for work assignments, budgeting, scheduling, risk assessment, cost collection, and performance statusing.

Figure 12.8 illustrates how the WBS relates the work required to produce the individual components (from the Product Breakdown Structure) to the work required to integrate those components into the system.

The WBS has been successfully employed by government agencies such as the Department of Defense (DoD) and NASA for many years and is now a standard planning technique for projects of all kinds. The Project Management Institute's *Practice Standard for Work Breakdown Structures* is a guide to the development of an appropriate WBS. Both product and service WBS forms are covered by the standard.[1]

For government projects, the Request for Proposal usually provides a top-level WBS that the project's WBS must interface with. MIL-STD-881A (former DoD WBS standard) embodies WBS requirements as well as examples. It accurately states that the WBS provides a system management structure for:

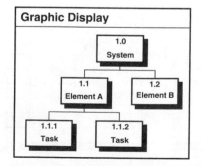
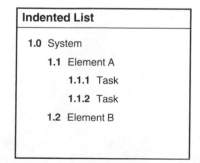

Figure 12.7　The work breakdown structure (WBS).

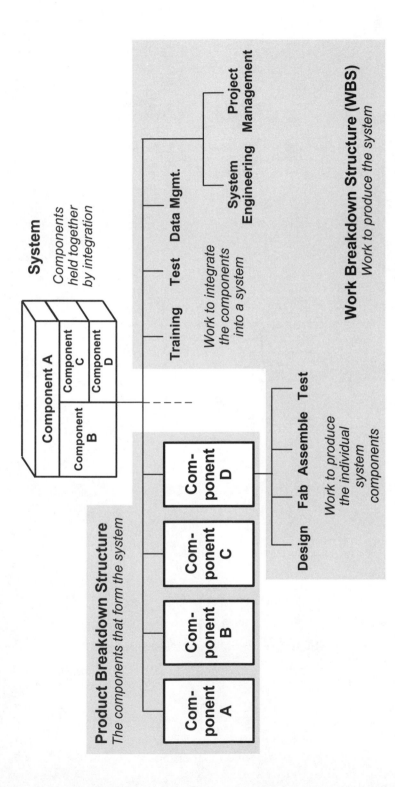

Figure 12.8 The work breakdown structure related to the system and product breakdown structure.

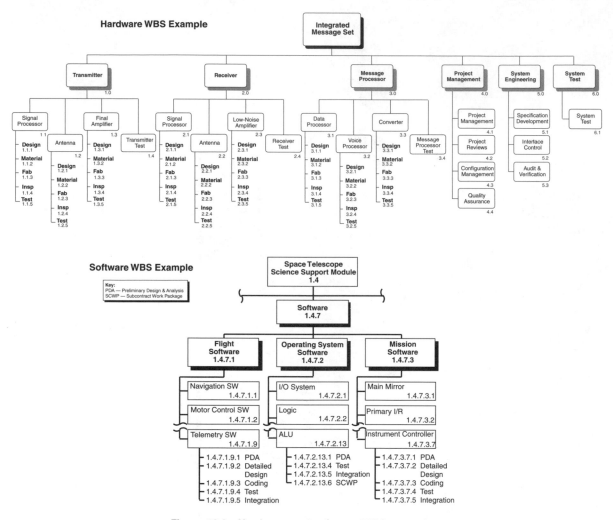

Figure 12.9 Hardware and software WBS examples.

System decomposition	Budgeting
Specifications and drawings	Scheduling
Configuration management	Responsibility

The guidelines in Figure 12.9 reflect our experience in refining this planning technique:

- For development projects structure the WBS by product and elements of the product.
- For service projects and for the study and operations periods structure the WBS by functional disciplines.
- Include all authorized tasks.

Component Test

This task consists of preparing test procedures, test facility, test personnel, and test conduct including documentation and resolution of all test discrepancies. The output from the task is a satisfactorily completed test, resolution of all test anomalies, and the final test report.

Figure 12.10   WBS dictionary excerpt.

- Cost collection is usually one level below budget performance reporting to facilitate problem cause identification.
- Identifiers for like tasks should be similar. Example: x.x.x.4 Material.
- All tasks for an element should be collected with the element identifier.
- WBS depth (number of levels) depends on the risk to be managed and reported.
- Level-of-effort tasks are usually at the second level, which may include project management, systems engineering, system integration, and system-level testing.
- The product level should consist of entity nouns and the task level should apply verbs such as *design, fabricate code, assemble,* and *test.*

The WBS is supported by the WBS dictionary, which links the WBS elements to the task definition—work packages. As Figure 12.10 shows, the WBS dictionary is a narrative description of each work task identified in the WBS. The descriptions drive the task estimating and are the basis of task assignments.

The work package contains a complete task description, including what, when, how, by whom, and also includes the budget and schedule allocations. It may incorporate the WBS dictionary entry or reference it. The work package represents another important link in the planning—the connection between the WBS and the functional organization or contractor assigned to the task, which is accomplished by the Work Authorization Agreement.

A work package is prepared for each element at its lowest level in the WBS.

WBS TASKS AND THE PROJECT DASHBOARD

The establishment of WBS tasks determines the instruments of the project's dashboard. For each task there should be an associated budget and work accomplishment plan. Then, as work is accomplished and labor charges are accumulated against the task, the expenditures compared to the budget (fuel gauge) will become apparent as well as the progress of accomplishments as compared to the milestone plan for the task (odometer). A well-managed project will have these instruments for all significant tasks and the project manager will drive the project in accordance with their readouts.

DEVELOPING THE PROJECT NETWORK AND SCHEDULES

There are three types of schedules to resolve: deliverable accomplishment, personnel, and budget. This section deals primarily with deliverable schedules, bounded by the required start and stop dates for each task. They form the basis for the other supporting schedules. Personnel schedules identify the timing for required personnel involvement and facilitate resource planning. Cost schedules define the allocation and spending for each task as a function of time. Their primary purpose is to facilitate funding management.

Scheduling usually involves more iterations than any other function in the planning process. This is mainly due to the trade-offs that must be made among the constraints of time, cost, technical requirements, available personnel, and risk. Another complicating factor is that all task interdependencies may not be obvious when scheduling is developed at the task level.

The WBS tasks are the foundation for the project network and schedule as shown in Figure 12.11.

The scheduling process iterates through these steps:

- Link the tasks to form a project network.
- Identify opportunities for project improvement.
- Identify and evaluate risks.
- Develop opportunity and risk management actions and add to the network.
- Factor in task duration times.
- Determine the critical path.
- Shorten the critical path.
- Commit to meeting the task schedules.

Historically, there have been two principal methods for constructing network diagrams, the Program Evaluation and Review Technique (PERT) and the Critical Path Method (CPM). In their very basic but easy-to-use book, the Bakers characterize these methods as follows:

PERT and CPM emerged in different ways in the late 1950s. PERT was developed by Lockheed and Booz, Allen, and Hamilton for the

---

PMBOK® Guide

PMBOK® Guide Sec 6.2.2 *Activity Sequencing* identifies three types of dependencies:

1. Mandatory (those inherent in the nature of the work).
2. Discretionary (also known as preferred logic, preferential logic, or soft logic based on best practices).
3. External (relationships between project and non-project activities).

PMBOK® Guide

PMBOK® Guide Sec 6.5.2.6 *The Critical Chain Method,* discusses this technique which accounts for the effect of resource availability.

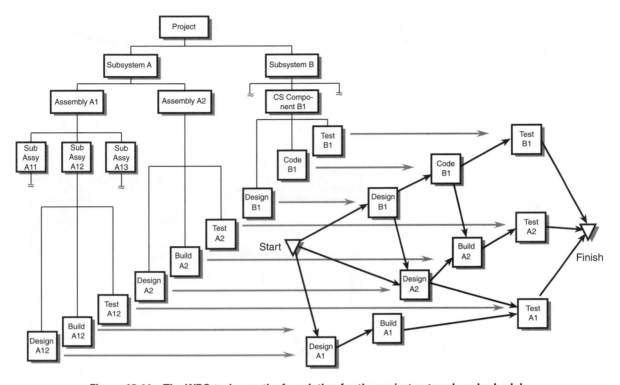

Figure 12.11   The WBS tasks are the foundation for the project network and schedule.

U.S. Navy Special Projects Office. The CPM was developed at about the same time by Morgan Walker and James Kelly for E.I. Du Pont. . . . (The primary difference is in the way the two techniques treat time estimates for tasks.) . . . [T]he networks are largely the same in terms of sequencing possibilities. In CPM, one time estimate is used for creating the schedule; PERT uses a more analytical system based on three time estimates that are used to determine the most probable time for completion.[2]

The distinction is that the PERT network allows a three-point estimate for the duration of each task (nominal, earliest completion, and latest completion). With the three-point estimates you can perform Monte Carlo simulations for the network and determine the nominally expected completion date (the output of the CPM), the probability of achieving that date, and the date for 95 percent or 99 percent probability of completion. The widespread availability of high-speed, high-capacity desktop computers makes this process readily available and potentially useful to the project team. Microsoft Excel can perform Monte Carlo simulations.

Technically, the COW technique result is similar to PERT/CPM, but the process is much more visual and interactive, leading to more reliable schedules.

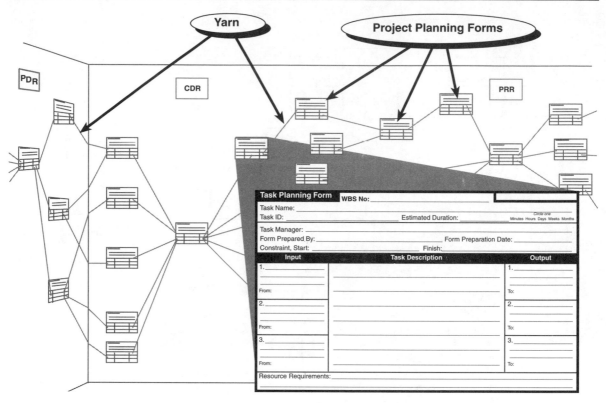

Figure 12.12   The cards-on-the-wall (COW) method.

Computer-based PERT or CPM affords very limited opportunities for team interaction during network construction. Computer-based network construction, regardless of the specific software, is usually built from work packages and input by a single person working alone at the keyboard and viewing the resulting network on the computer screen. The problem with using a computer at this early stage is that the team is not creating the network. We prefer a more interactive network diagramming technique that begins with a method we have dubbed cards-on-the-wall (COW). In this method, the team literally hangs each work package on the wall, by project phase, and interconnects them using markers or yarn to reflect the interdependencies (Figure 12.12). We prefer the wall as a work space because it allows the team to cluster in areas of interest of the evolving network to discuss the logic. We use "wetware" (the brains of the team) for creating the network and software for capturing that network and computing the critical path. We've devised a form for creating the network, as shown on a section of the network wall in Figure 12.12.

Our COW technique uses:

- A 5″ × 8″ project planning form for each task,
- Yarn or string for interconnecting the cards, and
- Ample walls to hang and arrange the cards.

The COW technique consists of interconnecting the tasks (cards) to reflect the optimum order of tasks and their interdependencies. Among the benefits of this interactive, visual procedure are:

- Participative decision making.
- Fewer "I forgots."
- Shared risks.
- Shared concessions.
- Quality results.
- *And most important:* team ownership of the plan.

In a recent planning session, someone commented that it was a shame that the walls weren't magnetic. "But they are," said the leader, looking at the cluster of people over at the wall discussing how to shorten a link in a critical path, "they have animal magnetism." We've never seen people crowd around a computer terminal talking about how to reorder tasks, but we've seen lots of groups cluster around a wall draped with cards and yarn, arranging "logic" to make an impossible schedule feasible.

Schedules at the task level usually employ a linear format or bar chart such as the Gantt chart. Figure 12.13 shows the relationship between the project network and the task schedules. Bar charts that include task interconnects are often called *time phased networks*. This is the most effective form for day-to-day project management.

The next step after network construction is determining the *critical path*—the task sequence that paces the project. When asked to identify his project's critical path, one rather defensive project manager we encountered asserted, "This project has no critical path, if it does, we will eliminate it."

We define the *critical path* as the sequence of project activities for which there is minimum or zero slack. The critical path for a vacation preparation is shown in bold in Figure 12.14. For convenience, we talk of "the" critical path. In fact, there may be several critical paths, and there are frequently many other "near-critical" paths. The following discussion applies to all of these situations.

The critical path paces the project schedule.

—— *PMBOK® Guide* ——
PMBOK® Guide Sec 6.2 *Activity Sequencing* covers the Precedence Diagramming Method (PDM) described here and also the Arrow Diagramming Method (ADM) in which activities are shown on the arrows connecting activity dependency junctions.

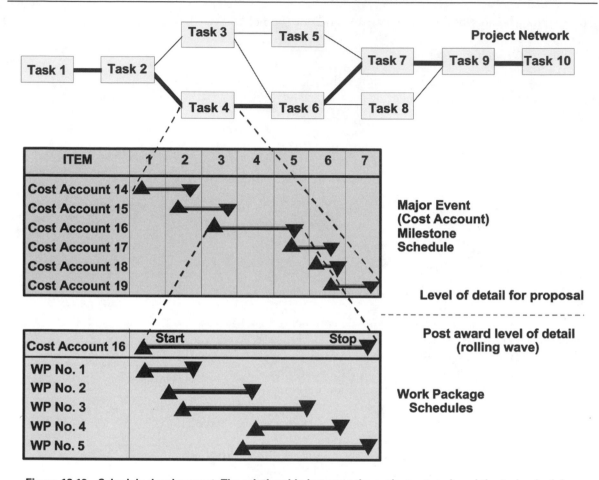

Figure 12.13 Schedule development: The relationship between the project network and the task schedules.

After adding contingency spans and opportunity and risk management tasks, the critical path needs to be reevaluated. Analyzing resource requirements for concurrent activities and using the critical path as the time scale will usually reveal suboptimal lumping of personnel resources (the critical chain). At the same time these tasks are being considered for resource leveling or smoothing, the following actions to reduce the critical path should be considered:

- Eliminate or shorten tasks on the critical path.
- Replan serial paths to be parallel.
- Overlap sequential tasks.

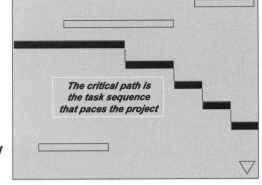

Pack clothes

Prepare boat

Have car fixed

Pick up supplies

Install hitch

The critical path is the task sequence that paces the project

Pick up boat

Pick up friends

Arrange house security

Cancel newspaper

Figure 12.14 Critical path example: Vacation preparation.

- Increase the number of workdays or work hours.
- Shorten tasks; the best candidates are those:
  —That are long, or easy, to speed up.
  —For which you have available resources.
  —That cost the least to speed up.
  —That your organization controls.

Actions taken to shorten the critical path usually have other impacts. Using the vacation preparation example (Figure 12.14), the critical path could be shortened by having the hitch installed while the car is being fixed, or you could rent a car to pick up supplies while the car is being repaired. In the first case, if the car is having the fuel injection system repaired, the mechanic may not have the skill to install the hitch, hence a risk would be added. In the second case, renting a car adds cost. You could also have your friends pick up the supplies (add project resources) or, as one student proposed, you could go on vacation without your friends (change requirements). In each case you must ask yourself, "Is it worth it to shorten the schedule?"

Sometimes risk reductions and critical path reductions are synergistic. You can expect to move lower-risk tasks off the critical path, which can contribute needed resources to the higher-risk tasks, thereby reducing the critical path and/or the risk. The optimum balance is achieved when both sets of tasks end up on the new, shorter critical path.

Next, resource leveling and optimization can be performed. These steps can be performed with the help of computers once the

Each action to shorten the critical path should be justified.

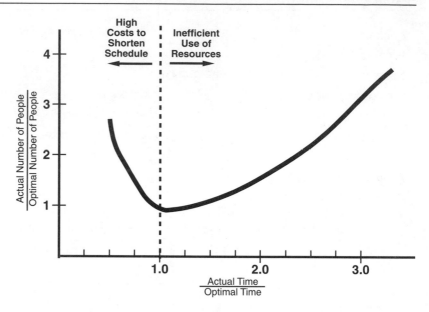

Figure 12.15   Schedule compression/expansion effects.

network is constructed. However, resource restrictions or problems are usually localized, and good judgment and common sense will produce meaningful results. Reducing the critical path and optimizing resource allocation can significantly affect a task's cost as illustrated graphically. Shortening a task schedule below the optimum point can lead to an increase in its cost (Figure 12.15). On the other hand, optimization at the network level may consist of offsetting a relatively small increase in task cost with a significant savings at the project level. For example, the incremental cost associated with compressing one task may result in equivalent burn rate savings for the total project.

——— PMBOK® Guide ———
PMBOK® Guide Sec 6.3 *Activity Resource Estimating* and Ch 7 *Project Cost Management* provide additional information on estimating and costing the planned work.

PLANNING THE RESOURCES

While this section focuses on the two limiting resources in most projects, personnel and funds, a unique physical resource can also impact the schedule. Take nothing for granted. Just when you need a special piece of test equipment that hasn't been used for six months, you can be sure Murphy will need it too. And Murphy's team reserved the equipment when they planned their project much earlier. Another property issue to plan for in government projects is the use of Government Furnished Equipment, Services, and Material (generally called GFE). First, contractual commitments must be negotiated for the GFE delivery dates. Second, permission must be granted by the government agency that owns the equipment (or services or material) that authorizes use of the material on your project. In one instance, one of the authors won a contract that involved manufacturing of components on special equipment owned by the U.S. Army. Unfortunately, prior permission for the use of the equipment had not been obtained. When asked for permission to use the machinery, the Army project office said, "Of course. What is the Army project number?" Answer: "It is a U.S. Air Force contract." Response: "Air Force? What Air Force? We don't have an Air Force. Permission denied." Incomplete planning and preparation almost always lead to a bad outcome.

To illustrate the time-phased resource requirements at the task, personnel category, and total project levels, Gantt charts are useful. They are derived from the PERT/CPM network, but use a conventional time scale, which may be more easily understood by the team. Having already adjusted tasks to smooth resource requirements, enhance opportunities, or reduce risks and/or the critical path, the next step is to return to the task level and define the personnel assignments and schedules.

The WBS is the basis for identifying task responsibilities (Figure 12.16). As a checklist, the Task Responsibility Matrix (Figure 12.17) is useful in summarizing which personnel and organizations have been assigned primary and support responsibilities for each task, and who will participate in the COW process. Figure 12.18 is an example of a planning form that extracts the monthly personnel needs from the task Gantt chart at the functional organization level and combines them with other resource requirements.

ESTIMATING, COSTING, AND PRICING

An essential part of planning is calculating the most probable cost to complete the project and then determining the market price. This process is often called cost estimating, but is more accurately described as estimating, costing, and pricing because each is a distinct process and is usually performed by domain specialists.

Estimating is usually performed by the task managers most familiar with the work to be done. Estimates are made regarding person hours, pounds and feet of material, number of lines of code, and so on. As much as possible, estimates are based on sound information

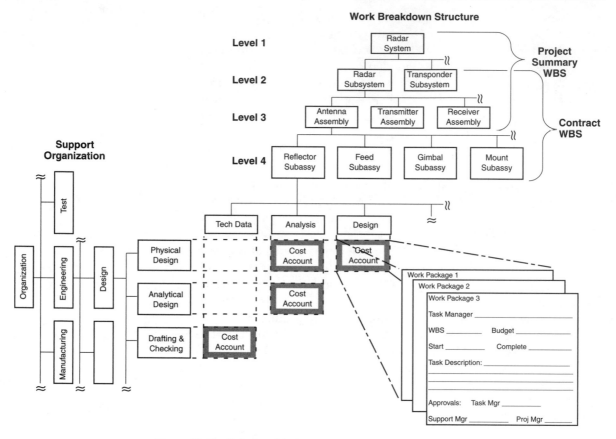

Figure 12.16   Relationship between WBS and organization.

such as build-to drawings or direct past experience, but in most cases the estimates are extrapolations, some of which depart significantly from the extrapolation baseline.

Costing is the conversion of the estimates into currency. Cost analysts are trained experts in making this conversion. While making the conversion they take into account the current hour or material to currency conversion, expected inflation or deflation over the period of the project, and all relevant burdens such as overhead and general and administrative charges. When the hours and all other resources have been costed with their appropriate burdens, then the cost of the project has been estimated. There are several tools in the marketplace to aid in costing hardware and software based on attributes such as weight, lines of code, or function points. Many companies also maintain a past-history database to substantiate estimating and costing.

Figure 12.17   Individual task responsibility matrix.

Task	Engineering	Manufacturing	System Integration	Test	Finance	Contracts
1	S	S	S	S	S	R
2	R	S	S	S		
3	S	R	S	S	S	S
4	S	S		R		

R = Responsible
S = Support

Organization Task Estimate	MFG No.		Contract		CCN No.	Doing Org. Name		No.
	Date Of RFP		Program			Responsible Org. Name		No.
WBS No:	Subject/Title of Task							
Work Package No:	Time - Phased Labor Hours							

Yr	Jan	Feb	Mar	Apr	May	Jun	Jul	Aug	Sep	Oct	Nov	Dec

Material description	$	Computer HRS	Other
Task description		Skill Mix	
		Basis of Estimate	

Prepared By	Doing Org. Manager's Signature	Responsible Org. Manager's Signature	Control
_____	_____Date_____	_____Date_____	**17633**

Figure 12.18   Resource planning form.

Pricing is a strategic decision made by management. It consists of adding or subtracting profit from the cost number. Negative profit is applicable when the project desires to capture a new market and is willing to invest to do so. Some companies have bid a total fixed price of zero to ensure capturing a high-value market. As the profit is increased, the probability of winning in a competitive environment decreases. Hence, this decision is one of marketplace strategy and risk tolerance. Figure 12.19 illustrates the estimating, costing, and pricing process.

The payoff of the detailed planning and scheduling is in securing support and commitment on the part of the team, functional organizations, subcontractors, general management, and the customer or user. The key negotiations, made easier by detailed scheduling, are those with the functional and task managers. The resulting agreement, the heart of the project's controlled work release system, should be documented in the form of a Project Work Authorizing Agreement (PWAA) shown earlier. The PWAA contains task definition, budget, schedule, performer's commitment, and project

> Authorization agreements and subcontracts authorize the project work and, collectively, represent and authorize the implementation plan.

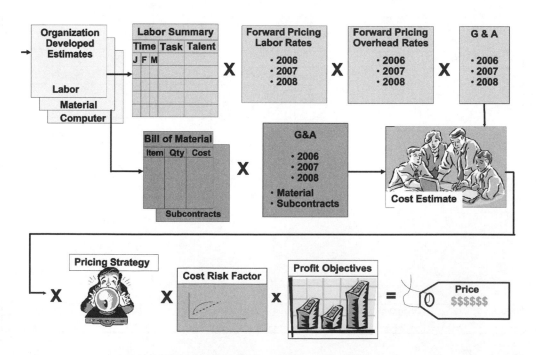

Figure 12.19   Estimating, costing, and pricing process.

office authorization. Subcontracts add terms and conditions clauses. The approved PWAA results from having:

Open and direct negotiations	Budgets accepted
Tasks understood	Contingencies identified
Milestones agreed	Caveats documented

Our project cycle template includes a Project Initiation Review decision gate. The objectives are to secure executive management approval of the implementation plan and to obtain management commitment of resources. The items to review include: contractual statement of work or memorandum of agreement for internal projects, deliverables, incentives; project strategy and tactics; implementation plan; opportunities, risks, and actions; functional organization commitments; and resources required.

KEEPING THE PLAN CURRENT

The project manager is responsible for:

- Assuring that all plans are consistent with current strategy, constraints, and the project's environment.
- Establishing the methods, techniques, and tools used in planning.
- Using the techniques and tools to update the plan.

The harder it is to plan, the more you need to.

The techniques and tools, especially software applications that support these responsibilities, are constantly improving. Before committing to a new software tool that may come up short as the project grows, you may do well to heed the following precautions:

- Beware of nonstandard data input and output formats.
- Some products are conceived and promoted as a full-management tool, but may only provide a scheduling algorithm.
- Test run the software.
- Use implementation tools. There are many computer-based tools available to mechanize the planning process and capture the project's data. These tools facilitate the planning process all the way from product decomposition through network development, critical path analysis, and schedule definition. They also provide for cost estimation, budget development, personnel planning, and resource leveling. Most tools will facilitate status reporting and associated rebaselining, if necessary.
- Talk to users who manage projects similar to yours.
- Set up operating procedures and standards.
- Insist that the standards be used.

PLANNING ELEMENT EXERCISE

The objective of this exercise is to provide experience in developing a project network and in identifying and calculating the critical path for a simple but relevant project.

Scenario: Develop a logic network and the critical path for the turnaround of a commercial 140-passenger airliner from final landing approach to takeoff clearance. A sample WBS for the airplane turnaround is provided.

WBS for the Aircraft Turnaround Project

1.0 Passengers and crew.
    1.1 Passengers.
        1.1.1 Unload arriving passengers.
        1.1.2 Load "Pre-board" passengers.
        1.1.3 Load terminal-area passengers.
        1.1.4 Obtain head count.
    1.2 Flight crew.
        1.2.1 Unload arriving crew (if required).
        1.2.2 Load departing crew.
2.0 Baggage.
    2.1 Unload arriving baggage.
    2.2 Load baggage from terminal.
3.0 Cabin service.
    3.1 Food.
        3.1.1 Unload empty food carts.
        3.1.2 Load new meals and beverages.
    3.2 Cleaning.
        3.2.1 Pick up trash.
        3.2.2 Vacuum or sweep cabin.
    3.3 Sanitation.
        3.3.1 Clean lavatories.
        3.3.2 Empty toilet sump tanks.
4.0 Fuel.
    4.1 Determine fuel load required.
    4.2 Load fuel.
    4.3 Verify fuel onboard.
5.0 Operations Integration.
    5.1 Landing control.
        5.1.1 Obtain permission to land.
        5.1.2 Land aircraft.

5.2 Takeoff control.

    5.2.1 Obtain permission to takeoff.

    5.2.2 Takeoff.

5.3 Taxi control.

    5.3.1 Obtain permission to taxi after landing.

    5.3.2 Taxi to gate.

    5.3.3 Obtain permission to taxi prior to takeoff.

    5.3.4 Taxi to takeoff holding point.

5.4 Gate control.

    5.4.1 Obtain permission to open door.
Ensures that the exit ramp is in place before opening the door.

    5.4.2 Open cabin door.

    5.4.3 Obtain permission to close door.
Ensures that all ticketed passengers in gate area are on board, and that all maintenance and service personnel have completed their tasks and have left the plane. The pilot and ticket agent must both concur plane is ready.

    5.4.4 Close cabin door.

5.5 Deicing application if required.
The deicing operation is done after all passengers are on board and the cabin door is closed. Deicing can be done at the gate or on the taxiway near the terminal. It must be completed within 15 minutes prior to actual takeoff.

    5.5.1 Apply deicing if required.

    5.5.2 Verify deicing application is within time limit.

6.0 Project management.

    6.1 Data management.

        6.1.1 Gather turnaround time statistics.

        6.1.2 Report performance.

    6.2 Manage "Turnaround Improvement Project."

The following functions should be provided for:

Air Traffic Control.

Ground Control.

Passenger and Crew Management.

Food Management.

All operational tasks in the WBS are linked into the serial/parallel relationships and then timed (example: Clean airplane—12 minutes) that will satisfy a turnaround time of 40 minutes. Plan events from aircraft touchdown to aircraft liftoff. You must budget three minutes from touchdown to gate arrival and three minutes for departure from gate to liftoff, and allow two minutes additional for deicing in winter.

The results should be (1) determination of the critical path activities and (2) what tasks should be addressed to further shorten turnaround time.

13

OPPORTUNITIES AND THEIR RISKS

California is a great place to live, complete with excellent climate, ethnic diversity, vibrant economy, and unlimited recreational possibilities. The opportunity of enjoying these benefits comes at the risk of earthquake devastation. Over the years, homeowners mitigated this risk by carrying earthquake insurance at modest rates. They had little need to call on the benefits until October 17, 1989, when California was hit by the magnitude 7.1 Loma Prieta earthquake causing huge insured losses with deductibles as low as $1,000. The claims impact to insurance companies was profound and the insurance industry began canceling homeowner policies and declining earthquake insurance. The California Earthquake Association was formed to provide homeowners with earthquake insurance with a deductible of 15 percent of the replacement value. But an important provision changed the insurance value proposition: In the event of a large quake without enough money to go around, benefits are to be prorated. While California is still a place of opportunity, the risk is considerably higher than pre–Loma Prieta.

PMBOK® Guide

This chapter is consistent with the content of *PMBOK® Guide* Ch 11 *Project Risk Management* although there are definition differences that will be noted.

INCOSE

This chapter is consistent with *INCOSE Handbook* Sec 5.8 *Risk Management Process.*

"A ship in a harbor is safe, but that's not what ships are built for."

William Shedd

Ships are built to pursue opportunities, as are projects.

Risks are born of opportunities. Without opportunities there are no risks.

THE OPPORTUNITY—RISK RELATIONSHIP

Over the past three decades, there has been a gradual paradigm shift in risk management. The 1960s and 1970s introduced the concept of risk management and the idea that project teams should anticipate risks and plan to reduce their impacts. This led to risk identification, top ten risk lists, and even risk management plans, although uniform

When you're encouraged to *take risk,* make sure to keep the driving *opportunity* in perspective.

adoption and implementation were slow. Then in the 1980s and 1990s, opportunities began to be addressed along with risks.

A review of current texts on risk management reveals that books written in 2000 and 2001 may mention opportunity and may even devote a paragraph to it. Then in 2002 and 2003, the emphasis climbs to a page or two, but opportunities are treated as things that happen with good results as opposed to being the very thrust of project management. A prominent risk management text defines opportunity, "as a possible occurrence that will have a positive effect on the project." It goes on to say that, "opportunities should be identified to balance out the negative occurrences (risks) as well as to take advantage of additional benefits of the project." We take issue with this perspective.

Project management is all about pursuing an opportunity to solve a problem or fulfill a need. Opportunities enable creativity in resolving concepts, architectures, designs, strategic and tactical approaches, as well as the many administrative issues within the project. It is the selection and pursuit of these strategic and tactical opportunities that determine just how successful the project will be. Of course, opportunities usually carry risks. Each will have its own set of risks that must be intelligently judged and properly managed to achieve the full value of each opportunity.

This chapter is not about risk management, but rather about managing opportunities and their risks to enhance ultimate project value. We see problems and risks much as Henry Kaiser did, as just opportunities in work clothes.

In project management, *opportunities* represent the potential for improving the value of the project results. The project champions (the creators, designers, integrators, and implementers) apply their "best-in-class" practices in pursuit of opportunities. After all, the fun of working on projects is doing something new and innovative. It is these opportunities that create the project's value. *Risks* are defined as chances of injury, damage, or loss. In project management, risks are the chances of not achieving the results as planned. Each of the strategic and tactical opportunities pursued have associated risks that undermine and detract from the opportunity's value. These are the risks that must be managed to enhance the opportunity value and the overall value of the project.

Opportunity and risk management are essential to—and performed concurrently with—the planning process, but require the application of separate and unique techniques that justify this distinct project management element.

When we pursue the opportunity to arrive at a destination early by speeding down the highway, we accept the risk of incurring an

———— *PMBOK® Guide* ————
The *PMBOK® Guide* Ch 11 *Project Risk Management* states that risks can have a positive or negative outcome. Our approach recognizes that opportunities seek a positive outcome and their associated risks diminish that opportunity.

The value of the opportunity must justify the incurred risks.

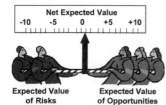

Net Expected Value
-10   -5   0   +5   +10

Expected Value   Expected Value
of Risks   of Opportunities

expensive traffic fine and higher insurance rates. To speed, our accelerator foot instinctively stabilizes at the exact position where we perceive the probability and benefit of arriving early is exactly equal to the probability and consequences of getting caught. We naturally and regularly make this trade and balance the expected outcomes with our accelerator foot for this combination of opportunity and risk.

The power of this concept is in the ability to adjust the opportunity to reduce or eliminate an undesired risk. One of the authors wanted a multiuse vehicle with all-wheel drive to get to the ski slopes. The opportunity was to purchase a sports utility vehicle (SUV), but the local newspaper and television vividly portrayed the risk of rollover. Risk was significantly reduced by simply adjusting the opportunity from an SUV to a minivan with all-wheel drive and a lower center of gravity that significantly reduces the rollover potential. Many project situations can be addressed by adjusting the opportunity to fit the risk tolerance of the project.

It is sometimes difficult to identify the opportunity that causes the risk (the "causing opportunity"). For instance, inhabitants of the southeastern United States are subjected to hurricanes almost every year. The causing opportunity, of course, is enjoying the benefits of living within the hurricane zone. Many people knowingly make that decision and consider the risk worthwhile. Similarly, other people prefer San Francisco as a place of residence in spite of the well-known risk of earthquakes.

If you have difficulty identifying or evaluating the causing opportunity, the risk just might not be important enough to accept and manage. In this case, consider eliminating the item or circumstances creating the risk.

> When we pursue opportunity, we normally incur risk. The opportunity to experience the thrill of an exciting sport like hang gliding or scuba diving brings with it the attendant risks. Many people instinctively make the trade that the thrill is worth the risks. Others decline.

LEVELS OF OPPORTUNITY AND RISK

In project management there are two levels of opportunities and risks. Because a project is the pursuit of an opportunity, the first category, the macro opportunity, is the project opportunity itself. The approach to achieving the project opportunity and the mitigation of associated project-level risks are structured into the strategy and tactics of the project cycle, the selected decision gates, the teaming arrangements, key personnel selected, and so on.

The second level encompasses the tactical opportunities and risks within the project that become apparent at lower levels of decomposition and as project cycle phases are planned and executed. This can include emerging, unproven technology; incremental and

> Opportunities and risks are endemic to the project environment. However well planned a project may be, there will always be residual project risk.

evolutionary methods that promise high returns; and the temptation to circumvent proven practices in order to deliver better, faster, and cheaper.

In the heat of project battle, it is easy for opportunities and risks to slip by or to slip in inadvertently. It is the project manager's responsibility to maintain a high level of awareness among all project participants, especially during various activities, such as:

- Project definition,
- Concept definition,
- Architecture definition,
- Strategic and tactical planning,
- Artifact selection and development,
- Hardware and software development,
- Manufacturing and coding,
- Supplier selection,
- Verification,
- Shipping and handling,
- Deployment, and
- Change evaluation.

> There is no simple way to prevent disasters. Nothing short of a systematic, detailed process will work.

Regarding the career-limiting effect of underestimating future risks, March and Shapira have articulated this management dichotomy: "Society values risk taking but not gambling, and what is meant by gambling is risk taking that turns out badly. . . . Thus, risky choices that turn out badly are seen, after the fact, to have been mistakes. The warning signs that were ignored seem clearer than they were; the courses that were followed seem unambiguously misguided."[1]

> If you don't identify opportunities, they won't be in your field of view.

The rest of this chapter is about maximizing opportunities and dealing directly with the inevitability of their risks—the foreseeable ones as well as the "unknown unknowns" that occur throughout the project.

> If you don't actively attack risks, the risks will actively attack you.

PROJECT-VALUE-DRIVEN OPPORTUNITY AND RISK MANAGEMENT

Project value can be expressed as benefit divided by cost. Opportunities and their risks should be managed jointly to enhance project value. This is based on the relative merits of exploiting each opportunity and mitigating each risk. In the context of the opportunity and the resultant project value, you make that kind of evaluation in your personal life every time you estimate how much you will drive per year (your opportunity) to decide how much insurance you should carry and with what level of deductible, which is the amount of residual risk you are willing to accept (your risk tolerance).

We carry a spare tire to mitigate the risk of a flat tire by reducing the probability and impact of having a delayed trip. The high value we place on getting where we want to go far exceeds the small expense of a spare. When deciding to pursue the opportunity of a long automobile trip, we may take extra risk management precautions, such as preventive maintenance and spares for hard-to-find parts.

The assessment of opportunity and risk balance is situational. For instance, few of us today have a car with more than one spare tire (multiple spares were a common practice in the early 1900s). However, a friend of one of the authors decided to spend a full month driving across the Australian Outback in late spring. He was looking for solitude in the wilderness (the opportunity). On advice from experienced friends, he took four spare tires and wheels. They also advised him that the risk of mechanical breakdown was very high on a 30-day trip, and the consequence would almost certainly be fatal. However, the risk of two vehicles breaking down at the same time was acceptably low. So he adjusted the opportunity for absolute solitude by joining two other adventurers. They set out in three cars. Everyone survived in good health, but only two cars returned, and two of his "spare" tires were shredded by the rough terrain. The mitigation approach proved effective.

We define *opportunity and risk management* as the process to enhance the opportunities and reduce their risks by:

- *Identifying* potential opportunities and their risks.
- *Assessing* associated probabilities of occurrence and the impact (benefit or consequence) of the occurrence to the project's value.
- *Deciding* to:

Do nothing	OR	Take causative action for opportunity, preventive action for risk.	OR	Take contingent action in response to a predefined trigger.

Opportunity management is driven by the desire to excel and risk management is driven by the desire not to fail or fall short of the objectives. The major driving forces for each are shown in Figures 13.1 and 13.2.

—— *PMBOK® Guide* ——
The *PMBOK® Guide* Ch 11 *Project Risk Management* identifies six processes:

1. *Risk Management Planning.*
2. *Risk Identification.*
3. *Qualitative Risk Analysis.*
4. *Quantitative Risk Analysis.*
5. *Risk Response Planning.*
6. *Risk Monitoring and Control.*

——— INCOSE ———
INCOSE Handbook Sec 5.8 *Risk Management Process* defines *risk management* as:

- *Risk Identification.*
- *Risk Planning.*
- *Risk Assessment.*
- *Risk Prioritization.*
- *Risk Handling and Mitigation.*
- *Risk Monitoring.*

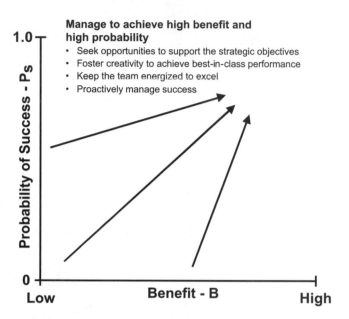

Figure 13.1 Opportunity management objectives—driven by the desire to excel.

Opportunity and risk management depends on a solid foundation of planning and proactive management of the plan. Good planning practices are:

- Develop (and use) an implementation plan that is:
  —Developed—and committed to—by the project team.
  —Kept current.
- Use proven processes tailored to your project.
  —Systems engineering methodology.
  —Software development methodology.
  —Hardware development methodology.
  —Reliability and quality methodology.
- Manage the business and technical baselines.
  —Keep participants informed of the evolving baseline.

The project team may feel they have already "managed" the risks by creating the initial opportunity/risk management plan. But opportunity and risk management is ongoing—it evolves as the proj-

Since many opportunities and risks are discovered in the decomposition process, it is impossible to identify all opportunities and their risks at the outset.

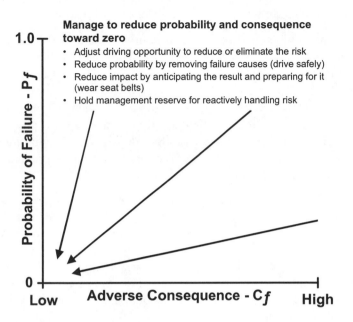

Figure 13.2   Risk management objectives—driven by the desire not to fail.

ect proceeds. Plans must be updated as new opportunities and risks are identified and the impacts are evaluated.

Opportunities and risks are interrelated and the risks must be justified by the opportunity pursued. The following eight-step opportunity and risk management process justifies decisions based on expected value analysis:

1. Identify the opportunities and risks.
   - What opportunities are available? What benefits?
   - What are their risks? What consequences?
   - Describe with "If . . . , then . . ." statements.
   - Group by like categories, such as funding, safety, schedule, and so on.
2. Assess both probability and impact. Forecast the expected value.
3. Prioritize according to expected project value.
4. Develop candidate management actions to enhance opportunities and mitigate risks.
5. Estimate the cost of both immediate and contingent actions.

Each opportunity and its risk should be evaluated as a whole, taking into account relative probabilities and offsetting benefits and consequences.

6. Compare changes to expected value against action costs (Mitigation Leverage).
7. Decide on actions required and obtain concurrence.
8. Document and incorporate decisions in all planning.

Some project managers and executives make a distinction between eliminating risks versus insuring against them (such as liability insurance) or deciding on an action versus planning a contingency. In our view, these are simply alternative cases of opportunity and risk management and need to be evaluated as such. For example, we consider insurance as one possible mitigating action for product liability risks. The examples that follow demonstrate techniques that are unique to opportunity and risk management. Opportunity and risk management actions fall into four categories:

1. *Accept the opportunity and its risks* with no exceptional action. We use this approach when we cross a street at a crosswalk with no exceptional actions to enhance the experience or reduce the risk.
2. *Avoid the risk,* which can often be accomplished by adjusting the opportunity to eliminate the risk cause. Driving carefully within the speed limit with seat belts fastened is an example of risk avoidance.
3. *Retain the opportunity and transfer the unacceptable portion of the risk* to a third party usually with only a small effect on the expected value of the opportunity. This is commonly achieved by insurance such as collision insurance and homeowners insurance.
4. *Mitigate the risk and retain the opportunity.* Reduce the probability or consequences of the risk to an acceptable level by one or more actions. In technical projects, redundant circuits and high reliability parts are possible mitigation actions.

IDENTIFYING OPPORTUNITIES AND THEIR RISKS

A major challenge of the project manager is team motivation. The "risk list" is a demoralizing force as the team engages in ongoing discussions to identify all the things that could go wrong. As Rita Mulcahy phrased it in her book *Risk Management,* "opportunities should be identified to balance out the negative occurrences (risks) as well as to take advantage of additional benefits of the project."[2] Mulcahy recognizes the negative morale that can result from incessant risk management viewed exclusive of the creating opportunities.

The "managing opportunities and their risks" approach maintains harmony and balances the evaluations. A risk that key personnel may not be available when required sounds serious. If the real situation is that the best supplier in the country has agreed to do the work (opportunity), but their best personnel may not be available (risk), then a key personnel clause in the contract may be sufficient to mitigate the risk. Having the opportunity and risk tied together puts the problem in context and balance.

On the Boeing 777 development, Boeing engineers wanted to seize the opportunity of using aluminum-lithium to save weight, gain payload capacity, and maximize fuel economy (opportunity). However, machining the material caused cosmetic cracks that would have to be explained in their maintenance manuals (risk). Discussions were held at the highest levels of management to evaluate the value trade-offs and impact to the 777 program. Aluminum-lithium was rejected as too risky to the market image of Boeing. It was a significant project-value-based judgment, as well as a vivid case of systems thinking.

> To evaluate risk without regard to the driving opportunity is almost meaningless and could be irresponsible.

A simple approach is to reward those who identify opportunities and risks. A cost-effective technique is a prominent posting (perhaps outside a manager's door) of all the opportunities and their risks in a manager's domain. A brief statement of what actions will be taken (or if no action is to be taken, why not) and who has the action should be included in the listing. The listing has powerful effects. It:

- Shows that the manager is serious about pursuing and managing creativity.
- Rewards participants (printed recognition is an effective, inexpensive reward).
- Stimulates others to think of opportunities.
- Precludes redundant efforts.
- Prompts others to offer suggestions for how to mitigate identified risks.

It can be helpful to subdivide the myriad of possible opportunities and risks into categories. Opportunity categories are strategic and tactical, like deciding what business to be in (strategic) and then pursuing the business (tactical). Figure 13.3 illustrates examples in each category. Using emerging technology or new development tools are examples of tactical opportunities that bring with them the risk of unsuccessful implementation.

Risk categories include risks to project implementation and risks to, of, and by the product, such as lack of sufficient funding (implementation) and incorporating dangerous toxins (product). Figure 13.4

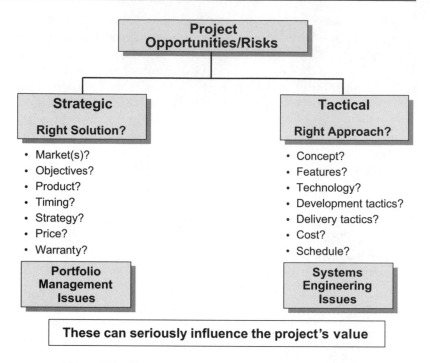

Figure 13.3   The two categories of opportunities and risks.

illustrates examples in each category. This is only a representative list—all relevant areas must be considered. Each of these areas should be evaluated in the context of the causing opportunity.

Identify the opportunities and risks for each project-cycle phase by systematically applying the appropriate techniques based on analysis, planning, and history. Techniques based on analysis include:

- Opportunity and risk checklists (the categories and lists in Figures 13.3 and 13.4 offer a beginning checklist).

- Rules of thumb and standards of performance.

- System decomposition and critical items (Vee off-core analysis).

- Hazard analysis.

- Failure modes analysis.

- Interviews with experts.

There is a wide variety of texts available that provide insight and checklists on identifying risks having to do with project administration, that is, risks associated with schedule, critical path, funding, resources, personnel, and so on. Tom Kendrick's book, *Identifying and*

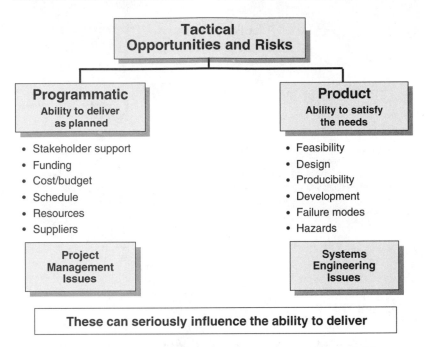

Figure 13.4 The two categories of tactical opportunities and risks.

Managing Project Risk,[3] and Rita Mulcahy's book, *Risk Management,*[4] are excellent references.

Figure 13.5 illustrates three areas of risks relative to the opportunity of product solution creation on development projects.

The first are "risks to the solution," such as shipping and handling. We are all very familiar with the use of foam popcorn and bubble wrap to mitigate the handling risk when shipping a fragile product. This category also includes the need for contamination control in semiconductor manufacturing, in pharmaceutical development and production, and in spacecraft development. In secure projects, security risks are critical and risk management must ensure the project's opportunity is not compromised by inadvertent disclosure. A recent mishap, when the NOAA N Prime $200 million satellite fell off of its tilt stand and crashed to the floor, is an excellent example of the handling risks not being properly managed. In this case, operators bypassed good workmanship practices and did not follow established procedures.

The second category is "risks of the solution," which become imbedded within the product only to surface later and cause project failure. There are many famous illustrations of this type of poorly

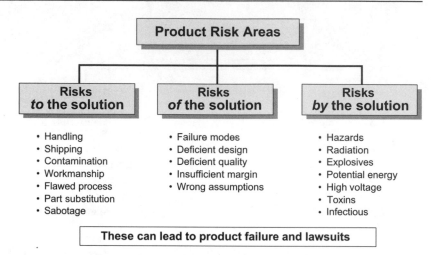

Figure 13.5   Areas of product risk.

managed risk. The Hubble telescope, the space shuttle *Challenger*, the Ford Pinto, the submarine *Scorpion*, and all the vehicles and other products that are the subject of product recalls were deployed with flaws built in to their products. Good design and verification practices should have caught and fixed every one of these flaws before first deployment. However, other stakeholders may have overriding priorities. A tragic case of this opportunity/risk relationship occurred in the 1970s. Lee Iacocca, head of the new Ford Pinto car development, was committed to pursuing the opportunity to enter a new market segment in competition with Japan and Germany for a low-cost car. He mandated 2,000 pounds and $2,000 as the value criteria that had to be met with no exceptions. It was soon discovered that the car would explode on rear impact because of gas tank location and design. To address that risk, the company could have made an $11 per car modification. However, they elected to accept the risk and pay for injury and deaths because the liability cost would be less than the tank modification cost. This unfortunate decision was based solely on a cost of the opportunity versus the cost of the consequences and resulted in several hundred lost lives.

The third product category is "risks by the solution" where the solution contains risks that can cause injury to the product or to those using the product. Nuclear power plants, radiation benches, weapons, and hospitals are all solutions that can cause injury to the innocent. Hospitals now shorten rehabilitation time to quickly exit patients from the potentially infectious environment of the hospital.

All of these areas must be considered in opportunity and risk planning in order to achieve a high probability of success.

Hazard analysis is a risk identification technique used to ensure all system hazards have been identified and anticipated in plans. Once identified, all hazards to personnel and to the system are either accepted, reduced by design, or contained by practice. For example, a high-pressure gas hazard can be reduced by designing the equipment with a large safety factor. Alternatively, the risk of explosion can be contained by placing sand bags or other protection between the hazard and personnel.

Failure Modes and Effects (and Criticality) Analysis (FMEA and FMECA) are risk identification techniques used to ensure all significant failure modes have been identified and anticipated. These techniques employ the following:

- Selection of a ranking or prioritizing scheme for project failure modes concern and attention.
- Identification of all single-point failure modes and ranking of them.
- Analysis of additional failure modes and the resultant operational effects.
- Determination of those failure modes requiring elimination, redundancy, and/or increased reliability.
- Implementation of the corrective action.

When ranking FMEA risks, it is helpful to have clear categories. Consider the following category examples:

Category #1—Loss of life.

Category #1R—Loss of life but the mode has redundancy.

Category #2—Mission fails.

Category #2R—Mission fails but mode has redundancy.

Category #3—Mission is compromised.

Category #3R—Mission is compromised but failure mode has redundancy.

Other effective risk identification techniques are usually based on planning and on past lessons learned. Scenario planning is a "low-tech" technique for "visualizing" opportunities and risks, and is useful in project planning judgment. It consists of querying:

- "What if . . . ?" followed by ". . . then what?"
- What opportunities might be pursued?
- What could go wrong?

This technique can also be used to build a decision tree based on broad market and economic trends: "If the economy does this, I'll do that." These scenarios can often identify important assumptions that traditional forecasting tends to miss. It represents another systematic way to consider future possibilities. Planning techniques also include:

- Project network interaction analysis.
- Critical path content and near critical path analysis.
- Schedule slack adequacy and position.

The techniques based on history are the most natural to apply. They include:

- Similar efforts and their lessons learned,
- Expert interviews,
- Technical surveys, and
- Development test results.

Generalized historical templates can work well in some industries. For example, construction projects are highly repetitive compared with research and development. Because the work patterns of one project may be similar to selected ones from the past, the same types of risks are likely to occur and lessons learned are especially relevant.

Alternatively, misperceptions or misinterpretations about prior projects will sometimes lead project teams to overestimate their ability to control future risks or to exploit future opportunities. It has often been left up to project leaders to identify risk based on their own experiences and perception of the situation. Such projects were at the mercy of whatever their experiences and perceptions were. As one engineer put it, "The alligator that was the closest to you was the one you worried about the most. You didn't look at the other 'gators in the swamp, even though they were bigger and meaner." A common misperception is that successful experiences with simpler projects scale to complex ones. Every new project has to be analyzed in detail to understand those unique properties that distinguish it from its predecessors. This needs to be an ongoing team effort, and it relies heavily on lessons learned.

> Not only is each project unique, but the uniqueness is often the source of its risk.

ASSESSING PROBABILITY AND IMPACT

A goal of identifying and anticipating all opportunities and risks would be overwhelming. The result of anticipating every possible opportunity and risk could bury the team in questionable information and turn the project into a hand-wringing exercise. This dramatizes the importance of prioritization.

There are a number of sophisticated and powerful tools available for opportunity and risk analysis, such as decision trees and Monte

Carlo simulations. These tools and others are described in texts such as Clemen's book, *Making Hard Decisions*,[5] and Tom Kendrick's book, *Identifying and Managing Risk*.[6]

However, for most decisions we face in a project environment a much simpler technique (called expected value) can be used, and it is described as follows.

The expected value (EV), sometimes called weighted value, expected outcome, or risk factor, is a technique for quantitatively comparing both opportunities and risks. It provides the project manager with a measure for sizing management reserves for investment and protection. The EV of opportunity and risk is equal to the probability of occurrence multiplied by the impact. For example:

Probability of occurrence of an opportunity $= 0.6$
Benefit of the opportunity $= \$720,000$ if it does occur
Therefore, expected value $= (0.6) \times (\$720,000)$
$= \$432,000$

Expected value provides a method for quantitatively comparing both opportunities and risks. The primary use of EV is to prioritize potential actions. When applying EV, be sure to use consistent units. For the purposes of prioritizing, "burn rate" (usually expressed as a daily expense rate) may be used to measure schedule impact in dollars. The following is an example of prioritizing two risks involving potential schedule slip and burn rate.

> When applying expected value, common sense and good judgment are required because the calculations, usually based on subjective information, will have low accuracy.

Risk 1 Expected Value

$(0.8) \times (\$100,000) = \$80,000$

Risk 2 Expected Value

$(0.4) \times (\$60,000) + (0.4) \times (45\text{-day slip}) = \$24,000$ (cost) plus 18-days (schedule)

Assuming a \$2,000/day burn rate, a 45-day slip would cost \$90,000

Expected value, on a cost basis,
$= \$24,000 + (0.4) \times (\$90,000)$
$= \$60,000$

——— *PMBOK® Guide* ———
The *PMBOK® Guide* Sec 11.3 *Qualitative Risk Analysis* and 11.4 *Quantitative Risk Analysis* differentiate qualitative risk analysis from quantitative risk analysis. Qualitative prioritizes risks and quantitative is numerical analysis of the risk effect on the project.

On the basis of this analysis, Risk 1 should be of higher priority than Risk 2. The risk can be managed by influencing the *probability* of occurrence and/or the *impact* of the outcome.

A complete listing of the possible influencing activities with their associated costs should be developed (Figure 13.6). From this, you can decide on the appropriate actions. There are basically two types of actions to consider: causative or preventive, and contingent.

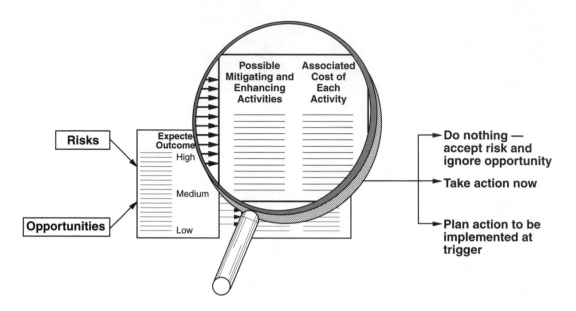

Figure 13.6　Management of opportunity and risk actions.

Causative actions enhance opportunity expected value and preventive actions reduce risk expected value. Contingent actions are the same as causative or preventive actions, except that no action other than preparation is taken until a predetermined trigger initiates the action.

Causative and Preventive Actions	*Contingent Actions*
Adjusting the opportunity to reduce the risk.	Red-line limits in test procedures (terminate test if exceeded).
Redundancy to eliminate single-point failure modes.	Establish thresholds for variance analysis and corrective action (triggers a focused review).
Higher quality to increase reliability.	Planned tactical changes contingent on a competitor's performance.
Increased margins to improve safety.	Unsolicited proposal based on competitor's poor performance.
Enforced use of common software languages and	

Causative and Preventive Actions	*Contingent Actions*
standards across subcontractor and prime team.	Red-line limit triggered change of test conditions.
Expert review to ensure best approach.	Technical performance measurement triggered weight reduction.
Overtime to shorten critical path.	Circuit breaker interruption of power overload.
Overdesign for possible future growth (preplanned product improvement).	

The cost effectiveness of candidate actions can be evaluated using mitigation leverage or enhancement leverage factors defined as follows. The leverage values can be used for comparison and as an aid in action selection.

DECIDING ON REQUIRED ACTIONS AND INCORPORATING THEM INTO THE PLAN

$$\text{Enhancement Leverage} = \frac{\text{EV after} - \text{EV before}}{\text{Benefit enhancement cost}}$$

$$\text{Mitigation Leverage} = \frac{\text{EV before} - \text{EV after}}{\text{Risk mitigation cost}}$$

It is often impractical to accurately estimate the probabilities of occurrence and impacts of potential events. In these cases, decisions may be based on a qualitative assessment for both the probability of occurrence and the benefit or consequence. In the sample risk decision matrix in Table 13.1, based on qualitative assessments, carrying a spare car ignition key in your wallet or purse is a high-impact, low-probability instance (for some, a high-probability instance).

All opportunity and risk management actions must be incorporated into the project plan and kept current (Figure 13.7). Carrying a spare key for the car you sold two years ago is an example of an excellent risk management decision turned bad through neglect (what's worse, you are confidant that you're secure until you discover the wrong key in a crisis).

On cost-reimbursable contracts, it is wise to obtain customer concurrence with opportunity and risk management actions because the customer will likely be paying for them.

—— *PMBOK® Guide* ——
The *PMBOK® Guide* Sec 11.5.2 *Risk Response Planning* identifies three strategies for negative risks:

1. Avoid.
2. Transfer.
3. Mitigate.

and three strategies for positive risks:

1. Exploit.
2. Share.
3. Enhance.

Table 13.1 Sample Risk Decision Matrix

		Low	Medium	High
Probability of Failure	**High**	**Establish contingency plans** *Status regularly*	**Establish contingency plans** *Act immediately if cost effective*	**Unacceptable** *Take immediate action*
	Medium	**Acceptable, Do Nothing** *Status regularly*	**Establish contingency plans** *Status frequently*	**Establish contingency plans** *Act immediately if cost effective*
	Low	**Acceptable, Do Nothing** *Status occasionally*	**Establish contingency plans** *Status regularly*	**Establish contingency plans** *Act immediately if cost effective*
		Low	Medium	High
		Adverse Consequence		

To be effective, this opportunity and risk management process should occur throughout the project cycle and at all levels of architecture decomposition. The resultant management actions must be:

- Overt, conscious decisions;
- Supported by justifiable rationale;
- Incorporated in the plan; and
- Implemented through work authorizations and subcontracts.

RELATING OPPORTUNITIES AND THEIR RISKS TO THE PROJECT CYCLE

As we emphasized earlier, opportunity and risk management is ongoing—it evolves as the project evolves. Perhaps one of the greatest project risks is not following the project plan (updated, as necessary). Not following the plan for the final ascent is the direct cause

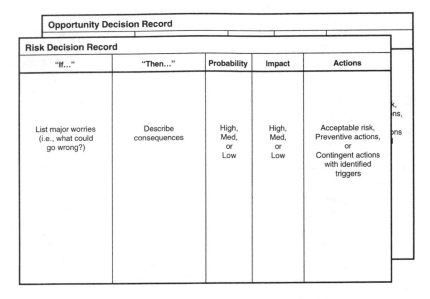

Figure 13.7 Opportunity and risk decision records.

of the fatal, tragic end of Rob Hall's Mt. Everest expedition in 1996 causing the death of 11 men and women.[7]

The sources and nature of opportunities and risks vary from period to period and from phase to phase. For example, the major risks during the study period may be the instability of the requirements, lack of understanding of the user problem, and funding, whereas training, logistics, and supplier quality may loom as the largest risks during the implementation period.

The Vee model provides a visual basis for identifying and managing opportunities and risks during both architecture and entity development. Figures 7.11 and 7.12 in Chapter 7 introduced the idea of using off-core activities for opportunity and risk investigation and management. Figure 13.8 lists critical issues to be studied off core during the user requirements understanding phase—an acknowledgement that users (or the organization representing the users) often do not have a clear understanding of their needs. Figure 13.8 also details the early portion of the core of the Vee, starting with the statement of user need. The diagram highlights the off-core studies that provide user requirements clarification and understanding.

Opportunities to be pursued may include innovations that extend the product's useful life through planned technology upgrades or value enhancements that reduce the cost or broaden the market.

Our personal insurance policies and the spare tires we carry in our cars are everyday examples of risk management.

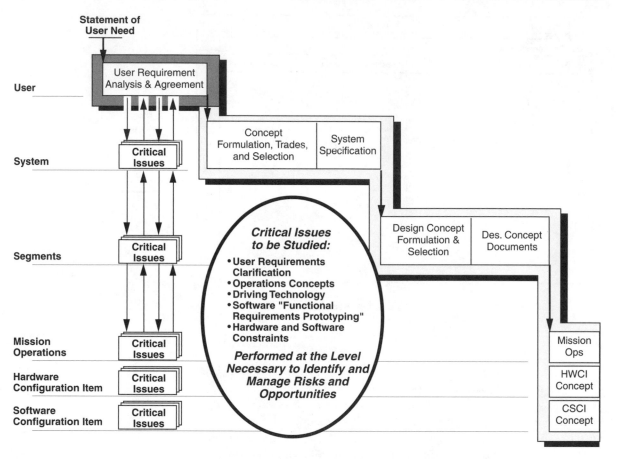

Figure 13.8   Critical issues of the user requirements definition phase.

An example of the latter occurred several years ago on a client's project to develop a new calculator for the U.S. financial community. As part of the off-core user requirements clarification, a meeting was held with a group of financial analysts. The users requested adding a button to the keyboard for dividing the displayed result by 365, the U.S. standard for interest-bearing days. This feature was an opportunity for a competitive edge and was adopted. Still another opportunity occurred soon thereafter that more than doubled the available market. A development team member suggested reconfiguring the keyboard to also accommodate the 360-day European standard. The change was easily accomplished at this early stage, but would have had a major impact after coding or manufacturing had started.

Off-core studies usually begin early in the project cycle and may be very simple investigations requiring only a few hours to explore opportunities and to ensure that risks are acceptable. However, if the solution is challenging the state of art, the studies themselves can be very involved projects requiring years of effort (the Reagan era "Star Wars" space defense initiative project is an opportunity exploration example).

> Off-core studies do not seek a final solution, but rather a demonstration that at least one solution is feasible.

Studies may be analytical or they may require development of a software or hardware model to resolve system capabilities, constraints, and technology or integration issues. These models may need to go to the lowest level of detail in selected areas. One example is creating a software algorithm to prove that a data search of a large, distributed database can be performed within a specified period. The authors were involved in developing a database management system that could perform a complex search of six million entries in three seconds. The off-core feasibility studies focused on functionality rather than performance, resulting in an algorithm that was successfully tested on 100,000 entries. Unfortunately, the project failed when the fully implemented system required up to one minute to perform a complete search (even though the typical search met the three-second limit).

> Projects that fall short of user expectations, even though they surpass the state of the art, are not likely to succeed.

After completion of early project phases, it is often necessary to revisit the decisions as external events change or as new insights are discovered through off-core studies in lower level detail. Calendar time and solution maturity move from left to right, so the revisiting process does not occur by going back up the core of the Vee but rather by moving vertically to the system specification update, concept update, or user requirements update.

The functionality that the user expects must be flowed down to, and responded to, by entities of the system. Piece parts and lines of code must be provided in order to complete those entities. At each of the subtier levels, there may be critical issues that should be explored to minimize the risk that, when these details are finally designed and verified, they fall short of the expected functionality or performance. Other critical issues include the expansion of opportunity and risk evaluation to include affordability assessment, environmental impact, system risk, failure modes, and hazard analysis.

The upward and downward opportunity and risk iterations continue through the design-to (PDR) and build-to (CDR) gates. During the decomposition and definition process, major areas of risk are identified and approaches are developed to manage them. As shown in Figure 13.9, it is not necessary that the same solution to a given problem be followed throughout. As the project moves from

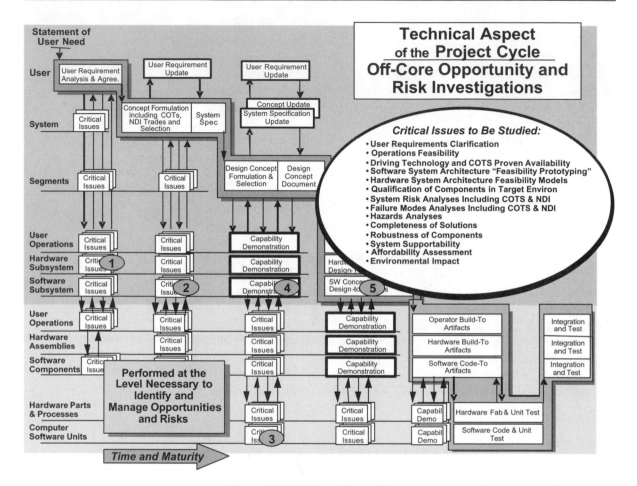

Figure 13.9   Off-core alternatives.

phase to phase, a new and better approach may be conceived. Consider the detailed view of the off-core studies illustrated in Figure 13.9. The following five steps correspond to the numbers in ovals on the diagram:

1. During the User Requirements Definition Phase, it may be necessary to descend to the subsystem level to verify that there is at least one way to meet the requirements, and a hardware solution is found.

2. As concepts are evaluated during the Concept Definition Phase, off-core studies reveal an opportunity to perform the function (in number one) using software, rather than hardware, yielding a more flexible design approach.

3. During segment concept definition studies, concern is raised about the risk of inadequate software performance, so the routine must be modeled to provide confidence.
4. When the software unit performance is proven acceptable, the software subsystem is modeled and opportunities to shape the design for future product enhancements are explored.
5. In the next phase, the software concept is defined in appropriate detail to create the design-to documentation and to put it under baseline control.

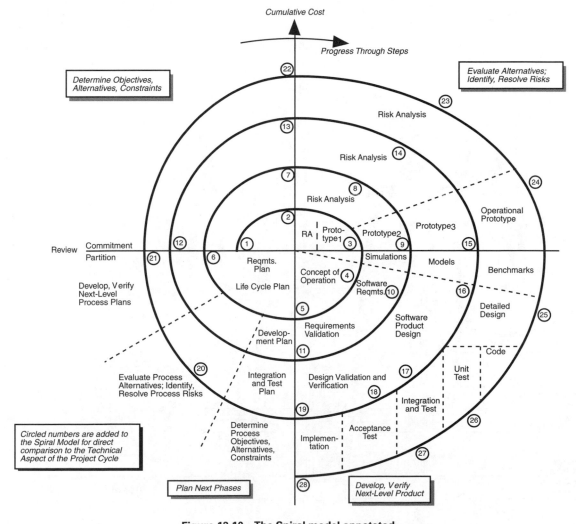

Figure 13.10 The Spiral model annotated.

There is no requirement for the concept at step 2 to mature into the baseline at step 5. On the other hand, there could be an iterative evolutionary development of a concept from step 2 to elaboration at step 4 to a baseline at step 5.

The Spiral Model

The two Vee models provide abstract views of both the architecture and entity development of complex solutions. Another popular view of entity software development is the Spiral model discussed in Chapter 7. While the spiral is basically a sound model, it tends to obscure the need for continuous attention to opportunity and risk management all the way through solution development (rather than just prior to concept definition). In fact, the Spiral and the Vee models

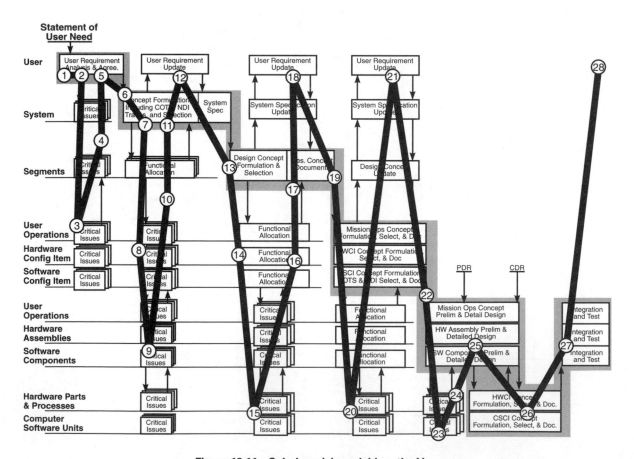

Figure 13.11   Spiral model overlaid on the Vee.

are two perspectives of the same process. Figure 7.8 shows the Spiral as Boehm created it. Figure 13.10 adds numbers along the spiral for reference. Figure 13.11 shows the spiral overlaid on the Entity Vee, illustrating their similarity. Note that the Spiral provides almost no detail in the integration, verification, and validation sequence.

APPROACH TO THE USE OF COTS AND NDI

When a project solution incorporates Commercial-Off-The-Shelf (COTS) products or Nondevelopment Items (NDI) precluding the need for an engineering design, the Vee for COTS used in the system would descend only to the COTS or NDI component level (Figure 13.12). However, off-core critical issue studies below the component level are required to investigate capability, to ensure interface compatibility, and to determine required modifications to achieve desired performance (remember modified COTS is no longer COTS).

In one example, a project team relied on traditional high-reliability piece part and component procurement to achieve the necessary reliability levels. According to the project manager, "commercial diodes, transistors, and integrated circuits were prescreened prior to selection (approximately 4% of all diodes, 3% of all transistors, and 1% of

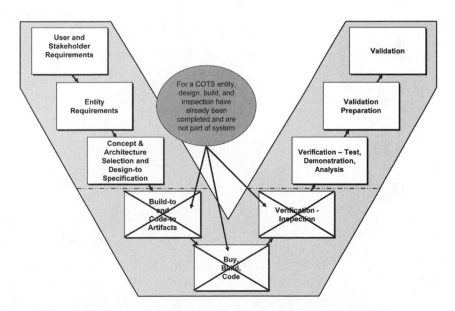

Figure 13.12   The full-depth Vee is not required for a COTS entity.

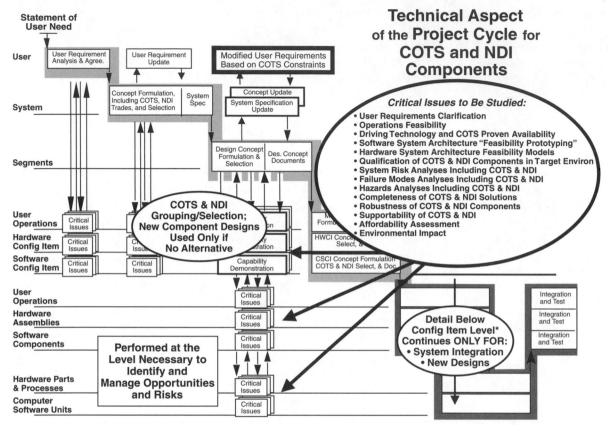

Figure 13.13   Critical issues to be studied for commercial off-the-shelf (COTS) and nondevelopment items (NDI).

all integrated circuits failed the screening test). . . . Sensor reliability analysis was conducted using (traditional) reliability standards to identify potentially weak elements for replacement."[8] These risk management activities are the off-core critical issue studies shown in Figure 13.13.

COTS and NDI—Proper Use Leads to Success

When asked to describe the top *success factors* contributing to project success, three successful project managers replied with the following factors:

1. Empowerment, where the project manager has full authority and control (executive management didn't meddle). The project manager should control the procurement process, as well; the contracting officer or contracts administrator should be responsible to the project manager.
2. Leadership.
3. Full willingness to seize opportunities, such as making effective use of COTS and NDI, but insistent on understanding the case-by-case risks involved in doing so.
4. Managerial, technical, and financial skills and motivation.
5. Burning desire to succeed, coupled with a passion for quality.
6. Collocated team (including all the engineers and technicians) for all essential functions.
7. An environment that rewards open and direct communications.
8. Preference for testing rather than analysis during development. Build and test an engineering model.
9. Reduced formal controls (on component traceability, quality, and documentation) to the minimum acceptable—based on risk.
10. A small team with clear responsibilities.

A comparison of these points with the operating procedures for the skunk works, a highly efficient aircraft development organization, shows a significant commonality.[9] The operating rules are consistent with the *essence* of good, traditional project management. The reason they succeeded is not that they abandoned obsolete processes, but rather that they tailored and streamlined the project management and systems engineering processes to their needs.

In addition, one team had a well-defined quantitative risk analysis process. They used Monte Carlo analyses to provide data for risk management decisions. Although the team did not express it this way, the details of Figures 13.12 and 13.13 apply here.

The BUYER Project

The multimillion-dollar BUYER project is a COTS software system to provide procurement support throughout a medium-sized commercial organization.

After attempting unsuccessfully to build a homegrown system in the 1980s, a decision was made to purchase a COTS product and tailor it to the organization's needs. Three unsuccessful COTS attempts over a decade led to project termination in 1997. Had the project team used the concepts in Figures 13.12 and 13.13, problems would have been revealed earlier and more systematically instead of being a continuous string of surprises. A list of lessons learned was compiled, from which the following points have been extracted:

- Poor requirements lead to poor plans.
- For COTS software projects, use incremental, phased development.
- For COTS software, pick the product, *and then* pick a contractor based on its experience with *that* COTS product.
- Use of COTS products may require performance compromise.
- A COTS product is not really COTS if the vendor is modifying it.
- COTS software is not really COTS if it doesn't run on your target hardware and system software.
- Involve the user in the development process.

In the first two attempts, the BUYER project failed because the selected COTS packages did not meet user requirements; in an environment of continuously changing user requirements, however, no development approach could have succeeded. In the third attempt to produce a system, the team finally got the necessary management support to baseline a stable set of solution-independent user requirements.

The last iteration of the BUYER project failed because, unknown to the team, key software that ran successfully in a commercial UNIX environment was only available in an alpha version for the new target environment (Windows NT). The problem was *not* the use of COTS, but rather the incomplete implementation of systems engineering. The project team jumped on an attractive COTS solution without performing off-core studies (Figure 13.13) to identify and mitigate the risks associated with the Windows NT opportunity.

Intelligent, hard-working people devoted years to make the BUYER project a success to no avail. They certainly displayed a burning desire to succeed (the fifth success factor). In fact, the BUYER team did most things right, and they got close to meeting all operational requirements. But, as the saying goes, "close only counts in hand grenades and horseshoes." The BUYER team simply failed to implement proven systems engineering and project management principles.

The Therac-25 Project

Therac-25 is a computerized radiation therapy machine used to treat cancer patients. It was first used in commercial hospitals in 1982. The goal of the manufacturer was to replace two older models with a new design that was more useful to the hospital because it combined both low- and high-energy modes of operation into a single unit. It was also designed to be cheaper to produce and operate. The Therac-25 project used Nondevelopment Item (NDI) software in its design. This project is particularly relevant in considering the balance of opportunities and risks, because the risks in using NDI are so often overlooked.

An excellent study of the cause of the Therac-25 failures reported, "between June 1985 and January 1987, six known accidents involved massive overdoses by the Therac-25—with resultant deaths and serious injuries. They have been described as the worst series of radiation accidents in the 35-year history of medical accelerators."[10] This 24-page article should be mandatory reading for any systems engineer involved in reuse of hardware or software for new applications.

The Therac-25 development used software from two earlier models (Therac-6 and Therac-20). Both earlier systems used the PDP-11 computers (as did the Therac-25), and both older systems had been in use for a decade without problems. Selected software was used without modification in the new machine. The developer did not recognize that this "previously developed product" was not being used in exactly the same way, however. Both the Therac-6 and Therac-20 models had software *and hardware* safety interlocks. The new Therac-25 had only software safety interlocks to save cost. After the Therac-25 accident investigation was completed, a reexamination of the Therac-20 showed that the old software had exactly the same failure mode but the hardware interlock intervened to prevent the hazard.

Leveson and her coauthor highlighted important lessons about software reuse: "A naïve assumption is often made that reusing software (NDI) or using commercial off-the-shelf (COTS) software increases safety because the software has been exercised extensively. Reusing software modules does not guarantee safety in the new system . . . and sometimes leads to awkward and dangerous designs . . . Rewriting the entire software to get a clean and simple design may be safer in many cases."[11] In addition, they found that, along with other problems, good systems engineering was lacking in the Therac-25 design and development, and proven software engineering practices and processes were not followed. *There was no effective peer review during the Therac-25 system development phase.*

The Therac development team used previously developed software to save development cost, to save development time, and to create a better product (the same goals sought by advocates of "better, faster, cheaper"). In this case, faster and cheaper did not lead to better.

Product Reliability

How good does the COTS product have to be? A score of 96 percent (success rate for high reliability diodes screened from a commercial line) is an excellent test score in school, but is it satisfactory for your project? Consider Mikel Harry's assessment of the consequences of an even tighter 99 percent successful performance requirement:

- 20,000 lost articles of mail per hour.
- Unsafe drinking water almost 15 minutes each day.
- 5,000 incorrect surgical operations per week.
- Two short or long landings at most major airports each day.
- 200,000 wrong drug prescriptions each year.
- No electricity for almost 7 hours each month.[12]

Most consumer COTS products fail to some degree, whether we talk about new cars or new Microsoft Office applications. The issue for systems engineers to resolve is whether or not the failures are of importance to their project. Most people would refuse medical treatment from a device or medical system that had a reliability level equivalent to current commercial software products sold for use on desktop computers.

The COTS product being reviewed for a specific application may not be suitable for its new use as it comes off the shelf. Systems engineering has the obligation to evaluate the risks and to decide on the appropriate actions. As the Therac-25 accidents revealed, assessing the suitability of a COTS or NDI solution is nontrivial.

OPPORTUNITY AND RISK ELEMENT EXERCISE

Make a list of all the risk mitigation actions that you personally practice in the normal conduct of your life. Categories for consideration are: insurance (life, homeowners, liability, collision, comprehensive, umbrella, etc.), insurance deductible provisions, security (alarm systems, motion detector lights, alertness, etc.), personal safety (life vests, seat belts, roll bars, hard hats, etc.), and many others. For each of these mitigation actions, identify the opportunity that you embraced that forced you to incur the risk, the risk mitigation, and the residual risk following your selected mitigation.

Action	Opportunity	Residual
Wear seat belts	Use car as transportation	Injury
Dental insurance	Healthy teeth	Exposure above coverage limits

People who prefer to live in potential disaster areas, such as flood, forest fire, earthquake, tornado, and hurricane zones accept the risks and the associated costs of storm shelters and insurance. Other risks are associated with lifestyles, such as smoking or commuting in areas with high accident rates.

An interesting exercise is to calculate the mitigation leverage for all of your insurance policy provisions, such as automobile (collision, liability, and comprehensive coverages), household (hazard provisions), and life insurance (smoking and other lifestyle factors).

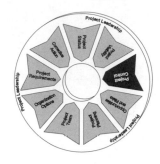

MANAGEMENT ELEMENT 6

14

PROJECT CONTROL

—— *PMBOK® Guide* ——
This chapter is consistent with *PMBOK® Guide* Sec 3.2 *Monitoring and Controlling Process Group,* Sec 4.5 *Monitor and Control Project Work,* and Sec 4.6 *Integrated Change Control.*

—— *INCOSE* ——
This chapter is consistent with *INCOSE Handbook* Sec 5.7 *Control Process,* Sec 5.9 *Configuration Management Process,* Sec 6.3 *Technical Project Control,* and Sec 7.6 *Quality Management Process.*

You can't manage cost and schedule without managing the technical content. It's where the time and money go.

When launched, Intelsat 6 rocketed to its parking orbit as planned. When signaled to separate from its booster and to further rocket up to synchronous orbit, nothing happened. The signal was sent, but the wire receiving the signal was not the correct one and the correct wire did not get the signal. The failure review board concluded that, "The hardware guys made a change and thought they had communicated that change to the software side of the house." But the communication breakdown occurred because an established change procedure was not used, the official said.[1]

To correct this situation, a space shuttle complete with an astronaut space walk was sent to retrieve the satellite and bring it back to Earth. Then a new Titan booster, with updated software, was used to put Intelsat 6 into the correct orbit. The cost of skipping the change procedure (about 30 minutes of meeting time) was over one billion dollars. This is but one dramatic case of high-tech systems failing for low-tech reasons. Unfortunately, over the years there have been an unacceptably large number of high-tech failures for low-tech reasons and the rate does not seem to be decreasing. Technical project control is about eliminating these types of errors and doing the job right the first time.

There is a fear among scientists and engineers that project controls such as standards and process will inhibit their right to creativity, which is their main purpose in life. Their fears are well founded as spurious and random creativity frequently causes projects to overrun and miss important deadlines. Successful development projects are rooted in efficient solution realization from user requirements development through deployment and operations. Project controls are designed to manage the ongoing creativity such that it contributes to what is needed and at the same time does not undermine what has already been baselined. This chapter is about focusing creativity such that it contributes to the success of the project by developing the right solution right the first time and does so with maximum efficiency thereby conserving cost and schedule.

> "A good system of control helps prevent undesirable surprises; it provides for turning the 'lemon' into lemonade."
>
> Henri Fayol[2]

In 1916, Henri Fayol recognized that project control is both proactive and reactive. "Control activities provide an opportunity for people to take the initiative in planning against deviations [proactive], to head off forces that might cause a deviation, to make corrections very quickly [reactive] when a deviation does occur, and finally, to redirect the firm to capitalize on a deviation when correction is less feasible."[3] Fayol referred to the final alternative as "making lemonade."

PROJECT CONTROL IS PROCESS CONTROL

> A tracking function is not a control function and can lead to project failure by giving the false impression that project controls are in place.

Most project management texts describe project control as comparing actuals to plan (status). While monitoring and tracking of cost and schedule data is one step toward reactive control, it is hardly project control without designing and implementing the proper control systems in the first place and responding with appropriate corrective action to significant variances.

We define project *control* as both proactive and reactive process control, a dual system designed and implemented to reduce risk:

> Project control needs to be proactive and reactive and seldom inactive. Contrary to popular opinion, reactive management is essential in managing projects.

- Proactive baseline control.
- Reactive performance control.
- Proactive control of the project plan and changes to the plan.
- Reactive control of variances in performance to the project plan.
- Management techniques that help ensure that results happen as planned, and that results not planned do not happen.
- Corrective action taken when unplanned results do happen.

This section deals with the functions of *defining* and *establishing* the five essential elements common to all control systems (Figure 14.1). They are:

1. *Things to be controlled.* The function that must be controlled to a standard of performance.
2. *Control standard.* The approved standard of performance.

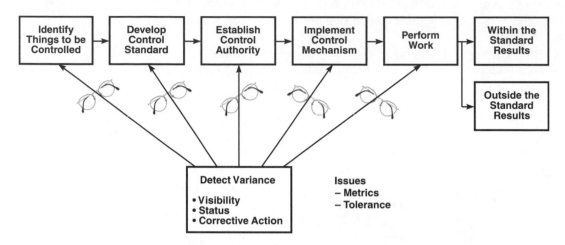

Figure 14.1   Project control is process control.

3. *Control authority.* The person or organization authorized to impose the standard and grant exceptions.

4. *Control mechanism.* The forum or technique that measures compliance to the standard.

5. *Variance indication.* The identification of flaws in the control process or violations of the standard.

Typical factors to be controlled:

Project baselines, business, cost, and technical.

Environment, physical and business.

Funding, amount and timing.

Hardware development process.

Manufacturing process.

Materials.

Parts.

Personnel conduct.

Quality.

Reliability.

Safety, both product and personnel.

Security.

Software development environment.

Software development process.

Test.

Time recording.

Work standards.

Control systems are designed to control achievement of the project plan. Of high importance are those controls required to manage significant risk and process-sensitive methods such as bonding agents and other processes where the environment and contamination can affect the quality of the result. Mature, well-established processes should be continually improved to achieve even higher consistency of results. New processes may require frequent audits to verify that the results are as expected. As the processes mature and are proven to be consistently reliable, the audits can be reduced and possibly eliminated. Examples of control functions are shown in Table 14.1.

Variance control (Figure 14.2) is designed to detect practices or performance considered substandard. Variances can result from flawed implementation of standards or deviations from the standards. This corrective action system relies on the management elements of Visibility, Status, and Corrective Action to close the reactive process control loop. All three are required for reactive control. We address each of these elements in separate chapters.

Control examples within the business baseline include schedule, funding, changes, personnel quality, headcount level, key personnel, work practices, and ethical conduct. Personnel safety control examples include high pressure, radiation, toxins, high voltage, slippery surfaces, sharp edges, overhead clearance, stair risers, and air quality.

Process controls are needed to manage important project functions and to control risk. Without appropriate process controls, details may get lost or overlooked. Smaller projects are often vulnerable due to overconfidence that the details can be informally "kept in mind."

Lessons learned relative to controls include:

- Large projects have complex communication paths;
  Details get lost, misinterpreted, or overlooked.
- Geographically dispersed projects often have informal communication paths;
  Details get lost, misinterpreted, or overlooked.

—— *PMBOK® Guide* ——
The *PMBOK® Guide* Sec 3.2.4 *Monitoring and Controlling Process Group* combines the monitoring and controlling of project work. Since the techniques and tools for determining status (monitoring) are considerably different from controlling and taking corrective action, we deliberately treat them as unique elements but essential for reactive project control.

Table 14.1 Example Control Functions

Function to Be Controlled	Control Standard	Control Authority	Control Technique	Variance Indication
Wiring	Electrical code	Building department	Inspection	Not to code—deficiency notice
Project work	Contract	Contract administrator	Work authorizations	Out of scope work
Schedule	Master schedule	Business manager	Work authorization	Off plan
Security	Need to know list	Security manager	Guard	Unauthorized access

	Activity	+	Visibility	+	Project Plan	=	Status	+	Corrective Action	=	Reactive Project Control
Case 1: No Visibility	?		No		?		No		No		No
Case 2: No Plan	Yes		Yes		No		No		No		No
Case 3: No Corrective Action	Yes		Yes		Yes		Yes		No		No
Case 4: Desired Approach	Yes		Yes		Yes		Yes		Yes		Yes

Figure 14.2   Reactive control of variances.

- High reliability projects must be built to exacting standards; *Details get lost, misinterpreted, or overlooked.*
- Long duration projects have personnel turnover; *Details get lost, misinterpreted, or overlooked.*
- Projects with subcontractors have communications and legal complexities; *Details get lost, misinterpreted, or overlooked.*

It follows that large, long, high-reliability projects using sub-contractors need comprehensive and effective process control. Analysis of failed projects often reveals the cause of failure to be lack of sufficient controls or circumvention of existing controls. In short, projects with inadequate process controls usually fail. Projects having the appropriate process controls have a good chance for success. But what is the "appropriate" level of control—the "sweet spot" where control is achieved without needless bureaucracy?

ACHIEVING THE APPROPRIATE LEVEL OF CONTROL

The appropriate level of control is achieved by pursuing the optimal balance between rigidity and discretionary freedom. It reflects and accommodates the need for agility and baseline change by managing those changes with a nonbureaucratic change control system. However, whatever system is used must be effective and binding on all affected parties. Configuration management, discussed in the following section, is perhaps the best example of an optimally designed control procedure.

"Ultimately, the success of a control system is determined by its effectiveness in getting people to make the necessary modifications in their own performance. Although the classical approach to control systems assumes that people will automatically act to correct their own behavior when directed to do so, this does not necessarily happen."[4]

Individuals may resist control systems for a variety of reasons, some of which are:

- Controls disrupt a person's self-image (they highlight things a person may have done poorly).
- People tend to avoid unpleasant involvement (such as behavioral changes).
- Goals of the control system may not have been universally accepted.
- Standards of expected performance may be too high.
- The controls seem irrelevant, bureaucratic, or lack completeness.
- An incompetent staff is administering the controls.
- Team norms may conflict with or violate company norms or standards.

One of the most pervasive reasons for resistance to controls is the equating of project controls with a lack of freedom. Controls, therefore, should never be arbitrary—they should make sense. But even the most logical controls may encounter resistance. We are increasingly scripted in a "zero sum" concept of personal freedom and control—the more we're controlled, the less we believe we are free. Enlightened managers know, however, that appropriate controls enhance and focus creativity rather than inhibit it. Such controls free the project team to be creative in finding the required solutions to the problems at hand, rather than being distracted by the day-to-day confusion of deciding what the project activity should be or how things should be done. Since this may not be the initial perception, particularly for inexperienced team members, it is the responsibility of the senior team members to gain general acceptance for the process control systems. To accomplish this, the team needs to be intimately involved in: process control definition and implementation; the reasons for the controls, the control activities and decisions; and access to relevant information at all organizational levels.

Some team members may still have to be sold on the potential benefits to gain their acceptance and to maintain a high level of teamwork. In this regard, the productivity and quality improvements that accrue from designing, selecting, and tuning the controls through team consensus can be particularly convincing.

Peter Drucker stresses the importance of *congruency:*

> Meaningful control systems . . . are discernible and appropriate for the complexity of the tasks being assessed and the size of the project effort. They are timely, simple to employ, and congruent with the events being measured.[5]

In summary, both proactive and reactive process controls should be:

- *Relevant.* Controls should never be arbitrary. Their purpose, rationale, and benefits should be clear. The controls should be designed and selected to manage the risks of the project. In general, the more visible and larger the commitment of project resources and the greater the human risk caused by the project, the greater the requirement for controls.
- *Efficient.* While designing the controls, determine the minimum required to assure performance. Avoid the tendency to measure and report information just because it's available (such data tend to mask and divert attention from more important items). Tailor the information to the needs of the team members who require the data to take action. Summarize and use graphics wherever possible.
- *Simple.* Keep the controls as simple as possible while maintaining their effectiveness.
- *Timely.* Controls need to be in place and tested before they're actually needed. The process should produce timely information to facilitate corrective action. This means determining the proper "sampling rate" to avoid obscured visibility at one extreme and information overload at the other.

To be effective, project control systems must be tailored to the nature, complexity, and risk of the situation and must be in place by the time the control is needed. There are many powerful controls such as configuration management or technical performance mea-

—— *PMBOK® Guide* ——
The *PMBOK® Guide* Sec 4.5.2 *Monitoring and Controlling Project Work* lists the following as tools and techniques.
- Project Management Methodology.
- Project Management Information System.
- Earned Value Technique.
- Expert Judgment.

The outputs of the process are listed as:
- Recommended Corrective Action.
- Recommended Preventive Actions.
- Forecasts.
- Recommended Defect Repair.
- Requested Changes.

Note that the project management information system and the earned value system provide visibility and status of past performance facilitating reactive but not proactive control as suggested by some of the outputs.

surement that can be very effective if implemented at the appropriate time. It is also important to recognize that there are situations when these tools are not appropriate. There are low-risk projects for which simple tools are adequate. In driving a car down a steep incline, it is appropriate to use a low gear as the primary control, but even the most ardent controls enthusiast would not advocate driving all the way across the United States using a low gear.

GENERAL CONTROL TECHNIQUES

General Guidelines

- One person should be placed in charge of specific areas, for example:
  - —*Project Manager:* Overall project requirements.
  - —*Chief Systems Engineer:* Technical requirements and technical baseline.
  - —*Business Manager:* Contracts and business baseline.
- Approved artifacts must be readily accessible. This is best accomplished by establishing a project information center or online repository with a responsible information manager. This subject is addressed in Chapter 15.

Technical Guidelines

- One person must control each task.
- There must be a controlled work release system.
- There must be an audit for compliance with project requirements.
- Variances must be negotiated with the project manager.

Cost Guidelines

- Team leaders must control to their budget.
- Variances must be negotiated with the project manager.

Schedule Guidelines

- All team leaders must sign off on the integrated schedule and Project Work Authorizing Agreements and control to them.
- Variances must be negotiated with the project manager.

Contract Control

The buyer controls sellers to standards set by contract types and incentives as summarized in Table 14.2.

Table 14.2 Summary of Contract Types

Type	Application	Control Provided
Fixed price	Reliable prior cost experience	Firm technical, cost, and schedule
Cost reimbursement	Research or development with advancing technology	Flexible objectives
Cost sharing	Seller shares cost in return for use of technology	Result ownership
Time and material	Not possible to estimate the task beforehand	Labor and material rates
Labor hour	Like time and material, but labor only	Labor rates
Indefinite quantity	Establishes price when quantity and schedule are uncertain	Item price
Letter	Limited project start without completed negotiations	Initial spending rate and amount

Data Control

A data manager should control contract data and approved baseline artifacts. Typical tools include a project library and a computer-based document management system.

Self-Control

Self-control operates at the most personal level. This kind of control is infectious.

"Setting a good example" includes:

- Being on time to work and to meetings.
- Demonstrating high personal standards.
- Remaining centered in times of stress.
- Delivering to all promises.

and controlling the pen by:

- Authoring straw-man documents.
- Proposing agendas.
- Recording action items.
- Reviewing and signing letters.

Management by Objectives

Management by Objectives (MBOs) can supplement, or in some cases substitute for, the Project Work Authorizing Agreements (PWAA) introduced earlier as the planning technique to control work authorization and release. Conversely, managing with definitive PWAAs can be thought of as MBO in its most effective form. In either approach, the corporate accounting system should provide cost accounting down to the task level in order to measure cost performance against the PWAA/MBO commitment and to provide early, in-process warning of variances and unfavorable trends.

In the absence of a WBS/PWAA system, a rigorous MBO system can accomplish many of their control functions. MBO is also a useful supplement to WBS/PWAA at a more detailed and shorter range associated with short time schedules and/or the first and second levels of the organization.

Many companies and government organizations have developed comprehensive MBO systems. Among their primary benefits, MBOs align individual contributions with the broadening objectives at each level of the organizational hierarchy, starting with the top strategic objectives. In that environment, project teams can benefit substantially by applying the same MBO structure to align project team goals down to functional unit goals and further to individual team member goals as well.

For an MBO system to be effective and self-motivating for the user, objectives need to be documented (typically on a quarterly schedule) and reviewed/revised regularly (usually weekly) and in detail. An effective system is characterized by objectives that are:

- Specific, clear, and unambiguous,
- Realistic, measurable, and verifiable,
- Consistent with available resources, and
- Consistent with company policies.

The best results are usually obtained by starting at the top levels. Every manager and all individual contributors draft their own objectives to fit with the level above while adding more detail and assumptions to represent their specific contributions. Each objective needs to include assumptions, measurement means, and verification methods. Joint commitments should be negotiated among the parties to arrive at identical objective statements. Team objectives are best negotiated with the team leader in a consensus driven session.

Embracing Micromanagement

Our Management Methods Survey reveals that micromanagement is universally scorned in all industries, workplaces, and in the press. Micromanagement is widely perceived as an incompetent manager

"Set a good example. It will please some people and amaze the rest."

Mark Twain

A loosely managed MBO system is worse than none at all.

nit-picking the work of a qualified subordinate who knows better. We characterize this scenario as "Nit Management" in that the perceived content and the consequences of the content to the project outcome appear miniscule.

One of the authors was on a senior manager's staff when our new boss arrived. The new boss spent two hours describing how to fill out a time card (pencil, not ink; block letters; each letter in the box, not overlapping the edges; etc.). Since none of us had to fill out time cards, nor had we for 20 years, this was an exercise in Nit Management at its finest.

However, "the devil is in the details," "no change is a small change," and, "people must not mess up" suggest that supervisory attention to detail may often be appropriate. TQM, Six Sigma, CMMI, and the learning organization are all about honing detailed processes to where results are efficient and repeatable with no "messing up." Intel has a philosophy of "getting it exactly right and replicating exactly." These are all examples of "positive" micromanagement in action.

The appropriate use of micromanagement is when the risk of failure is so high that you will not be satisfied until you are personally confidant that it has been managed properly. Experienced airline pilots go through a detailed checklist each time they are preparing to take off. Hopefully, this is not because they cannot remember how to fly the airplane, but rather the catastrophic consequences of omitting a step. A few years ago one airline reexamined their preflight procedures with a competitive goal to shorten the turnaround time from 45 minutes to 20 minutes. They deleted as unnecessary the step that required the pilot to initial the mechanic's worksheet showing the amount of fuel loaded onto the plane. This saved about five minutes in turnaround. The FAA reported that in the first two years after the change was made the airline had 12 flights that had taken off without enough fuel to reach their destination, forcing an emergency "unscheduled" landing at an intermediate airport. Maybe the pilot's micromanagement of the fuel log wasn't such a bad thing after all.

The following blunder cost the European Commission (EC) over $100 million:

> A lawyer's failure to operate a fax machine correctly has been blamed for the EC losing a multimillion-euro court case. The European Court of First Instance ruled in favor of five German banks that had been fined a total of $100 million by the EC.
>
> In 2001, they had been found guilty of running a cartel to fix foreign currency rates ahead of the introduction of the euro. The com-

panies—Dresdner Bank, Commerzbank, HVB, Beursche Verkehrs-bank, and Vereignsund Westbank—appealed this decision, and their case was concluded yesterday.

According to the *Financial Times,* the European Court of First Instance overturned the fine because an EC lawyer who attempted to fax a 100-page document outlining the Commission's case had accidentally placed it face upward in the fax machine.

This error meant the court received 100 blank pages, and the actual document was not received in time. With no other legal argument from the EC, the court had to rule in favor of the five banks.

With something this significant do you think micromanagement might have been appropriate? There are many process steps that should have been taken. Why didn't they make a phone call to confirm that the fax was received properly? With something this important, why wasn't there a second person there to assist and verify that the fax was being sent properly? The flawed process was the significance, not just putting the paper in upside down in the fax machine (which many of us have done at one time or another).

Another example is the multihundred-million-dollar satellite that fell off the test stand because tie-down bolts were missing. The issue is not that the bolts were missing, but rather that no one checked before moving the satellite. This is another instance where appropriate micromanagement would have saved the project.

> If the task at hand is critically important, then micromanagement is a technique worth considering.

Defining and following a correct process is vital to any project. Verifying that critical steps have been taken is equally important.

CONFIGURATION MANAGEMENT AND CHANGE CONTROL

Change happens. Requirements are almost always added, deleted, or changed. There are two ways to deal with these changes:

1. Prohibit them—not client responsive.
2. Control them proactively—client responsive.

> Configuration management is often a key project success factor, making it one of the most important proactive control processes.

Configuration management (Figure 14.3) is the process for controlling the evolving project baselines in a climate of change. Its purposes are to:

- Keep evolving baselines up to date and communicated.
- Keep the business, budget, and technical baselines congruent (Chapter 7, Table 7.1).

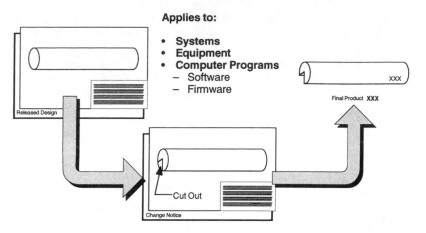

Figure 14.3   Configuration management.

- Ensure that the evolving solutions are consistent with the baselines.
- Manage the physical and functional characteristics of the solution and its entities.

Configuration management recognizes the inevitability of changes in the business case, funding, technical requirements, and configuration of hardware, software, and operations. It provides the techniques and tools to identify, control, and communicate those changes. It accounts for changes as they reverberate through the baselines, impacting technical performance, budgets, and schedules. Each time the project successfully passes a decision gate—a point of consensus between seller and buyer—the approved baselines that result are formally managed and subject to change management.

Common project management practice and industry standards focus on technical baseline management, just one critical aspect of configuration management and system integrity. As defined in the margin note, system integrity encompasses the business and budget aspects.

System Integrity: the congruency of the business, budget, and technical baselines. A developing system has integrity when its baselines are in agreement or congruent, which results from establishing a balance among the three aspects (business, budget, and technical) at the outset of the project and maintaining that balance as changes occur to any baseline.

The business, budget, and technical baselines in Table 7.1 are so interdependent that project success depends on keeping them in lock step. In this context, integrity exists only when the:

Margin notes:

Change control is intended to manage changes—not to prevent them.

—— *PMBOK® Guide* ——
The *PMBOK® Guide* Sec 4.3.2.2 *Project Management Information System* covers configuration management and change control within the Project Integration Management.

- Technical baseline is managed to satisfy the business baseline (strategic and tactical objectives), and
- Budget baseline is structured to allocate resources as needed to accomplish both the technical and business objectives.

If congruence does not exist, it means that one or more of the triple constraints will not be satisfied and the project may be deemed a failure.

Configuration management is based on controlling artifacts that range from oral statements to physical objects. The simplest forms of written artifacts are dated and signed handwritten notes or white-board representations (also dated and signed). More common examples are version-controlled electronic and paper specifications. Artifacts include hardware and software products with version identification and certifications attesting to their "configuration."

By definition baselines are under change control. Baselines appear at the top of the architecture and then descend, consistent with the solution decomposition, to the detailed parts, code, and processes used to produce the solution. The project management challenge is parallel elaboration of the many baselines such that they are:

- Consistent with, and responsive to, their parent baselines, and
- Congruent with their peer baselines.

Business/Mission Baselines

The project cycle discussion in Chapter 7 explained the concept of the business baseline and how it represents the business approach. In considering the configuration management of the business baseline, the following artifacts may require configuration management:

Contract.	Memorandum of Agreement.
Business case.	Schedule.
Marketing plan.	Schedule contingency.
Mission case.	Milestones.
Project charter.	Subcontracts.

While it's commonplace to control these project-level artifacts, it should also be recognized that candidates exist at every level of architecture decomposition and for every deliverable entity of the project. Hence, parent-child traceability is required to ensure proper flowdown, baseline integrity, and change evaluation at every level of the solution architecture.

The key for all project teams is to establish sound and achievable initial baselines and then to keep them congruent as the inevitable changes occur during project execution.

—— *PMBOK® Guide* ——
The *PMBOK® Guide* Sec 4.6 *Integrated Change Control* identifies three configuration management activities:

1. Configuration Identification.
2. Configuration Status Accounting.
3. Configuration Verification and Auditing.

Budget Baseline

The budget baseline addresses the required resources—obtaining and deploying them as needed to execute the project. It must be consistent with, and supportive of, both the business and technical baselines. Like the business baseline, it too must exist at every level of decomposition and must be responsive to parent and peer baselines.

In considering the configuration management of the budget baseline, the following artifacts may require configuration management:

Funding schedule.	Budgets.
Funding availability.	Burn rate.
Funding contingency.	Skill mix.

Technical Baseline

──────── *INCOSE* ────────
INCOSE Handbook Sec 5.9 *Configuration Management Process* and Sec 6.3 *Baseline Management* provide additional information on management of baselines.

The technical baseline addresses the evolution and elaboration of the technical solution at all levels of architecture decomposition. The technical baseline is responsive to the business baseline and tends to drive the budget baseline, since that is where most of the resources are consumed. While it is common to manage the technical baseline reasonably well at all levels of decomposition, it is not universal to flow down the associated business and budget baselines to all elements of the solution architecture.

In considering the configuration management of the technical baselines, the following artifacts may require disciplined management:

Requirements definition.	Design-to specification.
Concept definition.	Build-to documentation.
Architecture definition.	Code-to documentation.
Validation plan.	Logistics support plan.
Deployment plan.	Operations plan.
Concept specification.	Maintenance plan.
Verification plan.	Deactivation plan.
Verification procedures.	Other necessary procedures.

Effective configuration management—an ounce of prevention.

The major goal of a configuration management process, as diagrammed in Figure 14.4, is to ensure that approved baselines and changes to those baselines are in the best interest of the project.

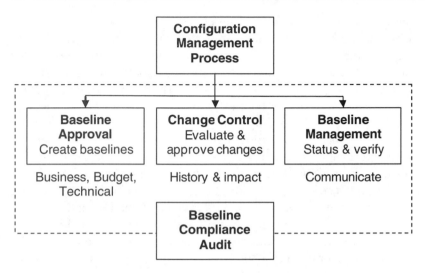

Figure 14.4   Key elements of configuration management.

Change Control

A vital element of configuration management provides the means to evaluate and approve changes to the baselines. The change control process can be as simple as a phone call between two programmers with a follow-up e-mail (part of the project documentation) or structured as a Change Control Board (CCB). An ad hoc meeting of the impacted stakeholders with documented minutes lies somewhere between. In any case, there needs to be an agreed to process that ensures:

- That all impacted parties agree to the process.
- That change agreements are documented and communicated.
- Compliance.

> Augustine's Law—No change is a small change—drives the need for change control.

It may be impractical to have a single control board for a large complex project, as it could easily become a bottleneck on the project's critical path. The practical solution is to have a layered control board aligned with the project's architecture. The board at each level should have the appropriate stakeholders, including a systems engineer to represent the overall and customer/user perspective.

In their chapter on managing configurations in *The Wiley Guide to Managing Projects*, Callium Kidd and Thomas Burgess trace the motivation for industry practices and related standards, such as EIA 649 and ISO 10007, to project failures and serious deficiencies. The

> Adjust your process to your project's size, risk, complexity, and your company/customer guidelines.

authors acknowledge that, while change controls are widely recognized as the best way to stay out of trouble, the appropriate level of rigor is controversial. "There needs to be a documented process for change, through which all changes must progress. The processing of changes through a single change board activity is where most organizations see unnecessary bureaucracy in the configuration management process. For this reason, it is important that clear rules exist whereby change classifications can help streamline the approval/implementation process, and changes that are considered minor, or low impact changes, can be directed to those empowered to do so."[6]

The change process usually begins with a change request that documents the change including the technical, budget, and schedule impact. The request precipitates a CCB review (Figure 14.5). The participants include the managers of each affected organization. The project manager chairs the CCB and is responsible for ensuring that:

- The decision is informed and objective.
- Each change is logged for traceability to the work package level of the WBS.
- All affected parties are notified of baseline changes.
- Upper management and the customer are officially informed of all baseline changes.
- Changes requiring customer approval are forwarded to the customer change board.

The CCB Agenda should include the following issues, which must be thoroughly understood for informed decision making:

- The details of the change and the need for it.
- The impact of the change on the performance, design, cost, schedule, support equipment, spares, contract, customer, and project team.
- The impact of making the change versus not making the change.
- Effectivity (e.g., date, versions, and specific units affected).

PMBOK® Guide

The *PMBOK® Guide* Sec 4.6 *Integrated Change Control* discusses the role of the change control board as part of Project Integration Management.

Usually the impact on people is the trickiest to assess objectively. For this reason, the customer impact and customer position are two different issues.

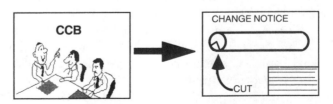

Figure 14.5 The change control board.

- Documentation affected by the change.
- Customer position (i.e., Is the customer supportive of the change?)

The project manager needs to factor the customer's situation into the decision process. Likewise, secondary impacts on the project team need to be accounted for in schedules. For example, the disruption resulting from redesigns are often underestimated. Conversely, a substitution or alternative approach could eliminate a source of conflict or risk.

Affected work authorizations must be revised to effect a change. Recognizing that a large project requires many PWAAs, rapid action is required to avoid having people working to an obsolete baseline. The opening case of this chapter presented an example of a major failure caused by a poorly implemented change. Use your most effective communication method to notify all affected parties that a change is forthcoming.

QUALITY CONTROLS AND TECHNIQUES

We define *quality* as conformance to the project's requirements. Quality is ultimately judged by the customer and end users, not by the project manager or other provider personnel. In this case, the *customer* may be any person or organization in the complete provider-customer chain extending from those internal to the project to the intended user.

It is the final user that determines product or service quality, that is, fitness for use. That viewpoint encompasses ease of learning, usability, serviceability, reliability, durability, and documentation effectiveness.

Traditional Quality Assurance

The traditional approach to controlling quality (Figure 14.6) focuses on the results of manufacturing operations where quality is most visible. For example, product quality assurance consists of an organization that screens the product (perhaps at several points in the manufacturing process) for adherence to its specifications (Figure 14.7). Suspect material is dispositioned as use-as-is, rework, or scrap—whichever is appropriate. Eventually, most design or process defects are recognized and corrected by the change control and corrective action process.

INCOSE
INCOSE Handbook Sec 7.6
Quality Management Process
provides additional informa-

PMBOK® Guide
The *PMBOK® Guide* Ch 8 *Project Quality Management* describes three processes:

1. Quality Planning.
2. Quality Assurance.
3. Quality Control.

A quality challenge is to develop specifications that will produce products that satisfy the customers' expectations.

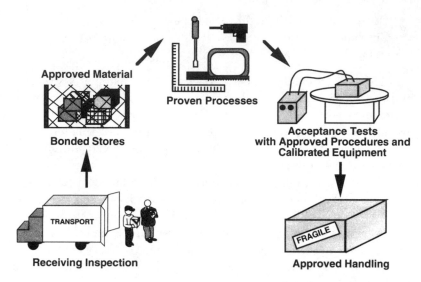

Figure 14.6   Traditional quality assurance.

A sensible and enduring standard for all industries is illustrated in Figure 14.7. Current ISO quality standards are based on these same sound concepts.

Total Quality Management

In many industries, quality is considered the foremost competitive success factor.

The need to improve profitability and to respond to increasing global competition have motivated both product and service industries to broaden the scope of quality assurance to reach the entire organization at all stages of the process. TQM is:

- Required from project initiation to completion.
- Required of everyone.
- Applied to every process and transaction.

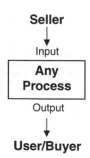

The quest for higher quality has been embodied in two closely related practices: TQM and Continuous Quality Improvement (CQI). TQM is a sound concept that is founded on the following three fundamentals:

1. Everything that people do can be described as a process that can constantly be improved. CQI emphasizes the process—the *system* for doing things—rather than the results themselves.

Provisions:

There should be a quality organization.

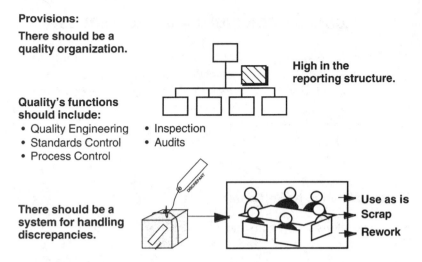

High in the reporting structure.

Quality's functions should include:
- Quality Engineering
- Standards Control
- Process Control
- Inspection
- Audits

There should be a system for handling discrepancies.

Use as is
Scrap
Rework

Figure 14.7   MIL-STD-9858A: Still a sensible standard for all industries.

2. To produce satisfactory results, each individual must have clearly defined expectations.

3. The person you deliver your output to is your customer and deserves to be satisfied. Every customer has the right to reject any unsatisfactory deliverable.

Most people are unaware of their own process and therefore do not consciously attempt to improve it for the customer's benefit, as well as for their own. Creating this awareness and motivation is part of the leadership responsibility of both the project manager and the systems engineering manager.

Attention to TQM principles can enhance other control techniques, notably MBO. The two concepts are complementary in the sense that TQM/CQI stresses the process while MBO stresses results.

To the extent that the project team is aware of, accepts, and conscientiously applies these fundamentals:

- Project output rises.
- Failure rates decline.
- Efficiency improves.

Software Quality Assurance

The Software Quality Assurance (SQA) function is responsible for auditing software development for compliance to the SQA plan. The availability of an audit trail, from automatically generated software configurations, enhances the efficiency of this audit that:

- Assures that prescribed development environment standards, procedures, and methods are being adhered to.
- Verifies process adequacy.
- Alerts the project manager to deficiencies.

TECHNICAL CONTROLS AND TECHNIQUES

The following controls expand on the basic control techniques previously described. The major selection criterion for these controls is the risk associated with each technical area, regardless of the proportion of project resources it represents. In general, the value of each technique depends on the project type, the risk associated with the technologies involved, and the project complexity.

Controls Unique to Software

Software-intensive projects have historically been poorly managed. We hear excuses like, "I didn't change that section, so there's no need to test it." (Invariably, "that section" fails because of a change in another section that was tested independently.) Worse yet is the assurance, "I only changed a few lines of code, so it was easy to verify manually."

An incident that received national attention in June 1991 provides a graphic example of the consequences of such "leaky" manual controls. The telephone services in Los Angeles, Pittsburgh, San Francisco, and Washington, D.C., were temporarily shut down. The reason turned out to be a faulty software change and flawed verification controls. A computer programmer, not understanding the potential consequences of his action, changed a few lines of code. Since only a few lines were changed, performance verification tests required by the company's configuration management policy were omitted. The three changed lines of software inadvertently caused the program to generate a repetitive message saying that the system required maintenance. Soon the system was swamped with such messages, blocking all calls.

Part of this problem is the intangibility of software until the code is highly functional. Other factors include the rapid change in development tools and technology, coupled with the explosive growth in size and complexity of software products. Although details of the conventions, techniques, and controls needed to manage the design process is beyond the scope of this book, the following techniques are common to most software development projects, regardless of size.

Before development is started, choices must be made among the myriad software development environments. False starts can sometimes be avoided by having this environment evaluated by an experienced expert. A Computer Resources Working Group is a name given to a panel established to judge the adequacy of the software

Having the development environment evaluated by an expert can avoid expensive false starts.

development environment before it is implemented and at major conversions or ports.

Two major areas requiring improvement in software change controls are integration and automation. Integration refers to the combination of all source, executables, objects, graphics, documents, and other applications that are related. The Software Development Library is a controlled collection of software, documentation, test data, and associated tools that include global resources common to the entire project as well as product modules. By adding automatic generation capability, the development system supports the regeneration of any level or version. This level of automation is capable of facilitating an automated audit trail as well, fulfilling an important quality assurance audit requirement.

The Software Engineering Institute's capability maturity models have been used for internal and external evaluation of internal software process or that of software suppliers. The CMM, and its integrated successor, the CMMI, appraises the software process maturity of an organization against criteria for five escalating levels. This is discussed in more detail in Chapters 2 and 21.

Design drawings can best be formally controlled through a subprocess of baseline controls whereby all affected disciplines approve initial releases and design changes. It is also vital that affected disciplines be involved in the design process itself. Known as concurrent engineering, this process was discussed in Chapter 11.

Design must be controlled for both technical requirements and development standards. Design controls occur at several organizational levels with commensurate formality. Supervisors, being familiar with the designer, the standards, and the design interface can, on a daily basis, adjust review depth and frequency to match the risk. Formal design reviews are addressed in Chapter 7.

Peer Reviews

Peer reviews vary in rate and formality, from informal walkthroughs and "chalk talks" to formal peer group presentations. Peer reviews can be highly effective and they can provide the additional benefit of cross training. A review board of a recent $60 million project failure identified lack of effective peer review during the design evolution as a significant contributing cause.

Expert reviews usually draw on objective experts from outside the project—often outside the organization. They occur less frequently than peer reviews and require considerable preparation on the part of both reviewers and the reviewed. The customer may also

> We strongly recommend peer review on everything of significance, even short memos.

conduct expert reviews. The government often contracts for independent technical experts to perform ongoing reviews of risky development projects.

Failure review boards evaluating failed projects almost always cite lack of peer reviews as a significant contributing cause of the failure. Peer reviews are not red teams or tiger teams, but rather a small collaborative group of domain peers examining work accomplished to ensure:

- Conformance to the requirements and accepted standards for the domain,
- Sufficient thoroughness with analytical backup,
- Adequate risk assessment,
- Attention to details, like using the correct measurement units (wrong units caused the failure of the Mars Climate Orbiter, which crashed into Mars), and
- Producibility.

While peer review tends to be informal in that the results are suggestions, they are a powerful control technique as any lack of response to the suggestions should have to be justified. Many engineers resist peer review as they don't enjoy having others critique their work.

THE CONDUCT AND RESOLUTION OF DECISION GATES

We defined decision gates in Chapter 7 and discussed their role in managing the project cycle. Their primary control objective is to ensure that the project team has completed and has baselined all required deliverables so as to avoid progressing to a phase for which the team is unprepared.

Decision gate conduct should lead to confidence in the project's progress by being:

Honest.	Constructive in challenges.
Open and interactive.	Mutually beneficial.
Helpful and supportive.	Synergistic.

Each decision gate should be defined with the following criteria:

Purpose of the decision gate.	Agenda and how conducted.
Host and chairperson.	Evidence that is evaluated.
Attendees.	Actions.
Location.	Closure method.

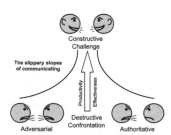

Decision Gates - Attitudes

It's easy to slip off of the best behavior.

The decision gate decision options are:

- *Acceptable*—proceed with project.
- *Acceptable with reservations*—proceed and respond to identified action items.
- *Unacceptable*—do not proceed; repeat the review.
- *Unsalvageable*—terminate the project.

On successful completion of a decision gate, the appropriate agreements (usually in the form of artifacts and products of a project cycle phase) will be added to the baseline and put under configuration management.

PROJECT CONTROL ELEMENT EXERCISE

Since controls are used to ensure responsiveness to predetermined standards they permeate all aspects of projects. Some controls are only proactive while others are both proactive and reactive. One example is the tachometer in your car: it is proactive in that it has been installed beforehand and alerts you when you are nearing the red line limit (the control standard). More modern systems now include ignition cutout to prevent violation of the red line limit, which is a complete proactive and reactive control system. A traffic light is only proactive while a building sprinkler system is designed to be both proactive and reactive.

Develop a list of control techniques both within and external to your project environment. Identify those that are

- Only proactive.
- Only reactive.
- Both proactive and reactive.

Control Technique	Proactive	Reactive
Traffic light	X	X
Bracing for a fall		X

MANAGEMENT
ELEMENT 7

—— PMBOK® Guide ——
This chapter is consistent with the *PMBOK® Guide* Ch 4 *Project Integration Management* and Ch 10 *Project Communication Management*.

———— INCOSE ————
This chapter is consistent with *INCOSE Handbook* Sec 5.2 *Planning* and Sec 5.7 *Control Process*.

"Not only is there but one way of doing things rightly, but there is only one way of seeing them, and that is, seeing the whole of them."

John Ruskin

15

PROJECT VISIBILITY

Can there be status without visibility? Under pressure to report favorable status, project managers are sometimes tempted to look the other way, foregoing visibility. Ferdinand de Lesseps became a national hero in France based on his success as manager of the Suez Canal project in the 1860s. Because of his reputation, he was chosen to head the French effort to build the Panama Canal. The privately funded construction began in 1881. The investors, primarily French families (well over ten thousand), relied on de Lesseps' glowing reports on the progress of the construction. In July 1885, he announced that the canal was over 50 percent complete and right on schedule. He was prone to inflate reports from subordinates, sometimes reporting status without any input. In fact, at the time of his 50 percent report, "less than a tenth of the canal had been dug. . . ."[1] Since de Lesseps lived in France and had only been to Panama once (five years earlier, before the work started), he clearly was caught in the syndrome of reporting status without visibility. In the twenty-first century, this practice continues, as evidenced by Enron, WorldCom, and many others.

Status without visibility is irresponsible at best, and is criminal at worst. The Panama Canal company declared bankruptcy in 1889. De Lesseps and four directors were convicted of fraud in 1893 and sentenced to five years in prison. Enron officials are also experiencing prison life.

The motto, "Trust, but verify," underlies the need for accurate and meaningful visibility as a basis for managing any project. "Trust me! I'm working on it" is a sure indicator of trouble, and a warning to go look for yourself. Visibility by itself, however, only lets you know what the team is working on, and how busy they are. To be useful, you must compare what you see with what is planned, which provides the project status covered in the next chapter. If timely status indicates deviations from plan, you now have information necessary to take appropriate corrective action to return to the plan. But it all begins with visibility.

The lack of total visibility is obscurity, referred to by Robert A. Heinlein as the "refuge of incompetence" and by Vauve-Nargues as the "realm of error." In the project environment it is both, and consequently, a major cause of project failures.

Project visibility, as shown in Figure 15.1, is the means by which the project team and other stakeholders are made aware of project activity to facilitate timely statusing and effective corrective action. While its main purpose is to lead directly to reactive management, good visibility also supports proactive management by making sure controls are in place and are effective. Visibility objectives are to:

Project visibility is how you and your team know what's *really* going on.

- Determine activity.
  —Planned tasks.
  —Unplanned tasks.
  —Work habits.
  —Control processes.
- Communicate—up, down, and laterally.
- Verify status—Is it as reported?
- Determine and influence morale and team spirit—"How is it going? Is there anything that you need?"

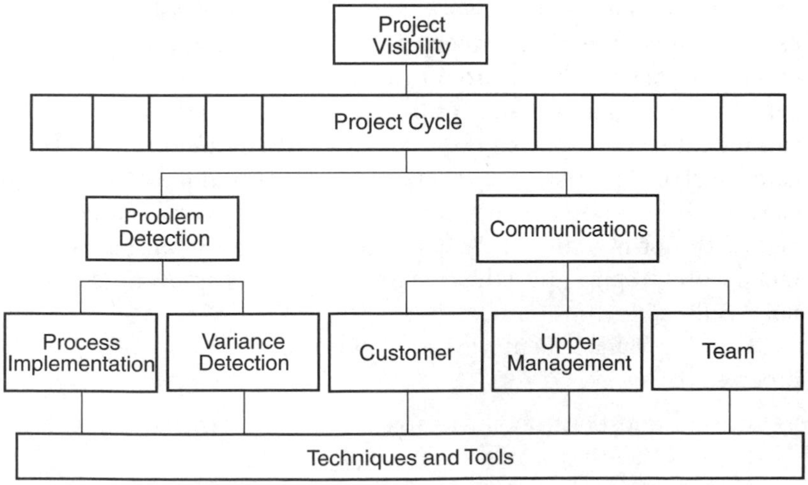

Figure 15.1 Project visibility decomposition.

Project visibility includes the facilitation of information gathering and dissemination techniques such as:

Meetings.	Glance Management.
Reports.	Project Information Center.
Tiger Teams.	Top Ten Problem List.

These techniques are driven by the timing, need, and geographic location of the required data. They change as the project progresses through the project cycle.

GLANCE MANAGEMENT

———— *INCOSE* ————
INCOSE Handbook Sec 5.5
Monitoring/Assessment Process identifies that taking the pulse of actual performance against planned is its main purpose.

Glance Management encompasses management-by-walking-around (MBWA) and other informal techniques used for follow-up and daily awareness by an appropriate project member, particularly the project manager, chief systems engineer, and subject-matter experts. We chose the name to reflect a major visibility lesson learned. Far too many project failures are caused by fatal problems or omissions that could have been detected by a follow-up "glance" by a cognizant expert. Experts can instantly identify small, yet critical, details by simply glancing at the situation. There is an appropriate German term of *augenblict,* which means in the blink of an eye. One of the authors had a major house renovation done, after which all six skylights leaked. When questioned, the contractor admitted he delegated the job to an inexperienced workman who failed to apply flashing. Almost anyone would have noticed the missing flashing in the blink of an eye but the workman did not know flashing was necessary. Quite often, that trained eye is simply a matter of experience or a broad view of the environment, such as the case of a communications system that was subject to frequent, but random errors. The technical team was poring over software listings and using sophisticated instrumentation and troubleshooting techniques to find the cause. While surveying the site, the project manager noticed that one of the printers had defective metal plating. Small particles of metal were dropping into the control unit causing spurious electrical noise pulses.

Glance Management involves periodic sampling of work in progress by:

- Casual questions about a project detail—perhaps in a chance hallway meeting or in the parking lot.
- Engaging in conversations before or after meetings, or at group functions.

- Skip-level meetings sitting in on a lower-level meeting.
- Quick scans of copies of routine correspondence (FYI or for your information) for telling phrases.
- Maintaining a reputation for an open door and an open mind.
- MBWA—walking through the project area and actively observing.

Prior to the *Challenger* failure, an O-ring Tiger Team *glanced* at the booster joint design and proclaimed, "Wrong application of an O-ring." Contrary to best practices, the O-ring was not always under compression due to a dynamically varying gap between the adjoining booster structures. This same flexing of the booster structure rendered the backup O-ring ineffective. Although a recognized concern for almost ten years, no corrective action was taken until after the *Challenger* accident. Had someone with authority used glance management to *initiate action,* perhaps the *Challenger* failure would have been avoided.

MBWA is a visibility technique with important leadership and team-building benefits. Even though its primary purpose is to improve visibility, it is useful for assessing morale and for obtaining general information. The MBWA method consists of stopping to talk with team members while taking different routes through the project area. To promote openness, it is important to give answers to questions that may be asked and to inform the appropriate managers and supervisors of what you conveyed. Be sure to diffuse political situations and avoid immediate problem solving. Also be careful not to usurp the authority you have delegated to those supporting you. Here are some MBWA guidelines and protocol:

- Make plant tours—your own facility and contractor/subcontractor facilities.
- Go where the action is.
- See and be seen.
- Observe, but do not direct.
- Talk to personnel working on your project.
- Verify status—spot check details and look for evidence of work in progress (drawings completed, software in test, or parts machined).
- Use this opportunity for team building:
    - —Show interest and ask people to tell you what they are doing and what they might need to be more effective.
    - —Confirm that team members understand their part in the process.
- Carefully and decisively use the information gathered. It may be used to assist the existing management in their management

Carefully and decisively use the information gathered.

—— *PMBOK® Guide* ——
The *PMBOK® Guide* Ch 9 *Human Resource Management* cites providing timely performance feedback as a key management action.

process or it may be used to change the existing management if they are found to be ineffective with no hope of improving.

MBWA can be especially effective when two or three work shifts are operating around the clock. The second and third shifts often feel left out of the mainstream: "Hardly anybody from day shift ever comes in." On one such project, the project manager and marketing manager, separately, made periodic visits to the work areas during second and third shifts. They were surprised by the number of valuable inputs they received. Even more surprising was the general morale improvement that even carried over to the day shift.

On another project, the chief systems engineer used this technique very effectively by deliberately parking his car in different parking lots depending on the active phase of the project. During the manufacturing phase, parking on the opposite side of the plant forced several trips through manufacturing operations during which workers would call his attention to various conditions and anomalies. Workers soon knew to expect the MBWA, taking pride by showing examples of their work and being prepared with questions. When activity moved to integration and verification, the parking lot was changed, and resulted in the same good collaboration results with the verification team.

All glance management techniques share a common risk—giving the impression of invasive scrutiny. Everyone dislikes being interrogated or watched too closely. This is where leadership techniques come into play. Glance management, especially MBWA, works best when visibility is both ways—when it includes recognition, praise, and casual advice—as well as questions.

THE PROJECT INFORMATION CENTER

Any visibility system should include a Project Information Center—a dedicated area or web page that displays the current status of all project activities against the plan. The use of a name like Short Cycle Room can convey an important theme and is a constant reminder to project personnel of the importance of schedule (Figure 15.2).

Beware of stale data! The information center must be kept current, otherwise it is of little or even negative value.

The main benefactors of the Information Center are project personnel with schedule and budget responsibility and/or interest. All users benefit from this visibility at a glance. It also provides a means for making the project more visible to stakeholders and others who may miss, or not be included in, meetings. By reviewing posted notices and selected correspondence, the observer can

Figure 15.2   A dedicated Short Cycle Room.

quickly scan for pertinent new information. The Project Information Center is an ideal location for all hands and project manager's reviews. On small projects, it can be the project manager's office or a conference room.

An alternative implementation method is to use a web-based information dissemination site with e-mail, baseline document libraries, and search capability. However, this approach lacks the opportunity for motivation, interaction, and cheerleading provided by a dedicated physical area.

—— *PMBOK® Guide* ——
The *PMBOK® Guide* Sec.
10.2.2 *Information Distribution* supports these concepts.

TIGER TEAMS FOCUS ON CONCERNS

In some organizations, Tiger Teams have an unearned negative reputation usually propagated by those who were subjected to one without adequate preparation. Therefore, to maximize chances for success, the project team must be educated as to the purpose, methods, and expected positive use of Tiger Teams.

Tiger Teams provide focused visibility on selected areas of concern. Usually composed of domain experts, their purpose is to objectively identify the problem sources and to recommend solutions. Solution implementation is usually the responsibility of the project team. While anybody can suggest the need for a Tiger Team, it is usually initiated by the project manager, upper management, customer, or functional managers.

Typical areas of concern for the Tiger Team include:

Design approach.	Management approach.
Interface compatibility.	Quality.
Software approach.	Cost.
Schedule approach.	Personnel turnover.
Failures.	

Tiger Team members should be experts and "quick studies."

Tiger Teams are composed of project personnel and invited experts with a demonstrated ability to accumulate the facts rapidly, objectively evaluate the status, and impartially report their findings. Participants may include seller and/or buyer personnel, outside consultants, or customer experts.

The benefits of using Tiger Teams to evaluate status include:

- Objective visibility into an area of concern.
- Focused approach to improve performance.
- Third-party assistance in securing increased resources.
- Tiger Team follow-up on success of recommendations.

Precautions when using Tiger Teams include:

Tiger Teams are for fixing problems, NOT for fixing blame.

- Expected use of Tiger Teams should be publicized by project management at the outset and during the course of the project.
- Tiger Teams must operate in a team (not adversarial) relationship with the project team.
- Tiger Teams must have "free rein."
- Project manager must stay aware and support both project and Tiger Team personnel.

MEETINGS—THE PROJECT MANAGER'S DILEMMA

Meetings are the major vehicle for performing many management roles:

Informational	*Interpersonal*	*Decisional*
Gathering.	Motivating.	Investigating.
Disseminating.	Inspiring.	Consensus making.
Clarifying.	Praising.	Evaluating.
Training.	Committing.	Decisin making.

Whether one-on-one or involving the entire project team, meetings are a significant technique for gathering and disseminating information. As such, they can easily consume 40 percent to 60 percent of a project manager's time. High-value meetings are critical to project success. However, meetings that just waste the team's time can result in decreased morale. For meetings to be effective, they must serve a specific, well-defined purpose.[2] Too many meetings and poorly conceived and poorly executed ones can be a major demotivator. When considering whether or not to hold a meeting, ask yourself:

- What is the objective of the meeting?
- Is there a better way to achieve the objective?
- Is this meeting really necessary?
- What would the consequences of not holding it be?
- How to mitigate the consequences?

We will return to the interpersonal and decisional meeting aspects in Chapter 18. Here's a checklist of recommended conduct:

- Distribute an agenda in advance of the meeting.
- Invite only those required.
- Schedule the start for an odd time such as 7:56 A.M.
- State the purpose of the meeting and stick to it:
    —Exchange information.
    —Determine status.
    —Solve a problem.
    —Make a decision.
- Start on time—don't wait for late people.
- Keep the meeting on track and control the progress.
- Summarize the results and assign action items.
- Follow up on action items.
- Ensure that all meetings are summarized including those meetings you are not responsible for.

Informational Meetings

An informational meeting is the opportunity to update the team's collective knowledge. This knowledge includes perceptions and experiences as well as facts. As with traditional staff meetings, a series of smaller, nested meetings, as identified in Table 15.1, can be effective in tailoring the information range and depth of detail to the particular group.

> Some informational objectives are better handled by other visibility techniques such as informal discussions, a telephone call, or a memo.

Table 15.1 Examples of Informational Meetings

Type	Frequency	Typical Duration
News flash	Daily or each shift	10 to 15 minutes
All-hands	As required	Several minutes to 20 minutes
One-on-one	Weekly	One hour
Plan violators	Weekly	Less than 30 minutes each
Project manager's review	Weekly	Two hours
Executive review	Monthly or quarterly	One to two hours
Customer review	Monthly	Varies—scope dependent

News Flash Meetings

News flash meetings are most effective when conducted daily at the start of each shift or a few minutes before the lunch break.

News flash meetings are used to streamline communication for schedule critical projects and to resolve issues immediately. Issues requiring further discussion are addressed right after the news flash meeting. News flash meetings work best with a small group—usually the direct reports to the project manager. Some managers prefer that all participants remain standing throughout to instill urgency and discourage long-winded discussions. Others prefer to assign seats, making it easier to know who, or what organizations, are not present and to position adversaries adjacent to one another to facilitate communication. An effective agenda is:

- What did not happened as planned?
- What action is required?
- What is not going to happen as planned?
- What action is required?
- What help is required of management?

All-Hands Meetings

All-hands meetings involve a larger group—usually the entire project team. Attendance by key personnel is mandatory. These meetings are typically convened to announce a major development such as a new contract, a technical breakthrough, or the need for extra effort. They offer an excellent opportunity for team building.

One-on-One Meetings

One-on-one meetings should be held weekly by every supervisor with each direct report to exchange information and deal with personal and performance issues. They are most effective when time is limited. Therefore, each employee needs to prepare a priority list to ensure that the high priority items get addressed within the allotted time.

Plan-Violator Meetings

Plan-violator meetings are held by the project manager to gain visibility. Once you understand what is going on, then this meeting extends beyond visibility to include active statusing and determining corrective action for areas not on plan. The manager that, for the prior week, is off schedule, headcount, or budget plan must personally meet with the project manager. The violation, cause, and proposed recovery are reviewed. Subsequent meetings update the recovery process. The business manager sets the variance threshold that triggers this meeting. The major benefits are:

> Headcount variance is often the earliest indicator of more serious problems.

- Causes task managers to pay attention to the plan and their progress.
- Provides review of previous week's headcount and schedule performance immediately following completion of the work week.
- Provides for prompt response to new problems.
- Keeps budget and schedule plans current.
- Keeps management knowledgeable.
- Lets the team know that you are paying attention and that you really care about results.

Project Manager's Weekly Review

The project manager's weekly review meeting extends beyond visibility to active statusing and corrective action. It involves all key project and functional support personnel. This meeting should be open to executive management as well as customer personnel. The agenda includes a thorough review of the status of the total project to surface conflict, areas of inaction, items awaiting disposition, and areas requiring special attention. The results include decisive actions by project management. The benefits include:

- Overall view of the project.
- Forum for organizational interaction to resolve project issues.

- Insight for support managers into project needs.
- Visibility for all key participants into top project issues, concerns, and problems.

It is often beneficial to hold this meeting on Friday mornings to determine what weekend effort can substantially shorten the critical path.

Executive Management Review

The executive management review is to provide upper management visibility into the status of the project. It usually consists of a presentation by the project's management on the overall health of the project. The format emphasizes accomplishments, particularly regarding contract requirements, and the efficient use of resources. This review is the opportunity for the project manager to alert executive management to bad news, potential risks, contingency plans, or corrective action, and any additional resources required.

Customer Review

The purpose of the customer review is to provide the customer an opportunity for constructive challenge of the progress against plan. This applies equally well to contract customers and to internal customers—namely, marketing. This review can be avoided altogether, or reduced in content, by including the customer in the weekly project manager's review. As with the executive review, key project team members present status against plan, problems analysis, and recovery actions, and seek concurrence from the customer as to the approach. Well-run projects routinely generate the type of data needed for this meeting, therefore, little new material needs to be prepared.

TECHNIQUES FOR ENHANCING VISIBILITY

The effectiveness of some visibility techniques can be situational—a matter of management style or project environment. Here are a few that work over a broad range of situations.

Top Ten Problem List

Publicize names of owners of the Top Ten problems. It will help them get the priority they need.

A Top Ten Problem List heightens the visibility of the most important concerns of the customer, project manager, functional managers, and task managers. These problems should be coded by each identifier as:

- Minor—I'm in control.
- Major—I need help.
- Showstopper—emergency action required.

All problems on the Top Ten List need to be statused daily by the responsible individual. The list is initiated by the task managers and propagates upward. The project manager's list should include majors and showstoppers that reach that level as well as pertinent items from the customer's list.

Use the Walls

Walls are an excellent display board for documentation review (RFP, proposals, user manuals, etc.) or design drawings. Use colored paper to indicate maturity (e.g., white for first draft, yellow for second, blue for the third). This technique has several benefits:

- Entire team has visibility.
- Helps identify inconsistencies, voids, overlaps, and schedule slippage.
- Highlights missing document sections.

Project Coordinators

Project coordinators augment the project manager's visibility for larger projects. A coordinator is chartered as a representative of the project manager who proactively ensures future events will occur as planned. He or she signals problem areas and recommends solutions. Project coordinators:

- Know how the organization "works."
- Provide expediting help to project and support organizations.
- Provide independent assessment of project information and status to the project manager.
- Ensure planning and milestones are satisfied.
- Ensure control procedures are being adhered to.
- Seek to shorten the critical path every day. A best practice is to title the coordinator the Critical Path Manager.

Customer In-Plant Representatives

Customer in-plant representatives reside with the supplier project team and provide two-way visibility because they:

- Understand customer expectations, needs, and capabilities.
- Provide continuous visibility into supplier and subcontractor activity and status.
- Can arrange with suppliers to have full plant access and random access accessibility.

The latter is accomplished by attending all in-plant visibility meetings and by other techniques such as MBWA. The techniques of glance management are particularly relevant to benefitting from customer visibility. A customer in-plant representative can address items that require guidance from the customer by immediately consulting with customer personnel. A secondary benefit is the escorting and briefing of customer visitors and their contacts.

TWENTY-FIRST CENTURY VISIBILITY TOOLS

Visibility tools include traditional devices and services such as:

Telephone.	Cellular phone.
Teleconferencing.	Video conferencing.
E-mail.	Fax.
Courier services.	Mail.
Internet.	Web conferencing.

The Internet has become the most important of all visibility tools. Bill Gates thinks so.[3] So do some project managers keeping abreast of a variety of projects overseas from their U.S.-based office. Photographs, taken twice a day with a digital camera and sent daily via the Internet, keep the team informed of progress worldwide and provide focused visibility on trouble spots. The personal computers, together with wireless local, wide-area networks, and the Internet have grown into powerful visibility tools. PDAs now provide integrated visibility through a range of phone and Internet services.

WHEN DESIGNING YOUR PROJECT'S VISIBILITY SYSTEM

Visibility is only the beginning. The visibility system must lead to statusing and timely corrective action.

Keep an open door and an open mind. The concept of visibility cannot coexist with significant secrecy, avoidance, or exclusion. Yet, these can take root and grow—particularly in the absence of strong leadership. The project manager needs to set an example by being open and willing to seek and accept expert advice, as well as bad news.

Avoid information overload. While it is better to be over-informed rather than under-informed, when carried to the extreme extraneous information causes overload and missed details.

Be selective. A visibility system can incorporate many techniques and tools. You need to determine the timing, critical need, and geographic location of the required information before designing and implementing the system you will use. These factors, and therefore the techniques, will generally change as the project progresses through its phases. It is important to carefully select the most cost-effective techniques and tools that get the job done.

PROJECT VISIBILITY EXERCISE

Considering your current or recent project experience, design a visibility system as follows:

1. Make a geographic map of the project activity locations with time zones.
2. Add the information flow requirements, format, and timing.
3. Add any other factors influencing the design.

Based on this trade space, design a system including method, format, and timing that will efficiently accomplish project visibility to all stakeholders.

16

PROJECT STATUS

Determining where you need to be in order to reach the intended destination—*the essence of project status.*

—— *PMBOK® Guide* ——
This chapter is consistent with the *PMBOK® Guide* Ch 10 *Project Communications Management* and Ch 11 *Project Risk Management.*

—— *INCOSE* ——
This chapter is consistent with *INCOSE Handbook Sec 6.3 Audits and Reviews,* and *Technical Performance Measurement and Metrics.*

"Nothing is good or bad, but by comparison."

Thomas Fuller[1]

Statusing must accurately reflect reality against the plan—not how busy the project team is.

"Would you tell me please, which way I ought to go from here?"

"That depends a good deal on where you want to get to," said the cat.

"I don't much care where—," said Alice.

"Then it doesn't matter which way you go," said the cat.

* * *

As the cat observed in Lewis Carroll's *Alice's Adventures in Wonderland,* it doesn't matter which way you go if you don't know your destination. Likewise, your current project situation is only meaningful from the perspective of where you need to be in order to reach your destination. Planning and status are inextricably linked.

Project status provides team members the ability to determine where they are against the plan—both present and projected—and the impact of this status on the anticipated project outcome. The main objective is to identify variances that require corrective action in order to recover to plan. To initiate corrective action quickly when deviations occur, the measurements must be:

- Relevant,
- Timely,
- Accurate,
- Comprehensive, and
- Compared to the plan.

Project activity without comparison to the plan may well be irrelevant, or even diversionary, in determining the need for corrective action. For example, the project manager may proclaim the team's long work hours and describe their dedicated efforts—even detailed work activities. Such reporting is often confused with status and contributes to information overload.

An effective status process:

—— *PMBOK® Guide* ——
The *PMBOK® Guide* uses the term monitor for the process we describe as status.

- Collects performance of critical metrics—matched to project complexity and risk.
- Compares baseline plan to current forecast and actual to plan.
- Evaluates the deterioration rate if no corrective action were to be taken.
- Tailors information to the needs of the team members interpreting it.

Status should be continuously known by task managers and by all levels of project management. Others who can affect project success, such as customers, subcontractors, and vendors, should provide status as to their critical obligations. Brief monthly status reports for distribution to executive management and functional support managers are a necessary communication technique for the project manager and the project team. Like many major corporations, Microsoft uses e-mail to distribute and comment on the monthly project status reports. Bill Gates and other top executives review them in appropriate detail. Gates reviews a hundred or so projects each month, and he "especially looks for schedule slips, cutting too many product features, or the need to change a specification."[2] The project manager creates monthly management reports based on detailed knowledge of the project's status using a common template that ensures completeness of information and ease of interpretation by the recipients. This chapter discusses the status methods the project manager should use to orchestrate the project to a successful conclusion.

STATUS MEANS TECHNICAL AND BUSINESS—COMBINED

To know the health of your project, schedule, cost, and other business factors must be evaluated together with technical performance, which requires the use of performance measurement techniques such as metrics and earned value. The following lists are representative of individual metrics often considered in each of the four factors:

—— *PMBOK® Guide* ——
The *PMBOK® Guide* covers metrics under the specific domain chapters (i.e., cost, schedule, scope, quality, time).

Schedule

Progress summary.

Master schedule.

Milestone accomplishments.

Earned value.

Assemblies and modules.

Tasks.

Subcontractors.

Parts and material.

Cost

Actuals versus budget.

Headcount.

Earned value versus expenditures.

Burn rate and overtime ratio.

Estimate to completion.

Estimate at completion.

Profit.

Dispersion ratio.

Technical

Development results.

Design release.

Technical review (closure on action items).

Technical performance measurements.

Interface control.

Quality.

Design change rate.

Other Business Factors

Contract change process.

Actions to/from customers.

Actions to/from management.

Actions to/from contractors.

Funding.

Top ten problems.

Security clearances.

Project manager's assessment.

(Note: Dispersion ratio refers to the equivalent full-time headcount divided by the number of different individuals charging to the project.)

Although each of these factors individually provides insight into aspects of the project, accurate status is only obtained when they are integrated. This integration requires tying the technical results to schedule, resources, and business impact. Without this integration, decisions may degrade one factor while trying to improve another.

CONDUCTING THE MAJOR STATUS REVIEWS

—— *INCOSE* ——
INCOSE Handbook Sec 6.3 *Audits and Reviews* addresses this area.

This discussion relates to status reviews for the examination of project health leading to a prescription for the cure, if appropriate. While decision gates may include reviews in both their name and the event, their purpose is approval of baseline elaboration. Status reviews result in action items directed at fixing problems.

The following three review types can represent a significant expenditure of team time and effort. They should be conducted as working meetings to avoid wasting time, particularly the repetition of carefully rehearsed scenarios.

This section addresses the details of format and agenda that facilitate the bulk of reactive management decisions. Detailed statusing does occur in smaller meetings—even one-on-ones—where corrective actions are sometimes decided. However, the project manager's review is the best opportunity for all relevant stones to be turned and assumptions to be challenged. The executive and customer reviews have two purposes: to aid visibility and provide a forum for corrective actions that need higher level management or customer concurrence and support. Figure 16.1 is a checklist for conducting these meetings.

EVALUATING STATUS

The foundation of status is technical accomplishment (which determines the schedule situation). Whatever method is used to collect status, it must reflect both the work accomplished and the acceptability of the results achieved to date. Without the assessment of the acceptability of the results, the status simply measures effort (how hard the team is working) and not how effective the team is in achieving the project objectives.

Once a calibrated understanding of technical accomplishment is determined, the schedule status reflects the difference between the planned time for successful accomplishment and reality. Although a delivery or review may occur when planned, it is not "on-time" unless it meets all defined objectives.

Likewise, the amount of resources consumed to fully accomplish technical objectives versus the resources planned for those objectives, provides the basis for cost status. Resources consumed against time is a measure of resource consumption, which is an important factor, but not relevant to project performance.

Once accurate technical, schedule, and resource consumption (cost) are determined, the business outcomes of the project may be estimated and appropriate actions taken. The following sections provide insight into how status may be taken and evaluated.

USING TPMS AND MARGIN MANAGEMENT TO OBTAIN TECHNICAL STATUS

Tying schedule and resource (cost) status to technical accomplishment requires effective means of determining the technical status.

INCOSE
See *INCOSE Handbook* Sec 6.3 *Technical Performance Measurement and Metrics (TPM).*

	Project Manager	Customer	Executive
General announcements	✓	✓	✓
Awards	✓		✓
Past and future meetings	✓	✓	✓
Organization (optional)		✓	✓
System concept overview (optional)		✓	✓
Action items from the customer	✓	✓	✓
Action items from upper management	✓		✓
Internal project action items	✓		
Master schedule with dateline and status	✓	✓	✓
Project milestone status	✓	✓	✓
Major accomplishments since last review	✓	✓	✓
Major customer-directed change status	✓	✓	✓
Engineering change request status	✓	✓	✓
Items awaiting customer disposition	✓	✓	✓
Top ten problem review	✓	✓	✓
Interface control action item status	✓	✓	✓
Systems engineering detailed status	✓	✓	
Technical Performance Measurement status	✓	✓	✓
Engineering release status	✓	✓	✓
Subsystem detailed status	✓	✓	
—Component by component status			
—Milestones accomplished vs. plan			
—Funds expended versus plan			
Contractor/Subcontractor technical status	✓	✓	✓
Contractor/Subcontractor key milestones	✓	✓	✓
Contractor/Subcontractor detailed status by item	✓		
—Budget, EAC, Variance			
Top level cost performance vs. budget	✓	✓	✓
Financial status—top level	✓	✓	✓
—Budget, EAC, Variance			
Plan for handling the reported variances		✓	✓
Manpower status vs. plan—top level	✓	✓	✓
Funding status		✓	✓
Management reserve			✓
Profit analysis		if internal	✓
Summary of new action items	✓	✓	✓
Key milestones for next 6 months	✓	✓	✓
Calendar of planned meetings	✓	✓	✓
Future business opportunities	✓	if internal	✓
Project manager's assessment		✓	✓
Customer's closing comments		✓	

Figure 16.1   Typical status agenda checklist.

In new development efforts, a method is needed to give early warning of development difficulties. For instance, if in the development of a new laptop computer, a high-speed computer chip is selected to meet performance objectives, the higher heat load could force those responsible for thermal control to use a larger cooling fan, which impacts system weight, physical volume, and power requirements. Cascading impacts such as this occur in almost every new design, so the risk of final system nonperformance is managed by establishing reasonable subsystem or component margins early in the design process. The project team should identify the driving technical parameters of their system (weight, average power, peak power, thermal limits, memory capacity, processing speed, system size, etc.). These key parameters are the technical performance measurement (TPM) set to be used to status and manage the technical development.

The microrover flight experiment on the Mars Pathfinder Project made very effective use of the TPM concept.[3] In their report, the authors note that, "by tracking the microrover's TPMs, the task manager gained insight into whether the delivered product would meet its performance requirements. There are several methods by which to track TPMs (i.e., system technical resources) and the task manager chose the development-phase margin management method. . . . The margin requirement is . . . expressed as a percentage of the TPM's allocation that declines toward zero consistent with design maturity. One of the advantages of margin management is that it allows management-by-exception—that is, so long as a TPM like mass has an actual margin that is within the requirement, contingent risk management action is usually not needed."

Figure 16.2 illustrates one of the TPMs (mass) used on the NASA Microrover System (Rover + Lander Mounted Rover Electronics or LMRE) (the team ultimately kept track of nine TPMs). The design margin requirement (established using the good judgment and experience of the team) started at 15 percent when the design was immature and performance predictions were speculation. It then dropped stepwise from 10 percent to 5 percent and finally to 1 percent as the design matured and speculation gave way to actual measurements. As shown, at critical design review (CDR) in February 1994, the system design was in a risk zone because the 11 percent actual margin violated the 15 percent margin requirement. Six months later, the best estimate indicated that the mass margin had violated the desired 10 percent limit, and weight reduction actions initiated at CDR were intensified. By February 1995, the design modifications succeeded in recovering to the desired margin. When

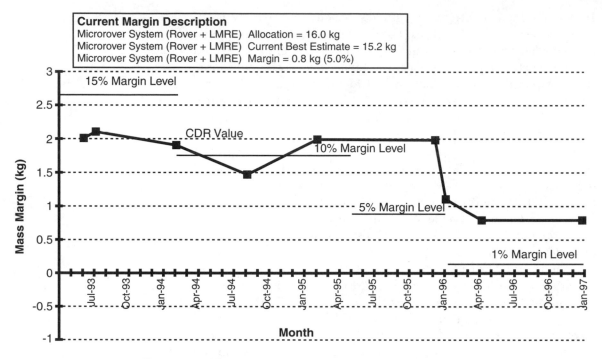

Current Margin Description
Microrover System (Rover + LMRE) Allocation = 16.0 kg
Microrover System (Rover + LMRE) Current Best Estimate = 15.2 kg
Microrover System (Rover + LMRE) Margin = 0.8 kg (5.0%)

Figure 16.2   Microrover mass—example of a TPM status chart.

the fully mature system was evaluated in April 1996, the margin was 4 percent, easily satisfying the minimum margin target of 1 percent. Timely action 20 months earlier (in August 1994) precluded a crisis late in the system development.

The microrover team highlighted several lessons learned. "First, it was very useful to begin tracking TPMs early even though there were changes in the TPMs included and their allocations. . . . Second, TPM/margin management was one of the most cost-effective risk management methods. A collection of simple graphical displays made it extremely easy to see looming problems. . . . Third, . . . the right number of TPMs to track in low-cost, high-risk . . . projects is small, but . . . should include key parameters used in any operations. . . ."

DETERMINING SCHEDULE STATUS

The quantity of milestones accomplished can be used as a schedule performance metric (Figure 16.3). The Milestone Deficiency Re-

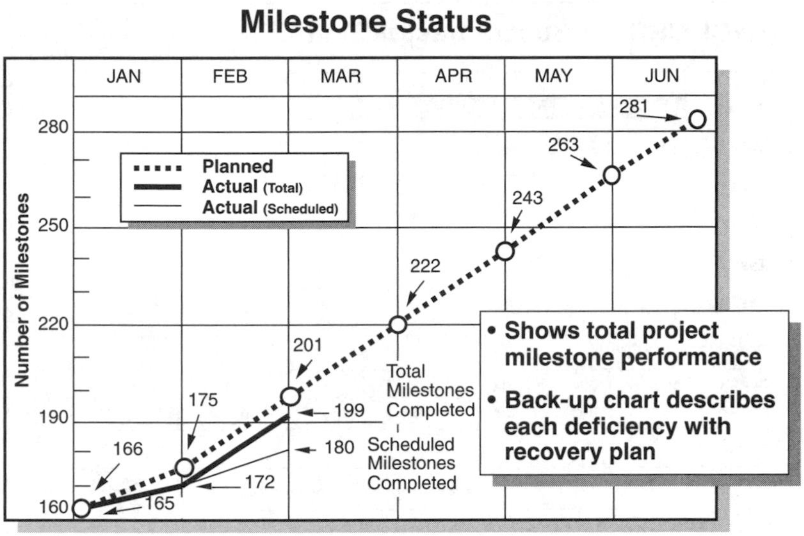

Milestone Status

Figure 16.3   Milestone status report.

port (Figure 16.4) should include an estimated completion date (ECD) and a recommended corrective action for each milestone that is past due. This way of highlighting exceptions, problems, and actions is very effective for most status measurements and reporting. The Configuration Item Status Report (Figure 16.5) illustrates

Milestone Deficiencies

Date Due	Project	M.S. No.	M.S. Title	Responsible	ECD	Plan
26 June	AJAX	SE-011	Release of Sys/ Segment Design Document	R. Smith	3 Aug	Revisit trade studies per action item 1072
27 June	AJAX	SE-012	Interface Spec.	H. James	10 Jul	Close TBDs from Associate

Figure 16.4   Milestone deficiency report.

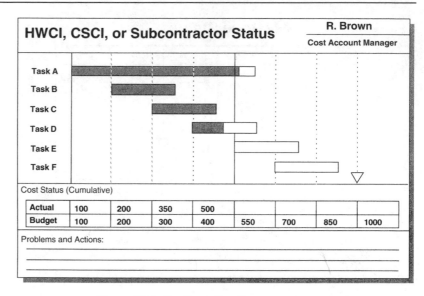

Figure 16.5   Configuration item status report.

the utility of pulling together and focusing on the tasks related to each deliverable and combined schedule, cost, and technical reporting. Again, statusing consists of reporting exceptions and actions, not activities.

Material shortage, which is critical to status, is shown here as a summary only (Figure 16.6). A separate page should be devoted to detailing each problem with actions completed and still open.

Before covering several comprehensive metrics for statusing project cost, consider a simple headcount cost indicator for payroll-intensive projects (Figure 16.7). As with other areas, there are several formats and metrics for statusing headcount. Typical parameters include part-time headcount ratios, on loan, and specific skill levels.

In this example, the project manager can use Total and Experienced headcount metrics to anticipate efficiency, cost, and schedule problems, because:

- Total personnel are exceeding plan.
- Experienced personnel are under plan.

With these expectations, the project manager should increase the experience or proficiency of the team.

The Top Ten Problem Summary (Figure 16.8) is a tool to highlight major problems which may result from a combination of factors. These can become worry lists and a place to track unsolvable

Part Number	Part Type	Quantity	Vendor	Next Assembly	Need Date	Prom Date	Resp. Individ.	Action
103-231	Elect.	42	Viking	1040	26 Sep	10 Oct	Fred H.	Visit vendor factory to pick up parts in person; daily phone calls to verify progress of tab and test of parts.
621-040	Firm-ware	1	S/W Creations	7131	26 Sep	15 Oct	Jenny C.	Firmware coding requirements clarification to be delivered to vendor by 10 Sept. Check out tests to be witnessed by our QA and engineering at vendor facility.

The last part in paces the project.

Figure 16.6   Material shortage list.

problems, but small problems solved may prevent future large ones. The summary should include the ECD, the number of weeks on the list, and the identity of the responsible person. A detailed chart should cover actions competed to date and actions planned with dates.

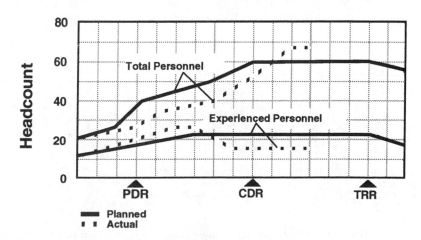

Figure 16.7   Headcount variance report.

Top Ten Problem Summary

No.	Problem Identification	Description	ECD	No. Weeks on list	Action/ Responsibility
71.	Update Project Products List (PPL)	Incorporate the changes from Rev A drawing release into the PPL	~~6/17,~~ ~~6/29,~~ ~~7/3,~~ 8/4	4	Frank A.
84.	Compatibility of SW with Rev A mechanical design	Ensure that software control system functions properly with Rev A mechanical modifications	8/1	1	Rich B.

◢—— **Detail Chart for each problem**

Figure 16.8 Top Ten Problem Summary.

PERFORMANCE MEASUREMENT SYSTEMS QUANTIFY THE SERIOUSNESS OF VARIANCES

Meaningful statusing depends on accurate and complete information.

Unless you are an accountant, it is very hard to see trends in tabular data. With graphical displays, significant items become vivid and trivial data can be appropriately obscured. Tufte, in his excellent 1983 work on the visual display of data, uses two figures that emphasize the value of graphics in detecting trends (Figures 16.9a and b).

	I		II		III		IV
X	Y	X	Y	X	Y	X	Y
10.0	8.04	10.0	9.14	10.0	7.46	8.0	6.58
8.0	6.95	8.0	8.14	8.0	6.77	8.0	5.76
13.0	7.58	13.0	8.74	13.0	12.74	8.0	7.71
9.0	8.81	9.0	8.77	9.0	7.11	8.0	8.84
11.0	8.33	11.0	9.26	11.0	7.81	8.0	8.47
14.0	9.96	14.0	8.10	14.0	8.84	8.0	7.04
6.0	7.24	6.0	6.13	6.0	6.08	8.0	5.25
4.0	4.26	4.0	3.10	4.0	5.39	19.0	12.50
12.0	10.84	12.0	9.13	12.0	8.15	8.0	5.56
7.0	4.82	7.0	7.26	7.0	6.42	8.0	7.91
5.0	5.68	5.0	4.74	5.0	5.73	8.0	6.89

N = 11
mean of X's = 9.0
mean of Y's = 7.5
equation of regression line: $Y = 3 + 0.5X$
standard error of estimate of slope = 0.118
$t = 4.24$
sum of squares $X - \overline{X} = 110.0$
regression sum of squares = 27.50
residual sum of squares of Y = 13.75
correlation coefficient = .82
$r^2 = .67$

Figure 16.9a Anscombe's quartet. All four of these data sets are described by exactly the same linear model. Used by permission. © Edward Tufte, *The Visual Display of Quantitative Data*, Cheshire, CT: Graphics Press, 1983.

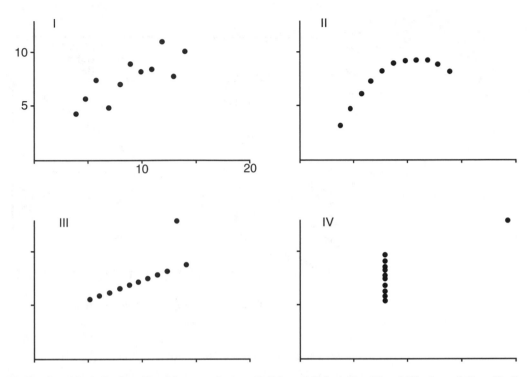

Figure 16.9b   Graphical display. Used by permission. © Edward Tufte, *The Visual Display of Quantitative Data,* Cheshire, CT: Graphics Press, 1983.

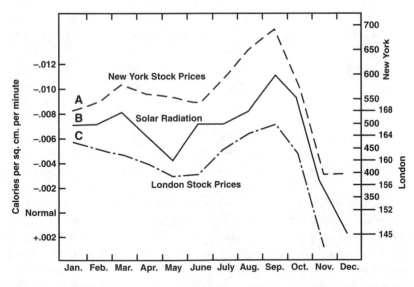

Figure 16.9c   Solar radiation and stock prices. Used by permission. © Edward Tufte, *The Visual Display of Quantitative Data,* Cheshire, CT: Graphics Press, 1983.

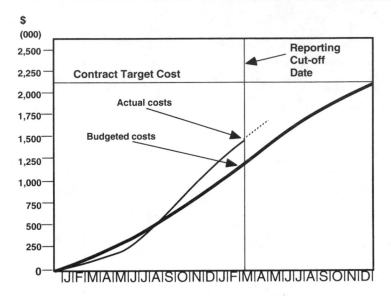

Figure 16.10   Superficial cost status.

He also warns against plotting data if it has no significance, as shown in Figure 16.9c.[4]

In his 1997 book, *Visual Explanations*, Tufte revisits the information presented to the Launch Review Board on the night before the fatal 1986 space shuttle *Challenger* launch.[5] He makes a strong case that the way the data were displayed obscured significant facts. It is worth reviewing Tufte's displays to help you consider how to improve the display of information.

Comprehensive performance measurement systems like earned value quantify the seriousness of the problems you should have known about and acted on much earlier. Performance measurement systems vary widely, depending on the organization's management information system and the techniques and tools available to the project. For highly effective status systems, time reporting to task codes is required to track the funds. In rapid growth years, many companies—especially technology start-ups where cost to capture a market is of little concern—may use crude, qualitative systems based on headcount estimates only. It is interesting to note that, on government projects, time reporting to the task level is manadatory all the way to direct charging managers. Figure 16.10 illustrates a cost status chart that fails to provide sufficient detail to decide on corrective action because schedule performance and technical milestone achievements are not included.

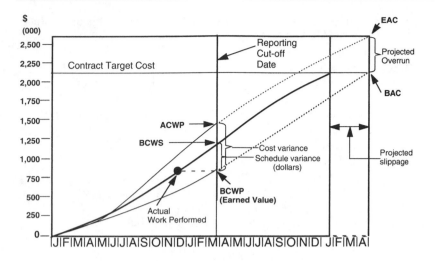

Figure 16.11   Earned value management system elements.

EARNED VALUE TIES STATUS
TO PLANNING

As competition increases and profit margins shrink, most organizations recognize the need to refine their performance measurements. Some commercial companies and many government agencies and their contractors use a system similar in framework to the one we describe here. This type of system requires detailed planning to predict cost and schedule expectations and interim milestones for each task. The insight provided is worth the effort, if the data are constructively used. In our experience, they've proven their value on projects with a budget as small as $500 thousand.

Earned Value Management (EVM) systems objectively evaluate status by comparing the budgeted value of work scheduled with the "earned value" of physical work completed and the actual value of work completed:

- EVM relates time-phased budgets to project tasks.
- EVM integrates cost, schedule, and technical performance.

Figure 16.11 illustrates the primary EVM elements.

When applied effectively as described here and in Chapters 8 and 11, the power of earned value as a predictive and preventive tool is available to be tapped. When used only as a status tool, however, the earned value approach will not *earn its own value* and could even contribute to project failure.

—— *PMBOK® Guide* ——
Earned value terminology is transitioning to PV, EV, and AC nomenclature to simplify the acronyms. Both sets of terms are in the *PMBOK® Guide*.

Garbage in—Garbage out. Meaningful statusing depends on good planning. Poorly planned projects simply cannot be statused.

BCWS	Budgeted cost of work scheduled.	The planned budget for the scheduled work.	Planned value (PV).
BCWP	Budgeted cost of work performed.	The planned budget for the completed work.	Earned value (EV).
ACWP	Actual cost of work performed.	Actual cost of performing the completed work.	Actual cost (AC).
BAC	Budget at completion.	The planned budget for all the work (a management reserve is often subtracted from the contracted or committed funding to arrive at a project budget).	
EAC	Estimate at completion.	Estimated total cost upon work completion.	
ETC	Estimate to complete.	Estimated remaining costs to complete the work.	

The *PMBOK® Guide* uses the somewhat less precise vocabulary shown in the last column.

Cost and schedule variances can both be expressed as dollars or percentage. Using the definitions that follow, negative indicates an overrun:

	In Dollars	*In Percent*
Cost variance	BCWP − ACWP	(BCWP − ACWP)/BCWP
Schedule variance	BCWP − BCWS	(BCWP − BCWS)/BCWS

—— *PMBOK® Guide* ——
The *PMBOK® Guide* Sec 7.3.2 *Cost Control* provides earned value terminology and equations.

The alternative methods for estimate to complete (ETC) and estimate at completion (EAC) are:

Performance projections.
Managerial judgment.
Bottom up (grass roots).
Statistical projections.

Performance projections assume that performance will continue at the same rate:

$$ETC = (BAC - BCWP) \times \frac{(ACWP)}{(BCWP)}$$

$$EAC = ACWP + ETC$$

Managerial projections for ETC are a matter of judgment. Typical methods are:

- Original budget plan to go (if original plan is valid).
- Current burn rate multiplied by the estimated time to complete (if these factors are reliable).
- Burn rate multiplied by schedule slip plus the original plan including normal personnel roll off for project shut down.
- Performance factor multiplied by the original budget plan to go (if efficiency rate is expected to continue).
- New bottom-up quote (scrubbed—if time permits since personnel will stop work to produce it).
- The EAC is determined by adding the ETC to ACWP.

There are several negotiable options for measuring work progress, expressed as the earned value (BCWP) by task. Four common definitions are listed next:

Option	*Amount of Task BCWP (Earned Value)*
0–100	Zero until task completion. (For this method, work packages should be small, probably less than 100 hours.) Distortion can occur since earned value is zero up until the task is complete.
50–50	One-half of Task BAC at start; final one-half is earned at completion. Distortion can occur since earned value is 50 percent at start with no work actually accomplished.
Percentage	Percentage of Task BAC based on interim milestones or task leader's estimate (BCWP at completion = Task BAC). For this method, work packages can be two to three times larger than those for the 0–100 option but require interim progress measurement milestones to achieve accurate status.

The 0 to 100 method is effective for small work packages. On large projects, there is a significant administrative effort required to manage the individual task cost accounts.

The percentage method based on interim milestone accomplishment is as accurate as 0 to 100 and requires fewer charge numbers.

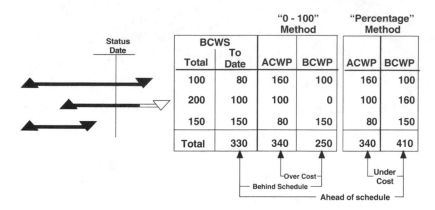

Figure 16.12   The 0—100 and percentage methods compared.

Level-of-Effort   BWCP is earned as effort is expended (BCWP = BCWS at any time). Used for level of effort tasks (should not exceed 10 percent to 15 percent of the total contract value).

These examples of using the 0 to 100 and percentage earned value (Figure 16.12) are shown here for the same three tasks. The earned value of the 0 to 100 option is distorted, since the second task is incomplete at the status date. The task earned value being zero makes the total look like bad news. In reality, the news is good. For the 0 to 100 method to be effective, the tasks should start and end within the reporting period so unfinished tasks will not distort the progress measurement.

The percentage example shows a more accurate status. With this method, the data reliability depends on the task leader's ability to accurately assess status of work progress. The preferred approach is to set interim milestones with accomplishment values and earned value accrued when milestones are satisfied, thereby eliminating the need to estimate percent complete. The assessment of software progress can be more difficult. The downloadable files available with this book include a set of spreadsheets for calculating earned value for software tasks. The forms automatically calculate percent complete based on the Xs appearing in the appropriate cells as entered by the programmer.

Interim milestones increase
measurement accuracy.

INTERPRETING THE TRENDS

In the previous sections, we selected charts that exemplify the key factors to status. These illustrations also provide templates that are adaptable to most projects. The performance of individual work packages is summed up to measure the aggregate performance of major WBS elements and the overall project. But status shouldn't be static. You need to pay careful attention to the trends, such as those in Figure 16.13, which can be leading indicators of trouble.

Two helpful indicators for trend analysis are CPI and SPI:

Cost Performance Index (CPI) = BCWP/ACWP
Schedule Performance Index (SPI) = BCWP/BCWS

Both CPI and SPI can be calculated cumulatively or for the most recent period. Both are helpful for flagging problems. These are interpreted in eight separate performance trend examples (Figure 16.14).

Timely, comprehensive project status information is important because it enables you to identify variances and quantify their seriousness.

Differences between planned and actual results need to be reviewed on at least a monthly basis, but weekly is advisable. Variances that exceed predetermined thresholds should be analyzed further to determine the reasons and the actions required to improve performance and recover to plan. The thresholds depend on the specific metrics. Example thresholds are:

If you can't measure it, you can't manage it!

± 20 percent and ± $20 thousand for the current period.
± 10 percent and ± $40 thousand for cumulative amounts.

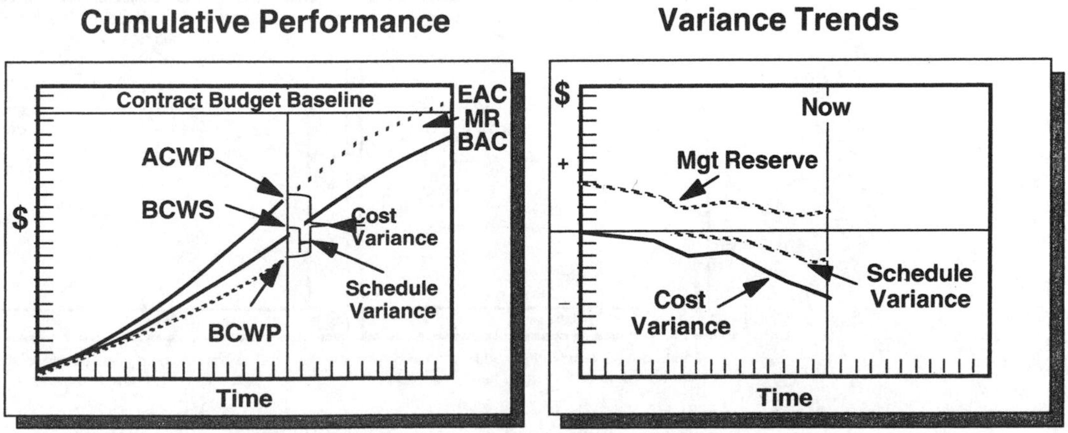

Cumulative Performance

Variance Trends

Figure 16.13   Trends provide leading indicators.

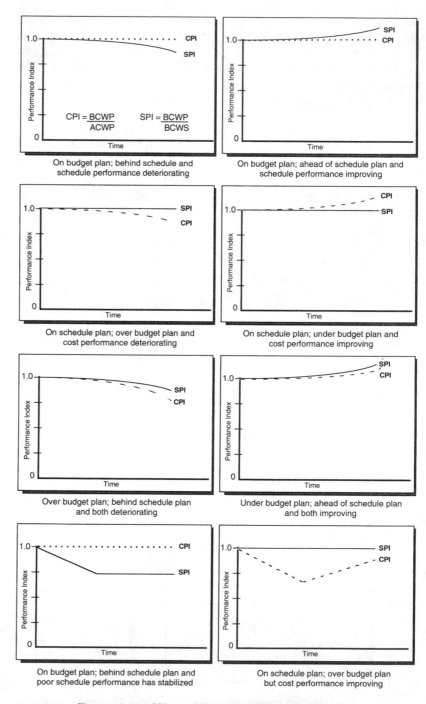

Figure 16.14 CPI and SPI trend analyses (may display cumulative or measurement period trend).

Status

8.4 Subcontractor Receiver Assembly

Cum **Cost** Var: **(33%) ($100K)**   Cum **Schedule** Var: **(66%) ($200K)**

This situation is serious. Our subcontractor has spent $400K (33% above the plan) and is two months behind schedule which equates to $200K. Investigation of this problem reveals that the subcontractor's key designers have left the company. The project is now overstaffed with unskilled personnel in a futile attempt to perform.

To recover we are planning to terminate the subcontract and perform this work internally. We have contacted the previous designers and they are anxious to assist on a consulting basis. The impact of the wasted effort to date plus termination costs and consultant costs will result in a variance to our budget of approximately $300K of which $75K will come from management reserve and $225K will be overrun.

Corrective Action

Figure 16.15   Status report example.

Variance analysis reports need to be specific as to variance cause. Figure 16.15 illustrates the status for an example task, together with the corrective actions, the subject of the next chapter.

PROJECT STATUS ELEMENT EXERCISE

Considering your current or recent project experience, evaluate the effectiveness of the status metrics used. Based on the evaluation, recommend additional metrics to aid in navigating the project.

Actual Metric	Importance
Headcount	Accomplishing staffing
Burn rate	Funds consumption

Desired Metric	Importance
Time to next milestone	Keep eye on the ball
Open action items	Keep in field of view

MANAGEMENT
ELEMENT 9

17

CORRECTIVE ACTION

—— *PMBOK® Guide* ——
This chapter is consistent with the *PMBOK® Guide* treatment of corrective action within the individual knowledge areas of scope, time, schedule, cost, quality, and so on.

—————— *INCOSE* ——————
The *INCOSE Handbook* treats corrective action similarly to the *PMBOK® Guide.* We believe it warrants special attention as the culmination of planning, visibility, and status.

There are many pressures to keep a project on schedule. In order to avoid admitting to a schedule slip, appropriate and timely corrective actions are sometimes delayed or eliminated altogether. Engineers were not allowed to pursue efforts to understand why some test data during the Hubble Telescope development evidenced that the mirror met requirements, while conflicting tests (on prior test equipment) indicated defects. The already overrun program could not "afford" the delay. Everything was assumed to be fine until eight years later when the telescope was put into orbit and first operational use revealed the defect previously detected in ground tests. Similarly, engineers were disturbed that the space shuttle booster field joints deformed differently than expected when under motor combustion pressure. They too were told that lack of funding prohibited further investigation. One joint subsequently failed on *Challenger*.

CORRECTIVE ACTIONS ARE TAKEN TO FIX VARIANCES

—— *PMBOK® Guide* ——
The *PMBOK® Guide* differentiates between *corrective actions* (bringing future performance in line with the plan) and *preventive actions* (actions to manage the probability and/or impact of issues—something we treat in opportunity and risk management).

Corrective actions are the valid and necessary reactive management actions to correct unacceptable variances detected (usually through statusing techniques) (Figure 16.15). Assessing status without following through with corrective action is meaningless. Therefore, the process described in this section—corrective action—usually takes place as a result of statusing.

Data have finally come to light that might explain the mysterious sinking of the USS *Scorpion* submarine. The evidence is strong that a battery in a Mark 37 torpedo burst into flames when a tiny foil diaphragm, costing pennies, ruptured in the battery. The crew of 99 died when the sub sank in May 1968. Earlier that year, a battery diaphragm failure occurred in a torpedo battery in a test lab and six people were sent to the hospital. Tracing back to 1966, the Naval Ordnance laboratory had bypassed its own safety and acceptance procedures in order to meet the demand for torpedo deliveries (with their batteries installed) to the fleet. The diaphragm was known to be a poor design and was difficult to make. Yield from one supplier was so low that 250 batteries had to be "accepted" despite failing required verification tests. One of the 250 batteries exploded in the laboratory. The ongoing "corrective action" was to deny that a problem existed, to continue with deliveries to the fleet, and to discipline anyone who tried to link any operational problems to the procuring command. It is presumed that one of the 250 exploded aboard *Scorpion*.[1] A safe diaphragm design was introduced in 1969.

> Statusing is comparing current performance to the plan—corrective action is doing something about the difference.

Commercial products also find their way to the marketplace with design defects. Children's toys are often subject to recall for choking hazards, cars are recalled for mechanical or safety defects, software products are released for sale—followed shortly by bug fixes. Many of these defects are discovered in the development or verification process, but timely corrective action is often not taken in order to be first to market. However, producers of consumer products are increasingly being held accountable for consequential damage caused by defects, such as poorly designed car seats for children.

> —— *PMBOK® Guide* ——
> The *PMBOK® Guide* identifies corrective actions (and occasionally preventive actions) as outputs of the nine knowledge areas.

Future investors will not be silent about an online trading company's liability when Internet trading is shut down for four days due to the online company's software problems. This happened in 1999 when incomplete testing of software changes caused the shutdown. In another situation reported by the Associated Press, "sports equipment maker Shimano American Corporation agreed to pay a $150,000 civil penalty to settle allegations that it failed to report in a timely manner bicycle crank defects that caused 22 injuries." The cranks were put on more than 200 models of mountain bikes over a two-year period.

Corrective actions may indeed have impact on project cost or schedule, especially if design flaws are not found until the product (hardware or software) is in final system verification or in operational use. The objective is to find problems early and fix them swiftly and completely. Schedule pressures, optimism, and the pressures by customers or management for the project manager to "go along with the crowd" are real issues that make effective corrective action easy to talk about but sometimes difficult to do.

> The goal is to find problems early and fix them completely and correctly—the first time.

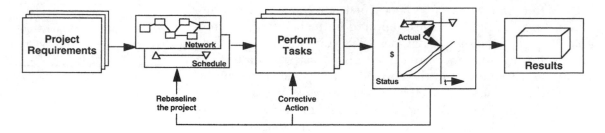

Figure 17.1 Corrective action closes the control loop.

In theory, if there is sound visibility and a solid plan, the only time a project status meeting would be required is when corrective action is necessary, as determined by a continuously available status system. Generally, those team members who are on plan would not need to attend such meetings. In practice, however, periodic status meetings with key team members are valuable, even if visibility and status systems appear to be sound and the project is on plan. Status meetings allow the team to see the project as a whole, and omissions—in project integration, for instance—can be identified and corrected early.

The effective use of positive reactive management considers many of the same attributes as an automatic control system or servomechanism (depicted in Figure 17.1):

- Fidelity—detection and accuracy.
- Disturbances—irrelevant data.
- Noise level—false input.
- Time lag—timeliness and validity.
- Lead time—early detection.
- Gain versus stability—too much gain can produce overreaction.

Corrective Action begins with periodic variance analysis to identify significant differences from the plan. The period and threshold for action is proportional to the criticality to the project. Near-term critical issues may need to be statused daily with tight thresholds while noncritical issues are relegated to monthly statusing with broader thresholds. The business manager should determine the periods and thresholds. Cost thresholds should be expressed in both percentage and absolute terms—say, for example, 20 percent or $20 thousand for current periods and 10 percent or $40 thousand for cumulative measurements.

Schedule thresholds could vary widely, depending on the time remaining to task completion and whether the task is on the critical path, a low-slack path, or a high-slack path. A one-week slip is a reasonable threshold for a critical milestone with one year to completion.

Budget underruns may be more critical than overruns.

Repeated schedule slips require special attention, lest they become the critical path.

DETERMINING THE CORRECTIVE ACTION

Approach

1. Analyze the problem:
    - The current impact.
    - The impact growth if no action is taken.
2. Prioritize all project problems from the most serious to the least serious.
3. Determine the best approach for each using the analytical decision process.

> Corrective actions should decisively solve the problem. They may require outside-the-box creativity.

In determining the "best" corrective action, classical root cause analysis is applicable. It consists of seeking answers to:

> Problems may have several underlying causes.

- What has changed from before the problem to after the problem?
- Were expectations unreasonable?
- Was the plan wrong?
- Were requirements ill defined?
- Were resources insufficient?
- Was there a lack of interest?
- Was there conflicting direction?
- Were communications faulty?

Identify Corrective Action Candidates

Cost overrun corrective actions seek to *reduce:*

- Requirements.
- Labor rates and/or hours.
- Overtime.
- Project length.

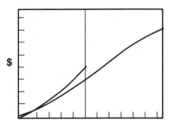

More imaginative cost options are to:

- Develop a more producible design.
- Install more efficient processes.
- Eliminate waste or superfluous tasks.
- Assign work to lower labor rate areas.

Schedule overrun corrective actions *add:*

- Work shifts and/or overtime.
- Personnel.

and *improve:*

- Tools.
- Processes.
- Network (shorten critical path).

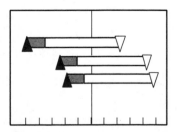

More imaginative schedule options are to:

- Overlap tasks.
- Use higher skilled personnel.
- Send work to high-efficiency specialty shops.

Technical corrective actions seek to resolve shortcomings:

- Add Tiger Team review.
- Challenge requirements.
- Reduce quantities.
- Add skilled talent.
- Add more capable tools.
- Improve supplier(s).
- Add training.

Business corrective actions seek to improve the business process and eliminate bureaucracy. They involve:

- Experts.
- Consultants.
- Executive management.
- Customer involvement.

Select the Highest Value Solution

Selecting among alternatives, like any difficult decision process, may require an objective selection system. First, establish evaluation criteria (musts and wants). Then assign relative weighting factors and score the alternatives against the criteria. Figure 17.2 illustrates an approach for selecting schedule recovery action.

> In some cases, taking no corrective action may be the best of the alternatives.

The tentative choice is usually the highest scoring alternative. However, the evaluation criteria and weighting factors, being somewhat subjective, may lead to a close, but biased, decision. A technique to evaluate the tentative decision is to assess other factors not contained in the decision criteria. Compare that assessment of implementing the tentative choice with the closest alternative(s). The process should also consider the consequences of doing nothing different—always an alternative worth evaluating. It is important to document the decision analysis for later justification.

Once the decision is made:

1. Develop an implementation plan.
2. Get the commitments.

The project manager approves the decision and is responsible for the timely implementation of the corrective action.

Evaluation Criteria		Alternative 1 **One 12 hr shift**			Alternative 2 **Two 8 hr shifts**			Alternative 3 **Three 8 hr shifts**			Alternative 4 **Two 12 hr shifts**		
Musts (Go-No Go): • Certified Software Testers • Available within 3 weeks								X X					
			Score			Score			Score			Score	
Wants	Weight (W)	Comments	Raw	R x W	Comments	Raw	R x W	Comments	Raw	R x W	Comments	Raw	R x W
Factors													
Maximizes productivity	10		5	50		7	70					10	100
Highly experienced in our software	8		10	80		8	64					8	64
Low average labor rate	8		7	56		10	80					5	40
Max Score (10xW) Total Score	260			186			214						204

Figure 17.2   **Evaluating alternatives by weighted scoring.**

SUCCESSFULLY IMPLEMENTING CORRECTIVE ACTION

The most prevalent error in reacting to variances is that corrective action is usually applied too little, too late, and with insufficient vigor. Problems must be dealt with promptly, decisively, and completely.

Some problems require major actions.

- Problems prevented are least expensive.
- Problems solved quickly are cheaper than delayed solutions.

Other common errors are:

- Corrective action is insufficiently imaginative to consider all viable options.
- The effect of labor burn rate and schedule slippage is usually ignored.

Problems that occur during high burn-rate periods are expensive (Figure 17.3). Extraordinary action may be justified to eliminate high burn-rate slippages. If too many critical path activities are in variance, or if the burn rate renders the variances nonrecoverable, it may be necessary to redefine the baseline plan since the current plan may be unachievable.

Expensive expert consultants may be a real bargain . . . if they eliminate schedule slips during high "burn-rate" periods.

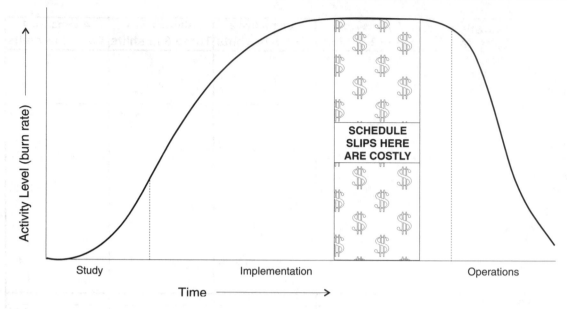

Figure 17.3   The high costs of schedule slips.

> Re-baselining the project is often the first task of the "new" project manager.

To ensure that all viable corrective actions are considered:

- Identify the total problem and impact.
- Develop alternative courses of action as straw man solutions.
- Select the highest value alternative.

Finally, to ensure that the plan is successfully implemented:

- Seek team consensus for the solution.
- Develop the implementation plan.
- Announce the plan.
- Status and control the corrective action plan along with the baseline plan.

CORRECTIVE ACTION ELEMENT EXERCISE

Considering your current or recent project experience, list all of the corrective actions you observed. Try to identify some in each of the categories of business, budget, and technical. Also critique how successful they were.

CA Technique	Objective	Success Rating
Tiger Team	Problem solving	9
Overtime	Shorten schedule	10

18

PROJECT LEADERSHIP

MANAGEMENT ELEMENT 10

"We all need to be ready for those moments when our leadership is on the line and the fate or fortune of others depends on what we do."[1] With this introduction to *The Leadership Moment,* Michael Useem tells nine gripping leadership stories and draws out the following principles:

Know yourself: Understanding your values and where you want to go will assure that you know which paths to take.

Explain yourself: Only then can your associates understand where you want to go and whether they want to accompany you.

Expect much: Demanding the best is a prerequisite for obtaining it.

Gain commitment: Obtaining consensus before a decision will mobilize those you are counting on after the decision.

Build now: Acquiring support today is indispensable if you plan to draw on it tomorrow.

Prepare yourself: Seeking varied and challenging assignments now develops the confidence and skills required for later.

Move fast: Inaction can often prove as disastrous as inept action.

Find yourself: Liberating your leadership potential requires matching your goals and talents to the right organization.

Remain steadfast: Faith in your vision will ensure that you and your followers remain unswerving in pursuit of it.

—— *PMBOK® Guide* ——
The *PMBOK® Guide* Sec 1.5.5 *Interpersonal Skills* identifies leadership as a skill needed for interpersonal relationship management along with:

• Effective communication.
• Influencing the organization.
• Motivation.
• Negotiation and conflict management.
• Problem solving.

—— *INCOSE* ——
The *INCOSE Handbook* Sec 1.7 *Systems Engineering Has a Human Orientation* cites leadership as essential for systems engineering, but does not expand further.

THE ESSENCE OF LEADERSHIP: VISION AND ACTION

"The only way in which anyone can lead us is to restore to us the belief in our own guidance."

Henry Miller

To paraphrase the author in his conclusion to *The Leadership Moment,* examining the behavior of strong leaders teaches us to think more strategically and act more decisively. "By watching those who lead the way—as well as those who go astray—we can see what works and what fails, what hastens our cause or subverts our purpose."

In its role as the uniting management element, the proper application of leadership must ensure that the other nine elements are accepted, passionately supported, and faithfully implemented. In this chapter, we address three primary aspects of project leadership:

1. Techniques for inspiring and motivating individual and team performance.
2. Situational leadership—the relationship of leadership to management.
3. Style—determining and communicating your leadership style.

Leadership is primarily a high-powered, right-brain activity.

In the context of project management, leadership represents the ability to inspire—to ensure that project members are motivated—on both the individual and the team levels. Several leadership professionals, quoted here, have captured the essence of inspiration and self-motivation. Regarding self-motivation, Peter De Vries wryly commented, "I write when I'm inspired, and I see to it that I'm inspired at nine o'clock every morning."

Leadership includes lifting a person's vision to higher sights.

As Peter Drucker defines it, "Leadership is not a magnetic personality—that can just as well be a glib tongue. It is not 'making friends and influencing people'—that is flattery. Leadership is lifting a person's vision to higher sights, raising a person's performance to a higher standard, building a personality beyond its normal limitations." He contrasts leadership, "doing the right things," with management, "doing things right."[2]

Managing is doing things right. Leadership is doing the right things, like leaning the ladder against the right wall.

Stephen Covey reminds us that management is clearly different from leadership. "Leadership is primarily a high-powered, right brain activity. It's more of an art; it's based on philosophy. Management is the breaking down, the analysis, the sequencing, the specific application, the time-bound left-brain aspect of self-government." His own maxim of personal effectiveness: "Manage from the left; lead from the right."[3]

Peter Drucker, Stephen Covey, and Warren Bennis associate efficiency with management, even in climbing the ladder of success. To paraphrase their observation, leadership determines whether the ladder is leaning against the right wall.

Motivational experts seek to explain why some projects succeed while others do not. These studies result in leadership-success models based on the project environment, the characteristics of the leaders being studied, and the leader's ability to influence others. Some have studied the basis for leadership power and influence, notably Hans Thamhain[4] and the Wilson Learning Corporation,[5] by having various influence factors ranked by managers, peers, and support personnel. To highlight the consistencies among their findings, we've focused on four influence categories. They're in the following list in the order of their effectiveness as rated by team members:

- *Organizational position or formal authority.*
- *The manager's personal factors*—Expertise, interpersonal skills, information, connections and alliances, trust, and respect. All credibility factors.
- *The project work itself*—Work interest and challenge; future assignments.
- *Rewards and penalties*—Salary and promotion; coercion and penalties.

While the order varies somewhat among surveys and industries, most participants rank the project manager's authority and expertise at the top along with the work itself. Surprisingly, salary and promotions are perceived only a little more positively than coercion and penalties, the latter being seen as the least influential.

One author's career-limiting experience takes a (somewhat obstructed) view of *organizational position.*

As a new lieutenant on active duty with the U.S. Army during peacetime, I was assigned to a combat engineering company at Fort Lewis, a large military base near a major city. I was assigned to lead a convoy of 107 vehicles through the military base, continuing 10 miles through the city, and on to a remote training area 90 miles away. The convoy consisted of jeeps, light trucks, one high-back communications van, and over 100 very heavy, very long, very slow vehicles, including heavy-duty dump trucks, flat-bed trucks with bulldozers, and rubber-tire-mounted cranes.

We set out at the appointed time, just at the start of the Tacoma rush hour. The convoy requirement was that we had to allow civilian vehicles to pass and to intermingle with the long line of trucks. As was appropriate, I was in the lead jeep, with my second in command in the jeep at the rear. The communications van was right behind me.

An hour later, a military police sergeant on a motorcycle, red lights flashing, pulled us over. The communications van, which I had been carefully watching—but could not see around—pulled over behind us. The police sergeant asked, "Lieutenant, are you the leader of this convoy?" "Yes, I am," I replied. He said, "Would you like to know where they are?" I got out of the jeep to discover that no army vehicle was in sight. Some of the longest vehicles "got lost" in the officers' quarters, wandering past the homes of the commanding general, the battalion commander, and others, causing a major traffic jam. Others of the lost 105 vehicles made it off the Fort, but got lost in the business areas of Tacoma. It took over two hours to round up everyone and reform the convoy.

A valuable lesson: Leadership is not about being in front.

When we discussed forming the project team, we emphasized that the project manager should be given as much authority as possible. But we need to add one important caveat. The *existence* of the authority is considered to be a positive influence; however, its *undue exercise* can be perceived as coercion—diminishing the net influence. Selective use of authority only when absolutely required will produce the best overall results.

> In the absence of adequate formal authority, strong personal skills and leadership techniques are indispensable.

THE MOTIVATIONAL TECHNIQUES OF PROJECT LEADERSHIP

Nothing requires leadership skills more than the challenges of motivation. The payoff is very high. According to the results of studies by the Public Agenda Foundation, a private research organization in New York, 88 percent of workers responded positively when asked if they considered it important to do their best job. However, 44 percent of those surveyed admitted that they "exert no effort over the minimum." And only 23 percent believe they work to their full capacity. The leader's motivation challenge is to tap that available discretionary effort.

The limitations of control and authority demand that project managers be able to differentiate motivational causes and effects and be able to accurately relate them to the specific project team and member needs. Misplaced or ill-conceived motivation often turns into demotivation—much worse than no motivation at all. The following groups of techniques, when properly applied, have proved effective in the project environment.

> Vision pursuit is the glue that holds all the other leadership techniques together.

Vision

Above all else, we demand that our leaders have a vision and be able to articulate and structure its attainment. Whether it's successful task completion or a company reorganization, the ability to convey the vision and then affect its realization is the glue that holds all the other leadership techniques in place. Leaders must accept the goals of the larger organization, of which their work is a part, and create the vision that supports the goals. They must understand the driving forces of the various stakeholders who will gain or lose by the vision's fulfillment. Finally, they must be able to communicate that vision to the team in relationship to their work.

Creating the Environment

How we manage vision attainment is the heart of the technique set. Attainment begins by creating the environment in which the work is to be accomplished.

Hallucinator: a visionary who cannot lead to realization of their vision.

Initially, this means defining management practices that will be used to manage the project and determining your style (discussed in detail at the end of the chapter).

In Chapter 5, we addressed the decision-making process as a major environmental and teamwork factor. The work of Douglas McGregor is also useful in characterizing the leadership environment.[6] He defined two types of environments (Figure 18.1): Theory X (authoritative) and Theory Y (challenge). Theory X is the militaristic environment based on the assumption that people really don't like to work and must be coerced into following orders, most of which originate with top management. But direct orders cannot

——— *INCOSE* ———
The *INCOSE Handbook* Sec 1.7 refers to leadership as a vision-based activity and cites the need for systems engineers to have systemic vision.

Figure 18.1   Theory X (authoritative) and Y (challenge) environments.

always be depended upon, as the following story, originally appearing in the Naval Institute's *Proceedings*, illustrates.

This "beacon of information" provides several metaphors regarding position power, perceptions of authority, and the need to act on complete information.

Two battleships assigned to the training squadron had been at sea on maneuvers in heavy weather for several days. I was serving on the lead battleship and was on watch on the bridge as night fell. The visibility was poor with patchy fog, so the captain remained on the bridge keeping an eye on all activities.

Shortly after dark, the lookout on the wing of the bridge reported, "Light, bearing on the starboard bow."

"Is it steady or moving astern?" the captain called out.

Lookout replied, "Steady, captain," which meant we were on a dangerous collision course with that ship.

The captain then called to the signal man, "Signal that ship: We are on a collision course, advise you change course 20 degrees."

Back came a signal, "Advisable for you to change course 20 degrees."

The captain said, "Send, I'm a captain, change course 20 degrees."

"I'm a seaman second class," came the reply. "You had better change course 20 degrees."

By that time the captain was furious. He spat out, "Send, I'm a battleship. Change course 20 degrees."

Back came the flashing light, "I'm a lighthouse."

We changed course.

Theory X often results in an adversarial relationship between manager and subordinates—totally inappropriate for most project teams. Theory Y assumes that people want to work and can be highly self-directed with an appropriate work environment and reward system.

Subsequent to McGregor's original work, William Ouchi introduced Theory Z to refer to the participative format that grew out of the Japanese "quality circles" movement and broadened with Total Quality Management.[7] It is typified by closely knit teams that develop common goals to which they are committed through shared values and a refined process (Figure 18.2).

Variations in performance often stem from the leadership style used by the accountable person—for example, the way the task work is assigned, planned, and statused.

For most projects each of these concepts has shortcomings. While Theory Z represents the project environment most closely—especially small, well-controlled projects—it has been found deficient in atmospheres of conflict. Larger projects involving multiple organizations, customers, and subcontractors work best when the environmental elements of both Theory Y (individual) and Theory Z (team) are combined. For your project, you need to determine the appropriate environment and decide how to set that environment in place.

Z - Management Environment

Figure 18.2   Theory Z (participative) environment.

Regardless of the specific style, a leader creates a problem-solving environment by:

- Building urgency and "admiring" the problem.
- Removing roadblocks so the team can do their things.
- Eliminating window dressing.
- Rising above bureaucracy and politics.

The same approach should be taken for a task managed by a self-directing team or by McGregor's worst nightmare, the X-style manager. That is, after assessing the team and the stakeholder expectations, adopt or adapt a project cycle for the project and announce what tailoring the team is expected to do to that cycle. Identify the training needed to increase the team effectiveness, both at the team and individual levels. You will also need to define the balance of decision-making authority among the team, you as the project manager, and higher-level management.

Due to the interdependent nature of project people and the teamwork culture, each team member wants to be involved and to feel responsible for proactive participation in management activities. These include planning, measuring, evaluating, anticipating, and alerting others to potential problems. To become committed to project goals, as Stephen Covey observes, ". . . they want involvement, significant involvement. And if they don't have involvement, they don't buy it. Then you have a significant motivational problem which cannot be solved at the same level of thinking that created it."

Project failures can frequently be traced to unrealistic technical, cost, or schedule targets. Such targets may be entirely arbitrary

> The leader knows the people on the team and recognizes their needs.

Involving team members in the goal-setting process facilitates team buy-in.

Goal setting by team members ultimately leads to greater self-confidence and more aggressive goals.

Meeting format and conduct is a significant aspect of creating the environment.

Major meeting demotivators include: lack of an agenda, indefinite start/stop times, and failure to stay on schedule.

A pattern of ineffective meetings is a sign of weak leadership.

or based on bad assumptions—setting team members up for failure. Furthermore, the goals that motivate one team member may not motivate another member. All tasks don't have to be inherently motivating—that's not sensible. But there have to be motivating factors, if by nothing more than participating in goal determination. This also helps ensure adequate opportunity and risk identification, analysis, and management.

We've found that it is better to aim high and to occasionally miss than to aim low. For example, Intel Corporation encourages employees to include goals in their management by objectives (MBOs) for which there is at least a 50 percent chance of accomplishing. An overall MBO score of 75 percent is considered good—encouraging a stretch. Even overly aggressive goals, if set by the team member rather than the leader, can stimulate the extra effort needed to meet them. And they pay an extra dividend—on-the-job training.

Meetings—lots of them—are an inherent part of the project management process. Nearly everyone complains about the time they waste in meetings. But meetings are the major vehicles for exercising leadership. In Chapter 15, we provided conduct guidelines for the various types, from one-on-one meetings to formal reviews. Well-conducted meetings can inspire and motivate the team, but too many meetings, or poorly conceived or poorly executed ones, can be demotivators.

Effective meetings are no accident. They demand management skills for preparation and leadership skills for conduct. For example, people who are needed for decisions, but who arrive late or not at all, waste everyone's time. Attendees who are not needed at all also feel that their time is wasted. On the other hand, one of the most needless and damaging demotivators is exclusion. Occasionally, a team member will be "spared" from an important meeting or a difficult task with no explanation. With proper explanation, that person might have been relieved not to be involved, but may feel left out—perhaps even penalized—with no explanation.

A problem-solving meeting is a contest. The leader's challenge is to convince others to: change their positions or realign priorities, overcome prejudices and accept another point of view, and extend commitments and increase vulnerability. But the leader needs to recognize and control counterproductive power struggles.

The leader should be an orchestrator, keeping the meeting balanced and on track. This often requires drawing out needed participation by others and preventing domination by overly vocal members, the leader included.

Studies by industrial psychologist Frederick Herzberg examine specific factors that motivate people in their work environment—

and those that don't.[8] Herzberg and his coauthors identify several maintenance or "hygiene" factors that are not motivational. Pay and working conditions (safety, security, and comfort) reduce motivation when absent. But maintenance factors were found to lead to discontent only when they are missing or perceived as deficient, otherwise they have very little attitudinal affect. They are never motivators.

The presence of motivational factors, such as the work itself and recognition, can significantly improve job satisfaction, goal orientation, and productivity. But they must not be manipulative. Alfie Kohn, in *Punished by Rewards,* observed "Do this and you'll get that, is not much different from do this or else."[9]

The maintenance and motivation factors are in the following list in order of their relative importance revealed by Herzberg's research:

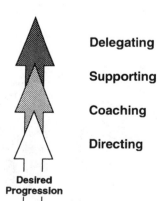

Motivational (Positive)	*Maintenance (Negative)*
Achievement.	Policy and procedure.
Recognition.	Supervision.
Work itself.	Salary.
Responsibility.	Interpersonal relations.
Advancement.	Working conditions.

Company-wide-employee-relations campaigns involve maintenance factors, whereas motivational factors are generally in the domain of the project manager and others in a direct leadership role.

> A leader's effectiveness depends on the ability to assess maturity levels and to adopt the appropriate delegation style.

Supervision Maturity

A good leader evaluates each team member's ability to accept delegation and supervise others. Every opportunity should be taken to match the job assignments with interest and skills, keeping in mind that a perfect match is impractical. This means assessing every member's individual job knowledge and maturity, then planning desired growth so that *detailed direction* can progress to *coaching* on important points; where *coaching* can transition to *supporting* as needed; and where *supporting* can mature to full *delegation.*

As the maturity level moves from low to high, leaders need to vary their style from directing to delegating. Hersey and Blanchard have developed a comprehensive situational leadership theory and process that helps in assessing maturity and determining the appropriate delegation style by considering the interaction between two major determinants (see Figure 18.3):[10]

Delegating

Supporting

Coaching

Directing

Desired Progression

Task behavior: The degree to which a leader *tells* people what, why, and how. Generally, task-oriented leaders set the goals and define the detailed steps to reach them.

Relationship behavior: The degree of *support* provided by the leader and the extent of feedback sought. Relationship-oriented behavior is characterized by good bilateral communications and active listening.

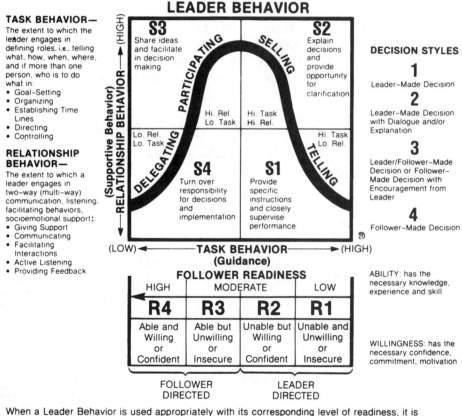

Figure 18.3 The Hersey situational leadership model. Reprinted from Paul Hersey and Ken Blanchard, *Management of Organizational Behavior: Utilizing Human Resources,* **Englewood Cliffs, NJ: Prentice Hall, 1993, sixth edition. All rights reserved.**

Follower readiness: The degree to which the followers need direction from the leader—individually and as a team. In the project environment, readiness depends on the level of experience and knowledge available for the specific project and the interpersonal growth from working together as a team, all of which can be expected to grow as the project moves through its phases. The four basic situational leadership styles are summarized in Figure 18.3, followed by their appropriate application:

- *Telling (S1):* This style is most appropriate for followers who are unable or unwilling to take responsibility because they lack knowledge or experience.
- *Selling (S2):* This style can be practiced when selling concepts to top management and customers. It can be effective in obtaining team buy in through selling the benefits of decisions. It is the natural training style.
- *Participating (S3):* This style is appropriate for a moderately mature team. The leader and followers share in the problem-solving and decision-making processes, with the main role of the leader being facilitator.
- *Delegating (S4):* This style matches the needs of teams or individuals who have reached a high maturity level. They have acquired both the motivation and ability to allocate project tasks and then to accomplish them with a minimum of supervision. The leader delegates and follows up.

Appropriate delegation is an effective technique for avoiding over management while, at the same time, improving job satisfaction. As a project or task manager, a particularly strong motivator is the confidence demonstrated by turning over one of your own plums to another team member.

> Delegate whole tasks—as large of a piece as possible—not bits and pieces.

If they're not ready now, then consciously grow personnel to the point where they can accept delegation. Mismanaging this growth process can mean either delegating too early and experiencing performance problems or giving overly detailed directions and being branded a nit manager. Whether a project manager or a junior team member, a sign of management maturity is knowing when to apply the following three approaches with your boss:

> People who can handle delegation usually don't complain.

1. "It's my responsibility, and I am taking care of it."
2. "It's my responsibility, and I am taking care of it. But you need to know what I am doing."
3. "It's my responsibility, but the best solution is beyond my authority and I need your assistance."

Interpersonal Traits

Leading people is, in part, the skill of knowing how to draw on the team's strengths and minimize the weaknesses. It takes time to understand others—to understand why a single act of ours can have a positive effect on some and the exact opposite effect on others. It's not merely a one-time event of being typecast by Wilson Learning[11] or Myers Briggs[12] or other good assessment tools and then wearing a label. It requires conscious attention to the needs of each team member and hard work to understand the complexities of the team members in order to work with them and benefit from that complexity.

Much of traditional motivation theory is based on Abraham Maslow's five hierarchical levels (physical, security, social, status, and psychic), each level becoming an intrinsic motivator after the lower-level need has been met. Any one of the levels may be dominant in a particular person. For example, some people are more responsive to psychic than to social incentives, regardless of how well their social needs have been met.

Needs can regress as the environment changes. Stephen Covey dramatizes the point:

> If all the air were suddenly sucked out of the room you're in right now, what would happen to your interest in this book? You wouldn't care about the book; you wouldn't care about anything except getting air. Survival would be your only motivation.
>
> But now that you have air, it doesn't motivate you. This is one of the greatest insights in the field of motivation: Satisfied needs do not motivate. It's only the unsatisfied need that motivates.[13]

Interpersonal clashes are inevitable, even in the most compatible teams. The techniques suggested here seek to channel the conflict in constructive ways so as to prevent a significant demotivator—prolonged or unresolved conflict.

The traditional conflict resolution methods are:

The process of constructive confrontation can be honed into a significant asset.

- Confrontation/Collaboration (Integration).
- Compromise (Negotiation).
- Smoothing (Suppression).
- Forcing (Power or Dominance).
- Withdrawal (Denial/Retreating).

Fact- and issue-based confrontation is the most favored mode for resolving conflicts, especially in dealing with superiors. Constructive confrontation has grown from a technique to a method complete with its own textbooks. But it is not a panacea.

Compromise is usually the best mode for dealing with functional support departments. At the other extreme, withdrawal is usually seen as capitulation, and is at best a temporary resolution. A skilled leader employs the full range of conflict resolution modes.

Brainstorming techniques are often used to attack the most difficult problems while enhancing interpersonal skills. The leader needs to ensure an open and noncritical atmosphere. For example, unusual or impractical ideas should be encouraged—they often lead to new combinations and improvements. Remember—the more ideas, the better.

> Group brainstorming can be very beneficial, but also very time consuming, so make sure it is time well spent.

The one-on-one meeting is one of the best techniques for exercising leadership on an interpersonal level. It provides the opportunity to demonstrate four important leadership qualities:

- Sensitivity to personnel issues.
- Accessibility and friendliness.
- Trust—respect for confidentiality.
- Training and coaching.

Reinforcement

Reinforcement refers to techniques used to remind team members of the vision and the continuing requirements of working as a team. Because the project process includes difficult aspects that may not yet be intuitive, team members may resist or circumvent them. At every opportunity, the leader should emphasize the benefits of the project management essentials. Posters and slogans around a team room reminding people of important things are good if there is follow through to make them credible. The project leader's spoken words and body language, and especially job performance, can reinforce those points.

> A leader's spoken and body language as well as job performance can provide reinforcement.

Setting the Example

Walk the walk, don't just talk the talk if you expect others to follow. It is less what you say and more what you do that influences behavior. Your attitude and body language set the tone for the entire team. You need to establish an atmosphere of openness by your willingness to seek advice, as well as bad news.

> Every action you take sends a powerful leadership style message to team members.

It's damaging to continually demand on schedule performance, and yet begin every meeting late. Act as you want your team to act: *upbeat, punctual, decisive, untiring, enthusiastic, fair,* and *dependable.*

> Never ask your team to do what you would be unwilling to do yourself.

Group activities such as planning and problem solving offer ample opportunity for setting examples. Make sure that you begin meetings on time and operate by the same standards that the team has committed to.

Rewarding Achievement

It may be time to put away the carrot and stick for good. Recent studies are calling into question the maxim of "You get what you reward." These studies show that, while some rewards can bring about short-term compliance, others often backfire in the longer term. Rather than getting sidetracked trying to resolve reward controversies, managers can benefit most by simply being aware of the issues. Much of the conflict confirms that people respond to widely varying rewards and some do not respond to external motivations at all. Our purpose is to characterize these forces so that they can be made part of everyone's awareness—managers and team members alike.

> Interesting assignments are often their own reward. People willingly work harder, as well as smarter, at interesting tasks.

Some rewards can be perceived as denials of self-control and freedom of choice, especially if they don't address a need. Even though there are many techniques for finding out what people want, managers hesitate to pursue them. You may not be prepared to deal with the answer. But you'll discover that asking about motivations, whether by a formal survey or a simple one-on-one question session, is motivating in itself. You need to follow-up to prevent being judged a hypocrite.

> Most people simply want to have interesting work and to be recognized for their accomplishments.

A Hilton Hotels' Time Values survey revealed that 70 percent of people earning over $30 thousand would trade a day's pay each week for an extra day of free time. This phenomenon exists even in the lower-pay brackets. Almost half of those surveyed earning less than $20 thousand would also make the trade.

> Most time-off incentives tied to productivity or schedule improvements get results.

You should take advantage of every opportunity to recognize good performance, but it's most effective when done in a group environment such as at meetings or reviews—even off-site pizza breaks. Be sure you're aware of the supporting details and that you don't leave somebody out. A further note of caution: intrinsic motivation, so fragile in the team environment, can be destroyed by anything that is perceived as being manipulative or controlling—even praise. Those who receive excessive praise can become so self-conscious that they have trouble concentrating. They may even duck challenges to avoid potential failure.

> It's important to recognize significant accomplishments frequently—but not routinely.

Rewarding individual performance doesn't necessarily result in a lack of teamwork. But cooperation does need to be one of the major performance rating factors. Accomplished leaders recognize and reward cooperation with teammates as an essential element of individual merit. One motivator for team performance is to do away

> Rewarding team performance can work as it does in sports—motivating stronger players to help weaker ones improve.

with individual reviews. Some managers consider an entire task group's effort as one performance.

Regardless of your reward philosophy or the details of your rewards, they need to be systematically aligned with the goals and values of your project, environment, and company.

Training

Trying to do a job you haven't been trained for is discouraging and demotivating. This applies double to the project manager who needs to be trained to select appropriate project personnel, depending on the project type and size, and then to contribute to their career development.

We are frequently retained by clients to train both their project teams and their executive management. We use techniques that bring groups together, encourage them to practice common goal setting and problem solving, and acknowledge their interdependencies. We've used managed delegation exercises, joint buyer-seller project planning, project simulations, and a host of other techniques. We often train in-house trainers—a group responsible to train others. But this doesn't work unless the trainers have extensive—and successful—project management experience and can credibly address detailed issues from that perspective. As one of our clients asserted: "Someone with that kind of capability is usually very busy managing a hot project."

> Training does not work as a one-shot seminar, regardless of how long or how intensive it may be.

Not all people are emotionally or technically equipped to take on the teaching role. A teaching attempt at the wrong time, or by the wrong person, can be seen as a form of judgment or criticism. Alternatively, being taught by your own management, if done well, can be extremely motivating. The higher the management doing the training, the more stimulating and effective it is in establishing a consistent culture (assuming that manager has progressed through the project trenches).

DETERMINING AND DECLARING YOUR LEADERSHIP STYLE

The practice of project management is increasingly influenced by human relations. Developing human relations skills, in turn, depends on awareness of your own operating style and behavior patterns as well as a willingness to adapt those qualities to the specific project environment.

A person's reaction to an unwanted fire offers a good metaphor for appreciating how extreme a rigid personal style can be:

- Reactive—Run for water.
- Inactive—Watch the blaze.
- Counteractive—Apply gasoline.
- Distractive—Send the fire trucks to the parade.
- Retroactive—"I could have told you to install sprinklers if you'd asked."

The proactive manager would have already installed a sprinkler system.

The project manager's ability to get the job done usually depends more on operating style than on any other factor—even more than power or authority. A true leader knows what is going on at all times and anticipates situations, consciously operating in the appropriate style. While most leadership *techniques* are directed toward motivation, leadership *styles* characterize the methods for applying the techniques.

There are numerous texts and self-study guides for analyzing one's own style tendencies and preferences. To conclude this chapter, we introduce two models that have proved to be particularly effective. The details of any specific self-typing or group analysis scheme are less important than the process itself—exploring your own preferences and stretching your range of styles. To benefit from that process, you first have to be self-aware.

Before analyzing further, you may find it useful to jot down your own behavior patterns, both formal and informal. As Frankl says, we "detect" rather than "invent" our missions in life. Think about the way in which you respond to different situations. Think about the situations in which you're comfortable—and others where you're uncomfortable. In which kind of relationship problems do you invest time and energy on a regular basis—which ones need more of your time? Identify your motivation source (personal need served) in each.

Wilson Learning Corporation's Interpersonal Relations Model has been widely used in the business environment for characterizing your own style. It is usually associated with a formal training seminar that includes a preliminary survey completed by selected peers. This is done through formal questionnaires similar in format to psychology and aptitude profiles. Your interpersonal style is determined by an evaluation of your peers' perceptions. In Figure 18.4 the results are displayed relative to a four-quadrant model.

Combining your primary style—Analytical, Driver, Amiable, or Expressive—with your secondary or backup style (one of the same

As the leader, you need to be motivated to adapt your own behavior rather than to "shape up" someone else.

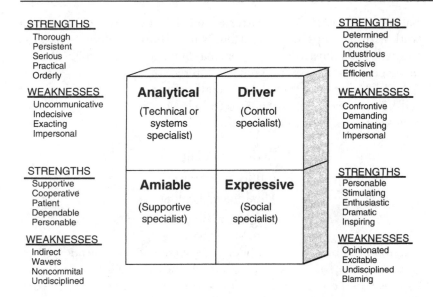

STRENGTHS
Thorough
Persistent
Serious
Practical
Orderly

WEAKNESSES
Uncommunicative
Indecisive
Exacting
Impersonal

STRENGTHS
Supportive
Cooperative
Patient
Dependable
Personable

WEAKNESSES
Indirect
Wavers
Noncommital
Undisciplined

STRENGTHS
Determined
Concise
Industrious
Decisive
Efficient

WEAKNESSES
Confrontive
Demanding
Dominating
Impersonal

STRENGTHS
Personable
Stimulating
Enthusiastic
Dramatic
Inspiring

WEAKNESSES
Opinionated
Excitable
Undisciplined
Blaming

Analytical
(Technical or systems specialist)

Driver
(Control specialist)

Amiable
(Supportive specialist)

Expressive
(Social specialist)

Figure 18.4   The basic Wilson Learning Model.

four quadrants in the basic model), places you in one of the 16 style categories, for example, an Expressive/Driver (Figure 18.5).

The usefulness of the Wilson model becomes clear when you consider the interactions among the various categories. The result is a much-improved insight and awareness, not only of your own styles,

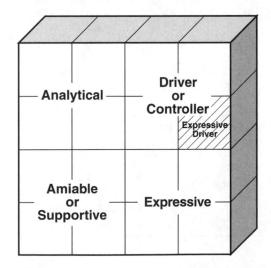

Analytical

Driver or Controller

Expressive Driver

Amiable or Supportive

Expressive

Figure 18.5   The 16 Wilson learning style combinations.

but more importantly the patterns and characteristics of those you work with. Perhaps most important is to anticipate interactions so as to adapt and adjust your own personal behavior to maximize chance of success in business and personal interactions.

The Myers-Briggs model is broadly supported in psychology and self-help. It uses a questionnaire to help you determine your dominant trait in each of four pairs of traits:

E/I	Extrovert or Introvert.
N/S	Intuitive or Sensing.
T/F	Thinking or Feeling.
J/P	Judging or Perceiving.

The model is based on the theory of psychological types described by C. G. Jung (1875–1961). Jung's model places you in one of 16 categories based on combining that one dominant trait from each pair. The characterizations in Figure 18.6 are adopted from Keirsey and Bates, one of several guides for interpreting the results.[14]

Rather than consolidating peer- and self-review into one composite result, you are encouraged to characterize yourself and to independently have others respond to the same questions about you. Additional insight can thus be gained by comparing your results for each trait with the perception of others. As with the Wilson model, most authors provide detailed advice and insight regarding the dynamics of one style interacting with another (e.g., an ENTJ interacting with an ISFP), whether the interaction is as team members, manager/subordinate, or spouses.

INFJ	INFP	ISTJ	ISFJ
Author	Questor	Trustee	Conservator
ENFJ	**ENFP**	**ESTJ**	**ESFJ**
Pedagogue	Journalist	Administrator	Seller
INTJ	**INTP**	**ISTP**	**ISFP**
Scientist	Architect	Artisan	Artist
ENTJ	**ENTP**	**ESTP**	**ESFP**
Field Marshal	Inventor	Promoter	Entertainer

Figure 18.6   Myers-Briggs' 16 types, characterized by Keirsey and Bates.

Regardless of your preferred style, your actual style at any time should be affected by such factors as the maturity level of team members and the gravity or priority of the situation. Variety and shifts in style are not only healthy—they're necessary. Leadership requires flexibility and adaptability in dealing with the task at hand, the personalities involved, events, and the situation.

Anticipate beneficial changes in your own style and declare what will trigger a change. A good time to announce these to the team is at the kick-off meeting. Here's an example: "I'll implement news-flash meetings, plan-violation meetings, daily stand-up meetings, and as needed, red teams and tiger teams. I'm an expressive/driver. I will operate in the Y-mode most of the time. I will be proactive and reactive—seldom inactive. I want to delegate as much as possible, but if I'm the one to recognize a slip in a delegated task, I'll switch to driver/directing mode."

> You need to develop the ability to vary your style.

> Once you determine your preferred styles, declare yourself and lead consistently with your stated standard.

LEADERSHIP ELEMENT EXERCISE

The objective of this exercise is to provide experience in describing your leadership style to others.

Based on the explanations of this chapter and your own leadership experiences, develop a single chart that clearly declares your leadership style to others. If you use unfamiliar terms or jargon, explain it for the uninitiated. Encourage feedback from peers, superiors, and subordinates as to its validity.

PART FOUR

IMPLEMENTING THE FIVE ESSENTIALS

We were about to name Part Four *Advanced Topics*, but agreed with our Wiley editor, Richard Narramore, that this rather ambiguous title could set false expectations. Part Four is not about depth of details or advanced theories. It is about the subtle combination of breadth and depth needed to build a process culture in the real world. We address overall implementation while selecting specific topics for drilling deeper to get to where the rubber meets the road (more on that in a moment).

Chapter 19 picks up from earlier chapters that introduced our visual models and proceeds through the tactics needed to master complex systems. Chapter 20 focuses on predictable, high-quality results and Chapter 21 wraps up by addressing the challenges of implementing cultural changes and of sustaining a successful culture in the face of growth and environment erosion.

That *process is freedom* may not always be intuitive. This reality is demonstrated dramatically by Hyundai's process route on its road from rags to riches, and conversely by Intel, a highly successful process-driven organization that may have lost its way along the same route of travel.

In 2004, Hyundai ($24 billion in revenue) startled the world by ascending from almost last place in automobile quality to first place. *Consumer Reports* magazine recently labeled the Hyundai Sonata as the most trouble-free 2004 model in the country. "It is

> Process is freedom.

> The investments and efforts made to revitalize the project environment, or to create one, can pay high dividends to the entire organization.

pretty amazing. I don't think we've ever documented in our studies an improvement quite like this," said Chance Parker, of J.D.Power and Associates, a marketing research firm.[1] The byline of a *Forbes* article sums up the situation: *"How Hyundai's carmaking prowess went from punchline to powerhouse . . ."*[2]

The prevailing industry opinion is that Hyundai has built a process culture that fosters teamwork and ensures that the right thing gets done right. The company releases designs that work, manages design stability throughout the life cycle, and uses new vehicle launches to make small continuous refinements to improve cost, quality, and reliability. Their teamwork culture views suppliers as valuable supply chain partners. Hyundai manages aggressive cost reduction targets as a joint responsibility with their suppliers, expending substantial effort and resources to assist suppliers in meeting cost targets without margin erosion.

By contrast, Intel ($34 billion in revenue) appears to have slipped from being the world leader in a process-driven industry to scrambling to sustain the culture that paved its road to success. Intel has been shipping defective parts late. In July of 2004, Craig Barrett, Intel CEO, found it necessary to write a letter to all 80,000 employees encouraging them to revisit the Intel culture and to reinstall "indicators, reviews, and management attention to start to turn these problems around by ensuring good planning, staffing and program management."[3]

These two situations highlight the role of organizational commitment, and its potential for misinterpretation, as reflected by top management behavior. During Andy Grove's tenure as Intel's CEO, the Intel cultural elements of training (every employee was challenged to devote 10% of his or her time to education or educating) and constructive confrontation (direct, forthright communication) were reinforced every day by Andy's personal presence in the classroom as teacher or student and at project reviews. Craig Barrett's external focus needed to sustain growth has lowered the bar on internal expectations at the same time that Hyundai Chairman, Mong-Koo Chung, has aggressively raised theirs. "He's not looking at [quality problems] on paper; he's very hands-on,"[4] says Robert Cosmai, chief executive of Hyundai Motor America.

Industry pundits debate how well these two companies will build, rebuild, or sustain their cultures over the long range. The messages are that culture building requires a committed, focused organization. Once in place, sustaining even the strongest and most productive process culture requires nurturing and involved leadership from top to bottom.

Whereas technology is surprisingly easy to clone, a well-integrated, high-performance project culture is an invaluable proprietary asset for sustaining high performance well into the future.

19

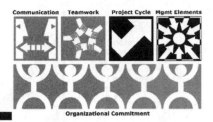

PRINCIPLES AND TACTICS FOR MASTERING COMPLEXITY

We have selected several key topics, introduced in prior chapters, to address in more depth. This chapter is intended for those responsible for the technical aspect of complex system development. It covers:

- Combining architecture and entity development to create the system solution—the Dual Vee.
- Agile development practices.
- Technical development tactics, including incremental and evolutionary development.
- Tactics and the critical path.
- Artifacts and their roles.

COMBINING ARCHITECTURE AND ENTITY DEVELOPMENT TO CREATE THE SYSTEM SOLUTION

Chapters 7 and 9 introduced the Architecture Vee Model that portrays the product breakdown of the system, illustrating decomposition and definition down the left Vee leg and integration and verification up the right Vee leg. Figure 19.1 incorporates the basic Vee attributes introduced in Chapters 7 and 9.[1]

INCOSE

The *INCOSE Handbook* defines these seven decomposition levels:

1. System.
2. Segment.
3. Element.
4. Subsystem.
5. Assembly.
6. Subassembly.
7. Part.

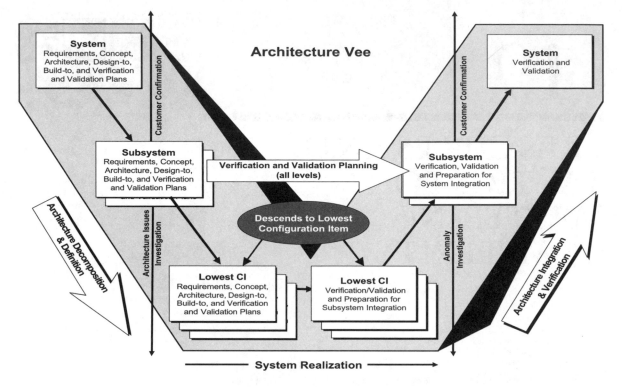

Figure 19.1   Architecture Vee Model.

The Architecture Vee Model

The Architecture Vee model extends downward according to the number of levels in the architecture. More complex projects may have several levels of segments, such as the first segment level and the second segment level or they may have multiple levels of elements. On the other hand, systems with a simpler architecture may have only two or three levels.

To develop complex systems—especially systems of systems—involves the orchestration of many concurrent tasks and intersecting processes. Development of every entity of the architecture, from the top-level system down to the lowest configuration items or lowest replaceable units is integral and concurrent with architecture development. For this discussion, lowest configuration item (LCI) is used to refer to the lowest level in the architecture from the perspective of the project's systems engineer. As such, the item can be assigned to an individual and it will be designed and verified to its configuration item (CI) specification. It will be statused by the project as a deliverable entity. The LCI may also be the lowest replaceable unit (LRU).

THE ENTITY SOLUTION AND
ARCHITECTURE PHASE SEQUENCE

To convert a set of user needs into a deployed system satisfying those needs requires that a solution be found for each entity at every level of architecture decomposition. Each rectangle in the Architecture Vee of Figure 19.1 contains a description of the development activities needed to create that entity. The series of eight figures, starting with Figure 19.2, illustrates the development sequence and the relationship of development steps at a particular level of decomposition with those of higher and lower levels of decomposition.

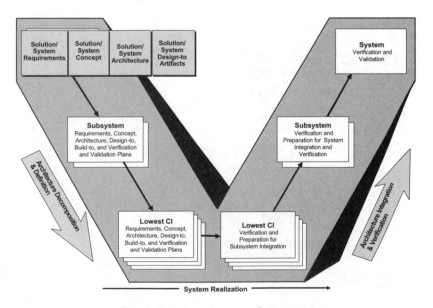

Creating a system solution starts at the upper left of the Architecture Vee with a first phase that defines user and system requirements. This is followed by three sequential phases, which define and baseline the system concept, the system architecture, and the system level design-to specification. At this point, system level development cannot proceed further until the entities at lower levels of decomposition are designed.

Figure 19.2   Development Sequence 1.

Defining requirements, concept, architecture, and design-to specifications at the system level makes requirements flowdown from the system level to the subsystem level possible. Requirements, concepts, architectures, and design-to specifications are developed for the subsystems that comprise the system. Collaboration among those managing the subsystems is necessary to ensure interface and design-to compatibility as well as ease of future integration and verification. The diagram shows the top-down progression of decision gates to manage the evolving architecture baseline.

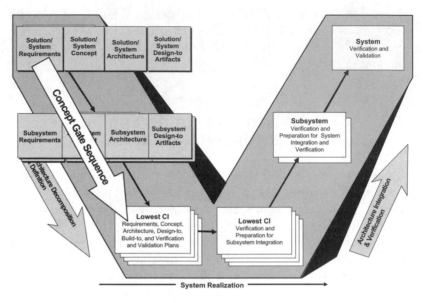

Figure 19.3   Development Sequence 2 (subsystem level).

Upon completing the subsystem design-to specifications, the effort shifts to the next lower decomposition level, the LCI development. Note that the design-to decision gate sequence starts at the system level and proceeds to lower levels of decomposition to ensure the correct flowdown of requirements.

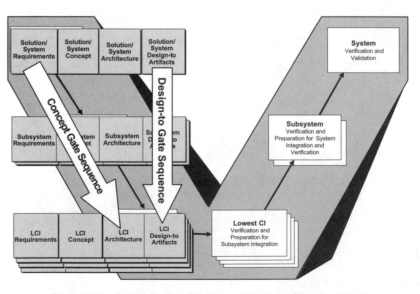

Figure 19.4   Development Sequence 3 (lowest CI entity level).

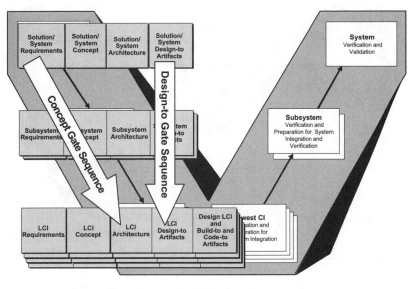

Figure 19.5   Development Sequence 4.

This diagram shows the simultaneous development of the build-to and code-to artifacts for all of the lowest configuration items. Of course, some LCIs, and even some subsystems, may not be designed if their design-to specifications can be met by procuring off-the-shelf items. Comprehensive technical management is needed to ensure compatibility of all LCI interfaces and intrafaces. With the completion of the build-to and code-to artifacts, including draft verification procedures, the build-to decision gate sequence is conducted to prove the feasibility of building, coding, integrating, and verifying the LCI designs and to baseline them.

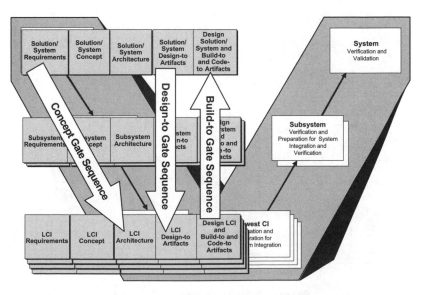

Figure 19.6   Development Sequence 5.

The LCI-level build-to baseline will be followed by the subsystem level baseline and then the system level. At the system build-to decision gate, evidence must be provided that proves that, if all the entities are built as designed, the system will perform as expected.

The satisfactory conclusion of the build-to gate sequence provides assurance that a viable solution exists and that it is realizable if the build-to designs and processes are carried out as prescribed.

This diagram shows the lowest configuration items being produced, verified, and validated at the LCI decomposition level. If COTS items are being integrated, they will already exist, but they must be verified and validated at the appropriate entity level.

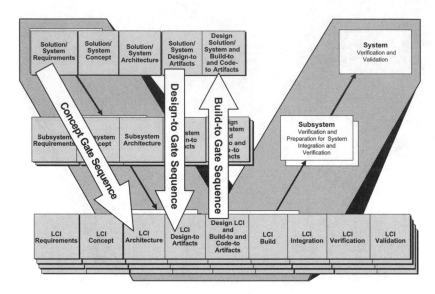

Figure 19.7 Development Sequence 6.

Once verified, the lowest configuration items are ready for physical integration into higher level subsystems. Integration hardware and software not already available will have to be created, for example, software to interface two COTS products or cables to interconnect two configuration items.

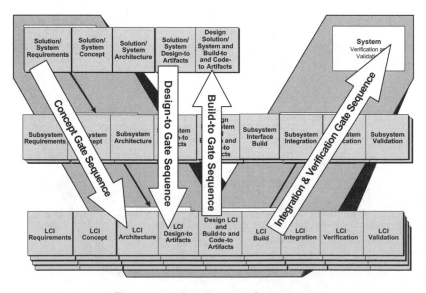

Figure 19.8 Development Sequence 7.

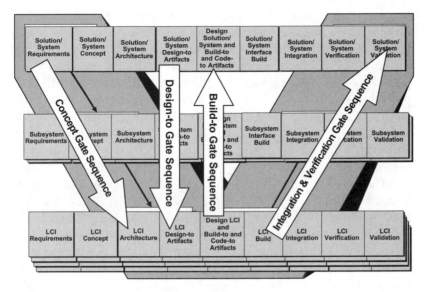

Figure 19.9 Development Sequence 8.

The integration and verification gate sequence is consistent with the buildup of the system, that is, from the bottom up. Finally, when subsystems are verified to perform as specified, full system integration is possible followed by system verification and validation.

The Entity Vee Model

The basic principles embodied in the Vee model can be used to illustrate the process for developing each entity. The Entity Vee model represents this process. Referring to Figure 19.10, the left leg represents the sequence of definition elaboration (decomposition analysis and resolution or DAR) and the right leg represents the sequence of assembly and performance assurance (verification analysis and resolution or VAR). All activities within one Entity Vee are at the same architecture level. The Entity Vee is repeated for every entity of the architecture from the system, down to the LCIs, such as computer software units or hardware components.

At each elaboration level, there is a direct correlation between activities on the left and right legs of the Vee. This is deliberate. The method of verification to be used on the right Vee leg must be defined at the time requirements are developed on the left; otherwise, requirements could be created that could never be verified. For example, "user friendly" is a perfectly valid requirement, but it

The right side of both Vees directly corresponds to the left—the rationale for the shape.

Verification must be planned at the same time requirements are developed; otherwise, the verification tends to address the "goodness" of the design rather than its compliance to the requirements.

is unverifiable. Instead, a requirement that a computer screen display have "no more that five lines of 14-point text" defines user friendly in measurable terms. Verification plans should be baselined to ensure verification requirements and methods are known and provided for at the design-to decision gate (PDR). Draft verification procedures based on the verification requirements, verification plan, and proposed entity design must be available at the build-to and code-to decision gate (CDR). This reduces the chances that requirements are specified and implemented in a way that cannot be measured or verified.

The vertical dimension is elaboration detail at an architecture level (for instance, at the subsystem level) and the core of the Entity Vee is entity baseline elaboration. Also included (similar to the Architecture Vee) are the activities associated with opportunity and risk management, pursued downward and off core to the level of detail necessary for issue evaluation and resolution. Unlike the commonly held view of the Waterfall Model, there is no prohibition against doing exploratory design and analysis at any point in the project cycle to investigate or prove performance or feasibility concepts. Unlike the Spiral Model, the Vee opportunity and risk investigations are performed either in series or in parallel with the on-core development work, rather than being conducted sequentially and prior to the overall development process. Hardware and software requirements-understanding models or technical feasibility models are encouraged early in the project cycle to pursue opportunities such as emerging technologies and to manage risk. For instance, to evaluate a concept requiring a manual override versus a concept with full automation, technical feasibility of the two concepts would be modeled. Selection might be based on response time versus cost and complexity of the system. Customer confirmation can provide valuable in-process validation of the preferred approach.

In the right leg, off-core investigations are used to resolve assembly and verification anomalies. This may require descending to design errors, a cold solder joint, or operator error and the like. Upward off-core user interactions obtain confirmation or rejection of the realized performance. Note that, in the Entity Vee, these interactions address individual entity solutions and not the integration of the architecture. That activity is modeled by the Architecture Vee. At any level of decomposition, the customer of an entity is the manager of the next higher level of decomposition. For example, the power subsystem manager is the customer of the person responsible for the battery.

Dual Vees: The Entity Vee Related to the Architecture Vee

To convert a set of user needs into a deployed system that satisfies those needs requires that a solution be found for each entity at each level of architecture decomposition. This can be visualized by positioning Entity Vees orthogonal to the Architecture Vee as shown in Figure 19.11. For each entity of the Architecture Vee there is a corresponding Entity Vee that addresses the entity development. For example, the Architecture Vee in Figure 19.1 shows two subsystems. The two Entity Vees shown represent the process for creating those two subsystems.

Figure 19.12 reiterates the relationship of the DAR and VAR processes to the Architecture Vee as discussed in Chapter 9 and illustrated by Figures 9.6, 9.7, and 9.8. Figure 19.12 elaborates further on the interrelationships by superimposing the DAR and VAR on the Entity Vees that they support.

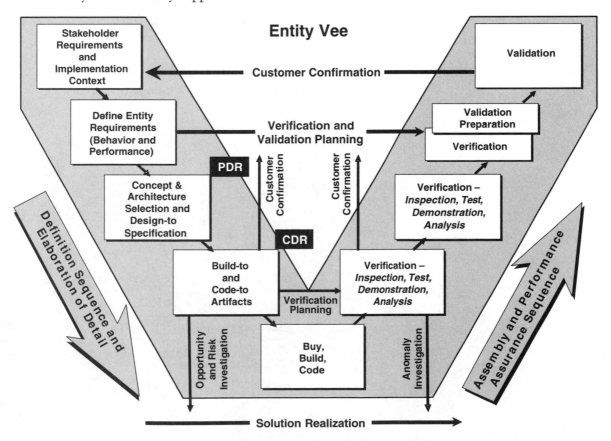

Figure 19.10   Entity Vee Model.

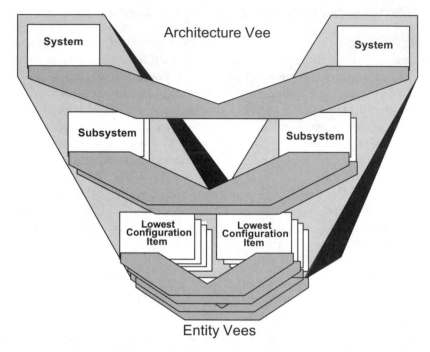

Figure 19.11   Architecture and Entity Vees intersecting.

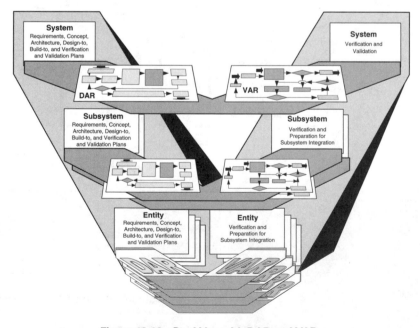

Figure 19.12   Dual Vee with DAR and VAR.

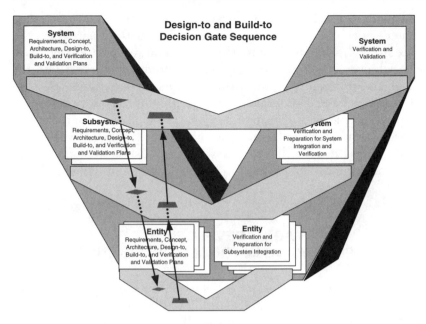

Figure 19.13   Design-to and build-to decision gate sequence.

Phasing of Decision Gates

Lowest configuration items and subsystems are developed and integrated into the architecture using interleaved phases. The activities are ordered in accordance with systems engineering best practices. Figures 19.3 through 19.9 reveal the sequence in detail. Figure 19.13 adds a three-dimensional view to clarify the phasing in relationship to the Entity Vees. The design-to and build-to decision gates are repeated to emphasize proper process sequence and flow:

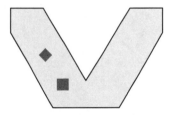

◆ Design-to (Preliminary Design Review, PDR).
■ Build-to (Critical Design Review, CDR).

For simplicity of illustration, only one Entity Vee is shown intersecting the Architecture Vee at each decomposition level. Note that the design-to sequence is top down, starting at the system level and proceeding down through decomposition to the LCI level. This sequence ensures that there is proper requirements allocation and flowdown from the system down through each decomposition level to the LCI.

When build-to and code-to artifacts, including draft verification procedures, are ready for baselining, the build-to decision gate sequence is conducted to prove the feasibility of building or coding the designs. The review also confirms that, if the solution is built according to the build-to artifacts, the required performance will be achieved. The build-to sequence is bottom up, starting with the LCI and proceeding upward through the decomposition levels to the system level. This sequence ensures that, if the entity designs at a particular level of decomposition are producible and satisfy their design-to requirements, the entities will integrate into the next higher-level entity. This review sequence ensures that the entire system is buildable, will perform as expected, and will satisfy the users.

AGILE DEVELOPMENT
PRACTICING IN-PROCESS VALIDATION

The preceding discussions have emphasized the benefits of orderly, hierarchical baseline progression followed by a corresponding verification sequence. Recognizing that the development process may require more flexibility in some circumstances, the wheel-and-axle process model provides a tailoring framework, based on opportunity to simplify development methods and to assess the risks in so doing. The extent of tailoring is determined by whether the opportunity to shorten the project cycle is worth the risk of doing the development steps out of sequence or in parallel.

The Agile Alliance is dedicated to developing iterative and agile methods, seeking a faster and better approach to software and system development, and challenging more traditional models. There are many references describing the agile concepts (www .agilealliance.com). Craig Larman addresses agile methods in the context of UML and iterative development.[2] The key objective is flexibility and allowing selected events to be taken out of sequence (as illustrated in Figure 19.14) when the risk is acceptable.

The features that distinguish agile development from the conventional approach are *velocity* and *adaptability*. While market strategies often emphasize that *time to market* or speed is critical, a more appropriate criterion is *velocity*, which adds direction to speed. By incorporating the customer into their working-level teams, the agile developers are ensuring that they are going in a direction that satisfies the customer's highest needs first. This is in-process validation in action. By adopting the following seven key practices of agile systems engineering, any organization can improve its velocity to customer satisfaction:

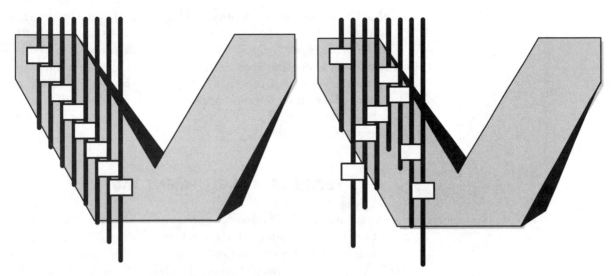

Figure 19.14   Hierarchical baseline elaboration (left) and Nonhierarchical baseline elaboration (right).

1. The project team understands, respects, works, and behaves within a defined systems engineering process. The process is systemic in the organization and implicit to the participants.
2. The project is executed as fast as possible with minimum down time or staff diversion during the project. Every opportunity is exercised to move the project forward, especially for the critical path activities.
3. All key players are physically or electronically collocated. Other contributors are available online 24/7.
4. There is a strong bias for automatically generated electronic documentation. Engineers rely on their tools and their Electronic Engineering Notebooks to record decision rationale. Artifacts for operations and replication are done only if necessary—not to support an existing bureaucracy or policy. Notebooks are team property and are available to all.
5. Baseline management and change control is achieved by formal, oral agreements based on "make a promise, keep a promise" discipline—participants hold each other accountable. Decision gate agreements are confirmed with a binding handshake. Formality relates to the binding of the action not the amount of documentation.
6. Opportunity exploration and risk reduction are accomplished by expert consultation and rapid model verification, coupled with close customer collaboration. Software development is done in a

rapid development environment, while hardware is developed in a multidisciplined model shop. There is no resistance or inertia to securing expert help; it is sought rather than resisted.

7. A culture of constructive confrontation pervades the project organization. Issues are actively sought. Anyone can identify an issue and pass it on to the most likely solver. No issue is left unresolved. The team takes ownership for success; it is never "someone else's responsibility."

TECHNICAL DEVELOPMENT TACTICS

Development and delivery decisions are usually driven by the business case in response to the demands of the market or the customer. These result in a business strategy that is then achieved through implementation tactics. While the project manager needs to be well versed in the business case, the systems engineer needs to fully appreciate the flexibility of the project to accommodate and benefit from the various tactical development and delivery approaches. To arrive at the best decision for the sake of the market and the project, the project manager and the systems engineer must collaborate until consensus is reached. Then, the decision must be baselined and communicated to the project team so that the tactics can be built into all planning.

The strategic goals of a project drive the development tactics. For instance, if the goal is to upgrade the solution over time with

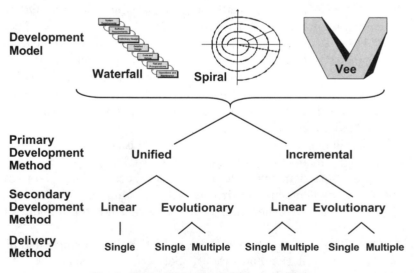

Figure 19.15   Technical development tactics.

newly developed improvements, then selecting an architecture with increments configured for easy upgrading and fielding may be the best tactical approach. Similarly, if the goal is to migrate technology into the solution over time, then an evolutionary development approach with delivery of successive versions is appropriate, each with potential for increased capability.

Figure 19.15 illustrates the decisions to be made for each architecture entity regarding development models, development methods, and delivery methods.

Waterfall and Spiral

At the highest level, the most effective models must be selected to address the development challenge. All three models shown in Figure 19.15 can be effective, but each emphasizes different aspects of system development. The objective of Royce's Waterfall model, discussed in Chapter 7 and illustrated in Figure 7.8, is to convert undisciplined software development into an orderly linear phased process and it does just that. However, as critics point out, it does not address complexities of architecture development or risk management. The Waterfall model is sometimes blamed for the significant software failures of the 1980s and 1990s since the model does not show iterative expansion and refinement of requirements.

The Spiral (Figure 7.9) is a widely used risk-driven model that addresses some of the shortcomings of the Waterfall model.[3] Boehm's objective was to focus on risk prior to development. Boehm dealt with risk by adding early requirements understanding, technical feasibility, and operational scenario investigations (prototyping) to the front end of Royce's Waterfall. The Spiral model is effective in emphasizing the risk-reduction objective, but it is silent on both architecture development and the development risks commonly experienced in the Waterfall phases.

The Dual Vee model, described earlier, is the third development model choice.

There are two primary development methods, unified or incremental (Figure 19.15). Unified is effective for entities where decomposition into an architecture with separate deliverable elements or modules is not practical. Examples include the physical structure of a spacecraft, a simple software application, and the concrete foundation of a building.

The alternative to unified development is to decompose the concept into an architecture having entities to be developed incrementally (i.e., separately for later integration; Figure 7.13). This tactic

Incremental development provides for staged development and delivery followed by upgrades to the increments as needed.

usually allows parallel development, assigning experts to each increment, and flexibility to accommodate funding and schedule constraints. Incremental development is used, for example, in product lines such as automobiles where engines, chassis, and transmissions are separately developed and then integrated into a complete automobile at the final assembly plants. Incremental development can plan for subsequent upgrading by increment. In the automobile example, increments that are later discovered to be faulty can be recalled and replaced in the field. In software, incremental development can start with the most important requirement and complete an increment that satisfies it. Then building on that verified increment, the thrust would be to satisfy the second requirement and so on. With this incremental approach, each increment is built on the previous set resulting in one single delivery. However, later upgrades to internal increments are not possible. The integrated set must be upgraded.

As illustrated by Figure 19.15, there are two alternative secondary methods, linear and evolutionary. Linear development is the single path approach where the requirements and the solution are sufficiently well understood to allow straightforward design and implementation without iteration or experimentation. The installation of electrical and plumbing systems in home construction is a linear approach developed over years of experience. No iteration or experimentation is required or desired.

Evolutionary development is appropriate where experimentation or investigation is necessary to determine the best solution. This approach works well for uncertain requirements, pursuit of opportunities and risks, or the pursuit of alternate concepts and solutions, and is common to research projects. A disadvantage of the evolutionary approach is unpredictability of progress. As a result, cost and schedule estimates are guesses. The evolution of Microsoft's Windows operating system is an example of evolutionary development providing a series of versions over the years with occasional increment upgrades to deal with user bugs and new security threats (Figure 19.16). Windows' past delivery record demonstrates that evolutionary development schedules are rarely met.

After selecting the development method, the delivery decisions can be made. For unified, linear development, only a single delivery occurs. Incremental, with or without evolutionary development, requires a decision to field the system in a single delivery or to deliver increments and versions of increments to gradually increase solution capability over time. This decision can be driven by the urgency for a solution to be fielded, the staggered availability of functional capability, funding limitations, regulatory constraints, or any other factors making staged fielding beneficial.

Evolutionary development provides for investigation and experimentation to develop a capability. Delivery is usually in entity versions, each delivering improved performance. Increments can be developed using the evolutionary approach.

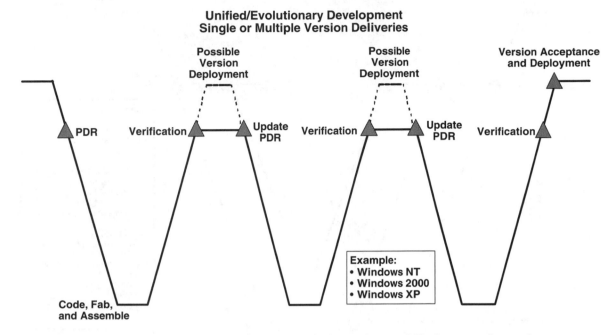

Figure 19.16 Evolutionary development: Used for increasing capability in successive versions.

The tailored project cycle must reflect the tactics of the development and delivery methods. Figures 19.16, 19.17, and 19.18 provide simplified Vee Model visualizations for three of the tactical method combinations.

By their nature, bridges and tunnels require single delivery. Light rail systems are usually built in increments delivered and connected over time to ultimately result in an entire transportation system (Figure 19.17). If requirements are unstable and the technology is emerging, then an incremental evolutionary approach will enable low-risk increments to proceed while experimentation and modeling is carried out on the high-risk increments (Figures 7.13 and 19.18).[4]

SELECTION OF TECHNICAL DEVELOPMENT TACTICS DETERMINES THE CRITICAL PATH

Much has been written about the definition and management of the critical path. It is widely understood that the critical path is the sequence of project activities that cannot be shortened, thereby determining the length of the project schedule. It is the task sequence with zero slack. Critical paths result from a combination of planned

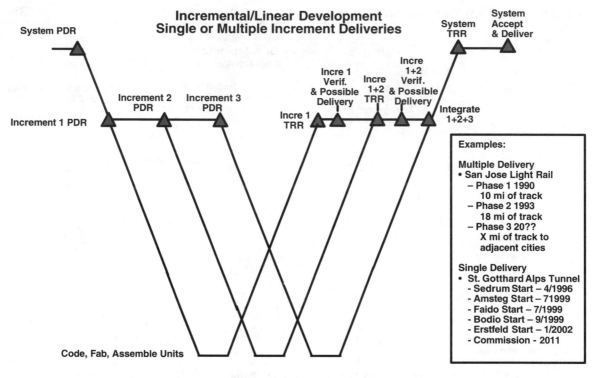

Figure 19.17   Incremental development—single or multiple delivery.

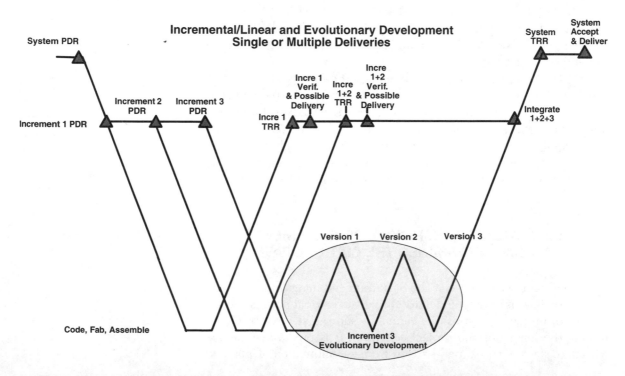

Figure 19.18   Incremental development—incremental delivery, with evolutionary iterations on increment 3.

activities and unplanned reactive activities such as late suppliers and quality problems.

As discussed in Chapter 12, the management of the critical path is usually focused on the task schedules and their dependencies, as represented by the structure of the project network. But prematurely focusing on precise calculation of the critical path may be missing the forest for the trees. The purpose of this section is to highlight the interdependency between the technical development tactics and the critical path throughout the project cycle.

Deployment strategies have a strong influence on the critical path, especially the early part. A strategy might be to capture market share by deploying a system solution quickly even though it might not initially achieve its full performance goals. Another strategy might be to field a system that is easily upgradeable after introduction to provide after-market sales. The resulting development tactics, selected for system entities, determine the connections among tasks and the relationships that form the project network. When the predicted task schedules are applied, their summation determines the length of the critical path.

In considering the development tactics, we sometimes misjudge the importance of integration, verification, and validation (IV&V) tactics. Projects that require the ultimate in reliability will usually adopt a bottom up step-by-step IV&V sequence of proving performance at every entity combination. High-quantity production systems may skip verification once the production processes have been proven to reliably produce perfect products. Yet other projects may elect a "threaded" or "big bang" verification approach. It is not uncommon for different project entities to embrace different task-dependent verification and validation tactics. The tasks associated with these tactical decision activities must also be incorporated into the critical path to accurately represent the planned approach. These system integration and verification activities will almost always be on the critical path. The next chapter addresses IV&V in detail.

ARTIFACTS AND THEIR ROLES

Project management artifacts are the results of communication among the project participants. Documentation is the most common artifact, but models, products, material samples, and even whiteboard sketches are valid artifacts. Artifacts are representations of facts and can be binding when used as such. Some projects managed in a bureaucratic environment develop too many artifacts without regard to their purpose and ultimate use. The three fundamental roles that artifacts fulfill are (Figure 19.19):

Official Document

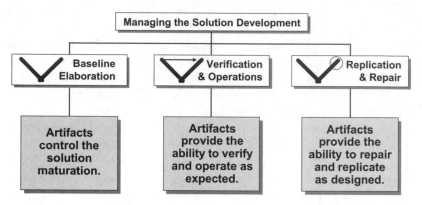

Figure 19.19   The three roles for artifacts.

1. Manage the elaboration of the development baseline. Since all team members should be working to the most current elaboration, it needs to be communicated among the team. The artifacts can range from oral communication to volumes of documentation. In a small skunk works team environment, whiteboard sketches are highly effective as long as they are permanent throughout the time they are needed (simply writing SAVE across the board may not be strong enough). These artifacts include system requirements, concept definition, architecture, design-to specifications, build-to documentation, and as-built documentation.

2. Communicate to the verification and operations personnel what they need to know to carry out their responsibilities. These artifacts communicate the expected behavior over the anticipated operational scenarios. These artifacts include user's manuals, operator's manuals, practice scenarios, verification plans, verification procedures, validation plans, and validation procedures.

3. Provide for repair and replication. These must represent the as-operated configuration, which should include all modifications made to the as-built baseline. These artifacts include the as-built artifacts together with all modifications incorporated, process specifications, parts lists, material specifications, repair manuals, and source code.

20

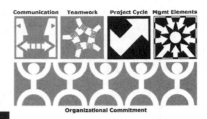

Communication Teamwork Project Cycle Mgmt Elements

Organizational Commitment

INTEGRATION, VERIFICATION, AND VALIDATION

Chapter 7 addressed integration, verification, and validation (IV&V) as represented by the Vee Model and in relationship to the systems engineering role. In Chapter 9, the planning for IV&V was emphasized in the Decomposition Analysis and Resolution process, followed by a broad implementation overview in the Verification Analysis and Resolution process. This chapter addresses the implementation of IV&V in more depth.

Successful completion of system-level integration, verification, and validation ends the implementation period and initiates the operations period, which starts with the production phase if more than one article is to be delivered. However, if this is the first point in the project cycle that IV&V issues have been considered, the team's only allies will be hope and luck, four-letter words that should not be part of any project's terminology manual.

We have emphasized that planning for integration and verification starts with the identification of solution concepts (at the system, subsystem, and lowest entity levels). In fact, integration and verification issues may be the most significant discriminators when selecting from alternate concepts. Equally important, the project team should not wait until the end of the implementation period to determine if the customer or user(s) likes the product. In-process validation should progress to final validation when the user stresses the system to ensure satisfaction with all intended uses. A system is often composed of hardware, software, and firmware. It sometimes becomes "shelfware"

Integration: The successive combining and testing of system hardware assemblies, software components, and operator tasks to progressively prove the performance and capability of all entities of the system.

Verification: Proof of compliance with specifications.
Was the solution built right?

Validation: Proof that the user(s) is satisfied.
Was the right solution built?

When an error reaches the field, there have been two errors. Verification erred by failing to detect the fielded error.

when the project team did not take every step possible to ensure user acceptance. Yet, this is a frequent result, occurring much too often. Most recently, the failure of a three-year software development program costing hundreds of millions of dollars has been attributed to the unwillingness of FBI agents to use the system (a validation failure). These surprise results can be averted by in-process validation, starting with the identification of user needs and continuing with user confirmation of each elaboration of the solution baseline.

IV&V has a second meaning: independent verification and validation used in high-risk projects where failure would have profound impact. See the Glossary for a complete definition. Examples are the development of the control system for a nuclear power plant and the on-board flight-control software on the space shuttle. The IV&V process on the shuttle project resulted in software that had an impressively low error rate (errors per thousand lines of code) that was one-tenth of the best industry practice. Proper development processes do work.

In the project environment, IV&V is often treated as if it were a single event. This chapter details each of these three distinct processes. *Integration* is discussed first. Then the discussion of *verification* covers design verification, design margin verification and qualification, reliability verification, software quality verification, and system certification. *Validation* covers issues in interacting with users, both external and internal to the project team. In closing, *anomaly management* addresses the unexpected.

INTEGRATION

The integration approach will drive the key details of the product breakdown structure (PBS), the work breakdown structure (WBS), the network logic, and the critical path. Interface specifications define the physical and logical requirements that must be met by entities on both sides of the interface. These specifications must cover both internal interfaces as well as those external to the system. A long-standing rule is to keep the interfaces as simple and fool proof as possible.

Integration takes place at every level of the system architecture. The PBS (see examples in margin opposite Figure 20.1) identifies where these interfaces occur. In Figure 20.1, the N^2 diagram illustrates relationships between system entities and relates the entities to the PBS. The entities are listed on the diagonal of the matrix, with outputs shown in the rows and inputs in the columns. For instance,

---

In cases of highest risk, Independent Verification and Validation is performed by a team that is totally independent from the developing organization.

Verification complexity increases exponentially with system complexity.

Integration: The successive combining and testing of system hardware assemblies, software components, and operator tasks to progressively prove the performance and capability of all entities of the system.

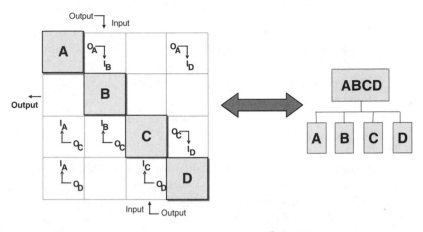

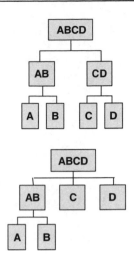

Figure 20.1   Interfaces illustrated by the N² and PBS diagrams.

Entity B has input from Entities A and C, as well as input from outside the system. In Figure 20.1, Entity B provides an output external to the system. Interfaces needing definition are identified by the arrows inside the cells. The BMW automobile manufacturer has successfully used a similar matrix with over 270 rows and columns to identify critical interface definitions.

Integration and verification planning, which must have project management focus from the outset, begins in the concept development phase. The planning must answer the following questions:

- What integration tasks are needed?
- Who will perform each task?
- Where will the task be performed?
- What facilities and resources are needed?
- When will the integration take place?

Integration and verification plans should be available at the design-to decision gate.

There are four categories of integration:

1. Mechanical:
   - Demonstrates mechanical compatibility of components.
   - Demonstrates compliance with mechanical interface specifications.
2. Electrical:
   - Demonstrates electrical/electronic compatibility of components.
   - Demonstrates compliance with electrical interface requirements.

Integration Planning

3. Logical:
   - Demonstrates logical (protocol) compatibility of components.
   - Demonstrates the ability to load and configure software.
4. Functional:
   - Demonstrates the ability to load, configure, and execute solution components.
   - Demonstrates functional capability of all elements of the solution working together.

Integration can be approached all at once (the "big bang") or incrementally. Except for very simple systems, the big-bang approach is generally considered too risky. Table 20.1 shows four incremental approaches. Three of these (top-down, bottom-up, and thread) are illustrated in Figure 20.2. Each approach is valid, and the choice depends on the project circumstances.

Interface management to facilitate integration and verification should be responsive to the following:

- The PBS portion of the WBS should provide the road map for integration.
- Integration will exist at every level in the PBS except at the top level.
- Integration and verification activities should be represented by tasks within the WBS.

Table 20.1 Incremental Integration Approaches

Technique	Features
Top-down	Control logic testing first.
	Modules integrated one at a time.
	Emphasis on interface verification.
Bottom-up	Early verification to prove feasibility and practicality.
	Modules integrated in clusters.
	Emphasis on module functionality and performance.
Thread	Top-down or bottom-up integration of a software function or capability.
Mixed	Working from both ends toward the middle.
	Choice of modules designated top-down versus bottom-up is critical.

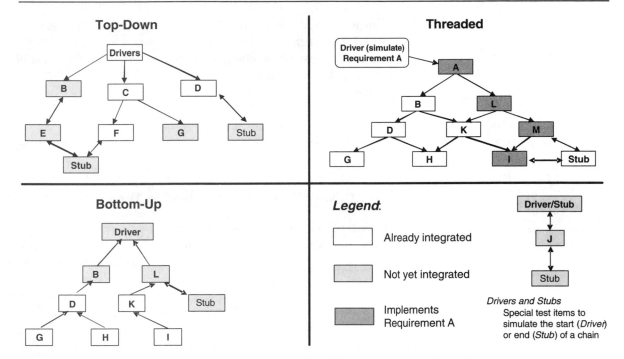

Figure 20.2 Alternative incremental integration approach tactics.

- The WBS is not complete without the integration and verification tasks and the tasks to produce the products (e.g., fixtures, models, drivers, databases) required to facilitate integration.
- Interfaces should be designed to be as simple and foolproof as possible.
- Interfaces should have mechanisms to prevent inadvertent incorrect coupling (for instance, uniquely shaped connectors such as the USB and S-Video connectors on laptop computers).
- Interfaces should be verified by low-risk (benign) techniques before mating.
- "OK to install" discipline should be invoked before all matings.
- Peer review should provide consent-to authorization to proceed.
- Haste without extra care should be avoided. (If you cannot provide adequate time or extra care, go as fast as you can so there will be time to do it over . . . and over. . . .)

Integration Issues

- Clear definition, documentation, and management of the interfaces are key to successful integration.

- Coordination of schedules with owners of external systems is essential for integration into the final environment.
- Resources must be planned. This includes the development of stub and driver simulators.
- First-time mating needs to be planned and carefully performed, step-by-step.
- All integration anomalies must be resolved.
- Sometimes it will be necessary to fix the "other person's" problem.

Risk: The Driver of Integration/Verification Thoroughness

It is important to know the project risk philosophy (risk tolerance) as compared to the opportunity being pursued. This reward-to-risk ratio will drive decisions regarding the rigor and thoroughness of integration and the many facets of verification and validation. There is no standard vocabulary for expressing the risk philosophy, but it is often expressed as "quick and dirty," "no single point failure modes," "must work," "reliability is 0.9997," or some other expression or a combination of these. One client reports that their risk tolerant client specifies a 60 percent probability of success. This precise expression is excellent but unusual. The risk philosophy will determine whether all or only a portion of the following will be implemented.

VERIFICATION

Verification management:
Proof of compliance with specifications.
   Was the solution built right?

If a defect is delivered within a system, it is a failure of verification for not detecting the defect. Many very expensive systems have failed after deployment due to built-in errors. In every case, there were two failures. First the failure to build the system correctly and second the failure of the verification process to detect the defect. The most famous is the Hubble telescope delivered into orbit with a faulty mirror. There are many more failures just as dramatic that did not make newspaper headlines. They were even more serious and costly, but unlike the Hubble, they could not be corrected after deployment.

Unfortunately, in the eagerness to recover lost schedule, verification is often reduced or oversimplified, which increases the chances of missing a built-in problem.

There are four verification methods: test, demonstration, analysis, and inspection. While some consider simulation to be a fifth method, most practitioners consider simulation to be one of—or a combination of—test, analysis, or demonstration.

Verification Methods Defined

Test (T): Direct measurement of performance relative to functional, electrical, mechanical, and environmental requirements.

Demonstration (D): Verification by witnessing an actual operation in the expected or simulated environment, without need for measurement data or post demonstration analysis.

Analysis (A): An assessment of performance using logical, mathematical, or graphical techniques, or for extrapolation of model tests to full scale.

Inspection (I): Verification of compliance to requirements that are easily observed such as construction features, workmanship, dimensions, configuration, and physical characteristics such as color, shape, software language used, and so on.

Test is a primary method for verification. But as noted previously, verification can be accomplished by methods other than test. And tests are run for purposes other than verification (Figure 20.3). Consequently, extra care must be taken when test results will be used formally for official verification.

Engineering models are often built to provide design feasibility information. The test article is usually discarded after test completion. However, if the test article is close to the final configuration, with care in documenting the test details (setup, equipment calibration, test article configuration, etc.), it is possible that the data can be used for design verification or qualification. The same is true of a software development prototype. If care

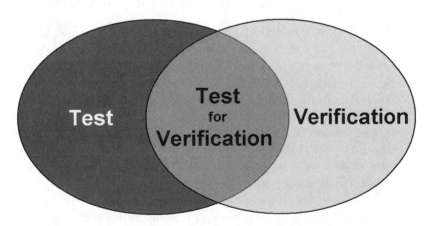

Figure 20.3   Test and verification.

is used in documenting the test stubs, drivers, conditions, and setup, it might be possible to use the development test data for verification purposes.

The management of verification should be responsive to lessons learned from past experience. Eight are offered for consideration:

1. A requirements traceability and verification matrix (RTVM) should map the top-down decomposition of requirements and should also identify the integration level and method for the verification. For instance, while it is desirable to verify all requirements in a final all-up systems test, there may be requirements that cannot be verified at that level. Often there are stowed items at the system level that cannot and will not be deployed until the system is deployed. In these instances, verification of these entities must be achieved at a lower level of integration. The RTVM should ensure that all required verification is planned for, including the equipment and faculties required to support verification at each level of integration. An example of a simple RTVM for a bicycle is shown in Figure 20.4.

2. The measurement units called out in verification procedures should match the units of the test equipment to be used. For example, considerable damage was done when thermal chambers were inadvertently set to 160 degrees centigrade although the verification procedure called for 160 degrees Fahrenheit. In another instance, a perfectly good spacecraft was destroyed when the range safety officer, using the wrong flight path dimensions, destroyed it during ascent thinking it was off course. Unfortunately, there are too many examples of perfect systems being damaged by error.

3. Redline limits are "do not exceed" conditions, just as the red line on a car's tachometer is designed to protect the car's engine. Test procedures should contain two types of redline limits. The first should be set at the predicted values so that if they are approached or exceeded the test can be halted and an investigation initiated to determine why the predictions and actual results don't correlate. The second set of redline limits should be set at the safe limit of capability to prevent failure of the system or injury to personnel. If these limits are approached the test should be terminated and an investigation should determine the proper course of action. One of the world's largest wind tunnels was destroyed when the test procedures that were required to contain redline limits did not.

Level	Rev	ID	Name	Make or Buy	Requirement		Predecessor	Verification			Auditor	Date
0	0	0.0	Bicycle System	M	0.0.1	"Light Wt" - <105% of Competitor	"User Need" Doc ¶ 1	0.0.1	Assess Competition			
0	0	0.0	Bicycle System	M	0.0.2	"Fast" - Faster than any other bike	"User Need" Doc ¶ 2	0.0.2	Win Tour de France			
1	0	1.1	Bicycle	M	1.1.1	8.0 KG max weight	0.0.1, Marketing	1.1.1	Test (Weigh bike)			
1	0	1.1	Bicycle	M	1.1.2	85 cm high at seat	Racing rules ¶ 3.1	1.1.2	Test (Measure bike)			
1	0	1.1	Bicycle	M	1.1.3	66 cm wheel dia	Racing rules ¶ 4.2	--	*Verif at ass'y level*			
1	0	1.1	Bicycle	M	1.1.4	Carry one 90 KG rider	Racing rules ¶ 2.2	1.1.4	Demonstration			
1	0	1.1	Bicycle	M	1.1.5	Use advanced materials	Corporate strategy ¶ 6a	--	*Verif at ass'y level*			
1	0	1.1	Bicycle	M	1.1.6	Survive FIVE seasons	Corporate strategy ¶ 6b	1.1.6	Accelerated life test			
1	0	1.1	Bicycle	M	1.1.7	Go VERY fast (>130 kpm)	0.0.2	1.1.7	Test against benchmark			
1	0	1.1	Bicycle	M	1.1.8	Paint frame Red, shade 123	Marketing	1.1.8	Inspection			
1	0	1.2	Packaging	B	1.2.1	Packaged for Shipment	0.0.4, Marketing					
1	1	1.2	Packaging	B	1.2.1	Photo of "Hi Tech" Wheel on Box	0.0.4, Marketing					
1	0	1.2	Packaging	B	1.2.2	Survive 2 m drop	Industry std					
1	1	1.3	Documentation	M	1.3.1	Assembly Instructions	0.0.4					
1	1	1.3	Documentation	M	1.3.2	Owner's Manual	0.0.4					
2	0	2.1	Frame Assembly	B	2.1.1	Welded Titanium Tubing	1.1.5, 1.1.6					
2	0	2.1	Frame Assembly	B	2.1.2	Maximum weight 2.5 KG	1.1.1, allocation					
2	0	2.1	Frame Assembly	B	2.1.3	Demo 100 K cycle fatigue life	1.1.6					
2	0	2.1	Frame Assembly	B	2.1.4	Support 2 x 90 KG	1.1.4, 1.1.6					
		•			•							
		•			•							
		•			•							

> - **The project team must verify that every requirement has been met. Verification is performed by:**
>   - *Test*
>   - *Demonstration*
>   - *Inspection*
>   - *Analysis*
> - **System Engineering is responsible for auditing the verification results and certifying that the evidence demonstrates that requirements have been achieved.**

Figure 20.4 Requirements traceability and verification matrix (RVTM) example.

During system verification, the testers unknowingly violated engineering load predictions by 25 times, taking the system to structural failure and total collapse. The failure caused a four-year facility shutdown for reconstruction.

4. A test readiness review should precede all testing to ensure readiness of personnel and equipment. This review should include all test participants and should dry run the baselined verification procedure, including all required updates. Equipment used to measure verification performance should be confirmed to be "in calibration," projected through the full test duration including the data analysis period.

5. Formal testing should be witnessed by a "buyer" representative to officially certify and accept the results of the verification. Informal testing should precede formal testing to discover and resolve all anomalies. Formal testing should be a predetermined success based on successful informal testing.

6. To ensure validity of the test results, the signed initials of the responsible tester or quality control should accompany each official data entry.
7. All anomalies must be explained with the associated corrective action. Uncorrected anomalies must be explained with the predicted impact to system performance.
8. Unrepeatable failures must be sufficiently characterized to determine if the customer/users can accept the risk should the anomaly occur during operations.

Design Verification

Design verification proves that the design for the entity will perform as specified, or conversely, that there are identified design deficiencies requiring design corrective action (Figure 20.5). Design verification is usually carried out in nominal conditions unless the design-to specification has design margins already built into the specified functional performance. Design verification usually includes the application of selected environmental conditions. Design verification should confirm the required positive events and the absence of negative events. That is, things that are supposed to happen do happen, and things that are not supposed to happen do not.

Software modules that are too complex (i.e., they have too many alternate paths) to verify all possible combinations of events contain a residual risk within those that have not been verified. Many organizations have been successful in using informal and formal software inspections to give confidence that software design verification goals have been achieved (Figure 20.6).

Figure 20.5   Design verification considerations.

Figure 20.6   Software formal inspections.

Advocates of Agile methods (including eXtreme Programming) emphasize thorough unit testing and builds (software integration) daily to verify design integrity in-process. Projects that are not a good match for an Agile methodology may still benefit from rigorous unit tests, frequent integrations, and automated regression testing during periods of evolving requirements and/or frequent changes.

Design Margin Verification: Qualification

Design margin verification, commonly called qualification, proves that the design is robust with designed-in margin, or, conversely, that the design is marginal and has the potential of failing when manufacturing variations and use variations are experienced. For instance, it is reasonable that a cell phone user will at some time drop the phone onto a concrete surface from about four or five feet. However, should the same cell phone be designed to survive a drop by a high lift operator from 20 feet (6 meters)?

Qualification requirements should specify the margin desired. Qualification should be performed on an exact replica of the solution to be delivered. For instance, car crash tests are performed on production models purchased from a retail dealer to verify that measured test results are meaningful to the user (the buying public). In general, the best choice is a unit within a group of production units. However, since this is usually too late in the project cycle to discover design deficiencies that would have to be retrofitted into the completed units, qualification is often performed on a first unit that is built under engineering surveillance to ensure that it is built exactly as specified and as the designers intended.

Qualification testing usually includes the application of environment levels and duration to expose the design to the conditions that may be accumulated in total life cycle use. Qualification tests may be performed on replica test articles that simulate a portion of an entity. For instance, a structural test qualification unit does not have to include operational electronic units or software; inert mass simulators may be adequate. Similarly, electronic qualification tests do not need the actual supporting structure since structural simulators with similar response characteristics may be used for testing. The exposure durations and input levels should be designed to envelop the maximum that is expected to be experienced in worst-case operation. These should include acceptance testing (which is quality verification) environments, shipping environments, handling environments, deployment environments, and any expected repair and retesting environments that may occur during the life of an entity.

Environments may include temperature, vacuum, humidity, water immersion, salt spray, random vibration, sine vibration, acoustic, shock, structural loads, radiation, and so on. For software, transaction peaks, electrical glitches, and database overloads are candidates. The qualification margins beyond normal expected use are often set by the system level requirements or by the host system. Twenty-degree Fahrenheit margins on upper- and lower-temperature extremes are typical, and either three or six dB margins on vibration, acoustic, and shock environments are often applied. In some cases, safety codes establish the design and qualification margins, such as with pressure vessels and boiler codes. Software design margin is demonstrated by overtaxing the system with transaction rate, number of simultaneous operators, power interruptions, and the like.

To qualify the new Harley-Davidson V Rod motorcycle for "Parade Duty," it was idled in a desert hot box at 100 degrees Fahrenheit (38 centigrade) for 8 hours. In addition, the design was qualified for acid rain, fog, electronic radiation, sun, heat, structural strength, noise, and many other environments. Actual beyond-specification field experience with an exact duplicate of a design is also admissible evidence to qualification if the experience is backed by certified metrics. Once qualification has been established, it is beneficial to certify the design as being qualified to a prescribed set of conditions by *issuing a qualification certification* for the exact design configuration that was proven. This qualification certification can be of value to those who desire to apply the same design configuration to other applications and must know the environments and conditions under which the design was proven successful.

Reliability Verification

Reliability verification proves that the design will yield a solution that over time will continue to meet specification requirements. Conversely, it may reveal that failure or frequency of repair is beyond that acceptable and anticipated.

Reliability verification seeks to prove *mean* time between failure (MTBF) predictions. Reliability testing may include selected environments to replicate expected operations as much as possible. Reliability verification tends to be an evolutionary process of uncovering designs that cannot meet life or operational requirements over time and replacing them with designs that can. Harley-Davidson partnered with Porsche to ultimately achieve an engine that would survive 500 hours nonstop at 140 mph by conducting a series of evolutionary improvements to an engine that initially fell short of meeting the requirement.

Life testing is a form of reliability and qualification testing. Life testing seeks to determine the ultimate wear out or failure conditions for a design so that the ultimate design margin is known and quantified. This is particularly important for designs that erode, ablate, disintegrate, change dimensions, and react chemically or electronically, over time and usage. In these instances, the design is operated to failure while recording performance data.

Life testing may require acceleration of the life process when real-time replication would take too long or would be too expensive. In these instances, acceleration can be achieved by adjusting the testing environments to simulate what might be expected over the actual lifetime. For instance, if an operational temperature cycle is to occur once per day, forcing the transition to occur once per hour can accelerate the stress experience. For software, fault tolerance is the reliability factor to be considered. If specified, the software must be tested against the types of faults specified and the software must demonstrate its tolerance by not failing. The inability of software to deal with unexpected inputs is sometimes referred to as *brittleness*.

Quality Verification

In his book *Quality Is Free,* Phillip Crosby defines *quality* as "conformance to requirements" and the "cost of quality" as the expense of fixing unwanted defects. In simple terms, is the product consistently satisfactory or is there unwanted scrapping of defective parts?

When multiple copies of a design are produced, it is often difficult to maintain consistent conformance to the design, as material suppliers and manufacturing practices stray from prescribed formulas or processes. To detect consistent and satisfactory quality—a product free of defects—verification methods are applied. First, process standards are imposed and ensured to be effective; second, automatic or human inspection should verify that process results are as expected; and third, testing should prove that the ultimate performance is satisfactory.

Variations of the process of quality verification include batch control, sampling theory and sample inspections, first article verification, and nth article verification. Quality testing often incorporates stressful environments to uncover latent defects. For instance, random vibration, sine sweep vibration, temperature, and thermal vacuum testing can all help force latent electronic and mechanical defects to the point of detection. Since it is difficult to apply all of these environments simultaneously, it is beneficial to expose the product to mechanical environments prior to thermal and vacuum environments where stressed power-on testing can reveal intermittent malfunctions.

Software Quality Verification

The quality of a software product is highly influenced by the quality of the individual and organizational processes used to develop and maintain it. This premise implies a focus on the development process as well as on the product. Thus, the quality of software is verified by determining that development followed a defined process based on known best practices and a commitment to use it; adequate training and time for those performing the process to do their work well; implementation of all the process activities, as specified; continuous measurement of the performance of the process and feedback to ensure continuous improvement; and meaningful management involvement. This is based on the quality management principles stated by W. Edwards Deming that "Quality equals process—and everything is process."

-ilities Verification

There are a number of "-ilities" that require verification. Verification of -ilities requires careful thought and planning. Several can be accomplished by a combined inspection, demonstration, and/or test sequence. A verification map can prove to be useful in making certain that all required verifications are planned for and accomplished. Representative "ilities" are:

Accessibility	Hostility	Reusability
Adaptability	Integrity	Scalability
Affordability	Interoperability	Securability
Compatibility	Liability	Serviceability
Compressibility	Maintainability	Survivability
Degradability	Manageability	Testability
Dependability	Mobility	Transportability
Distributability	Portability	Understandability
Durability	Producibility	Usability
Efficiency	Recyclability	Variability

Certification

Certification means to attest by a signed certificate or other proof to meeting a standard. Certification can be verification of another's performance based on an expert's assurance. In the United States, the U.S. Food and Drug Administration grades and approves meat to be sold, and *Consumer Reports* provides a "Best Buy" stamp of approval to high-value products. Certification often applies to the following:

- *The individual* has achieved a recognized level of proficiency.
- *The product* has been verified as meeting/bettering a specification.
- *The process* has been verified as routinely providing predictable results.

The ultimate project certification is the system certification provided by the chief systems engineer that the solution provided to the customer will perform as expected. This testimonial is based on the summation of the verification history and the resolution of all anomalies. Figure 20.7 is an example certification by a chief systems engineer.

Date: _____

I _____ certify that the _____ system delivered on _____ will perform as specified. This certification is based on the satisfactory completion of all verification and qualification activities. All anomalies have been resolved to satisfactory conclusion except two that are not repeatable. The two remaining are:

1. _____

2. _____

All associated possible causes have been replaced and regression testing confirms specified performance. If either of these anomalies occurs during the operational mission there will not be any effect on the overall mission performance.

Signed _____
Chief Systems Engineer (CSE)

Figure 20.7 CSE system certification example.

VALIDATION AND VALIDATION TECHNIQUES

Validation: Proof that the user(s) is satisfied.
Was the right solution built?

Most projects produce hardware, software, and/or firmware. What is not wanted is shelfware. *Shelfware* is a product that fails to validate, and the user puts it on a shelf or in a warehouse.

Validation is proof that the users are satisfied, regardless of whether the specifications have been satisfied or not. Occasionally, a product meets all specified requirements but is rejected by the users and does not validate. Famous examples are the Ford Edsel, IBM PC Junior, and more recently, Iridium and Globalstar. In each case, the products were exactly as specified but the ultimate users rejected them, causing very significant business failures. Conversely, Post-It Notes failed verification to the glue specification, but the sticky notes then catapulted into our lives because we all loved the failed result. The permanently temporary or temporarily permanent nature of the glue was just what we were looking for, but it hadn't been specified.

Traditionally, validation occurs at the project's end when the user finally gets to use the solution to determine the level of satisfaction. While this technique can work, it can also cause immense waste when a project is rejected at delivery. Too many projects have been relegated to scrap or a storage warehouse because of user rejection. Proper validation management can avoid this undesirable outcome.

When considering the process of validation, recognize that except for the product level having just the ultimate or end user, there are direct users, associate users, and ultimate users at each decomposition level and for each entity at that level, all of whom must be satisfied with the solution at that level. Starting at the highest system level, the ultimate user is also the direct user. At the outset, the ultimate users should reveal their plans for their own validation so that developers can plan for what the solution will be subjected to at delivery.

A user validation plan is valuable in documenting and communicating the anticipated process. Within the decomposition process, as each solution concept and architecture is developed, the ultimate users should be consulted as to their satisfaction with the evolution of the architecture. In the Agile iterative development process the customer is an integral part of the development team, so there is potentially continuous feedback. In large system projects and traditional development, a customer representative resident with the development team can provide ongoing feedback.

The approved concepts become baselined for further decomposition and rejected concepts are replaced by better candidates. This process is called *in-process validation* and should continue in accordance with decomposition of the architecture until the users decide that the decisions being made are transparent to their use of the system.

This ongoing process of user approval of the solution elaboration and maturation can reduce the probability of user dissatisfaction at the end to near zero. Consequently, this is a very valuable way to achieve and maintain user satisfaction throughout the development process and to have no surprise endings. Within the decomposition process, validation management becomes more complex. At any level of decomposition, there are now multiple users (Figure 20.8). Figure 20.9 presents a different view, but with the same message.

The end user is the same. However, there are now direct users in addition to the end user, and there are associate users who must also be satisfied with any solution proposed at that level of decomposition. Consider, for instance, an electrical energy storage device that is required by the power system within the overall solution. The direct user is the power subsystem manager, and associate users are the other disciplines that must interface with the storage device's potential solutions. If a chargeable battery is proposed, then the support structure system is a user, as is the thermodynamic system,

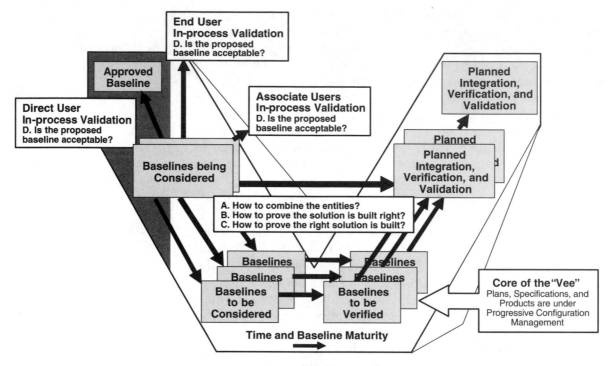

Figure 20.8   Three types of users.

among others. In software, a similar situation exists. Software objects have defined characteristics and perform certain specified functions on request, much like the battery in the prior example. When called, the software object provides its specified service just as the battery provides power when called. Associate users are any other element of the system that might need the specified service provided by the object. All direct and ultimate users need to approve baseline elaboration concepts submitted for approval. This in-process validation should ensure the integration of mutually compatible elements of the system.

In eXtreme and Agile programming processes, intense user collaboration is required throughout the development of the project to provide ongoing validation of project progress. Ultimate user validation is usually conducted by the user in the actual user's environment, pressing the solution capability to the limit of user expectations. User validation may incorporate all of the verification techniques that follow. It is prudent for the solution developer to duplicate these conditions prior to delivery.

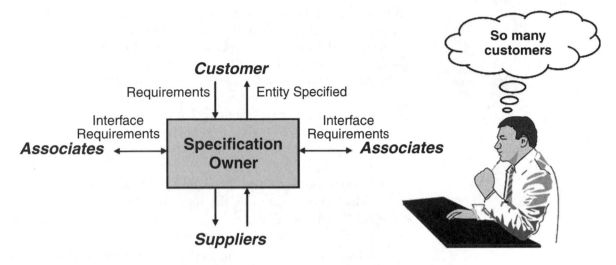

Figure 20.9   Three roles of the specification owner.

ANOMALY MANAGEMENT—
DEALING WITH THE UNEXPECTED

Anomalies are deviations from the expected. They may be failure symptoms or may just be unthought-of nominal performance. In either case, they must be fully explained and understood. Anomalies that seriously alter system performance or that could cause unsafe conditions should be corrected. Any corrections or changes should be followed by regression testing to confirm that the deficiency has been corrected and that no new anomalies have been introduced.

The management of anomalies should be responsive to the past experience lessons learned. Four are offered for consideration:

1. Extreme care must be exercised to not destroy anomaly evidence during the investigation process. An effective approach is to convene the responsible individuals immediately on detecting an anomaly. The group should reach consensus on the approach to investigate the anomaly without compromising the evidence in the process. The approach should err on the side of care and precaution rather than jumping in with uncontrolled troubleshooting.
2. When there are a number of anomalies to pursue, they should be categorized and prioritized as Show Stopper, Mission Compromised, and Cosmetic. Show Stoppers should be addressed first, followed by the less critical issues.

3. Once the anomaly has been characterized, a second review should determine how to best determine the root cause and the near- and long-term corrective actions. Near-term corrective action is designed to fix the system under verification. Long-term corrective action is designed to prevent the anomaly from ever occurring again in any future system.

4. For a one-time serious anomaly that cannot be repeated no matter how many attempts are made, consider the following:
   - Change all the hardware and software that could have caused the anomaly.
   - Repeat the testing with the new hardware and software to achieve confidence that the anomaly does not repeat.
   - Add environmental stress to the testing conditions, such as temperature, vacuum, vibration, and so on.
   - Characterize the anomaly and determine the mission effect should it recur during any phase of the operation. Meet with the customer to determine the risk tolerance.

IV&V: THE OUNCE OF DISASTER PROTECTION

Integration, verification, and validation are the "proof of the pudding." If done well, only successful systems would be completed and deployed since all deficiencies would have been discovered and resolved. Unfortunately, deficient IV&V has allowed far too many defective systems to reach the operations period where they have caused death, injury, financial loss, and national embarrassment. We can all do better.

21

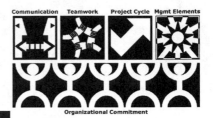

IMPROVING
PROJECT
PERFORMANCE

The preceding chapters focused on ensuring project success by enabling and empowering the project team. This chapter looks beyond project success toward building a learning organization that can sustain project success as the performance bar keeps rising. As Irving Berlin put it, "The toughest thing about success is that you've got to keep on being a success." Successful organizations cannot stand still.

The next section explores performance improvement by examining the criteria upon which success is usually based. Subsequent sections explore opportunities for propelling performance upward.

> People ask for the secret to success. There is no secret, but there is a process.
>
> Nido Quebin

PROJECT SUCCESS IS ALL ABOUT TECHNICAL, COST, AND SCHEDULE PERFORMANCE

Technical, schedule, and cost performance are not naturally compatible. They are opposing forces, in dynamic tension, as the bowed triangle in the margin illustrates. Achieving balance among the three requires compromise based on knowledge of the project's priorities and performance health. In system development, the technical content of the project drives the cost and schedule.

The technical performance factors are the verification factors defined in Chapter 20, including quality (the degree to which the delivered solution meets the baselined requirements) and the appropriate "ilities." Regarding schedule and cost performance, it's

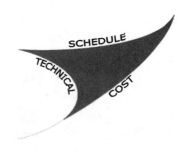

instructive to examine the bigger picture, our complex system development legacy, and the reasons for the performance trends.

The U.S. aerospace industry provides us with a rich and varied legacy of complex system development projects. The first operational U.S. fighter jet, the P-80, was developed from concept to first flight (in 1945) in 143 days.[1] The U-2 went from concept to first flight (in 1955) in just eight months. The SR-71, which was still one of the most advanced aircraft in the world in 2000, 43 years after its first flight, was developed from concept to its first flight (in 1962) in 32 months. The SR-71 also pushed the state of the art in many areas, including the structural use of titanium.

The Corona project, America's first reconnaissance satellite, took three years and 11 months from project start to the first totally successful flight (in 1960); this span includes 13 launches before achieving full success. The Corona program started before any man-made objects had been put into orbit, so everything from concept to reliability was first of a kind. These four projects share a common trait in that all had a national mandate and resources (which had to be continuously justified) to get the job done right.

The P-80, U-2, and SR-71 were all developed in the Lockheed skunk works.[2] The Corona was developed in a skunk works-like environment, with Kelly Johnson, founder of the skunk works, as an advisor.[3] While Lockheed may be the only organization that supported skunk works operations for an extended time (50 years), David Aronstein discusses three other independent aerospace skunk works operations (two American, one German) that embodied the same rules and outstanding successes.[4] The skunk works concepts were also common and effective in the computer industry. IBM, Control Data, and Intel all maintained significant skunk works operations.

The skunk works environment and principles can improve the performance of any project, especially complex system developments by addressing:

- Organizational commitment.
- Tailored systems engineering and project management processes.
- A small, empowered, and cohesive team.

It is critically important for projects to practice the basic principles, especially those that don't have the highest enterprise support enjoyed by a skunk works. As a small part of a larger organization, skunk works are usually able to handpick the top talent and garner other precious resources as needed.

The very isolation that benefits a skunk works can be its undoing. In the case of one Intel skunk works project, the resulting product concept turned out to be a solution looking for a problem (also known as the "silver platter syndrome"). We know of one Lockheed group that undertook a study of the origin of the stone axe in the Amazon Basin.

One of the consequences of the successes of the process models of the 1960s is that they led, in the 1970s and 1980s, to more rigid, untailored processes. As noted by Cialdini,[5] Ralph Waldo Emerson in his essay "Self-Reliance" said, "A *foolish* consistency is the hobgoblin of small minds" [italics added]. There are many instances in the experience of the authors and our colleagues where an unthinking adherence to process led to wasted time and money. In the 1970s and 1980s, projects typically stretched out many years and costs grew significantly (Figure 21.1).

Lest we think that these problems are unique to aerospace or to collocated teams, there are many examples from commercial experience as well. In one instance, a project team in a major U.S. corporation, working in a dispersed environment (over ten sites), shortened key internal processes from 30 days to 2 days; the overall project span decreased from a predicted 5 to 6 years to a completion in 18 months. The secret: improved communication and interaction through collocation of the key project team members. Breaking the

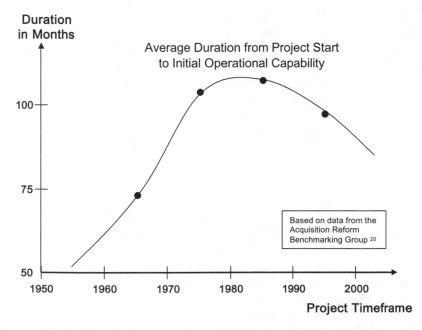

Figure 21.1 Project spans for major defense acquisition programs.

mold of inefficient practices is key. The advances in the Internet and the evolving use of distributed, collaborative engineering concepts and tools can facilitate similar effective team interaction, even when they are not physically collocated. The ability to have informal and frequent technical dialogue is the essence of collocation, which is one of the powerful principles of a skunk works.

In another instance, a major corporation desired to introduce a "hot, new idea" for a food product. At the time the idea was proposed, they were well ahead of the competition and could have captured a majority of a very lucrative business. However, it took eight years for them to get this high-priority product to market, which is longer than it took to build the Golden Gate Bridge in San Francisco or to build the world's first satellite. The problem was that they had no process.

In the early 1990s, the U.S. Department of Defense (DoD) mandated that its standards and specifications be replaced by commercial ones—even though commercial counterparts were nonexistent in most cases. The objective was to break down barriers between the DoD and commercial suppliers. A side benefit is that it forced rethinking of existing paradigms and developing new processes from scratch. That is also one of the challenges posed by the "better, faster, cheaper" legacy. NASA has demonstrated that "better, faster, cheaper" (BFC) can lead to dramatic success as evidenced by the Mars Pathfinder mission.[6] The key is that any process must be tailored to the project at hand, and that systems engineering must thoughtfully orchestrate the tailoring. In earlier chapters, we cited several examples of BFC gone wrong. Many of the NASA project failures have been traced to concentration on "cheaper" budgets and shorter schedules to the exclusion of technical performance and reconciling technical, cost, and schedule performance.

An example of the consequences of inappropriate tailoring of the project cycle is found in the *Lewis* spacecraft launched by NASA on August 23, 1997. All contact with the spacecraft was lost three days later. There were specific engineering and operational causes of the failure.[7] However, from a process standpoint, one of the primary causes was the abandonment of informal peer reviews two years prior to flight. (Note that this was also a root cause of the Therac failure cited in Chapter 13.) The contractor reduced the number and scope of internal reviews to save costs and could do so because the customer did not require them. From the perspective of our model, they did inadequate off-core risk management. The lack of peer reviews on the *Lewis* spacecraft allowed the risks to go unchecked all the way into orbit.

Planning for Complexity: Another Ounce of Prevention

At any level of complexity, the management process must be up to the task and carefully followed. The processes should be as simple as the situation allows. Management rigor increases with the project size, risk, or complexity as illustrated in Figure 21.2. In general, more complex or higher-risk projects require tighter controls, such as requirements traceability and more rigorous baseline management. Furthermore, as size and risk increase, so do the needs for more extensive planning and documentation.

Ship of Gold: A Case Study of Systems Engineering and Project Management Working Seamlessly

Kinder's book, *Ship of Gold in the Deep Blue Sea* (www.shipofgold .com) provides a fascinating case study of a project that succeeded

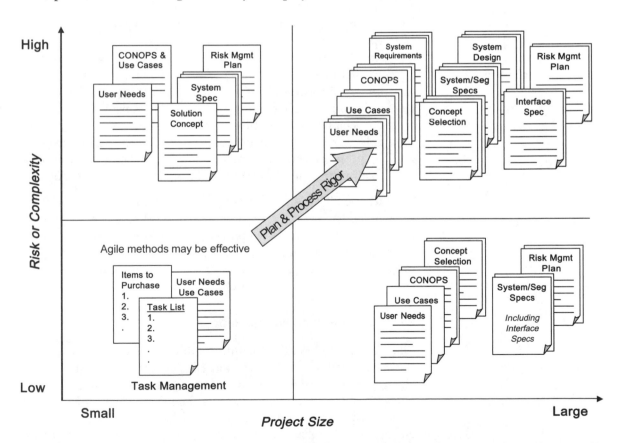

Figure 21.2 Plan and process rigor increases with project size, risk, or complexity.

because it applied the principles we have been discussing.[8] The project provides a vivid illustration of the power of business and technical integration and the rewards of viewing risks as opportunities in work clothes. The book is a thought-provoking story of the recovery of gold from a ship, the *Central America,* that sank in the deep ocean (8,000 feet or 2,440 meters). Treasure hunters typically work in an undisciplined fashion with no detailed project plan. In stark contrast, Tommy Thompson, the entrepreneur and project manager, ran the multiyear recovery project in a very businesslike and structured way, as carefully described by Kinder. There were few guidelines from prior projects as to how to proceed and there were many obstacles to success that demanded the highest technical, cost, and schedule performance:

- The challenge of finding the ship, with no precise recorded location at the time it sank in one of the nineteenth century's worst hurricanes.
- The challenge of designing recovery equipment when deep-sea experts insisted, "it cannot be done."
- Expert opinion in the mid-1980s, when this project took place, was that deep-sea recovery would cost hundreds of millions of dollars with little chance of success. Thompson's project cost less than $15 million. To achieve this, the project had to be managed as a business venture. Investors expected a clear accounting for their funds and a positive return on their investment.
- The project required secrecy and precise scheduling since other ventures were actively trying to beat Thompson to the gold.

Although Thompson did not use our terminology, he intuitively recognized the need for an incremental development with periodic decision gates. His intuitive process was tailored to his specific objectives and he practiced the principles of our model: an integrated project management and systems engineering process applied effectively without drowning in administrative details.

Toward More Accurate Planning

Plans are only as good as the information and assumptions on which they are based and, therefore, must be updated as the information changes and becomes more accurate and as the planning horizon becomes better understood. Cost estimates are critical planning inputs, yet are notoriously inaccurate at the project inception, especially for the software tasks. Appendix D provides a software development cost estimating process that has proven effective in addressing this problem. The process is now being successfully applied to complex system developments. But as the next section emphasizes, it is important to recognize differences between estimates and budgets and to resolve those differences to improve both schedule and cost performance.

SUSTAINING PERFORMANCE IMPROVEMENT

Measuring performance determines where improvements are needed. *Improving performance* requires organizational commitment.

Institutionalizing Best Practices

Professional organizations have taken a more scientific approach to understanding project success and failure. They evaluate work practices and use them to develop and apply capability maturity and process improvement models. The SEI Capability Maturity Model Integrated, which incorporates systems engineering to assess the work practice maturity of software and systems development teams, is discussed in more detail in the following section. The model is based on the theory that more effective people, processes, tools, and measurement lead to higher performance and probability for project success. The PMI Organizational Project Management Maturity Model (OPM3) is a standard for organizational assessment and process improvement that has three interlocking elements: Knowledge, Assessment, and Improvement. INCOSE is crafting a maturity model for systems engineering for use in assessing organizational capability in the systems engineering domain. While these capability models assess and measure the presence of practices within an organization, they may overlook the team members' underlying resistance to the best practices.

Exposing the Hidden Enemies

A negative attitude and lack of confidence in process management often turns out to be a self-fulfilling prophecy:

> At a software engineering course for aspiring managers, the participants were asked: "If your team of programmers developed airplane onboard flight control software, and one day when you were flying, you found out before takeoff that this plane was one of those equipped with *your* software, how many of you would get out?"

Project success depends on the team members' attitude as much as on the leader.

All except one person raised their hands. The course instructor asked the only one left whose hand was not raised, "What would you do?" She said, "Stay in my seat—if my team wrote the software for this plane, it wouldn't move, let alone take off."

While this true story is told with tongue in cheek, it comes close to characterizing the attitudes of many frustrated team members in this era of "vaporware" and getting to market at any cost. In an attempt to understand why some teams succeed and others do not, experts have studied the magic of the natural-born leaders. These studies produced project manager attribute models similar to those we referenced in Chapter 18. Although relevant and important, this leadership approach alone, based on the characteristics of the leaders in the studies, does not yield teams that are consistently successful. This approach fails to consider the importance of the process, tools, and the team members' attitudes toward essential project management techniques.

Sustained performance improvement depends on winning over the hidden enemies of project management.

Teams within organizations known for their expertise in project management would sometimes violate basic best practices resulting in failures of the worst kind as described in previous chapters. When we became aware that most of these project failures were not caused by the problems of advanced technology, but rather by the failure to implement fundamental and basic project management techniques, we looked for root causes, or the "ultimate why."

In each of these cases, a fundamental project management practice was overlooked, ignored, or circumvented. In every case, the properly applied project management technique would have prevented the project failure.

We set out to discover what caused project teams to ignore proven practices. Fortunately, our business causes us to routinely interface with substantial numbers of skilled project personnel including government agencies and contractors, commercial hardware and software companies, and graduate students, at several universities, pursuing project management careers.

No competent project manager would think of managing a project without these important techniques, effectively practiced.

We typically survey participants entering our training programs. The survey collects the participant's candid attitudes about "how they value" a selected group of important project management techniques prior to receiving training. The summary of responses (Figure 21.3) from approximately 20,000 participants represent the percentage of "positive" responses for some of the most important techniques. Our premise with this questionnaire is that personnel who are negative, neutral, or have no opinion toward a technique cannot be expected to pursue and support the technique in the proj-

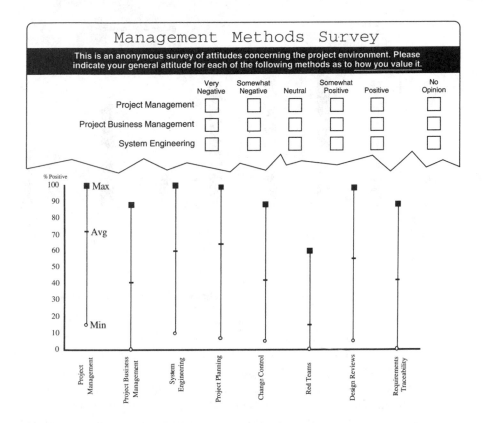

Figure 21.3   Management methods survey form and summary of results.

ect environment. The "somewhat positive" person may support the technique if implemented by others, but will usually not be the initiator or orchestrator. The only person who is a possible candidate for championing the technique and cultivating its effectiveness in the project environment is the person who checks "positive." And even if positive, the person might not have the leadership skills required to instill a technique in a resistant climate.

The survey results are sobering on two accounts—the wide range of group results and the low averages. The negative biases carried into the room when the survey was taken are alarming, especially considering that clients send only their best project personnel to a week or two of advanced project management training. The 45 percent averages for project business management, change control, and requirements traceability means that less than half of the 20,000 participants felt decidedly positive toward these techniques. Inadequate attention to one or more of these specific techniques

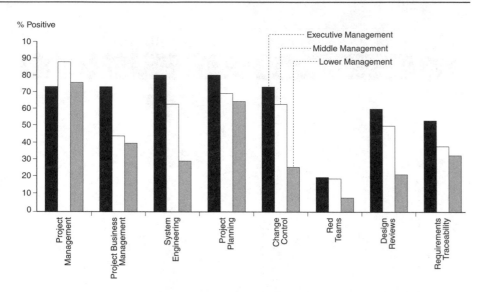

Figure 21.4   How three management levels value important techniques.

caused the failure of the Intelsat commercial satellite, the *Challenger* disaster, and the Denver airport delay and cost overrun.

Further analysis reveals that the main factors contributing to the nearly 85 percent dynamic range for most factors is the corresponding knowledge of—and experience with—the technique and the management level of the respondent. The perceived value of project management techniques diminishes at lower levels of the organization hierarchy (Figure 21.4).

Fortunately, this trend can be reversed with proper training and positive experience with the techniques. In early applications of the survey, we administered it both before and after training without discussing the reasons for the survey. The results showed a positive attitude increase to 70 percent or higher for most techniques as a result of understanding the use and the application of the technique. This attitude improvement demonstrates the power of training and of being informed. It is important for project leaders to measure the attitudes of their team at project start-up by applying this survey. Armed with this knowledge, selectively seek to improve the understanding of the techniques that received low scores.

PROCESS IMPROVEMENT DONE RIGHT

What makes one organization successful in its process improvement efforts while others flounder for years expending millions of dollars without getting any benefits? It is very tempting to say management commitment, but that doesn't tell the whole story. That commitment has to be made *for the right reasons*. This means tying the process improvement program to real business goals that are focused on bottom-line performance. Whether the desired performance is profit, cycle time, or quality improvements, the organization that understands its problems and starts its process improvement focused on fixing those problems is the one that will generally succeed.

Among the several established process improvement frameworks, three have demonstrated significant value in the project environment and beyond: ISO 9000, Six Sigma, and the SEI-CMMI. Each of these frameworks provides a platform for continuous process improvement, and each has different strengths, purposes, and goals.

ISO 9000 is a series of international standards that identify the minimum activities that an organization must have in place in order to control quality. An ISO 9000 Quality Management System is a framework that includes systematic methods, documented processes, and defined responsibilities. The ISO 9000 approach encompasses:

- A quality system that describes how the company fulfills the requirements for each element of a given standard.
- Practices consistent with documented quality policies and procedures.
- Maintenance of quality records.
- Performance of regular quality audits.

ISO 9000 is very broad and addresses all aspects of the enterprise, from administration to manufacturing.

Six Sigma improves performance by focusing on those process aspects that are critical to quality from the customer perspective. A major Six Sigma goal is to eliminate process variation. Six Sigma uses a project methodology known as DMAIC (Define, Measure, Analyze, Improve, and Control) to allow project efforts to bring measurable and repeatable results. Six Sigma views businesses as being composed of processes that start with customer needs and end with delighted customers using the organization's product or service.

The SEI-CMMI framework has been discussed earlier. It evolved from the need to assess an organization's software development capability and process maturity into a comprehensive framework for establishing and improving processes critical to complex system development. Because of its specific alignment with system development projects, this chapter focuses on the SEI-CMMI process improvement framework.

Effective Process Improvement Needs the Right Motivation

Consider a company that is having profitability problems and has determined that one problem is realistic cost estimates. It decides to start a process improvement program to get better at cost estimating and, hopefully, be more profitable. They decide to use the continuous representation of the CMMI and pick the project planning (PP) process area to guide its efforts. Using the best practices in the PP process area, the company discovers that its real problem isn't estimating—it's not recognizing the difference between estimates and budgets and the importance of reconciling the differences. It makes some minor, but critical, changes to its planning process and starts seeing its bottom line improve. This encourages it to look at other process areas that seem to address other problems. Eventually, it implements all of the Maturity Level 2 process areas, which are tied to the basic management practices we have been discussing in this book. The company undergoes a CMMI appraisal and becomes rated at Maturity Level 2.

Contrast the previous experience with Company XYZ, a government contractor. It would like to expand its business with some new government contract opportunities that require it to be rated at CMMI Maturity Level 2 in order to compete. It immediately adopts a sweeping process improvement program to become level 2 rated within three months. Company XYZ doesn't understand the issues involved with culture change and the time it takes to progress through the forming/storming/norming/performing stages of building effective teams. The SEI statistics show that it takes from 6 to 18 months to move up one level with the median being 12 months. A three-month program is doomed to fail. This is not to imply that being rated at any given maturity level is an invalid reason for initiating a process improvement program. However, for Company XYZ to reap the performance improvement benefits of a process improvement program requires a broader commitment: a goal to manage processes better to ensure profitable delivery within the schedule, which necessitates getting to Maturity Level 2 as a means rather than as the end.

It's All about Performance Improvement

The principles and recommendations covered in this book are distillations of the cumulative experiences of successful project practitioners. Many organizations have attempted to discover how these successful managers and engineers were able to succeed in the face of gloomy industry trends described in books such as Edward Yourdon's *Death March*.[9] The premise in many of these books is how difficult it is to design and build modern, technologically complex systems. Yet, few of these projects and teams used a disciplined approach that combined all the best practices covered in this book.

The situation was so endemic to the industry 25 years ago that the DoD chartered the SEI to improve the capabilities and development maturity of U.S. defense contractors. The SEI performed a survey of successful contractors and discovered that they had a number of common characteristics referred to as best practices. Not surprisingly, it was rare that a single organization implemented all the best practices, yet there was a direct correlation between success and the number of best practices in use. The DOD needed a method to assess the extent to which this collection of best practices was implemented in order to determine the relative risk of awarding a contract. The resulting SEI-CMMI and its evolution are described in Appendix B.

Readers familiar with the CMMI model reading this book for the first time will be struck by how closely all of the discussed concepts are reflected in the CMMI. Conversely, readers of the CMMI for the first time who are familiar with this book will see how implementing the concepts in this book will make implementing the CMMI easier.

Overcoming the "Band-Aid" Approach to Performance Improvement

Most organizations implementing the CMMI start with a gap assessment consisting of an internal assessment to identify their strengths and weaknesses relative to the model. The gap assessment usually results in a list of items that are either not implemented or are only partially implemented, along with a recommendation for correction. The usual management approach is to prioritize this list and start creating new processes to fill in the gaps. This naturally results in a "band-aid" approach to implementing the CMMI. Each gap or weakness gets a band-aid to fix the immediate problem, and there's a mix of existing processes and small fixes with little thought to integrating all the processes together for efficiency. After the organization has achieved its initial goals and has started working toward higher levels of maturity, it usually finds it can combine the "band-aid" fixes into fewer, more efficient processes. It is not uncommon to see shrinkage of greater

It is not uncommon to see shrinkage of greater than 50 percent in the total page count of a Maturity Level 3 organization from their Maturity Level 2 processes.

than 50 percent in the total page count of a Maturity Level 3 organization from its Maturity Level 2 processes.

As an example of this phenomenon, consider Generic Practice 2.6 (GP 2.6) from the CMMI. This GP is found in each of the 25 process areas contained in the model and it states:

GP 2.6 Manage Configurations

Place designated work products of the project planning process under appropriate levels of configuration management.

The primary intent of this practice is to ensure that project teams identify all the artifacts they will create (work products) and describe how they will be controlled. The range of control can include the lowest level of no control, the intermediate levels of saving the artifacts in a file structure or repository or putting version numbers on them, all the way to formal configuration management with change control boards. A typical and concise way to show compliance with GP 2.6 is a table that identifies the specific work products and the level of control to be used for each. Such a table might look like this for the project planning process area:

Work Product	Level of Control
Meeting announcements	No control
Meeting minutes/agendas	File—date stamp and save in a repository
Project estimates and Plan	Version—unique identification
Work breakdown structure	Configuration Management—baseline control with board approval

This type of table or similar information is usually found in the Project Plan. A similar table might be found in a Configuration Management Plan with different work products. Other tables might be found in other types of plans or documents as the priorities of closing the gaps dictate. In the worst case, a project team could accumulate 25 versions of this basic table, one for each process area in the model.

However, most organizations soon realize that this is relatively static information across project teams and they can combine all the tables into one super table in a template given to their project teams. Table 21.1 is an example of one such template.

As the table is put into practice on various project teams, they will notice project-specific items that need to be added. Ongoing feedback should ensure that, over time, the basic template will expand to the point that every possible work product is included. At that point, project managers can select the ones that are applicable

Table 21.1 Configuration Management Process Improvement Template

Work Product	Type of CM	Location	Comments
Miscellaneous artifacts			
Staff meeting agenda	File		
Staff meeting minutes	File		
E-mails discussing issues/action items, etc.	File		
Line management organization charts	Version		
Organizational ID of roles and responsibilities	Version		
Project Status Meetings			Also called MMRs, QMR, PSRs...
Regular review presentation packages	File		
Minutes of reviews	File		
Agendas for regular reviews	File		
Plans			
Project plan	Version		
Project schedules	CM Control		May be included in project plan
Project estimates	Version		
Project budgets	CM Control		May be in Work Authorizations
Organization charts	Version		
Configuration management plans	Version		
Quality assurance plans	Version		
Verification/validation plans	Version		
Training plans	Version		
Work authorizations	CM Control		
Requirements artifacts			
User statement of need	File		
User requirements	Version		
User operational concept	CM Control		
System requirements specification	CM Control		
Component-level requirements specification	CM Control		
Lower-level requirements specifications	CM Control		
Requirements traceability matrix	Version		
Technical analyses	Version		
Change requests	File		
CR log	File		
CCB minutes	File		
Review artifacts			
Presentation packages	File		
RIDs and logs	File		
RFAs and logs	File		
Attendance sheets	File		
Minutes	File		
Design artifacts			
Architecture drawings/specifications	CM Control		
Component-level design documents	CM Control		
Wiring diagrams	CM Control		
Technical data packages	Version		
Algorithm descriptions	Version		
Make/buy decision analyses	Version		
Product integration plans/procedures	Version		
Product artifacts			
Software code modules	CM Control		
Software make/build instructions	Version		These may be under CM control
Verification/validation plans/procedures	CM Control		
Verification/validation reports	File		
Test databases	Version		

to their project and delete the others. A task that might have taken several hours is now reduced to a few minutes. The reader is challenged to find the obvious missing work products from the sample table provided.

To illustrate this shrinkage effect even further, there is a practice in the project planning process area that covers planning for data management. This practice states:

PP SP 2.3 Plan for Data Management

Plan for the management of project data.

Similarly, there is a practice in the Project Monitoring and Control process area that tracks progress against the Data Management Plan. It states:

PMC SP 1.4 Monitor Data Management

Monitor the management of project data against the project plan.

It is a simple matter to add a few columns to the work product table to show when the work products will be created, where they'll be stored, who will get copies, and any other information the project deems necessary to satisfy both these practices. In essence, this one table can fulfill the requirements for 27 practices (GP 2.6 in 25 process areas plus the PP and PMC SPs shown previously).

Mapping the CMMI to the Five Essentials

The CMMI process areas are typically seen as being independent by organizations starting out in process improvement and this can lead to a band-aid approach in their implementation. However, the wheel and axle model can be used to illustrate how these process areas are interrelated. Further to the previous discussion about mature organizations growing out of the band-aid stage, the wheel and axle model can be used to illustrate a composite view of all the process areas in the staged Maturity Level 2 representation of the CMMI. This mapping is discussed further in Appendix B.

Sustaining Performance Improvements with a Process Improvemet Program

The concept of shrinkage that we've been describing also occurs in the Maturity Level 3 process areas. Most germane to this discussion are how well the six engineering process areas are included within the Vee model. The engineering process areas include:

- Requirements Development (RD).
- Requirements Management (REQM from the level 2 Maturity Level).
- Technical Solutions (TS).
- Product Integration (PI).
- Verification (VER).
- Validation (VAL).

While the process areas themselves are not a process and don't necessarily imply a time sequence, they map perfectly to the Vee (Figure 21.5).

The message of starting at the upper left leg of the Vee by eliciting requirements and then planning the project incorporates the RD process area, as well as the first specific goals from PI, VER, and VAL. The first Specific Goal from these three process areas addresses early planning for how the resulting products or systems will be integrated, verified, and validated at the opposite side of the Vee.

Continuing down the left leg of the Vee through stepwise refinement of requirements into concept and architecture down to build-to design and implementation shows how the practices within RD and TS are intended to flow together and result in product implementations of the requirements. The off-core activities describing how the Vee accommodates investigations at any time shows how

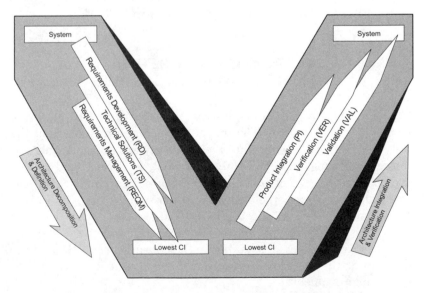

Figure 21.5   Six engineering process areas and Vee model.

a REQM process is to be incorporated into the overall product cycle at any point.

Continuing up the right leg of the Vee illustrates the process of integrating subentities into higher-level entities and eventually into the complete system as required by the PI process area. The Vee demonstrates how verification and validation are accomplished at each level of integration.

Thus, in a single model, the Vee illustrates how the engineering process areas are interrelated and can be combined into one comprehensive process that incorporates 40 specific practices from the six process areas (not counting the generic practices).

The importance of understanding the entire picture and being able to relate the component processes to each other should not be underestimated. It's typical for organizations to have a large number of process descriptions when starting out as they apply the band-aids to their gaps, only to see the number shrink back as process improvement takes hold and the individual process descriptions are combined with artifacts supporting multiple practices as described earlier with the work products table.

Use of our five-essentials model and the Vee can help organizations starting out in process improvement to avoid some of the early inefficiencies in establishing processes. With the big picture in mind, it will be easier to avoid the temptation to apply band-aid fixes to CMMI process gaps. The models also allow the organization to tailor the big picture approach to their business goals and objects early and further reduce the effort to implement CMMI.

PUTTING IT ALL TOGETHER
TO MASTER COMPLEX SYSTEMS

Being able to internalize the overall project management process removes the need to follow the individual steps on faith or by edict.

Chapter 2 employed systems thinking to view the bigger picture of the project environment. That chapter concluded by looking at the waves of the future—the convergence of project management, systems engineering, and process improvement. In Parts II and III, we presented management process models, principles, and techniques as an integrated set, without regard to their specific domain. In Part IV we have covered advanced principles of systems engineering and identified the synergies between process improvement and the wheel and axle process model. It is in the convergence of these three domains at the enterprise level that the real potential for performance improvement lies.

Complexity Made Simple

Overwhelming complexity is often cited as the reason project management processes defy our intuition. But complexity alone does not preclude intuition. Intuition develops from observing and understanding key principles. For example, the behavior of a gyroscope is not intuitive to most of us. But to an inertial guidance specialist, gyroscopes are second nature.

Intuition is developed by observing the environment, understanding the driving characteristics, and learning reasonable ranges for them. As an example, consider the plight of the main character in an old movie. As part of the plot he was to pretend that his sister had just given birth. A woman asked him how much the newborn weighed. Caught by surprise, he suggested the baby weighed 20 pounds. The woman reacted in horror, "Oh, no!" Our hero quickly corrected his mistake, "Oh, of course I meant 20 ounces." The woman reacted in horror, "Oh, no!" If you don't have sufficient intuition to get within an order of magnitude, you are in the wrong position. Take heart—intuition can be developed if you work at it and concentrate on the essentials.

Managing a project without some intuition is like looking at a road map through a drinking straw. Generating that intuition is perhaps the most important contribution of our Vee models and the wheel and axle. The obvious correctness of the models instills confidence in the process. A team that understands the value of a credible process, and follows it because the members believe in it, will be far less likely to omit an important step or to perform a practice incorrectly.

> Project management is the best training ground for general management.

BEYOND SUCCESS:
SUSTAINING A HIGH PERFORMANCE CULTURE

The investments and efforts made to revitalize the project environment, or to create one, can pay high dividends to the entire organization. One project team can be the catalyst for culture changes that can represent the enterprise's most significant competitive advantage in this technology-driven, time-compressed era. Whereas technology is surprisingly easy to clone, a well-integrated, high-performance project culture is an invaluable proprietary asset for sustaining high performance well into the future.

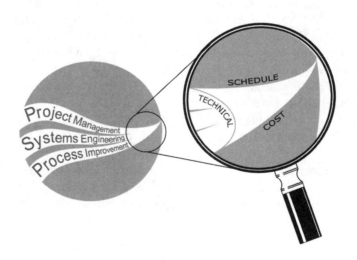

APPENDIX A

WEB SITE FOR FORMS AND TEMPLATES

Most of the forms and templates that appear in this book, plus others, together with related white papers, references, and links to other online resources are available on our web site. Go to www.csm.com/vpm3e and log on using the three-letter password Vee (case sensitive).

Document and Project Deliverable Templates

USER AND SYSTEM CONCEPT OF OPERATIONS DOCUMENT
Version X FOR (PROJECT NAME)

1. **Scope**
   1.1 Identification.
   1.2 Overview of User Needs (User ConOps).
   1.3 Overview of the Proposed System (System ConOps).
2. **Referenced Documents**

Part 1 - USER CONCEPT OF OPERATIONS

3. **Overview of the Current System or Situation**
   3.1 Description of the Current System.
   3.2 Operational Environment and Connectivity to Other Systems.
   3.3 Operational Policies and Constraints
   3.4 Users and Potential
   3.5 Users and Potential

4. **Desired Changes**

   4.1 Description of Desi
       a. Capability C
       b. System Prod
       c. Technology
       d. Interface Ch
       e. Personnel C
       f. Environmen
       g. Operational
       h. Support Cha
       i. Other Chan

   4.2 Priorities Among D
       a. Essential Fe
       b. Desirable F
       c. Optional Fe

   4.3 Justification for Des

   4.4 Features Considered

   4.5 Assumptions and C

Competency and Attitude Assessments

Rating Factor	Wt	Basic	Score	Wtd	Advanced	Score	Wtd	Expert	Score	Wtd
Project Management Training		Has had some Project Management Training			Has had the Company's or equivalent Project Management Training			Has the Company's, PMI, or equivalent certification in Project Management		
Project Management Experience		Has served as a deputy or assistant Project Manager			Has been a successful Project Manager			Has managed several successful programs		
Contracting		Is knowledgeable of			Has participated in			Has considerable		

SW Planning and Estimating Spreadsheets

APPENDIX B

THE PROFESSIONAL AND STANDARDS ENVIRONMENT

This appendix briefly characterizes the professional societies, regulatory bodies, and standards organizations that influence project practitioners, the project vocabulary, and the solution space. For further details, refer to Part 3 of *Communicating Project Management* and to www.csm.com/vpm3e, which also provides links to further references and to each organization's web sites.

THE PROFESSIONAL ENVIRONMENT

The table on page 404 summarizes three organizations that, through continued growth in scope, influence, and collaboration, are expected to shape the future of the project management and systems engineering professional environment:

INCOSE—International Council on Systems Engineering.
PMI—Project Management Institute.
SEI—Software Engineering Institute.

INCOSE expanded to international scope in 1995 and launched its certification program in August 2004. INCOSE works with, and through, international standards organizations rather than publishing its own standards. INCOSE has collaborated with the Electronics Industries Alliance (EIA) on several broad standards, including

	INCOSE	PMI®	SEI
Scope and impact	Over 5,000 members from over 30 countries. Collaborative agreements include American Institute of Aeronautics and Astronautics, EIA, IEE, ISO, and SEI.	Over 100,000 members from 125 countries. Cooperative agreements include the Construction Management Association of America and IIE.	SEI-authorized appraisers have evaluated thousands of organizations (2/3 commercial) and tens of thousands of projects with productivity gains of 20% to 28% when advancing from Level 1 to Level 3.
Professional credentials and certification	Certified Systems Engineering Professional (CSEP) introduced in August 2004.	Project Management Professional (PMP®) certification, maintained by earning PDUs.	SEI authorizes Lead Appraisers to rate organizations as to maturity and capability using a five-level model.
Competency model or framework	Collaborated on EIA/IS 731 Systems Engineering Capability Model (SECAM)	OPM3 expresses enterprise maturity in terms of Project, Program, and Portfolio.	Capability Maturity Model Integration (CMMI®) Product Suite addresses hw/sw and systems engineering disciplines
Best practices	Systems Engineering Handbook SysML in development	A Guide to the Project Management Body of Knowledge (PMBOK® Guide)	
Representative standards	EIA-632, Processes for Engineering a System	Practice standards, such as those for work breakdown structures	Standard CMMI Appraisal Method for Process Improvement (SCAMPI^SM)

EIA/IS-731 Systems Engineering Capability Model, a source standard for the SEI CMMI Product Suite.

Holding a PMI PMP certification is the de facto basis for judging an individual's knowledge about project management, especially in the United States. PMI publishes *A Guide to the Project Management Body of Knowledge (PMBOK® Guide)*, to identify and describe that subset of the body of knowledge in project management that is "generally recognized as good practices on most projects most of the time."

The SEI is a research and development center sponsored by the U.S. Department of Defense and operated under contract to Carnegie Mellon University. The SEI mission is to advance the practice of software engineering and to make predictable the acquiring, developing, and sustaining of software-intensive systems, from design through operation.

The integrated systems engineering/hardware/software CMMI® Product Suite was introduced in August 2000 to replace the Software Capability Maturity Model (SW-CMM) in use since 1987. The SEI authorizes CMMI Lead Appraisers through a formal program of training, mentoring, observation, and performance criteria.

One view of the genealogy of the SEI CMMI Product Suite follows:

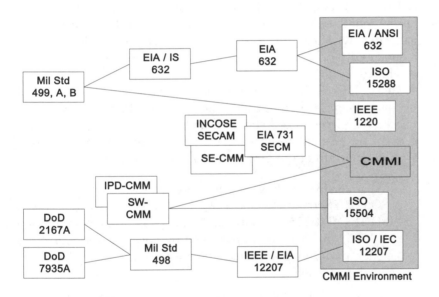

It illustrates one of the major collaborative and integrative efforts among the professional and standards organizations involved in project management and systems engineering.

A large number of professional organizations and societies share their lessons learned, develop their own best practices, and offer various forms of support and mentoring to their members. They range in size from the Agile Alliance to the 28 separate professional societies that make up the half-million-member Institute of Electrical and Electronics Engineers (IEEE). Several others are identified in Chapter 2.

REGULATORY BODIES AND
STANDARDS ORGANIZATIONS

The regulatory and standards bodies identified next are three of the most influential in the project solution space:

Electronics Industries Alliance (EIA).

International Organization for Standardization (ISO).

U.S. Department of Defense (DoD).

The EIA is the primary industry association representing the U.S. electronics community and its six trade associations. The EIA has an affiliate relationship with the Internet Security Alliance, a collaborative effort with the SEI's CERT Coordination Center (CERT/CC). Two standards have a broad and continuing influence on the solution space. EIA 632 standard and the International Organization for Standardization (ISO) 15288 standard, while complimentary with different roles and details, have greatest impact when combined.

The ISO is a worldwide, nongovernmental federation of national standards bodies established in 1947. ISO 9000 is the internationally recognized standard and reference for quality management in business-to-business dealings. The ISO standards that most directly affect the project solution space include:

- ISO 15288 System Engineering—System Life Cycle processes.
- ISO 12207 Software Engineering—Software Life Cycle processes.
- ISO/IEC TR 15504—Software process assessment (published in 1998): A series of nine standards covering the capability model, performing assessments, assessor competency, and process improvement.

Historically, the U.S. Department of Defense (DoD) has been directly involved in the solution space with standards such as Mil Std 498/499 and DoD 2167A/7935A. In more recent years, DoD influence has shifted to acquisition policy, such as requiring contractors to be rated at a specified CMMI level and/or conformance with DoD 5000 management principles and requirements generation.

The DoD acquisition processes and procedures are directed and guided by three key documents:

1. DoD Directive (DoDD) 5000.1,
2. DoD Instruction (DoDI) 5000.2, and
3. Defense Acquisition Guidebook (DAG).

The Defense Acquisition System Directive (DoDD 5000.1) identifies management principles for all DoD programs. The Defense Acquisition System Instruction (DoDI 5000.2) establishes a management framework for translating needs and technology opportunities into acquisition programs/systems. The Defense Acquisition Guidebook (DAG) is non-mandatory and provides guidance on procedures for operation of the acquisition system and is based on an integrated management framework formed by three primary decision support systems: the Requirements Generation System, the Defense Acquisition System, and the Planning, Programming, and Budget System (PPBS).

DoDI 5000.2 states that "Evolutionary acquisition is the preferred DoD strategy for rapid acquisition of mature technology for the user. An evolutionary approach delivers capability in increments, recognizing, up front, the need for future capability improvements. The objective is to balance needs and available capability with resources, and to put capability into the hands of the user quickly. The success of the strategy depends on consistent and continuous definition of requirements, and the maturation of technologies that lead to disciplined development and production of systems that provide increasing capability towards a materiel concept."

In the DoD vernacular, "evolutionary" is an acquisition strategy that defines, develops, produces or acquires, and fields an initial hardware or software increment (called a phase or block) of operational capability. Evolutionary acquisition is based on technologies demonstrated in relevant environments, time-phased requirements, and demonstrated capabilities for deploying manufacturing or software. Evolutionary acquisition provides capabilities to the users in increments. The capability is improved over time as technology matures and the users gain experience with the systems. The first increment can be provided in less time than the "final" capability. Each increment will meet a useful capability specified by the user; however, the first increment may represent only 60 percent to 80 percent (or less) of the desired final capability. Each increment is verified and validated to ensure that the user receives the needed capability.

The two basic evolutionary approaches are referred to as Spiral Development and Incremental Development, an unfortunate and confusing choice of terms since the well-known Spiral Model is applicable to both. In the DoD Spiral Development, the "end-state requirements are not known at program initiation." The final functionality cannot be defined at the beginning of the program, and each increment of capability is defined by the maturation of the technologies matched with the evolving needs of the user. In the case of Incremental Development, the final functionality can be defined at the beginning of the program, with the content of each increment determined by the maturation of key technologies.

The DoD Spiral Development closely corresponds to our Incremental/Evolutionary Method (with multiple deliveries) defined in Chapter 19, which may be modeled using the Spiral, but depending on other characteristics of the project, may best be modeled with the Waterfall or Vee.

The DoD Incremental Development closely corresponds to our Incremental/Linear Method, which again, can be represented by any or all of the defined models.

APPENDIX C

THE ROLE OF UNIFIED MODELING LANGUAGE™ IN SYSTEMS ENGINEERING

James Chism, Chairman,
INCOSE Object Oriented Systems Engineering
Methodology (OOSEM) Working Group

Large complex systems must be structured in a way that enables scalability, security, and robust execution under stressful conditions, and their architecture must be defined and communicated clearly enough so that they can be built and maintained. A well-designed architecture benefits any program, not just the largest ones. Large applications are mentioned first because structure is a way of dealing with complexity, so the benefits of structure (and of modeling and design) compound as application size grows large. *The OMG's Unified Modeling Language™ (UML®)* helps you specify, visualize, and document models of software systems, including their structure and design, in a way that meets all of these requirements.[1] That's great for software engineers, but does it help with systems engineering?

To develop any complex system requires a team of engineers working at the system level to analyze the needs of the stakeholders, define all the requirements, devise the best concept from several alternatives and architect the system to the component level. The system team must also provide to the designers all of the models and visualizations that describe the architecture down to the lowest decomposed level. David Oliver in his book *Engineering Complex Systems with Models and Objects*[2] states: "These descriptions must be provided in the representations, terminology, and notations used by the different design disciplines. They must be unambiguous, complete and mutually consistent such that the components will integrate to provide the desired emergent behavior of the system." So how does one use UML that was originally designed primarily for software personnel to help the systems engineer?

UML is a graphical language for modeling software systems and it was adopted as V1.1 by the Object Management Group (OMG) in 1997. Since then UML has become a de facto standard of the software community and the language has continued to improve through V2.0 as of 2004. It is a robust language with built-in extension mechanisms capable of addressing many needs. UML is supported by the OMG that has a well-defined technology adoption process and broad user representation that should assist in future development of the language. So how does this help the systems engineer and what is wrong with the current structured approach to systems engineering?

First, there are many systems being developed that use the Object Oriented (OO) approach for software development. As such, the current structured approach to systems sngineering poses a definite communication blockage between the SE and the software developers due to the visualizations used by the traditional approach. Basically, there is the lack of a common notation, semantics, and terminology as well as a definite tool incompatibility. This gap needs to be bridged to take full advantage of the OO approach and make full use of UML. So in addition to the structure language (UML), you need a systems engineering method consistent with that language and additional systems engineering notation to be effective.

In November 2000, the INCOSE Object Oriented Systems Engineering Methodology (OOSEM) Working Group was established to help further evolve the methodology. The working group is sponsored by the INCOSE Chesapeake Chapter and led by Jim Chism.

The OOSEM working group goals are to:

- Evolve the object-oriented systems engineering methodology.
- Establish requirements and proposed solutions for extending UML to support systems engineering modeling.

- Develop education materials to train systems engineers in the OO systems engineering method.

OOSEM includes the following development activities:

- Analyze needs.
- Define system requirements.
- Define logical architecture.
- Synthesize candidate allocated architectures.
- Optimize and evaluate alternatives.
- Validate and verify the system.

These activities are consistent with the typical systems engineering Vee Model and process that can be recursively and iteratively applied at each level of the system hierarchy. Fundamental tenets of systems engineering, such as disciplined management processes (i.e., risk, configuration management, planning, and measurement) and the use of multidisciplinary teams, must be applied to support each of these activities to be effective.

OOSEM utilizes a model-based approach to represent the various artifacts generated by these activities as opposed to a document-driven approach with traditional systems engineering. As such, it enables the systems engineer to apply a very disciplined approach to the specification, design, and verification of the system, and ensures consistency between the requirements, design, and verification artifacts that are understood by the OO software developer. The added rigor of the model-based approach helps to analyze the system and surface technical issues early and communicate the issues in a precise manner. The modeling artifacts can also be refined and reused in other applications to support product line and evolutionary development approaches. However, the OOSEM Working Group as well as others determined that even UML 2.0 did not contain sufficient robustness to encompass the needs of systems engineering to support analysis, requirements, specification, design, and verification of complex systems. As a result, in addition to the features of OOSEM, Sandy Friedenthal and others are working with the OMG and INCOSE to develop a Systems Engineering Modeling Language (SysML) to enhance the use of UML by Systems Engineers.

So what is SysML? "SysML will customize UML 2 to support the specification, analysis, design, verification, and validation of complex systems that may include hardware, software, data, personnel, procedures, and facilities" according to the SysML partners (OMG doc #ad/03-11-02). That effort began on September 13, 2001, with a meeting of an OMG chartered group called the Systems Engineering

Domain Special Interest Group (SE DSIG). The goals of that group were to:

- Provide a standard SE modeling language to specify, design, and verify complex systems,
- Facilitate integration of systems, software, and other engineering disciplines, and
- Promote rigor in the transfer of information between disciplines and tools.[3]

In addition to the following UML 2.0 diagrams: activity diagram, assembly diagram, class diagram, behavior diagram, structure diagram, object diagram, package diagram, sequence diagram, state machine diagram, timing diagram, use case diagram; the SysML partners are recommending the addition of the following diagram types: parametric diagram and requirements diagram. The activity diagram and the assembly diagram will require extension to enhance their use for systems engineering. The design approach for SysML is to reuse a subset of UML and create extensions as necessary to support the specific requirements of the UML based on the SE RFP.

"The parametric diagram provides a mechanism for integrating engineering analysis, such as performance and reliability analysis, with other SysML models. It also provides an effective mechanism to identify critical performance parameters and their relationships to other parameters, which can be tracked throughout the system life cycle."[4]

In addition to these SysML attributes that will be added, new features of UML 2.0 will include parts, ports, and components that will allow an added capability to recursively decompose systems into their constituent components as well as to decompose behaviors in the activity and sequence diagrams. It is expected that SysML will be formally adopted by OMG in 2005.

How does OOSEM enhance the UML role for Systems Engineering? As an example, we have chosen the topic "Analyze Needs," since this initiates the systems engineering effort on a project. We then provide a comparison table of the traditional representations to the OOSEM visualizations used (UML diagrams).

ANALYZE NEEDS

This activity characterizes the problem space by defining the as-is systems and enterprise, their current deficiencies and potential improvement areas, and the to-be enterprise model, mission/enterprise use cases, and associated mission requirements.

An enterprise model depicts an overall enterprise and its constituent systems, as well as the enterprise actors (entities external to the enterprise). The constituent systems include the system to be developed or modified as well as other systems that support the enterprise. The as-is enterprise is analyzed to determine its limitations using causal analysis techniques. The to-be enterprise model is established based on proposed changes to the as-is enterprise to address the deficiencies. The mission objectives for the enterprise/mission are used as a basis for deriving top-level mission use cases. The use cases and mission scenarios capture the key functionality for the enterprise. Measures of effectiveness are identified to support the enterprise/mission objectives, and used as a basis for trade-off and analysis.

Analyze Needs	
OOSEM Visualization Used	Traditional SE Representation
As-is operational depiction	
As-is users	
As-is enterprise model	
As-is scenarios	
As-is system requirements	
As-is system design	
Causal analysis	
Reuse candidates	
To-be operational depiction	Mission needs statement, concept of operations
To-be enterprise model (operational, full life cycle)	
Mission scenarios	OV-1; system threads; work flows
System use cases	Functional flow decomposition, business scenarios; work flows
Mission time line	Mission time line
Mission parametric and trade-off analysis	Mission analysis via simulation and mission scenarios. Trade-off analysis
Requirements traceability matrix (RTM)	Requirements traceability to original documents with decomposition typically done in requirements tool (DOORS, CORE, POPKIN, etc.)

OTHER AREAS OF SYSML APPLICATION

In addition to the SE process "Analyze Needs," there are five other areas that have been elaborated. Space restrictions limit us to listing the SE process areas covered in SysML:

- Analyze needs (covered earlier).
- Define system requirements.
- Define logical architecture.
- Synthesize candidate allocated architectures.
- Optimize and evaluate alternatives.
- Verify and validate the system.

SUMMARY

The OOSEM approach combines traditional systems engineering approaches with object-oriented techniques and the application of the UML modeling language. It is not a pure OO method as used by the software community, but is a hybrid between structured and OO techniques. Some of the features that have been incorporated into OOSEM to enhance traditional systems engineering methodologies:

- Use of UML and OO concepts for a model-based approach.
- Use of enterprise model to support specification of mission requirements and constraints.
- Use of causal analysis techniques to determine limitations of as-is enterprise and system.
- Elaborated context diagram for capturing black box system requirements.
- Control function for specifying control requirements.
- Store requirements specified at the system level.
- Requirements variation analysis.
- Logical decomposition and logical architecture versus functional decomposition.
- Formalizing the use of partitioning criteria for developing the architecture.
- Verification system development approach.

While the role of UML enhances the discipline with semantics and a modeling language it is necessary but not sufficient. The OOSEM approach, the use of SysML and the upgraded tools that need to include all of these methods and languages will make the approach sufficient. As a result the role of UML becomes the foundation of a structured and disciplined approach to systems engineering modeling.

APPENDIX D

A SUMMARY OF THE EIGHT PHASE ESTIMATING PROCESS

**Ray Kile, Chief Systems Engineer
for The Center for Systems Management and
developer of the REVIC parametric
cost estimating model.**

The Eight Phase Estimating Process (Kile, 1987) was developed initially to provide structure to a training course for organizations desiring to use the REVIC model, but it soon proved far more useful as a means of elaborating the risk inherent in a cost estimate. Subsequently, the Eight Phase Estimating Process provided a number of key practices that are currently documented in the CMMI.

PHASE 1: THE DESIGN BASELINE PHASE AND WORK BREAKDOWN STRUCTURE

The Design Baseline Phase starts as soon as the systems engineers, or equivalent, have determined a candidate architecture and design for the proposed system. The requirements have been gathered and allocated to the components within the candidate architecture and a complete Work Breakdown Structure (WBS) has been developed for the project. The output product from the Design Baseline Phase is a table or listing of the components along with the required functionality of each and the WBS. The products from this phase should be reviewed by the appropriate level of management and placed under configuration control.

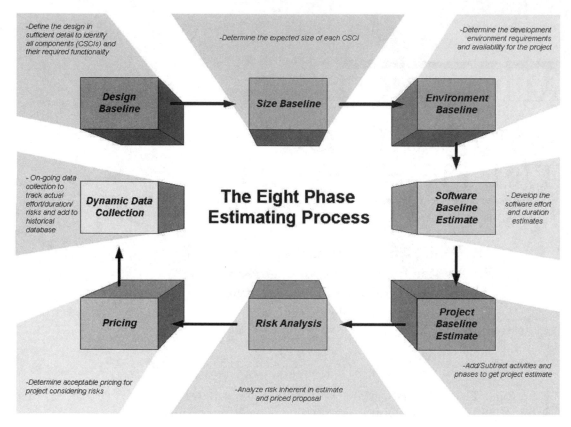

-Define the design in sufficient detail to identify all components (CSCIs) and their required functionality

-Determine the expected size of each CSCI

-Determine the development environment requirements and availability for the project

- On-going data collection to track actual effort/duration/ risks and add to historical database

- Develop the software effort and duration estimates

Design Baseline

Size Baseline

Environment Baseline

Dynamic Data Collection

The Eight Phase Estimating Process

Software Baseline Estimate

Pricing

Risk Analysis

Project Baseline Estimate

-Determine acceptable pricing for project considering risks

-Analyze risk inherent in estimate and priced proposal

-Add/Subtract activities and phases to get project estimate

PHASE 2: THE SIZE BASELINE PHASE

Once the Design Baseline has been established, the next task is to develop the size estimates for the components of the system. While estimating the size, risk information can be captured in the form of either ranges in the estimate or as a standard deviation using methods like PERT. It should be noted that the term *size* is used in the generic sense as a measure of the volume of the work. For software components within the WBS, size might naturally be expressed in terms of lines of code, function points, number of objects, number of modules, number of change requests, and so on. Hardware components can express size as weight, volume, component complexity, and others. Systems may express size as number of components, number of interfaces, performance requirements, and others. Each type of component has a different method for estimating and the size measure should be interpreted as the input attributes to the estimating method. The resulting size statements should also be reviewed by management and placed under configuration control.

PHASE 3: THE ENVIRONMENT BASELINE PHASE

The next step is to specify the Environment Baseline. The environment referred to are the total conditions that will prevail during the development of the system being built. This includes both the hardware and software tools and training that will be provided by the organization, as well as the skills and experience of the personnel who will be assigned the task. Every parametric estimating methodology has a set of parameters that are used to adjust the estimates for differences in the environment. During the Environment Baseline Phase, all the information collected to date will be used along with knowledge about the organization that will develop the system to establish the appropriate settings for these parameters.

You may think that this phase could have been accomplished at any point in time since organizations normally remain relatively stable in terms of their tools, training, and personnel. However, the size of the product to be developed will have a definite impact on the environment for several reasons. First the organization's ability to handpick personnel and staff a project with experts and highly experienced personnel is far easier for a small project requiring only 5 to 10 personnel than for a large project needing 50 to 100 or more personnel. Similarly, the number of tools and ability to provide specialized training becomes diluted with size. Thus, size estimation must occur before the environment can be firmly established.

PHASE 4: THE BASELINE ESTIMATE PHASE

By the time we have reached the Baseline Estimate Phase, we now have all the inputs necessary to run our parametric effort/cost and duration models and manual estimating methodologies. Each set of input types (sizes, environments) have been independently generated, reviewed, and approved to form the associated baselines. Each baseline is linked to the products of previous phases and is traceable back to the original requirements. In this phase, we use the input parameters in conjunction with the estimating methodologies and see for the first time the predicted effort and duration for the various components of the project. It is also at this point in the process that an effort/cost or duration problem will become apparent. In the past, the typical response was to somewhat arbitrarily change the size or environmental parameters to make the estimates match management's expectations. In our disciplined process we now introduce a rule to preclude this break in the chain of traceability.

Rule 1: Never change the output of a given estimating process phase without a corresponding change to the inputs of that phase.

To illustrate the rule, consider the situation where we have just determined that we have a budget overrun. In order to reduce the cost and follow Rule 1, we must first change one of the inputs to the phase. In other words, we must change the environment or the size information. We now introduce another rule.

Rule 2: Always try to change the previous phase's products first before proceeding up the process chain.

This rule says that we should back up the process chain one phase at a time when we need to make changes to the outputs of any particular phase. For the example given, where we have a cost problem, we should go to the previous phase first to try to effect a change. We dutifully revisit the environment and see if there is anything we can change to improve the situation. Perhaps we decide that if we can handpick staff we can raise the productivity and reduce costs. We must then document the rationale for the change and reaccomplish the management review to establish a new Environment Baseline. When we then reenter the Baseline Estimate Phase and reaccomplish the estimating methodology with the new environmental settings, we may find that the improvement in productivity now meets the cost constraint.

In accordance with Rules 1 and 2, we may have found that we had no justification for changing any of the Environmental Baseline parameters without a corresponding change to the Size Baseline, so we proceed back to the Size Baseline Phase. However, here we find that the size information in the baseline is directly traceable to the design components and their required functionality. Following Rule 1, we can't arbitrarily change the size estimates based on wishful thinking, and must go all the way back to the Design Baseline Phase. In this case, in order to reduce the cost to meet the budget, we must either eliminate a required function or down-scope the means of satisfying the requirement. In each case, we must capture the rationale for the changes and maintain a document trail for subsequent analysis.

PHASE 5: THE PROJECT ESTIMATE PHASE

All parametric models and estimating methodologies come with specific assumptions about both what development life cycle phases (e.g., design, code, verification) and types of activities (e.g., systems engineering, project management, testing) are included. When the characteristics of your project do not match those assumed by the model adjustments will have to be made. The purpose of the Project Estimate Phase is to add those things to the estimate that are not included in the methodology' assumptions and to take those things out of the estimate that the methodology assumes but are not in the project's scope.

Some examples illustrate the problem. Most parametric estimating models don't include the up-front systems engineering time required to perform system level requirements analysis. If this work is to be included in the project, we must add the effort and duration required to the model's estimates. Also, many models were calibrated from government projects that had a large amount of documentation. Our project may not require that much documentation and we will have to reduce the effort (and duration). Another example of activities mismatch is the inclusion, or not, of line management in the effort predictions. Most models include the first line project manager, but do not include any other management type labor. Finally, most models don't include the costs associated with establishing or maintaining development facilities, or other costs such as travel and materials.

PHASE 6: THE RISK ANALYSIS PHASE

In the Risk Analysis Phase, we will take all the risk information collected and try to determine in both a quantitative and qualitative manner what risks are inherent in this project associated with the estimate. This phase is usually run in parallel with the next phase, the Budgeting Phase, and the risk analysis should also consider the risk inherent when management decides to price the system differently from the estimate. Note that this risk analysis is not the same as a technical risk assessment leading to a risk management plan, although the risks identified and mitigation actions planned should be included in all project plans including the project's risk management plan.

Various methods of sensitivity analysis can be performed including Monte Carlo methods, use of standard deviations to get estimate spreads, and simply varying the input parameters to give the best and worse case estimates. However the risk information is generated, the goal is to make the quantitative and qualitative information support managers who must trade off desire to get the project against the possibility of an overrun in budget or schedule.

Once management has decided on the budget for this system, the risk analysis takes a slightly different form. We can now go through the estimate inputs and determine what changes would be needed to produce the system for the proposed price. For example, we might say that in order to meet the proposed price we would have to have the authority to handpick all the staff. Or we might say that we need to reduce the size by eliminating or reducing some functionality. This information should then be documented in a risk memorandum and used by the project team in their risk management planning.

PHASE 7: THE BUDGETING PHASE

The purpose of the Budgeting Phase is to use the available estimate and risk information to arrive at an acceptable budget and schedule for the project. Management has two conflicting goals during this phase. The first goal is to win the project or get approval to proceed. The second goal is to ensure there won't be an overrun of budget or schedule. As management tries to optimize probability of getting approval for the project by lowering the budget, they are simultaneously increasing the probability of an overrun. Similarly, if management wants to ensure there won't be an overrun by raising the budget to include some management reserve, they are reducing the probability of gaining approval.

Once management has decided on the budget, the risk analysis activities in phase 6 are reengaged to determine the risk inherent in the difference between the project estimate and the project budget. Management should carefully consider the risks and ensure that appropriate risk planning and mitigation are included in the project's plans and schedules.

PHASE 8: DYNAMIC DATA COLLECTION PHASE

The purpose of the Dynamic Data Collection Phase is to close the loop by gathering data for calibration of the estimating methodology for future estimates. This includes both the gathering of data from the current project as it is progressing to help manage the project and adding completed project data to a database used for re-calibrating the methodology. This phase also continuously tracks the impact on effort, cost, and duration as risks become reality.

For ongoing projects, data collection can be used to calibrate the methodology on the fly. Actual experience on the project through a major milestone can be used to predict the remaining effort or duration in a manner analogous to using actual cost data to calculate the Cost and Schedule Performance Indexes for Earned Value projects.

APPENDIX E

OVERVIEW OF THE SEI-CMMI

**Ray Kile, Chief Systems Engineer
for The Center for Systems Management**

As described in Chapter 21, the U.S. Department of Defense (DoD) initiated the development of the SEI's Capability Maturity Model (CMM) that evolved to the CMMI. The CMM organized the industry's best practices into a framework for assessing the extent to which they were implemented by an individual organization as a means for the organization to guide its performance improvements. After initial successes with the CMM, the DoD recognized that the management disciplines imposed by the CMM were equally applicable to systems development, but many organizations were ignoring it because of the heavy software-only flavor. Other discipline models such as the Federal Aviation Administration's iCMM® and the Systems Engineering CMM (SE-CMM) were merged into the resulting Capability Maturity Model Integration (CMMI). The new model greatly expands the engineering aspects of the original model while retaining all the original management practices.

Process Improvement

1. The continuous adjustment of process steps to improve both efficiency and results.
2. A program of activities designed to improve the performance and maturity of the organization's processes, and the results of such a program. [SEI]

These definitions describe a general approach to improving any process. A distinction should be clearly made between a general process improvement program and the CMMI model. Many organizations have chosen to pursue process improvements in business and manufacturing areas and are geared toward reducing costs, shortening production cycles, and many other goals expressed by management. These improvement programs all start with the existing status quo and attempt to improve the condition of interest. The CMMI model starts with a different premise. It is a collection of best practices gathered from industry and government organizations over the years that reflect a set of characteristics that good organizations should have. The CMMI represents a set of initial conditions that the organization can compare itself against in order to decide upon a prioritized set of actions to "improve." In essence, they are the initial desired end state. However, merely satisfying a best practice doesn't end it, since the model only describes the "what" that should be done and not the "how." Organizations typically find that their initial approach to implementing a practice from the model may not be the most efficient in terms of effort, cost, schedule, or quality and continue with their process improvement programs long after reaching an initial rating. There are various approaches available to describe how to run a process improvement program, including the SEI's IDEAL model, which can be downloaded from the SEI's web site at www.sei.cmu.edu.

CAPABILITY MATURITY MODEL INTEGRATION (CMMI)

The purpose of CMMI is to provide guidance for improving an organization's processes and its ability to manage the development, acquisition, and maintenance of products and services. The CMMI places proven practices into a structure that helps an organization assess its organizational maturity and process area capability, establish priorities for improvement, and guide the implementation of these improvements. (*Source:* SEI)

The CMMI model supports two basic views of improvement through its representations, Staged and Continuous. Each representation contains the same process areas and best practices; however, the organization and approach are different. An organization that is experiencing problems in a given area can look to the Continuous representation and work on individual process areas that have potential for fixing its problems. For example, an organization that is having problems with cost and schedule overruns might look to the

Project Planning process area. There it will find recognized best practices that describe how to estimate the scope of its projects along with the cost and schedule estimates, reconcile the differences between those estimates and externally imposed budget/ schedule constraints, and clearly document the resulting plans.

The Staged representation, on the other hand, provides a predefined road map for addressing the organization as a whole and organizes the process areas in stages that reflect a well defined group of project and organizational characteristics. The first stage reflects projects planning how to do the work, documenting those plans, performing the project according to those plans, and putting the feedback mechanisms in place to recognize when it's going astray.

In the Staged approach, an organization works on seven process areas to reach the second maturity level, 14 more to get to the third level, and two more for each of the fourth and fifth levels, a total of 25 process areas if the organization pursued it all the way. In the Continuous approach, the organization may chose to work on only one process area at a time, get it's processes in good shape according to that process area's best practices and then move on to another process area, or not.

The emphasis in the staged approach is reaching a specified Maturity level, while the emphasis in the Continuous approach is reaching a specified capability level for a individual process area. This is summarized in the two diagrams that follow. In the Staged approach, there are five maturity levels and the organization has either reached the maturity level or not, there is no credit for partial fulfillment. The Continuous approach shows that the organization can have different goals for individual process areas.

Provides predefined road map for *organizational improvement*, based on proven grouping of processes and associated organizational relationships.

STAGED (by Maturity Level)

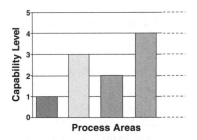

Provides flexibility for organizations to choose *which* processes to emphasize for improvement, as well as *how much* to improve each process.

CONTINUOUS (by Process Areas)

CMMI Model – Two Representations

CONTINUOUS REPRESENTATION

Continuous representation: A capability maturity model structure wherein capability levels provide a recommended order for approaching process improvement within each specified process area.

The diagram that follows shows the structure of each process area within the Continuous representation:

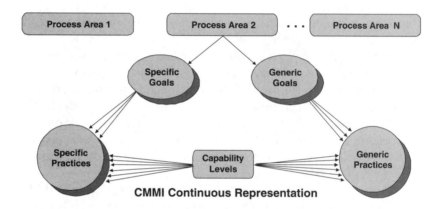

CMMI Continuous Representation

Each process area contains a number of specific and generic goals. The specific goals express a desired capability that addresses the implementation of the process area. Within the model, the goals are the only required items. To satisfy the intent of any goal, we expect the organization would implement certain practices. For example, within Project Planning the first specific goal states:

Estimates of project planning parameters are established and maintained.

To satisfy that goal, we would expect that certain things would have to be done; establishing the scope of the project, determining the project's life cycle that will be used, estimating costs and schedules, and so on. These things become the specific practices.

The Generic Goals express a desired capability that addresses the organization's infrastructure that needs to be in place to support projects. These Generic Goals are identical in each of the 25 process areas, although they may be interpreted slightly differently. For example, the second generic goal states:

The process is institutionalized as a managed process.

We expect that a managed process is one that is required by management (a policy), has a plan, has adequate resources to accomplish, has someone specifically assigned the responsibility to do it, has trained people performing it, has considered the impacts on stakeholders, controls its work products, is monitored and corrective actions taken when deviations of actual to planned are noted, is objectively evaluated, and is continuously reviewed by management. These expectations are reflected in the Generic Practices.

For any given process area, the extent to which the Specific Goals and Generic Goals are fully satisfied determines the organization's Capability Level for that process area. Any individual process area can range in capability from levels 1 through 5 (process areas start at level 0) by satisfying all specific goals (capability level 1) and then the generic goals (generic goals 1 and 2 for capability level 2, generic goals1, 2, and 3 for capability level 3, etc.).

STAGED REPRESENTATION

Staged representation: A model structure wherein attaining the goals of a set of process areas establishes a maturity level; each level builds a foundation for subsequent levels.

Within the Staged representation, the process areas, specific goals, and generic goals are identical. There are some minor differences in the number of specific practices for some of the process areas, but not enough to significantly affect the description. The difference as shown in the diagram that follows is that there are preselected groupings of process areas within a given Maturity Level:

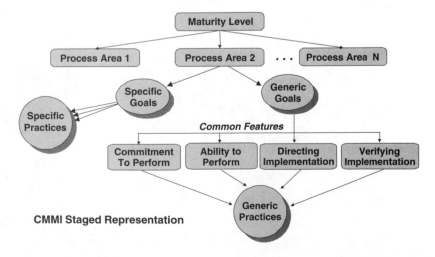

CMMI Staged Representation

Everything else is the same. The separation of the generic practices into common feature groupings is intended to clarify how the practices relate to the organization's commitment and ability to perform the process area, as well as how it directs the implementation and subsequently verifies the implementation was done correctly. The generic goals are identical to the Continuous representation, however in the Staged representation there is no need to have any individual process area satisfy the generic goals for level 4 or 5. Once all the process areas within a given maturity level have been satisfied through capability level 3, the organization is said to have reached Maturity Level 3.

This discussion has covered the high-level concepts of the CMMI model. Interested readers should go to the Software Engineering Institute's web site, www.sei.cmu.edu/cmmi, and download the full model for more details.

GLOSSARY

ONE HUNDRED COMMONLY MISUNDERSTOOD TERMS

This glossary contains terms that are often misunderstood within the project management and systems engineering domains. It also includes important terms that appear throughout this book. *Communicating Project Management*, a companion to this book, published by John Wiley & Sons, 2003, contains over 1,900 definitions, some with illustrations.

affinity diagram A problem-solving technique for relating ideas, issues, or other items that result from brainstorming. The affinity diagram is formed by categorizing the items (often in the form of "sticky notes" or index cards) in order to serve as a catalyst for breakthrough ideas and to reveal relationships.

agile development A software development method that focuses on individuals and interactions over processes and tools, working software over comprehensive documentation, customer collaboration over contract negotiation, and responding to change over following a plan.

analytical hierarchy process (AHP) A decision process based on pair-wise comparison of decision criteria followed by applying a mathematical process to calculate the relative importance of each criterion. Then scoring alternatives, again using pair-wise comparison, against those criteria to determine the best overall candidate.

architecture The framework and interrelationships of elements of a system. Typically illustrated by both a pictorial and a decomposition diagram depicting the segments and elements and their interfaces and interrelationships.

artifact A product or result. Can be samples, models, documents, white board sketches, and even oral descriptions.

baseline The gate-controlled step-by-step elaboration of business, budget, functional, performance, and physical characteristics, mutually agreed to by buyer and seller, and under formal change control. Baselines can be modified between formal decision gates by mutual consent through the change control process. Typical baselines are Contractual Baseline, Budget Baseline, Schedule Baseline, User Requirements Baseline, Concept Baseline, System Specification Baseline, Design-to Baseline, Build-to Baseline, As-Built Baseline, As-Tested Baseline, and As-Fielded Baseline.

baseline budget   The buyer/seller agreed-to budget and budget management approach that is under formal change control. Can include the funding source, time-phased budget, total funding, time phased funding profile, management reserve, and method for handling funding needs beyond the funding limit.

baseline—business   The buyer/seller agreed-to business requirements and business approach that are under formal change control. Can include the Acquisition Plan, Contract, Subcontracts, Project Master Schedule, Implementation Plan, System Engineering Management Plan, Contract Deliverable(s) List, and the Contract Documentation Requirements List.

baseline—technical   The buyer/seller agreed-to technical requirements and technical approach that are under formal change control. Can include the User Requirements Document, User CONOPS, System Requirements Document, Concept Definition Document, System CONOPS, System Specifications, "Design-to" specifications, "Build-to" documents, and "As-built," "As-tested," "As-accepted," and "As-operated" configurations.

best practices   Processes, procedures, and techniques that have consistently been demonstrated to contribute to achieving expectations and that are documented for the purposes of sharing, repetition, and refinement.

beta test   The testing, evaluation, and constructive feedback to the developers of a new product by a select group of potential users prior to product release.

black box testing   Verification of entity inputs and outputs only.

cohesion   The degree of interactivity and interdependence among solution elements.

concept evaluation criteria   The musts, wants, and weights used to judge alternative concepts.

configuration item (CI)   A hardware, software, or composite entity at any level in the system hierarchy designated for configuration management. CIs have four common characteristics: defined functionality; replaceable as an entity; unique specification;

formal control of form, fit and functionality. Each CI should have an identified manager and may have CI-unique design reviews, qualification certification, acceptance reviews, and operator and maintenance manuals. See lowest configuration item (LCI).

consent-to meeting   A meeting, with all parties directly involved in a decision, held to critically examine readiness to proceed. Not all consent-to meetings are decision gates, but all decision gates are consent-to meetings.

Constructive Cost Model (COCOMO)   Nonproprietary software cost and schedule estimating model originally developed by Barry Boehm (Software Engineering Economics, 1981). Produces an estimate of the number of man months required to develop common software products at three levels of complexity: basic, intermediate, and detailed.

Critical Chain Method   Eli Goldratt's theory of constraints (TOC) based planning approach that moves most individual task contingencies to the end of the critical path and applies resource availability as a driving factor in schedule achievement and critical path determination. The process surfaces resource constraints that must be addressed to achieve schedule.

Critical Design Review (CDR)   The series of decision gates held to approve the build-to and code-to documentation, associated draft verification procedures, and readiness and capability of fabricators and coders to carry out the implementation. All hardware, software, support equipment, and tooling should be reviewed in ascending order of unit to system. More appropriately called Production Guarantee Review since proof is required that the fabrication and coding called for can actually be carried out and that it will yield results that meet the design-to specifications. The evidence provided is typically samples of the critical processes to demonstrate credibility and repeatability.

decision gate   A preplanned management event in the project cycle to demonstrate accomplishments, approve and baseline results, and approve the approach for continuing the project. (Also known as a control gate.)

decision tree   A decision analysis technique consisting of a diagram showing sequence of alternatives considered and those selected.

decomposition and definition   The hierarchical, functional, and physical system partitioning into hardware assemblies, software components, and operator activities that can be scheduled, budgeted, and assigned to a responsible individual for the development of the associated design-to, build-to, and verification documentation.

decomposition diagrams—HW and SW   The noun levels of the WBS that illustrates the structured decomposition and integration of a system.

delivery method   The choice between holding all system increments and versions of increments until full integration and delivery (single delivery) or the fielding of partial capability through staged delivery of increments and versions of increments and developing capability over time (multiple delivery). Bridges and tunnels require single delivery while light rail systems and software often use multiple deliveries.

development method   The selection of unified, incremental, linear, and/or evolutionary development.

development model   The selection of the Waterfall, Spiral, or Vee, as the model for managing the development process. Selection depends on the approach to risk management and other factors.

development tactics   The selection of the development model(s) and methods, together with the delivery method, for a development project.

dispersion ratio   The ratio of total equivalent headcount charging to a project for a specific period divided by the number of different individuals charging in the same period. An important metric to reveal the extent of part-time individuals working on a project. A value of 1 would indicate no part-time personnel while a value of 0.5 would indicate that the average person is only working half-time on the project.

evolutionary development   A development method in which successive versions are produced to respond to discoveries surfaced by the previous versions. Applied when requirements are uncertain and/

or when technology experimentation is required. The alternative method is linear development.

failure mode, effects, and criticality analysis (FMECA)   An analysis of the potential failure modes, the resulting consequences, the criticality of the consequences, and actions to reduce the probability of serious failures (i.e., single point catastrophic failures).

fishbone diagram   An analysis tool that provides a systematic way of evaluating effects and the causes that create or contribute to those effects. The fishbone diagram assists teams in categorizing the many potential causes of problems or issues in an orderly way. The problem/issue to be studied in the "head of the fish." The succeeding "bones" of the "fish" are the major categories to be studied: the 4 Ms: Methods, Machines, Materials, Manpower; the 4 Ps: Place, Procedure, People, Policies; the 4 Ss: Surroundings, Suppliers, Systems, Skills. Dr. Kaoru Ishikawa, a Japanese quality control statistician, invented the fishbone diagram.

House of Quality   A mapping technique for relating the ability of design features to satisfy prioritized requirements. A matrix of cells, appearing like a house, has rows containing the requirements and columns containing the design features. The intensity of the cell hue indicates the degree of requirements satisfaction. The plus and minus symbols in the cells of the triangular house roof highlight strong or weak correlation in the satisfaction of requirements by multiple design features.

increment   One of a series or group of planned additions or contributions.

incremental development   A hardware/software development method that produces a partial implementation and then gradually adds preplanned functionality or performance in subsequent add-on increments. The alternative method is unified development.

independent verification and validation (IV&V)   The process of proving compliance to specifications and user satisfaction by using personnel that are technically competent and managerially separate from the development group. The degree of independence of the IV&V team is driven by product risk. In cases of highest risk, IV&V is performed by a team that is totally independent from the developing organization.

Integrated Definition for Functional Modeling (IDEF0) A multiple page (view) model of a system that depicts functions and information or product flow. Boxes illustrate functions and arrows illustrate information and product flow. Alphanumeric coding is used to denote the view: IDEF0—system functional model; IDEF1—informational model; IDEFX—semantic data model; IDEF2—dynamic model; IDEF3—process and object state transition model.

linear development A method for developing a system solution that is well understood and accomplished in a single pass as opposed to that requiring experimentation and multiple versions to achieve a satisfactory solution. The alternative method is evolutionary development.

logic diagram A diagram depicting the sequential and parallel interrelationships (functions or data) between entities or activities. Often used to show system functionality, software functionality, hardware system interactions, and project management serial and parallel sequences and interactions. Behavior diagrams, functional flow diagrams, data flow diagrams, and project schedule networks are examples.

lowest configuration item (LCI) The lowest architecture entity from the perspective of the responsible developer. For instance, the car battery would be an LCI for the car designer. The battery case would be an LCI for the battery developer.

mock-up A physical or virtual demonstration model, built to scale, to verify proposed design fit, critical clearances, and operator interfaces. In software, screen displays are modeled to verify content and layout.

model A representation of the real thing used to depict a process, investigate risk, or to evaluate an attribute, such as a technical feasibility model (risk) or a physical fit model (attribute). Models may be physical or computer based, for example, thermal model, kinetic model, finite element model.

model—advanced development model A term for a research model that is built to prove a concept.

model—engineering model A technical demonstration model constructed to be tested in a simulated or actual field environment. The model meets electrical and mechanical performance specifications, and either meets or closely approaches meeting the size, shape, and weight specifications. It may lack the high-reliability parts required to meet the reliability and environmental specifications, but is designed to readily incorporate such changes into the prototype and final production units. Its function is to test and evaluate operational performance and utility before making a final commitment to produce the operational units. Also called *Engineering Development Model.*

model—hardware and software feasibility model A hardware or software model constructed to prove or demonstrate technical feasibility. Technical feasibility should be proven at the Preliminary Design Review.

model—interface simulation A hardware or software interface simulation model used to verify physical and functional interface compatibility.

model—manufacturing demonstration A sample to demonstrate the results of a critical process. The objective is to confirm the ability to reliably manufacture using the process and to achieve the required results. Results are often provided as evidence at the Critical Design Review.

model—mock-up A physical demonstration model, built to scale, used to verify proposed design fit, critical clearances, and operator interfaces. Mock-up verification results should be available at the Critical Design Review.

model—preproduction model Entity built to released drawings and processes, usually under engineering surveillance, to be replicated by routine manufacturing. Provides manufacturing with a model to demonstrate what is intended by the documentation.

model—production model A production demonstration model, including all hardware, software, and firmware, manufactured from production drawings and made using production tools, fixtures, and methods. Generally, the first article of the production unit run initiated after the Production

Readiness Review (PRR). A prototype model, also built from production drawings, may precede the PRR to provide confidence to authorize fabrication of the production model.

model—requirements understanding   A software or hardware model developed by a provider to demonstrate the understanding of a buyer's problem or to help in resolving what the buyer wants.

model—risk reduction   All models are used to reduce the risk in some area of concern.

model—technical demonstration model   An experimental device constructed and operated in a laboratory environment to demonstrate application of a scientific or engineering principle. Sometimes called a "Breadboard Model." A more elaborate model, sometimes called a "Brassboard" is used where certain physical properties, such as dimensions, are critical to performance as in RF devices.

model—test simulator   A functional replication of the system used to verify that the test equipment and test facility is configured properly to test the real system.

Monte Carlo analysis   A technique to estimate the likely range of outcomes from a random process by simulating the process a large number of times with random values. When applied to static PERT scheduling it helps predict how the real schedule might behave. Random durations are applied to each activity in the network and the probability is calculated for each activity on a critical path. In a complex schedule it provides insight into which activities should receive special attention to ensure they occur as planned. Also referred to as Monte Carlo Simulation.

N^2 diagram or chart   A graphical depiction of the functions within a system, together with the one-way interactions between each function ordered in a matrix, with function or entities on the center descending diagonal cells. Since functions occupy each diagonal cell, the total number of cells is equal to the square of the number of function, hence the name. Interface functions and constraints are shown in the cells that correlate to both interfacing entities and the graphic is read clockwise. For example, cell A1 would output to cell B2 and cell B1 would contain the interface functions. Blank cells indicate that there are no interfaces between those two entities.

optimizing process   A quantitatively managed process that is improved based on an understanding of the common causes of variation inherent in the process. A process that focuses on continually improving the range of process performance through both incremental and innovative improvements.

pairwise comparison   The process of ranking items by comparing all pairs and, through mathematical analysis, determining the relative ranking. *See Analytical Hierarchy Process.*

Pareto Chart   A column chart where columns are types of defects and column height is frequency of occurrence. Used to pinpoint where corrective action should be applied to most effectively improve quality by reducing the greatest number of defects. *Also called Pareto Diagram.*

pedigree   The documented heritage of material or components usually tracing from the raw material to the finished entity.

Preliminary Design Review (PDR)   The series of decision gates held to approve the concepts, design-to specifications, associated verification plans, and approaches to developing build-to and code-to documentation for all configuration items (CIs). All hardware, software, support equipment, facilities, personnel, and tooling should be reviewed in descending order of system to assembly. More appropriately called Performance Guarantee Review since it must be proven that the specified performance is achievable. This is usually done by laboratory tests, analytical models, or field tests.

preplanned product improvement (PPPI)   Provisions that anticipate and provide for future increased capability. This may require the predecessor versions to have excess capability or special provisions to accommodate subsequent enhancements.

process performance baseline   A documented characterization of the actual results achieved by following a process, which is used as a benchmark for comparing actual process performance against expected process performance. [SEI]

project business management The function that commonly manages cost, schedule, legal, contracts, subcontractors, human resources, safety, and security. The function works closely with systems engineering to keep the technical, business, and budget baselines congruent.

project products list (PPL) A matrix summary of what entities and services must be provided to accomplish the project including quantities required for each form of the entity. Example: mock-up, field test unit, deliverable, spare, and so on. The PPL forms the basis for planning, estimating, assigning, material ordering, and so on.

project products list fact sheets (PPLFS) A narrative description of each entry of the project products list. The narrative should be written by the most knowledgeable expert and should include sufficient information to facilitate planning, estimating, and scheduling.

project work authorizing agreement (PWAA) The work release system document that defines and authorizes work tasks to be performed for a project. The PWAAs and subcontracts are the end product of implementation planning. The PWAA should contain the following five elements: task description (input required, task to be performed, and output resulting from successful completion); time-phased budget; schedule, with appropriate intermediate milestones, and if appropriate, detailed work packages to enable earned value reporting; signature of the task leader indicating commitment to do the task within the time and budget constraints; signature of the project manager indicating that the task is authorized.

prototype—hardware A specification-compliant, production readiness demonstration model developed under engineering supervision that represents what manufacturing should replicate. All design engineering and production engineering must be complete, and the assembly must be under configuration control.

prototype—software A term, currently with multiple meanings. A "rapid prototype" is usually a software requirements demonstration model, which provides a simulated representation of the software functionality and operator interface. The model facilitates early buyer-developer agreement on the design approach. A software prototype may also be a technical demonstration model. Except with "Evolving Prototypes," the code is usually discarded once the model has served its purpose.

qualification Proving that the design will survive in its intended environment with margin. The process includes testing and analyzing hardware and software configuration items to prove that the *design* will survive the anticipated accumulation of acceptance test environments, plus its expected handling, storage, and operational environments, plus a specified qualification margin. Qualification testing usually includes temperature, vibration, shock, humidity, software stress testing, and other selected environments. Qualification by similarity may be used if the item in question is sufficiently similar to a qualified item and the use is also sufficiently similar so as to not invalidate the previous qualification evidence and decision.

qualification certificate A configuration item specific document that defines the extent of the qualification of the CI. It provides subsequent users details of the qualification environments and history.

quality function deployment (QFD) The mapping of requirements satisfaction to product entities and features resulting in a requirements satisfaction effectiveness map. For instance, the hefty chrome gear shift lever with hand stitched leather knob in a high priced sports car has little to do with the shifting capability of the transmission but has a large impact on the look and feel of the sports car. Similarly the "thunk" sound of the doors closing radiates quality while having little contribution to strength or safety. The QFD House of Quality effectiveness map reveals where the various desirable attributes are being realized.

red team Objective peer or expert review of documentation and presentation material to identify deficiencies and recommend corrective action. A red team review is usually used to evaluate and score proposals before submittal, but is applicable to any documentation and presentation material. A red team is not the forum for a debate and the document owner decides which of the red team recommendations will be implemented.

regression test   Tests to ensure that imposed corrective actions to correct a deficiency have not inadvertently altered other functions. May require complete retesting to achieve the required confidence.

requirements   Needs or necessities; something demanded or obligatory. For clarification purposes, a descriptor should always precede requirements; for example, user requirements, system requirements, operational requirements, contract requirements, and test requirements.

requirements traceability verification matrix (RTVM)   A document that maps the parent-child relationships of requirements and the results of verification.

schedule performance index (SPI)   In the earned value system, the schedule efficiency index of the ratio of actual schedule achievement (BCWP or the earned value) to the planned schedule achievement (BCWS or planned value) for a specified period. SPI = BCWP/BCWS. An SPI of 1.0 indicates that schedule progress is according to plan. An SPI of less than 1.0 indicates that the rate of progress is behind plan. An SPI of more than 1.0 indicates progress rate is ahead of plan.

scope   The sum of products, services, and results to be provided. The PMI *PMBOK® Guide* defines Project Scope as the work that must be performed to deliver a product, service, or result with the specified features and functions.

significant variance   A variance from the plan that exceeds the predefined threshold and therefore requires variance analysis complete with planned corrective action.

Six Sigma   A quality program developed by Motorola that focuses on meeting six-sigma quality that equates to only allowing 3.4 defects per million opportunities.

skunk works   A collocated project environment usually isolated from other operations and/or distractions, to shorten communication paths and to keep highly skilled functional contributors close to one another and to the project activity centers.

spiral—evolutionary   The DoD nomenclature for development that produces and fields solutions that are later enchanced by added or replaced increments.

Spiral model   A software development model authored by Dr. Barry Boehm in 1980 to promote the management of requirements, feasibility, and operational risk prior to proceeding with traditional phased software development. The model also encourages user and stakeholder involvement in early risk resolution. Although developed for the software profession the model is also applicable to hardware development.

stakeholder   Anyone that can affect or be affected by the project.

stubs and drivers   Temporary software products created to simulate unavailable parts of the system during development and testing.

system   A combination of any or all of hardware, software, facilities, personnel, data, and services to perform a designated function with specified results. The highest member of the example system decomposition hierarchy.

system concept of operations (CONOPS)   A description of how the selected solution is expected to operate. It typically includes a narrative description, data flow diagrams, primary operation plan, secondary operations, and timelines. A day in the life of the system. Also known as System CONOPS (1).

system decomposition hierarchy   A set of ranked terms defining the composition of a system. The number of levels will be determined by the complexity of the system. The *INCOSE Handbook* defines these seven decomposition levels from highest to lowest: system, segment, element, subsystem, assembly, subassembly, part.

system integrity   Congruency of the business, budget, and technical baselines. A developing system has integrity when its baselines are in agreement or congruent and results from establishing a balance among the three aspects (business, budget, and technical) at the outset of the project and maintaining that balance as changes occur to any baseline.

system of systems   (1) A set or arrangement of interdependent systems that are related or connected to provide a given capability. (2) An arrangement of independent systems that can be arranged and interconnected in various ways to provide different capabilities.

Systems Modeling Language (SysML)   A general-purpose notational language for specifying, describing, and visualizing complex systems. SysML builds on UML.

technical aspect of the project cycle   The technical management approach to achieving the project solution shown as an aspect of the project cycle and often depicted in a Vee format to illustrate decomposition on the left and integration on the right.

unified development   The development method for a single entity, such as a concrete foundation or spacecraft structure, that is not divided into increments. The alternative method is incremental development.

Unified Modeling Language (UML)   A general-purpose notational language for specifying, describing, and visualizing complex software, especially large, object-oriented projects. UML builds on previous notational methods such as Booch, OMT, and OOSE.

user concept of operations (CONOPS 2)   The user's planned use of any solution in the operational environment. It may include the physical environment, operational environment, operating scenarios,

and requirements for logistics, provisioning, and maintenance. This document should be created early in the project cycle during the User Requirements Definition Phase.

validation   Proof that a developed system meets actual user needs and that the user is satisfied.

Vee model (Dual)   A system development model authored by Dr. Kevin Forsberg and Hal Mooz to illustrate integrated architecture and entity solution development.

verification   Proof of compliance with specifications. Verification may be determined by test, inspection, demonstration, or analysis.

verification, validation, and test (VV&T)   The methods to prove that the solution meets both specification and user requirements. This common acronym is misleading in that "test" is a method of verification.

Waterfall model   A software development model authored by Dr. Win Royce in 1969 to promote a sequentially phased software development process. The model promotes knowing the requirements before designing and designing before coding, and so on. The objective was to provide a repeatable process to the then undisciplined (generally ad hoc) software development environment. Although developed for the software profession the model is also applicable to hardware development.

white box testing   Verification of an entity's internal behavior as well as inputs and outputs.

NOTES

INTRODUCTION

1. Hans Hoffman, *Search for the Real* (Cambridge, MA: MIT Press, 1948).

CHAPTER 1

1. *Society of Satellite Professionals Journal* (June/July 2004).
2. Hal Mooz, Kevin Forsberg, and Howard Cotterman, *Communicating Project Management* (Hoboken, NJ: Wiley, 2003).

CHAPTER 2

1. *A Guide to the Project Management Body of Knowledge* (PMBOK® Guide) Project Management Institute (Philadelphia, PA: 2004).
2. Hal Mooz, Kevin Forsberg, and Howard Cotterman, *Communicating Project Management* (Hoboken, NJ: Wiley, 2003).

CHAPTER 3

1. Gary Kinder, *Ship of Gold in the Deep Blue Sea* (New York: Vintage Books, 1998), p. 92.
2. Ibid.
3. Henri Fayol, *General and Industrial Management* (New York: IEEE Press, 1984). A translation of the original French version published in 1916.
4. Michele Jackman (with Susan Waggoner), *Star Teams, Key Players* (New York: The National Association for Female Executives Professional Library, Holt and Company, 1991).
5. Gary Kinder, *Ship of Gold in the Deep Blue Sea* (New York: Vintage Books, 1998), p. 92.

6. Dennis Kinlaw, *Superior Teams* (Hampshire, England: Gower Publishing Ltd., 1998).
7. Ibid.

CHAPTER 4

1. James Womack, *Lean Thinking*.

CHAPTER 5

1. *Final Report of the Columbia Accident Investigation Board* (Washington, DC: NASA, August 2003), p. 187.
2. Hal Mooz, Kevin Forsberg, and Howard Cotterman, *Communicating Project Management* (Hoboken, NJ: Wiley, 2003).
3. Stephen W. Littlejohn, *Theories of Human Communication* (Belmont: Wadsworth Publishing Company, 1995).
4. Richard L. Lanigan, *Phenomenology of Communication: Merleau Ponty's Thematics in Communicology and Semiology* (Pittsburgh, PA: Duquesne University Press, 1988).
5. *Final Report of the Columbia Accident Investigation Board* (Washington, DC: NASA, August 2003), pp. 199–201.
6. Dianna Booher, *Communicate with Confidence!* (New York: McGraw-Hill, 1994), p. xvi.
7. Ibid.
8. Philip J. Harkins and Warren G. Bennis, *Powerful Conversations: How High-Impact Leaders Communicate* (New York: McGraw-Hill, 1999).
9. Robert Kegan and Lisa Laskow Lahey, *How the Way We Talk Can Change the Way We Work:*

Seven Languages for Transformation (San Francisco: Jossey-Bass, 2000).

10. Juanita Brown and David Isaacs, "Conversation as a Core Business Process," *The Systems Thinker* (Cambridge, MA: Pegasus Communications, 1996/1997), pp. 1–6.

11. Brown and Isaacs, "Conversation as a Core Business Process."

12. Dianna Booher, *Communicate with Confidence!* (New York: McGraw-Hill, 1994), p. xvi.

13. *Report of the Presidential Commission on the Space Shuttle Challenger Accident* (1986), pp. 94–95.

14. Robert Slater, *Jack Welch and the GE Way: Management Insights and Leadership Secrets of the Legendary CEO* (New York: McGraw-Hill, 1999), p. 15.

15. William Duncan from his Foreword to *Visualizing Project Management*, 2nd ed. (Hoboken, NJ: Wiley, 2000).

16. *Final Report of the Columbia Accident Investigation Board* (Washington, DC: NASA, August 2003), p. 187.

17. John L. Beckley, *The Power of Little Words* (Fairfield, NJ: The Economics Press, 1984).

18. Simon Winchester, *The Professor and the Madman* (New York: HarperCollins, 1998).

19. Sybil Parker, ed., *McGraw-Hill Dictionary of Mechanical and Design Engineering* (New York: McGraw-Hill, 1984).

20. R. H. Thayer and M. Dorfman, eds., *Tutorial: System and Software Requirements Engineering* (Washington, DC: IEEE Computer Society Press, 1990), pp. 606–676.

21. *A Guide to the Project Management Body of Knowledge* (Sylva, NC: Project Management Institute, 1996), pp. 159–171.

22. *Report of the Presidential Commission on the Space Shuttle Challenger Accident* (1986), p. 95.

CHAPTER 6

1. Stephen R. Covey, *The Seven Habits of Highly Effective People* (New York: Simon & Schuster, 1989).

2. Michele Jackman (with Susan Waggoner), *Star Teams, Key Players* (New York: The National Association for Female Executives Professional Library, Holt and Company, 1991).

3. Peter F. Drucker, *People and Performance: The Best of Peter Drucker on Management* (New York: Harper & Row, 1977).

4. Deborah S. Kezsbom, Donald Schilling, and Katherine A. Edward, *Dynamic Project Management* (New York: Wiley, 1988).

5. Dennis Kinlaw, *Superior Teams* (Hampshire, England: Gower Publishing Ltd., 1998), pp. 201–233.

CHAPTER 7

1. NASA GPG 7120.5 *System Engineering* (Greenbelt, MD: Systems Management Office, NASA GSFC, June 2004); NASA NPG 7120.5C *Program and Project Management Processes and Requirements* (Washington, DC: AE/Office of Chief Engineer, NASA HQ, March 2005).

2. DoDI 5000.2 *Acquisition Management* (DoD 2004).

3. ISO 15288, "Systems Engineering: System Life Cycle Processes" (ISO/IEC 2002).

4. Michael Cusumano and Richard Selby, *Microsoft Secrets* (New York: Simon & Schuster, 1995), pp. 192–207.

5. Frank Addeman, "Managing the Magic," *PM Network, The Professional Magazine of the PMI* (July 1999), pp. 31–36.

6. Helena Russell, *Partnership Pays: Project Management the Øresund Way* (Kent, UK: Route One Publishing, Ltd., 2000).

7. Jonathan S. Landay, staff writer, Knight Rider Newspapers, *Sacramento Bee* (December 16, 2004), p. 1.

8. David McCullough, *The Path Between the Seas* (New York: Simon & Schuster, 1977), pp. 117–118.

9. David McCullough, *The Path Between the Seas* (New York: Simon & Schuster, 1977), p. 235.

10. Web site for Øresundsbro Konsortiet, www.oeresundsbron.com.

11. Eberhardt Rechtin and Mark W. Maier, *The Art of Systems Architecting* (New York: CRC Press LLC, 1997).

12. R. Stevens, P. Brook, K. Jackson, and S. Arnold, *Systems Engineering: Coping with Complexity* (Hertfordshire, England: Prentice Hall Europe, 1998).

13. Winston W. Royce, "Managing the Development of Large Software Systems," *Proceedings, IEEE WESCON* (August 1970), pp. 1–9.

14. B. W. Boehm, "A Spiral Model of Software Development and Enhancement," *Tutorial: System and Software Requirements Engineering*, eds. R. H. Thayer and M. Dorfman (Washington, DC: IEEE Computer Society Press, 1990), pp. 513–527.

15. Michael Cusumano and Richard Selby, *Microsoft Secrets* (New York: Simon & Schuster, 1995), p. 192.

16. Craig Larman, *Applying UML and Patterns: An Introduction to Object-Oriented Analysis and Design and Iterative Development*, 3rd ed. (Upper Saddle River, NJ: Prentice Hall, 2005), p. 27.

17. Jim Lovell and Jeffrey Kluger, *Apollo 13* (New York: Pocket Books, 1994), Epilogue, pp. 372–378.

18. Kevin Forsberg, "'If I Could Do That, Then I Could . . .': System Engineering in a Research and Development Environment," *The Five Best Papers: Proceedings of the National Council for System Engineering Symposium* (St. Louis, MO, July 1995).

19. *Final Report of the Columbia Accident Investigation Board* (Washington, DC: NASA, August 2003); Frank Kuznik, "Blundersat," *Air & Space* magazine (Washington, DC: Smithsonian Institution, December 1993/January 1994).

20. Ben R. Rich and Leo Janos, *Skunk Works* (Boston: Little, Brown & Company, 1994).

CHAPTER 8

1. William G. Pagonis (with Jeffery L. Cruikshank), *Moving Mountains* (Boston: Harvard Business School Press, 1992), pp. 185–191.

2. Stephen R. Covey, *The Seven Habits of Highly Effective People* (New York: Simon & Schuster, 1989).

3. Ben R. Rich and Leo Janos, *Skunk Works* (Boston: Little, Brown & Company, 1994).

CHAPTER 9

1. "Advertisement and Specification for a Heavier-Than-Air Flying Machine," U.S. Army Signal Corps Specification No. 486 (Washington, DC: Smithsonian Institution, December 1907).

2. Tom D. Crouch, *The Bishop's Boys: A Life of Wilbur and Orville Wright* (New York: Norton, 1990), p. 347.

3. John Locke, *An Essay Concerning Human Understanding* (New York: Dover Publications, 1959).

4. Cynthia Monaco, "The Difficult Birth of the Typewriter," *American Heritage of Invention & Technology* (Forbes Inc., Summer 1988), pp. 10–21.

5. Clayton M. Christensen, *The Innovator's Dilemma* (New York: Harper Business, 2000).

6. John R. Hauser and Don Clausing, "The House of Quality," *Harvard Business Review* (May/June 1988), pp. 63–73.
   L. Guinta and N. Praizler, *The QFD Book: The Team Approach to Solving Problems and Satisfying Customers through Quality Function Deployment* (New York: AMACOM Books, 1993).

7. Bill Gates, *Business @ the Speed of Thought* (New York: Warner Books, 1999).

8. Michael Cusumano and Richard Selby, *Microsoft Secrets* (New York: Simon & Schuster, 1995), pp. 192–207.

9. Richard E. Fairley and Richard H. Thayer, "The Concept of Operations: The Bridge from Operational Requirements to Technical Specifications," *Tutorial: Software Requirements Engineering*, 2nd ed., eds. R. H. Thayer and M. Dorfman (Los Alamitos, CA: IEEE Computer Society Press, 1997), pp. 73–83.

10. Thomas L. Saaty, "Priority Setting in Complex Problems," *IEEE Transactions on Engineering Management*, vol. EM-30 (August 1983).

11. Charles H. Kepner and Benjamin B. Tregoe, *The New Rational Manager* (Princeton, NJ: Princeton Research Press, 1981).

12. "Introduction to Unified Modeling Language (UML)," Object Management Group (OMG), 2004. Web site http:/www.omg.org/gettingstarted/what_is_uml.htm; Craig Laran, Applying UML and Patterns, *An Introduction to Object-Oriented Analysis and Design and Iterative Development,* 3rd ed. (Upper Saddle River, NJ: Prentice Hall, 2005).

13. David Oliver, Timothy P. Kelliher, and James G. Keegan Jr., *Engineering Complex Systems with Models and Objects* (New York: McGraw-Hill, 1997).

14. Sanford A. Friedenthal and Cris Kobryn, "Extending UML to Support a Systems Modeling Language," INCOSE Symposium Paper (2003).

CHAPTER 10

1. Henry Miller, *Tropic of Capricorn* (New York: Grove Press, 1961), p. 176.
2. Peter F. Drucker, *People and Performance: The Best of Peter Drucker on Management* (New York: Harper & Row, 1977).
3. Suzanne K. Bishop, "Cross-Functional Project Teams in Functionally Aligned Organizations," *Project Management Journal* (Sylva, NC: Project Management Institute, September 1999), pp. 6–12.
4. Deborah S. Kezsbom, Donald Schilling, and Katherine A. Edward, *Dynamic Project Management* (New York: Wiley, 1988).

CHAPTER 11

1. James P. Lewis, *Team-Based Project Management* (New York: American Management Association, 1998), p. 71.
2. James P. Lewis, *Team-Based Project Management* (New York: American Management Association, 1998), pp. 22–28.
3. Tom I. Peters and R. H. Waterman Jr., *In Search of Excellence* (New York: Harper & Row, 1974).
4. Harold Kerzner, *Project Management* (New York: Van Nostrand Reinhold, 1984).
5. Ibid.
6. Ibid.
7. Stephen R. Covey, *The Seven Habits of Highly Effective People* (New York: Simon & Schuster, 1989), pp. 50–51.
8. Deborah S. Kezsbom, Donald Schilling, and Katherine A. Edward, *Dynamic Project Management* (New York: Wiley, 1988).

CHAPTER 12

1. *Project Management Institute Practice Standard for Work Breakdown Structures* (Philadelphia, PA: Project Management Institute, 2000).
2. Sunny Baker and Kim Baker, *The Complete Idiot's Guide to Project Management* (New York: Alpha Books, Simon & Schuster Macmillian, 1998), pp. 97–100.

CHAPTER 13

1. J. March and Z. Shapira, "Managerial Perspectives on Risk and Risk Taking," *Management Science*, vol. 33, no. 11 (November 1987), pp. 13–17.
2. Rita Mulcahy, *Risk Management: Tricks of the Trade for Project Managers* (Minneapolis: RMC Publications, 2003), p. 68.
3. Tom Kendrick, *Identifying and Managing Project Risk* (New York: AMACOM, 2003).
4. Rita Mulcahy, *Risk Management: Tricks of the Trade for Project Managers* (Minneapolis: RMC Publications, 2003), p. 68.
5. Robert T. Clemen, *Making Hard Decisions* (Boston: PWS-Kent Publishing Co., 1991).
6. Rita Mulcahy, *Risk Management: Tricks of the Trade for Project Managers* (Minneapolis: RMC Publications, 2003), p. 68.
7. Jon Krakauer, *Into Thin Air* (New York: Doubleday Dell, 1997).
8. Kevin Forsberg and Hal Mooz, "Risk and Opportunity Management and the Project Cycle," *Proceedings of the National Council for System Engineering Symposium* (July 1995).
9. Ben R. Rich and Leo Janos, *Skunk Works* (Boston: Little, Brown & Co., 1994).
10. Nancy G. Leveson and Clark S. Turner, "An Investigation of the Therac-25 Accidents," *IEEE Computer* (July 1993), pp. 18–41.
11. Ibid.
12. Mikel J. Harry, "The Nature of Six Sigma Quality," (Motorola Inc., Government Electronics Group, 1987).

CHAPTER 14

1. Aviation Week & Space Technology, "NASA, Intelsat Discuss Shuttle Rescue of Satellite Stranded in Useless Orbit" (March 26, 1990).
2. Henri Fayol, *General and Industrial Management* (New York: IEEE Press, 1984). A translation of the original French version published in 1916.
3. Ibid.
4. Leonard J. Kazmier, *Principles of Management* (New York: McGraw-Hill, 1969), p. 309.
5. Peter F. Drucker, *People and Performance: The Best of Peter Drucker on Management* (New York: Harper & Row, 1977), p. 498.
6. Callium Kidd and Thomas Burgess, *The Wiley Guide to Managing Projects* (Hoboken: Wiley, 2004), p. 502.

CHAPTER 15

1. David McCullough, *The Path between the Seas* (New York: Simon & Schuster, 1977), pp. 183, 185.
2. Michael Doyle and David Straus, *How to Make Meetings Work* (New York: Berkley Publishing, 1984).
3. Bill Gates, *Business @ the Speed of Thought* (New York: Warner Books, 1999).

CHAPTER 16

1. Thomas Fuller, *Gnomologia, Adagies and Proverbs, Wise Sentences and Witty Sayings, Ancient and Modern, Foreign and British* (Whitefish, MT: Kessinger Publishing, 2003).
2. Michael Cusumano and Richard Selby, *Microsoft Secrets* (New York: Simon & Schuster, 1995), pp. 28–29.
3. Ed Jorgensen, Jake Matijevic, and Robert Shisko, "Mars Pathfinder Project Microrover Flight Experiment: Risk Management End-of-Mission Report," *Jet Propulsion Lab Report* JPL D-11181-EOM (September 23, 1998).
4. Edward R. Tufte, *The Visual Display of Quantitative Information* (Cheshire, CT: Graphics Press, 1983).
5. Edward R. Tufte, *Visual Explanations* (Cheshire, CT: Graphics Press, 1997), pp. 38–53.

CHAPTER 17

1. Sherry Sontag and Chistopher Drew, *Blind Man's Bluff: An Untold Story of American Submarine Espionage* (New York: Public Affairs, Perseus Books Group, 1998), pp. 88–120.

CHAPTER 18

1. Michael Useem, *The Leadership Moment* (New York: Three Rivers Press, 1998), pp. 3, 266.
2. Peter F. Drucker, *People and Performance: The Best of Peter Drucker on Management* (New York: Harper & Row, 1977).
3. Stephen R. Covey, *The Seven Habits of Highly Effective People* (New York: Simon & Schuster, 1989), p. 147.
4. G. Gemmill, H. Thamhaim, and D. L. Wileman, "The Power Spectrum in Project Management," *Sloan Management Review*, vol. 12 (Fall 1970), pp. 15–25.

5. The Wilson Learning Corporation, Eden Prairie, MN.
6. Douglas McGregor, *The Human Side of Enterprise* (New York: McGraw-Hill, 1960).
7. William G. Ouchi, *Theory Z: How American Business Can Meet the Japanese Challenge* (Reading, MA: Addison-Wesley, 1981).
8. Frederick Herzberg, Bernard Mausner, and Barbara Snyderman, *The Motivation to Work* (New York: Wiley, 1959).
9. Alfie Kohn, *Punished by Rewards* (Boston: Houghton Mifflin, 1993).
10. P. Hersey and K. H. Blanchard, *Management of Organizational Behavior: Utilizing Group Resources* (Englewood Cliffs, NJ: Prentice Hall, 1993).
11. The Wilson Learning Corporation, Eden Prairie, MN.
12. Consulting Psychologists Press, Inc., Palo Alto, CA.
13. Stephen R. Covey, *The Seven Habits of Highly Effective People* (New York: Simon & Schuster, 1989), p. 241.
14. David Keirsey and Marilyn Bates, *Please Understand Me, Character & Temperament Types* (Del Mar, CA: Prometheus Nemesis Book Company, 1984).

PART FOUR

1. Don Hammonds, "Hyundai Goes from Also-Ran to Most Reliable," *Pittsburgh Post-Gazette* (March 26, 2005).
2. Joann Muller and Robyn Meredith, "Last Laugh: How Hyundai's Carmaking Prowess Went from Punchline to Powerhouse: And Is Shaking Up the World's Auto Industry," *Forbes* (April 18, 2005).
3. John G. Spooner, "Intel's CEO Wants an Employee Attitude Check," ZDNet News (July 27, 2004).
4. Joann Muller and Robyn Meredith, "Last Laugh: How Hyundai's Carmaking Prowess Went from Punchline to Powerhouse and Is Shaking Up the World's Auto Industry," *Forbes* (April 18, 2005).

CHAPTER 19

1. Kevin Forsberg and Hal Mooz, "The Relationship of System Engineering to the Project

Cycle," *Proceedings of the National Council for System Engineering Symposium* (Chattanooga, TN, October 1991), pp. 57–65.

2. Craig Larman, *Applying UML and Patterns: An Introduction to Object-Oriented Analysis and Design and Iterative Development,* 3rd ed. (Upper Saddle River, NJ: Prentice Hall, 2005).

3. B. W. Boehm, "A Spiral Model of Software Development and Enhancement," *Tutorial: System and Software Requirements Engineering,* eds. R. H. Thayer and M. Dorfman (Washington, DC: IEEE Computer Society Press, 1990), pp. 513–527.

4. Kevin Forsberg and Hal Mooz, "Application of the 'Vee' to Incremental and Evolutionary Development," *Proceedings of the National Council for System Engineering Symposium* (St. Louis, MO, July 1995).

CHAPTER 21

1. Ben R. Rich and Leo Janos, *Skunk Works* (Boston: Little, Brown & Co., 1994).

2. Ibid.

3. David C. Aronstein and Albert C. Piccirillo, *Have Blue and the 117A* (Reston, VA: American Institute of Aeronautics and Astronautics, 1997).

4. David C. Aronstein and Albert C. Piccirillo, *Have Blue and the 117A* (Reston, VA: American Institute of Aeronautics and Astronautics, 1997), Appendix C.

5. Robert B. Cialdini, *Influence, the Psychology of Persuasion* (New York: William Morrow, 1993).

6. Craig Sholes and Natalie Chalfin, "Mars Pathfinder Mission," *PM Network* (January 1999).

7. *Lewis Spacecraft Mission Failure Investigation Board Final Report* (Washington, DC: NASA Headquarters, February 1998).

8. Gary Kinder, *Ship of Gold in the Deep Blue Sea* (New York: Vintage Books, 1998).

9. Edward Yourdon, *Death March* (Upper Saddle River, NJ: Prentice Hall, 2003).

APPENDIX C

1. "Introduction to Unified Modeling Language (UML)" (Object Management Group, 2004), http://www.omg.org/gettingstarted/what_is_uml.htm.

2. David Oliver, Timothy P. Kelliher, and James G. Keegan Jr., *Engineering Complex Systems with Models and Objects* (New York: McGraw-Hill, 1997).

3. Sanford A. Friedenthal and Cris Kobryn, "Extending UML to Support a Systems Modeling Language," INCOSE Symposium Paper (2003).

4. Ibid.

INDEX